THE
ENTREPRENEURIAL
VENTURE

The Practice of Management Series
HARVARD BUSINESS SCHOOL PUBLICATIONS

The Craft of General Management
Readings selected by Joseph L. Bower

The Entrepreneurial Venture
Readings selected by William A. Sahlman and Howard H. Stevenson

Managing People and Organizations
Readings selected by John J. Gabarro

Strategic Marketing Management
Readings selected by Robert J. Dolan

THE ENTREPRENEURIAL VENTURE

READINGS SELECTED BY

William A. Sahlman and Howard H. Stevenson

Harvard Business School

HARVARD BUSINESS SCHOOL PUBLICATIONS
Boston, Massachusetts

Library of Congress Cataloging-in-Publication Data

The entrepreneurial venture / edited by William A. Sahlman, Howard H.
Stevenson.
    p. cm. — (The Practice of management series)
    Includes index.
    ISBN 0-87584-312-3 (pbk.)
    1. New business enterprises. 2. Entrepreneurship.   I. Sahlman,
William Andrews.   II. Stevenson, Howard H.   III. Series.
HD62.5.E56 1991
658.4'21--dc20   91-31891
                                                                      CIP

The Harvard Business School Publications Practice of Management Series is distributed in
the college market by McGraw-Hill Book Company. The readings in each book are available
individually through PRIMIS, the McGraw-Hill custom publishing service. Instructors
and bookstores should contact their local McGraw-Hill representative for information
and ordering.

"The New Venture" from *Innovation and Entrepreneurship* by Peter Drucker. Copyright © 1985
by Peter F. Drucker. Reprinted by permission of HarperCollins Publishers.

"The Family Venture" from *The Entrepreneurial Mind* by Jeffry A. Timmons. Copyright © 1989
by Jeffry A. Timmons. Reprinted by permission of Brick House Publishing Company.

"Aspects of Financial Contracting in Venture Capital," by William A. Sahlman, *Journal of
Applied Corporate Finance*, Summer 1988. Copyright © 1988 by Stern Stewart Management
Services. Reprinted by permission.

"Going Public" from the Coopers & Lybrand *Guide to Growing Your Business*, by Seymour
Jones, M. Bruce Cohen, and Victor V. Coppola. Copyright © 1988 by Coopers & Lybrand.
Reprinted by permission.

Printed in the United States of America.

95 94   5 4 3 2

WILLIAM A. SAHLMAN

William A. Sahlman is Dimitri V. D'Arbeloff–Class of 1955 Professor of Business Administration at Harvard Business School. His research focuses on the investment and financing decisions made in entrepreneurial ventures. Related areas of research include the role of financial institutions in providing risk capital and the venture capital industry.

In 1985, he introduced a second-year elective course at HBS called Entrepreneurial Finance. Sahlman has published articles in the *Harvard Business Review*, the *Journal of Business Venturing*, and the *Journal of Applied Corporate Finance*.

HOWARD H. STEVENSON

Howard H. Stevenson is Sarofim-Rock Professor of Business Administration at Harvard Business School. Professor Stevenson previously served as vice president of finance and administration and a director of Preco Corporation, a large, privately held manufacturing company. He also has served as vice president of Simmons Associates, a small investment banking firm specializing in venture financing.

Before 1978, he held various academic appointments at Harvard University, specializing in real property asset management and general management. He received his B.S. in mathematics, with distinction, from Stanford University and his MBA and DBA degrees from Harvard University.

His books include *New Business Ventures and the Entrepreneur*, with Michael J. Roberts and H. Irving Grousbeck, and *Policy Formulation and Administration*, with C. Roland Christensen, Norman Berg, and Malcolm Salter. He has published articles on entrepreneurship in the *Harvard Business Review*, the *Strategic Management Journal*, the *Journal of Business Venturing*, and elsewhere.

CONTENTS

PART ONE
THE ENTREPRENEUR: IMAGES AND SELF-IMAGES

Understanding the behavior and thought patterns of entrepreneurs can help managers in companies of all sizes foster creativity and flexibility in their organizations.

The founder and CEO of a high technology supplier describes the essence and elements of successful innovation in a large corporation.

**PART TWO
LAUNCHING THE NEW VENTURE**

**SECTION A
ASSESSING: WHAT ARE THE OPPORTUNITIES AND RISKS?**

PART THREE
MANAGING VENTURE GROWTH

SECTION A
BUILDING AN EFFECTIVE ORGANIZATION

SECTION B
FINANCIAL STRATEGY FOR THE GROWING VENTURE

SERIES PREFACE

The Harvard Business School has a long and distinguished publishing history. For decades, the School has furnished original educational materials to academic classrooms and executive education programs worldwide. Many of these publications have been used by individual managers to update their knowledge and skills. The Practice of Management Series, developed by Harvard Business School Publications, continues this tradition.

The series addresses major areas of the business curriculum and major topics within those areas. Each of the books strikes a balance between broad coverage of the area and depth of treatment; each has been designed for flexibility of use to accommodate the varying needs of instructors and programs in different academic settings.

These books also will serve as authoritative references for practicing managers. They can provide a refresher on business basics and enduring concepts; they also offer cutting-edge ideas and techniques.

The main objective of the Practice of Management Series is to make Harvard Business School's continuing explorations into management's best practices more widely and easily available. The books draw on two primary sources of material produced at the School.

Harvard Business School is probably best known for its field research and cases. Faculty members prepare other material for their classrooms, however, including essays that define and explain key business concepts and practices. Like other classroom materials produced at Harvard Business School, these "notes," as they are called at the School, have a consistent point of view—that of the general manager. They have a common purpose—to inform the actual practice of management as opposed to providing a theoretical foundation. The notes are an important source of selections for the books in this series.

The *Harvard Business Review* has long been recognized by professors and managers as the premier management magazine. Its mix of authors—academics, practicing executives and managers, and consultants—brings to bear a blend of research knowledge and practical intelligence on a wide variety of business topics. *Harvard Business Review* articles challenge conventional wisdom with fresh approaches and often become a part of enlightened conventional wisdom. The magazine speaks primarily to the practice of management at the level of the general manager. *Harvard Business Review* articles are another essential source of selections for this series.

Finally, this series includes selections published by other distinguished institutions and organizations. In instances where there were gaps in coverage or viewpoint, we have taken the opportunity to tap books and other journals besides the *Harvard Business Review*.

——— ACKNOWLEDGMENTS

The books in this series are the products of a collaborative effort. William A. Sahlman and Howard H. Stevenson, the Harvard Business School faculty members who wrote the introduction to *The Entrepreneurial Venture*, worked closely with a Harvard Business School Publications editor, Judith Maas, to select and arrange the best available materials. The content expertise, teaching experience, and diligence of Professor Sahlman and Professor Stevenson, together with Ms. Maas's editorial skill and commitment, have been crucial to the development of the book.

The Harvard Business School faculty whose work is represented in the books have generously taken the time to review their selections. Their cooperation is much appreciated.

Each of the books has been evaluated by practitioners or professors at other institutions. We would like to thank the following individuals for their careful readings of the manuscript for the collection on entrepreneurship: Zenas Block, New York University; William Gartner, Georgetown University; and Ian C. MacMillan, the University of Pennsylvania. Their evaluations and many useful suggestions have helped us develop and shape this book into a more effective teaching instrument.

We would like to thank Maria Arteta, former Director of Product Management for Harvard Business School Publications; Bill Ellet, Editorial Director of Harvard Business School Publications; and Benson P. Shapiro, Malcolm P. McNair Professor of Marketing and former faculty adviser to Harvard Business School Publications. The Practice of Management Series would not have materialized without their support, guidance, and insight.

INTRODUCTION

Entrepreneurship is a way of managing that involves pursuing opportunity without regard to the resources currently controlled. Entrepreneurs identify opportunity, assemble required resources, implement a practical action plan, and harvest the rewards in a timely, flexible way. In the rapidly shifting and highly uncertain environment of the 1990s, managing entrepreneurially is essential to create jobs and compete successfully.

There was a time when entrepreneurship was seen not as an end in itself, but as a stage that organizations passed through on the way to professional management. This view has changed. Entrepreneurial activity has flourished in unexpected ways, often generating more efficient and effective new technologies and more competitive products than large, traditionally managed corporations. By any measure, the rate of business start-up has soared. During the past 35 years, the number of new businesses created annually in the United States has risen from 93,000 to more than 900,000. The surge of interest in entrepreneurship over the past decade—from new publications to university courses to new venture programs in some of our largest, best-known corporations—testifies to the critical role that entrepreneurship now plays and is expected to play in shaping and strengthening our economy.

This book of readings is designed to serve as a handbook of friendly advice for those considering or engaging in the entrepreneurial process. It contains different voices, different perspectives, different insights, and sometimes even contradictory advice—a variety that captures the reality of entrepreneurship.

Advice inevitably reflects the training, experiences, and biases of the person giving it. While taking advice literally is almost always dangerous, so too is assuming that your opportunity, situation, and concerns are unique. Too often the entrepreneur wastes energy, time, and resources by failing to learn the inexpensive lessons provided by other people's experiences. Tuition in the school of hard knocks is costly, especially to entrepreneurs.

These readings explore common problems and opportunities in entrepreneurship. They come from a variety of sources and serve a variety of purposes. Some are intended to inspire; others provide technical information; still others are designed to help the reader master important skills. As you consider the various perspectives offered, ask yourself how the logic applies to you and your current or prospective business.

Each reading can stand alone or can be studied as part of a thematic unit. Taken together, the readings demonstrate that the entrepreneur is the ultimate general manager, responsible for orchestrating relationships among all parts of the enterprise. They underscore the versatility that entrepreneurs must cultivate to make their ventures succeed. They also will help you determine the key questions to ask at each stage of planning and building your venture, they will suggest milestones to measure your progress, and they will warn of the traps that have ensnared earlier explorers of the territory. The variety of readings offered here also will help you think about a new business venture from the viewpoints of its many stakeholders—the entrepreneur, the investors, the managers and employees, the suppliers, and the customers.

This collection can be used as both a travel guide and a reference source. Part One, "The Entrepreneur: Images and Self-Images," can help you think about the concept of being an entrepreneur. The term itself was coined in the eighteenth century by economist Richard Cantillon, who believed that the primary role of the entrepreneur was to bear risk. Since then, the definition has evolved in different and occasionally contradictory ways. Some people have focused on risk seeking and risk bearing, while others, notably economist Joseph Schumpeter in the early part of this century, have associated entrepreneurship with innovation. More recently, psychological profiles detailing the entrepreneur's distinctive character traits have been developed. The popular press often portrays the entrepreneur as a high-tech genius or a flamboyant promoter.

This text asks you to challenge the stereotypes, to consider entrepreneurship as a way of managing rather than as an economic function or a set of personal characteristics. Indeed, as the numerous examples in this book—as well as your own experience—will tell you, many entrepreneurs break the mold. Some, for example, bear risk grudgingly. (As a highly successful entrepreneur once put it, "My idea of risk and reward is for me to get the reward and others to take the risk.") Others owe their success, not to having a creative gift, but to extending ideas originated by others or to finding better ways to deliver products and services to customers. The first reading in the book, Stevenson and Gumpert's "The Heart of Entrepreneurship," introduces and illuminates the concept by contrasting entrepreneurial behavior with administrative behavior. The selections that follow—the Cook and Maytag interviews and Reich's

"Entrepreneurship Reconsidered: The Team as Hero"—develop the concept by depicting different entrepreneurial management styles in a range of settings.

Part Two, "Launching the New Venture," focuses on conceptualizing, creating, and planning the new enterprise. Since the most difficult part of the entrepreneurial process often is discovering a worthwhile idea, the readings in the section on assessing opportunities and risks offer insights on how to find an opportunity (a new idea, a better idea, or an existing business), how to judge its merits, and how to be certain that the idea is worth your time, money, and reputation. After all, many ideas are just that—ideas, not opportunities. As the readings by Drucker and Vesper emphasize, a blend of practical business sense, market knowledge, product expertise, resourcefulness, and imagination is needed to create or identify genuine opportunities.

This group of readings also addresses important procedural questions, such as how to conduct a start-up analysis, how to prepare for a meeting with a prospective seller and evaluate its results, and how to measure the potential value of an opportunity. Understanding the entire entrepreneurial process and gaining the appropriate skills before start-up is ever undertaken can help the reader steer clear of the waiting minefields.

Once an idea has been formulated, the next challenge is to enlist the support of others. Entrepreneurs can be so in love with their new ideas that they may overlook the necessity of selling these ideas and winning constituents. Thus, the second step in launching a new venture is determining the best way to explain the opportunity to potential supporters and to demonstrate why taking part would be beneficial for them. A comprehensive business plan, the features of which are explained in the Rich and Gumpert selection, is essential to winning investment and support from financiers. Block and MacMillan then describe a method for setting achievable and measurable goals during the planning stage. Bhide and Stevenson broaden the focus by describing how ventures can attract a range of stakeholders, from employees to customers. MacMillan tackles the same issue from a different perspective, emphasizing the role of an entrepreneur's political skills in mobilizing stakeholders.

Only after the entrepreneur has carefully assessed the opportunity, devised ways to enlist support, and set a series of concrete planning goals should the issue of financing arise. Once upon a time, banks enjoyed the stature of churches, revered for their power to bestow or withhold precious funds. Today, people speak of financial supermarkets offering a variety of products, prices, and services. It is the entrepreneur's job to become an astute consumer. The readings in the section on marshaling resources deliver a clear message: know your needs and seek the appropriate match. When it comes to capital, one size does not fit all.

To begin, the entrepreneur must be familiar with the common sources of capital, outlined here by Roberts and Stevenson, and understand his or her own financial requirements, a topic addressed by Stancill's "How Much Money Does Your New Venture Need?" The entrepreneur then must negotiate a deal that achieves the proper balance between risk and reward, a delicate task requiring skill, intuition, and especially empathy, as the remaining readings in this section suggest. What are the investors' expectations, motives, and goals? What overt and subtle messages are they communicating? Skill in reading signals and in knowing when to compromise and when to stand firm is critical to raising capital successfully.

To reap the rewards of careful idea assessment, venture planning, and fund raising, the entrepreneur must make the transition from founder to entrepreneurial manager, a theme explored by Drucker in "The New Venture." New responsibilities requiring new skills arise—assembling a management team; hiring, supervising, and compensating employees; developing and implementing budget and control systems; planning product and marketing strategies; and employing financial and legal advisers.

The readings in the section on "Building an Effective Organization" survey these topics, emphasizing the importance of anticipation and preparation. By understanding the problems in each stage of venture development, a subject studied by Churchill and Lewis in "The Five Stages of Small Business Growth," entrepreneurs can avert, or at least constructively manage, the crises that erupt as the new venture becomes a full-fledged business. Handler's "The Family Venture" considers the special management issues that arise when work and personal relationships converge.

In addition to managing internal and external relationships and resources, overseeing day-to-day operations, and charting strategies for the future, the entrepreneur must thoroughly understand the financial realities supporting new business ventures. One reality is that cash fuels the enterprise. As the readings on financial strategy demonstrate, managers must know how cash is measured, how much cash is needed today and how much will be needed tomorrow, and what the implications are of cash deficiencies and surpluses.

The first reading, Sahlman's "The Financial Perspective: What Should Entrepreneurs Know?," demonstrates how fundamental concepts from finance—cash, risk, and value—can help guide managerial decision making and enable entrepreneurs to keep their ventures thriving. The readings that follow focus on budgeting and debt policy, important dimensions of financial management. The collection concludes by exploring two possible outcomes of the start-up process: bankruptcy and going public. Each should be understood by the entrepreneur well in advance of taking action. The readings supply both technical information and practical advice; at the same time, they point out the important role that specialists play in helping entrepreneurs pursue the paths that are best for them and for their ventures.

The assembled readings cover the spectrum of the entrepreneurial experience, from idea generation to harvest. Obviously, certain readings are more relevant than others at any particular stage. A recurring theme of this collection, however, is anticipation. Becoming an entrepreneur means that you are willing to accept the prospect of complexity, contradiction, and change.

By understanding and preparing for the realities that lie ahead, the entrepreneur can greet the future with enthusiasm. Perhaps the greatest challenge, once the entrepreneur has leaped the hurdles and mastered the important skills, is to continue to pursue opportunity rather than simply to consolidate past victories. We hope the reader will find excitement in the entrepreneurial challenge and in the lifelong learning that is required to achieve success in entrepreneurial management.

WILLIAM A. SAHLMAN
HOWARD H. STEVENSON

PART ONE

THE ENTREPRENEUR:

Images and Self-Images

The Heart of Entrepreneurship

HOWARD H. STEVENSON AND DAVID E. GUMPERT

The term entrepreneurship calls to mind so many various images that a precise definition can be elusive. Popular views of the entrepreneur as do-it-yourselfer abound: the lone inventor working from a garage, the gourmet cook turning a home-based business into a restaurant, the experienced manager leaving the corporation to open a consulting practice. Such company founders are often portrayed as risk takers and mavericks. Politicians and editorial writers have seized on entrepreneurial spirit as the way to make companies—and the nation—more productive, innovative, and competitive. Looking to the entrepreneurial ideal, managers in companies large and small have responded by striving to foster creativity and flexibility in their organizations.

In this reading, Stevenson and Gumpert seek to interpret the concept by focusing on entrepreneurial thinking and behavior. Rejecting the notion that entrepreneurship is an all-or-nothing character trait of certain individuals or groups, the authors look specifically at how entrepreneurs capitalize on change, identify opportunity, and marshal resources. By highlighting the differences between the entrepreneur—the seeker of opportunity—and the administrator—the guardian of existing resources—the authors develop an anatomy of entrepreneurship for both start-up and established companies. They conclude by describing what government, schools, and businesses can do to create a climate in which entrepreneurship can flourish.

Suddenly entrepreneurship is in vogue. If only our nation's businesses—large and small—could become more entrepreneurial, the thinking goes, we would improve our productivity and compete more effectively in the world marketplace.

But what does *entrepreneurial* mean? Managers describe entrepreneurship with such terms as innovative, flexible, dynamic, risk taking, creative, and growth oriented. The popular press, on the other hand, often defines the term as starting and operating new ventures. That view is reinforced by the enticing success of such upstarts as Apple Computer, Domino's Pizza, and Lotus Development.

Neither approach to a definition of entrepreneurship is precise or prescriptive enough for managers who wish to be more entrepreneurial. Everybody wants to be innovative, flexible, and creative. But for every Apple, Domino's, and Lotus, there are thousands of new restaurants, clothing stores, and consulting firms that presumably have tried to be innovative, to grow, and to show other characteristics that are entrepreneurial in the dynamic sense—but have failed.

As for the idea of equating the beginning stages of a business with entrepreneurship, note a 1983 study by McKinsey & Company on behalf of the American Business Conference. It concluded that many mature, medium-sized companies, having annual sales of $25 million to $1 billion, consistently develop new products and markets and also grow at rates far exceeding national averages.[1] Moreover, we're all aware of many of the largest corporations—IBM, 3M, and Hewlett-Packard are just a few of the best known—that make a practice of innovating, taking risks, and showing creativity. And they continue to expand.

So the question for the would-be entrepreneur is: How can I make innovation, flexibility, and creativity operational? To help this person discover some answers, we must first look at entrepreneurial behavior.

At the outset we should discard the notion that entrepreneurship is an all-or-none trait that some people or organizations possess and others don't. Rather, we suggest viewing entrepreneurship in the context of a range of behavior. To simplify our analysis, it is useful to view managerial behavior in terms of extremes.

At one extreme is what we might call the *promoter* type of manager, who feels confident of his or her ability to seize opportunity. This manager expects surprises and expects not only to adjust to change but also to capitalize on it and make things happen. At the other extreme is the *trustee* type, who feels threatened by change and the unknown and whose inclination is to rely on the status quo. To the trustee type, predictability fosters effective management of existing resources while unpredictability endangers them.

Most people, of course, fall somewhere between the extremes. But it's safe to say that as managers move closer to the promoter end of the scale they become more entrepreneurial, and as they move toward the trustee end of the scale they become less so (or, perhaps, more *administrative*).

When it comes to their own self-interest, the natural tendency of most people is toward the promoter end of the behavior spectrum; they know where their interests lie and pursue them aggressively. A person's most valuable assets are intelligence, energy, and experience—not money or other material things—which are well suited to the promoter role.

A close relationship exists between opportunity and individual needs. To be an entrepreneurial opportunity, a prospect must meet two tests: it must represent a desirable future state, involving growth or at least change; and the individual must believe it is possible to reach that state. This relationship often identifies four groups, which we show in *Exhibit 1*.

---

1. Richard E. Cavanagh and Donald K. Clifford, Jr., "Lessons from America's Midsized Growth Companies," *McKinsey Quarterly* (Autumn 1983): 2.

EXHIBIT 1
Manager's Opportunity Matrix

		Desired future state characterized by growth or change	
		Yes	No
Self-perceived power and ability to realize goals	Yes	Entrepreneur	Satisfied manager
	No	Frustrated potential entrepreneur	Consummate bureaucratic functionary

Companies of all sizes encounter difficulty encouraging entrepreneurship when the individual's interest and the corporate interest don't coincide. Executives may enhance their position or boost their income by serving the status quo through short-term and readily measurable actions such as cost reductions or price cuts, even though such "accomplishments" may not help and may even hurt the company's long-term welfare.

To make the individual's tendency toward entrepreneurship match corporate goals and needs is no easy task for companies. First must come an understanding of the ways in which the promoter and trustee mentalities exert influence within the organization. In these pages we try to further such an understanding and develop a framework for analyzing the essential aspects of entrepreneurship in companies of all sizes. We then use the framework to offer suggestions for encouraging entrepreneurship.

ENTREPRENEURIAL PROCESS

Based as they often are on changes in the marketplace, pressures for extension of entrepreneurship tend to be external to the company. Limitations on entrepreneurial behavior tend to come from inside, the result of high-level decisions and the exigencies of hierarchy. In making decisions, administrators and entrepreneurs often proceed with a very different order of questions. The typical administrator asks:

- What resources do I control?
- What structure determines our organization's relationship to its market?
- How can I minimize the impact of others on my ability to perform?
- What opportunity is appropriate?

The entrepreneur, at the other end of the spectrum, tends to ask:

- Where is the opportunity?
- How do I capitalize on it?
- What resources do I need?
- How do I gain control over them?
- What structure is best?

The impact of the difference in approach becomes apparent as we trace the entrepreneurial thought pattern.

WHERE IS THE OPPORTUNITY?

Naturally, the first step is to identify the opportunity, which entails an external (or market) orientation rather than an internal (or resource) orientation. The promoter type is constantly attuned to environmental changes that may suggest a favorable chance, while the trustee type wants to preserve resources and reacts defensively to possible threats to deplete them. (See *Exhibit 2*, part A.)

Entrepreneurs are not just opportunistic; they are also creative and innovative. The entrepreneur does not necessarily want to break new ground but perhaps just to remix old ideas to make a seemingly new application. Many of today's fledgling microcomputer and software companies, for example, are merely altering existing technology slightly or repackaging it to accommodate newly perceived market segments.

The shakeout in the publications aimed at cable television subscribers in the 1980s illustrates good and bad readings of opportunity. In 1983 Time Inc. abandoned its TV-Cable Week after a pretax loss of $47 million. Still thriving is The Cable Guide, which is operated by two entrepreneurs marshaling a fraction of Time Inc.'s resources and working out of a town in Pennsylvania. By listing broadcast programs as well as those available on cable, TV-Cable Week aimed its content at viewers and thereby annoyed some cable operators. The Cable Guide focuses on cable-transmitted programs only, thereby pleasing the cable operators who distribute it.

Woolworth's difficulties demonstrate the challenge posed by changing opportunities. For many years the company thrived because it had the best retail locations in America's cities and towns. That approach worked fine as long as all the best locations remained in the centers of cities and in towns. As the best

EXHIBIT 2
The Entrepreneurial Culture vs. the Administrative Culture

	ENTREPRENEURIAL FOCUS		ADMINISTRATIVE FOCUS	
	Characteristics	*Pressures*	*Characteristics*	*Pressures*
A. Strategic Orientation	Driven by perception of opportunity	Diminishing opportunities	Driven by controlled resources	Social contracts
		Rapidly changing technology, consumer economics, social values, and political rules		Performance measurement systems
				Planning systems and cycles
B. Commitment to Seize Opportunities	Revolutionary, with short duration	Action orientation	Evolutionary, with long duration	Acknowledgment of multiple constituencies
		Narrow decision windows		Negotiations about strategic course
		Acceptance of reasonable risks		Risk reduction
		Few decision constituencies		Coordination with existing resource base
C. Commitment of Resources	Many stages, with minimal exposure at each stage	Lack of predictable resource needs	A single stage, with complete commitment out of decision	Need to reduce risk
		Lack of control over the environment		Incentive compensation
				Turnover in managers
		Social demands for appropriate use of resources		Capital budgeting systems
		Foreign competition		Formal planning systems
		Demands for more efficient resource use		
D. Control of Resources	Episodic use or rent of required resources	Increased resource specialization	Ownership or employment of required resources	Power, status, and financial rewards
		Long resource life compared with need		Coordination of activity
		Risk of obsolescence		Efficiency measures
		Risk inherent in the identified opportunity		Inertia and cost of change
		Inflexibility of permanent commitment to resources		Industry structures
E. Management Structure	Flat, with multiple informal networks	Coordination of key noncontrolled resources	Hierarchy	Need for clearly defined authority and responsibility
		Challenge to hierarchy		Organizational culture
				Reward Systems
		Employees' desire for independence		Management theory

retail sites shifted to suburban and highway malls, however, Woolworth's was caught off guard and other mass merchandisers grabbed the new top locations. To survive, Woolworth's was forced into a defensive strategy of developing secondary suburban properties while closing old city stores.

Woolworth's is typical of many companies that, preoccupied with the strength of their resource base, are unable or unwilling to perceive momentous environmental changes. These companies turn opportunities into problems for fear of losing strength. For the entrepreneurial mentality, on the other hand, external pressures stimulate opportunity recognition. These pressures include rapid changes in:

1. *Technology,* which opens new doors and closes others. Advances in producing microcomputer chips helped make possible the personal computer market but at the same time shrank the minicomputer market. This development posed problems for those producers that failed to perceive the change quickly.
2. *Consumer economics,* which alters both the ability and willingness to pay for new products and services. The sharp rise in energy costs during the mid-1970s made popular the wood-burning stove and chain saw, and spawned the solar energy industry, among others. But these same pressures set back those huge sectors of our industrial economy that thrived on the belief in cheap energy forever.
3. *Social values,* which define new styles and standards of living. The 1980s interest in physical fitness opened up markets for special clothing, "natural" food, workout centers, and other businesses.
4. *Political action and regulatory standards,* which affect competition. Deregulation of airlines and telecommunications has sparked opportunities for assorted new products and services while at the same time disrupting the economics of truckers, airlines, and many concerns in other sectors.

Unfortunately, innovation and the pursuit of opportunity impose a cost that many executives resist—the necessity of change. Like most other people, they tend to take comfort in routine and predictable situations. This is not because they are lazy; they are just more inclined to the administrative end of the organizational spectrum than to the entrepreneurial end. Among the internal pressures that move companies toward the administrative end are the following:

The "Social Contract"   Managers feel a responsibility to employ human, manufacturing, technological, and financial resources once they have been acquired. The American steel industry, which had the best plants in the world during the 1950s but failed to update them in the face of rising foreign competition, is a prominent example of the social contract gone awry.

Performance Criteria   Few executives are fired for neglecting to pursue an opportunity compared with the number punished for failing to meet ROI targets. Capacity utilization and sales growth, the typical measures of business success, are almost always based on use of existing resources.

Planning Systems and Cycles Opportunities do not show up at the start of a planning cycle and last for the duration of a three- or five-year plan. Better formal planning is often the enemy of organizational adaptability.

HOW DO I CAPITALIZE ON IT?

The ability to identify favorable circumstances is important but isn't enough to qualify a person as an entrepreneur. Many innovative thinkers never get anything done. Promoters, however, move quickly past the identification of opportunity to its pursuit. They are the hawkers with umbrellas who materialize from nowhere on Manhattan street corners at the first rumbles of thunder overhead.

For the trustee, commitment is time consuming and, once made, of long duration. Trustees move so slowly that they may appear to be stationary; once committed, they are tenacious but still very slow moving. Entrepreneurs have gamblers' reputations because of their willingness to get in and out of markets fast. But merely moving quickly does not guarantee success. First, entrepreneurs must know the territory they operate in, then they must be able to recognize patterns as they develop.

Successful risk takers have the confidence to assume that the missing elements of the pattern will take shape as they expect. Thus designers of CAD/CAM equipment felt free to engineer systems around disk drives that had yet to be built. From their knowledge of the industry, the designers felt confident the drives would be built and therefore they could get the right products on the market ahead of competitors. On the other hand, many utilities act like trustees. For example, they resist adoption of digital technology to streamline their operations and stick to electromechanical recording for readings of important data.

The pressures pushing companies toward either the entrepreneurial or administrative end of the spectrum with regard to the timing and duration of their commitment are a mixture of personal, organizational, and environmental forces. They are listed in *Exhibit 2*, part B.

Administratively oriented companies approach the question whether to commit to new opportunities more cautiously. Administrators must negotiate with others on what strategy to take and must compromise to achieve necessary approvals. This process produces evolution rather than revolution. The search for perfection is the enemy of the good. Administrators often see the need to change as the result of failure of the planning process.

This disposition helps explain why managers of American electronics concerns sometimes are seen looking on in amazement as their Japanese counterparts consistently bring new electronics products—from videocassette recorders to talking calculators—to market first. These Japanese companies and other successful market-oriented businesses know that change is inevitable and, therefore, keep their organizations learning.

By endlessly studying how to reduce risk, instead of trying to deal with it, administrative companies slow the decision making. The many decision constituencies necessary to satisfy proposals for new products and services lengthen the process. If there's a project that everyone down the line agrees has a three-fourths chance of succeeding, the odds of getting that project through eight approval levels are one in ten. Many executives will justifiably say to themselves, why bother? (The Japanese have learned how to make rapid decisions by consensus without bogging down in layers of bureaucracy.)

WHAT RESOURCES DO I NEED?

In grasping opportunities, some institutions with vast resources (such as government agencies, large nonprofit organizations, and big corporations) are tempted to commit resources heavily, to "go first class" all the way. In this way, the rationale goes, you reduce your chances of failure and increase your eventual returns.

From our observation, however, success is unrelated to the size of the resource commitment. More important is the innovativeness with which the institution commits and deploys those resources. The Apple and IBM personal computers were developed and produced by organizations that have little vertical integration. Few successful real estate developers have architects, contractors, or even space salespeople on the payroll. Yet many of these organizations rack up extraordinary ROIs and ROEs.

As necessity is proverbially the mother of invention, people who start businesses often make imaginative use of their limited resources. Computer engineers starting a peripheral equipment company will discover selling skills they never knew they possessed. The owner of a new restaurant quickly adjusts to waiting on tables. Entrepreneurs who are effective make the sparest allotment of resources.

Besides their reckless invasion of markets, people at the promoter end of our scale have reputations as gamblers because they throw everything they've got at opportunities. But in reality they throw in everything they have simply because they don't have enough. Successful entrepreneurs seek plateaus of success, where they can consolidate their gains before trying to acquire control over additional resources and further pursue the opportunity. They wish they had more to commit, but they do more with less anyway.

What level of resources is required to pursue a given opportunity? Tension prevails between the adequacy of commitment and the potential for return. Handling this tension is part of entrepreneurship's challenge and excitement. (See *Exhibit 2*, part C.)

Most of the risk in entrepreneurial management lies in the effort to pursue opportunity with inappropriate resources—either too few or too many. Failures in real estate investing, for example, occur when participants attempt projects larger than their resources can handle. When the investors can't come up with more funds to tide them over unforeseen obstacles or setbacks, they fail. Large corporations tend to make the basic error of overcommitting resources.

Some large companies seem to believe that they can handle all opportunities with the resources they have behind them. But that's not always so: witness Exxon's spectacular entry into the electric motor control business and its subsequent humiliating retreat. A different error made by large corporations is rejection of openings in emerging businesses because they are too small, thereby allowing new ventures an opportunity to gain footholds that cannot later be dislodged.

Looking beyond the size of the resource commitment, managers must consider its timing. At the administrative end of our spectrum, the tendency is to make a single decision for a total resource commitment. But during times of rapid change, such as we have experienced during the 1970s and 1980s, commitments in stages foster the most effective response to new competitors, markets, and technologies. Familiar by now is the staged entry of IBM into the full range of the microcomputer hardware and software market. Much of the genius of Procter & Gamble's marketing approach rests in trial, test, strategic experiment, and in-stage rollout of new products.

The pressures toward the gradual commitment of resources—toward the entrepreneurial end of our scale—are mostly environmental, and include:

An Absence of Predictable Resource Needs   Given the rapid pace of change in today's world, one must assume that in-course corrections will be necessary. The rapid advances have made technology forecasting hazardous, and projecting consumer economics, inflation rates, and market responses has become equally difficult. A multistage commitment allows responsiveness; a one-time commitment creates unnecessary risk.

External Control Limits   Companies can no longer say they own the forest and will therefore do with it what they want; environmental consideration must be taken into account. Similarly, increasingly strict zoning affects companies' control of real estate. International access to resources is no longer guaranteed, as the mid-1970s oil shortages made very clear. Corporate executives must respond by matching exposure to the terms of control. They have learned the lesson in international operations but seem unwilling to apply the lesson domestically.

Social Needs   The "small is beautiful" formulation of E. F. Schumacher and the argument that too large a gulf separates producers and consumers are very persuasive. Gradual commitment of resources allows managers to determine the most appropriate level of investment for a particular task.

In many of our large corporations, however, the pressure is in the opposite direction toward a single, heavy commitment of resources (at the administrative end of the scale) for the following reasons:

The Need to Reduce Risk   Managers limit the risk they face by throwing all the resources they can muster at an opportunity from the outset, even if it means wasting assets. Such a commitment increases the likelihood of early success and reduces the likelihood of eventual failure. This stress on concentrated marshaling of assets fosters the belief that the resources themselves bring power and success.

Fragile Tenure of Management   At companies in which executives are either promoted every one-and-a-half or two years or exiled to corporate Siberia, they need quick, measurable results. Cash and earnings gains in each period must surpass the last. You must achieve quick, visible success or your job is in danger.

Focus on Incentive Compensation   Concentration of resources upfront yields quick returns and easily measurable results, which can be readily translated into a manager's bonus compensation. Small-scale strategic experiments, however, often show little in the immediate bottom line and therefore produce no effect on pay tied to ROA or ROE while consuming scarce managerial time.

Single-Minded Capital Allocation Systems   They assume that the consequences of future uncertainty can be measured now, or at least that uncertainty a year from now will be no less than that at present. Thus a single decision point seems appropriate. Many capital budget systems make it difficult to get two bites of an apple.

In a typical case, a board of directors gets a request for $1 million net year for a start-up that, if successful, will need $3 million more in the future. The board, thinking in terms of full commitment, inquires into the return on $4 million. It fails to realize that it can buy an option and make a judgment at the $1-million stage without knowing the return on the extra $3 million. Such an approach inhibits the exercise of managerial discretion and skill, which lie in revising plans as needed and doing more with less. Hewlett-Packard and 3M are exceptions to this rule; they encourage multiple budget requests. Approval of a project means that the manager is unlikely to get all that is asked for the first time around.

Bureaucratic Planning Systems   A project can win the support of 99 people and then get scuttled by just one rejection. An entrepreneur, though, can be rejected 99 times but go ahead if one crucial respondent gives approval.

Once a project has begun, requests for additional resources return executives to a morass of analysis and bureaucratic delays. They try to avoid such problems by making the maximum possible upfront commitment.

An independent entrepreneur can field a salesperson when the need arises, but a corporate manager may put a salesperson in the field before necessary to avoid going through the approval process later. Easy access to small, incremental resources, allocated often on the basis of progress, has great power to motivate employees.

HOW DO I CONTROL THE RESOURCES?

When one thinks of a book publishing company, one imagines large numbers of editors, marketers, publicists, and salespeople. That is the way most of the nation's largest book publishers are set up. But many of today's young publishing ventures consist of just two or three people who rely heavily on outside professionals and suppliers. When one of these acquires a manuscript, it will often hire a freelancer to make editorial improvements. The publisher then contracts with a typesetting company to have the manuscript set in type, a printing and binding concern to produce the volume, and a public relations firm to promote the book. People who are the equivalent of manufacturers' reps sell the book to stores.

Not coincidentally, many large, well-known New York book publishers have struggled financially in recent years, while a number of the small young book publishing ventures have thrived. Although manuscript selection and marketing decisions certainly help determine success, two key factors are the ability to reduce overhead and the acumen to take advantage of cost-lowering technological changes in the printing industry by using outside resources.

Promoter types think that all they need from a resource is the ability to use it; trustee types think that resources are inadequately controlled unless they are owned or on the payroll. Entrepreneurs learn to use other people's resources well while keeping the option open on bringing them in-house. For example: on reaching a certain volume level, the maker of an electronic product decides that it can no longer risk having a particularly valuable component made by an outside supplier who may be subject to severe market or financial pressures. Each such decision pushes the entrepreneur toward the administrative arena. (See *Exhibit 2*, part D.)

Because they try to avoid owning equipment or hiring people, entrepreneurs are often viewed as exploitive or even parasitic. But this trait has become valuable in today's fast-changing business environment, for the following reasons:

Greater Resource Specialization   A VLSI design engineer, a patent attorney, or state-of-the-art circuit-testing equipment may be a necessity for a company, but only occasionally. Using rather than owning enables the company to reduce its risk and its fixed costs.

Risk of Obsolescence   Fast-changing technology makes ownership expensive; leasing or renting reduces the risk.

More Flexibility   Using instead of owning a resource lowers the cost of pulling out of a project.

Power and status, as expressed in a hierarchy, and financial rewards push organizations toward the administrative end of the spectrum and toward ownership. In many corporations, the extent of resource ownership and control determine the degree of power, the status level, and the amount of direct and indirect compensation. Administrators argue for the ownership of resources for many sound and valid reasons, among them:

Efficiency   Execution is faster because the administrator can order a certain action without negotiation. Moreover, by avoiding having to find or share the right outside resource, companies capture (at least in the short run) all profits associated with an operation.

Stability   Effective managers are supposed to insulate the technical core of production from external shocks. To do this they need buffer inventories, control of raw materials, and control of distribution channels. Ownership also creates familiarity and an identifiable chain of command, which becomes stabilized over time.

Industry Custom   If everyone else in an industry owns, it is a competitive risk to buck the tide.

WHAT STRUCTURE IS BEST?

A strangling organizational structure of stifling bureaucracy often stirs corporate managers to think about starting or acquiring their own businesses. Rebuffed by channels in attempts to get their employer to consider a new product or explore a new market, they long for the freedom inherent in a small and flexible structure.

When it comes to organizing businesses, there is a distinct difference between the promoter and the trustee mentalities. Via contact with the principal actors, the promoter tries to feel the way events are unfolding. The trustee views relationships more formally: rights, responsibilities, and authority are conferred on different people and segments of an organization. The trustee is prepared to take action without making contact with those that are affected by the decision.

Also influencing the approach to business organization is the control of resources. To help them coordinate their activities, businesses that use and rent resources by necessity develop informal information networks both internally and externally. But organizations that own and employ resources are easily and naturally organized into hierarchies according to those resources. Because hierarchy inhibits not only the search for and commitments to opportunity but also communication and decision making, networking evolves in most companies. Usually this networking is formalized in matrix and committee structures. (See *Exhibit 2*, part E.)

Commentators on organizations often criticize the entrepreneur's antipathy toward formalized structure as a liability stemming from an inability to let go. The entrepreneur is stereotyped as egocentric and unable to manage. In this view, the administrator may not be very spontaneous or innovative but is a good manager. In reality the entrepreneur isn't necessarily a worse manager than the administrator but has simply chosen different tools to get the task done. Fashioning these tools are the following pressures:

The Need to Coordinate Resources That Are Not Controlled   Entrepreneurs must motivate, handle, and direct outside suppliers, professionals, and others to make sure needed goods and services are available when they're supposed to be.

The Need for Flexibility   In today's atmosphere of rapid change, the development of much essential operating information outside the company makes communication with external resources even more important. The notion that hierarchy provides stability does not hold true, especially if one considers that in a typical company growing 30% annually, only 40% of the employees three years down the line will have been with the company from the start. A flat and informal structure enhances communication.

Employees' Desire for Independence   Many of today's managers are still influenced by the antiauthoritarian values of the 1960s and the self-fulfillment values of the 1970s. Furthermore, organizations with little hierarchy breed employees accustomed to authority based on competence and persuasion; they will resist attempts to introduce structure and to rationalize authority based on hierarchy.

Of course, hierarchical organizations arise for rational reasons. According to classic management theory, a formal, well-defined structure ensures attention to all the necessary planning, organizing, and controlling activities. Among the pressures against the entrepreneurial approach and toward the administrative are the following:

The Greater Complexity of Tasks   As planning, coordinating, communicating, and controlling functions become more involved, clearly defined authority and responsibility are needed to ensure adequate differentiation and integration.

Stratified Organizational Culture   If a desire for routine and order comes to dominate corporate attitudes, a more formal structure is attractive and reassuring.

Control-Based Reward Systems   As we indicated earlier, reward systems are often based on the amount of control executives have, as measured in the organizational structure. Thus incentives reinforce formality.

It's easier, of course, to avoid adding structure than it is to reduce existing structure. Many of the high-technology companies in California's Silicon Valley and along Route 128 in Massachusetts have been notably successful in keeping structure to a minimum by erasing distinctions between upper and lower management and encouraging such group activities as the Friday afternoon beer bust. The fewer the distinctions, the less inhibited lower-level employees will be about approaching top managers with complaints and suggestions about operations. Managers trained to expect an orderly world may feel uncomfortable in such an informal atmosphere, but the dividends in coordination and motivation can be important.

It is possible for companies with extensive structure to reduce it. Sears, Roebuck has trimmed its corporate staff way back and in the process has granted much autonomy to its operating units. Dana Corporation, like many other companies, has found that cutting out the "helping staff" has improved performance.

—— STIMULATING ENTREPRENEURSHIP

Our discussion should have made clear our belief that entrepreneurship is a trait that is confined neither to certain types of individuals nor to organizations. Obviously, it is found more in smaller and younger enterprises than in larger and older ones simply because the conditions favoring its development are more likely to be present.

For many people, the dream of being the boss and being financially self-sufficient is enough to stimulate the pursuit of opportunity. The venturesome are usually forced by capital limitations to commit resources gradually and to rent or use them rather than own them. Similarly, they recoil from the idea of bureaucracy; to them, it's vital to have an organization that can react quickly to new opportunities.

Even so, many of the nation's small businesses inhabit the administrative end of our spectrum. The owners shy from taking risks in pursuit of growth; perhaps they are preoccupied with other financial activities such as investing in real estate or the stock market, paying their children's college expenses, or providing for impending retirement. Perhaps they only want the business to provide a steady living, so they run their businesses in a way to guard what they have.

A society can do much to stimulate or inhibit the development of entrepreneurship. Government policy can do much to create opportunity. Decisions in recent years to lower the capital gains tax and deregulate certain industries have been instrumental in encouraging the establishment of many new businesses that otherwise would probably not exist today. Support of basic research in health, technology, and material science establishes a base on which opportunities are built.

Similarly, the way our colleges and universities teach business management affects approaches to entrepreneurship. Courses and departments in entrepreneurship, set up at many such institutions, will produce increasing numbers of young managers who are attuned to effective ways of pursuing opportunity and managing resources.

While government agencies and educational institutions can create conditions favorable for entrepreneurship to take hold, it is up to individual organizations to foster the conditions that allow it to flourish. That means encouraging the timely pursuit of opportunity, the most appropriate commitment and use of resources, and the breakdown of hierarchy.

Those goals of course are not easy to reach, especially if the organization must be turned around from its habitual administrative approach. We see in corporations the same type of opportunity matrix as we described for individual managers early in this reading and in *Exhibit 1*. As one can see in *Exhibit 3*, movement to the left requires a strategic focus and the instillation of belief throughout the organization that change is acceptable and even desirable. Movement upward presupposes that corporate officers think their organization has the capacity to acquire resources as needed. To foster this belief the leadership of the organization can:

Determine Its Barriers to Entrepreneurship   Is a manager's principal reward found in handling the company's existing resources? Are managers expected to pursue outside opportunities in its behalf only when they have extra time? Do management and director committees evaluate opportunities on an all-or-none, one-shot basis? Do superiors have to go through many levels to gain approval for capital budgets and adding personnel?

Seek to Minimize Risks to the Individual for Being Entrepreneurial   When people are promoted for behaving like trustees while promoter types are shunted aside if not eased out, there's little motive to be venturesome. The leadership can work at reducing the individual's cost of failing in the pursuit of opportunity, especially if the failure is externally caused. To convince skeptical managers that the risks have indeed been reduced, the leadership must not only recognize entrepreneurship as an organizational goal but also eliminate the bottom line as the main determinant of subordinates' success.

Exploit Any Resource Pool   The huge resources that many companies have can be committed intelligently. Indeed, the fact that they are huge can be

EXHIBIT 3
Corporate Opportunity Matrix

		Desired future state characterized by growth or change	
		Yes	No
Belief in capacity to influence the competitive environment	Yes	Adaptive entrepreneurial organization	Complacent, though successful, market leaders
	No	Reactive planners	Bureaucratic and lethargic organization

an important aspect of reducing the perceived risk to managers of pursuing opportunity. After all, resources per se reduce risks associated with exploiting opportunity. Excess resources can also support a thorough search process. And if enough opportunities are pursued, there can be ultimate success even if some fail.

Tailor Reward Systems to the Situation   For some, a primary motivating force is the possibility of becoming wealthy through ownership in a growing enterprise. For a start-up or early-stage venture, then, equity in the company may be the main incentive to entrepreneurial behavior on the part of the initial employees. Large organizations cannot hope to duplicate this lure without creating interest among those who are not offered such rewards. (Managers of these companies are often driven by other objectives anyway, including security and growing responsibility.) The leadership of established corporations, then, must think in terms of fostering team commitment and rewarding successful entrepreneurs with chances to do more of the same on a grander scale.

It is much easier and safer for companies to stay with the familiar than to explore the unknown. Only by encouraging change and experimentation can companies of all sizes adapt and grow in the midst of much uncertainty.

——— DISCUSSION QUESTIONS

1. According to the reading, entrepreneurs are traditionally perceived as being "innovative, flexible, dynamic, risk taking, creative, and growth oriented." Why do the authors try to expand the notion of entrepreneurship to embrace modes of behavior as well as character traits?

2. The authors argue that emphasizing formal planning and short-term targets discourages entrepreneurial initiative. Can the interests served by traditional planning techniques be balanced with the advantages of staying flexible?

3. Many companies pursue opportunities cautiously, seeking to minimize rather than manage risk. Think of some examples of risks you have taken in your business or personal life. What approaches and actions distinguish smart risk taking from reckless risk taking?

4. Compare the entrepreneur's and the administrator's views on acquiring and controlling resources. What are the benefits and tradeoffs of each perspective? Can vast resources be a disadvantage and limited resources an advantage?

5. Do you think that an entrepreneurial attitude can be acquired? How might initiative be fostered in workers and managers who previously have been expected to simply follow rules and regulations?

2   The Business of Innovation: An Interview with Paul Cook

WILLIAM TAYLOR

Economist Joseph Schumpeter described the entrepreneur as a person who "carries out new combinations"—a definition that gives the entrepreneur a wide arena in which to develop and implement new ideas. As the following interviews with Paul Cook and Fritz Maytag demonstrate, entrepreneurship can thrive in diverse settings and structures. Paul Cook, founder and chief executive officer of Raychem Corporation, heads an organization consisting of 30 plants in 12 countries; it supplies technical products to industrial customers in fields ranging from aerospace to telecommunications. Since its founding in 1957, the company has created numerous proprietary products based on core technologies. Fritz Maytag, founder and president of Anchor Brewing Company, works with a staff of 14 full-time and 7 part-time employees to produce six varieties of premium quality beer; his goal is to brew beer as simply as possible in a pure, traditional manner.

As both pioneers and executives, Cook and Maytag have had to translate their visions into action and to keep them fresh and alive. Cook here offers valuable lessons on corporate innovation: how to overcome such obstacles to creativity as size, the inevitable drudgery of new-product development, and even success itself; how to motivate people so they will continue to innovate; and how to investigate markets and look at new products from the customer's point of view. Maytag gives insights into the challenges and opportunities of managing in a small, family-like atmosphere: how company size can contribute to product quality, how to promote organizational learning, how to keep employees invested in company goals, and how to operate productively in an informal environment with few written rules. The contrasts between these men and their organizations challenge conventional images of the "typical" entrepreneur. At the same time, their imaginative ways of managing their enterprises underscore Schumpeter's conception of the entrepreneur.

What's the secret to being an innovative company?

Paul Cook: There is no secret. To be an innovative company, you have to ask for innovation. You assemble a group of talented people who are eager to do new things and put them in an environment where innovation is expected.

It's that simple—and that hard. There are, after all, a limited number of things management can ask for. We get innovation at Raychem because our corporate strategy is premised on it. Without innovation we die.

And I don't mean just from the engineers. Innovation is as much about sales or service or information systems as it is about products. We spend twice as much on selling as we do on research and development, so creativity from our sales force is just as important as creativity from the labs. How do you sell a product no one has seen before? How do you persuade a customer to accept us as a sole source for an important component? There's no one in any organization who can't be clever and imaginative about doing his or her job more effectively. We expect innovation from our secretaries and the people on the loading docks as well as from the scientists.

Still, few American companies are as innovative as they could be—or must be—to survive intense global competition. What's missing?

You won't get innovation without pressure. Most companies put pressure on their sales force to go out and get orders. They put pressure on manufacturing to cut costs, increase yields, improve quality. But they forget the importance of pressure when it comes to new products and processes. We want to grow this company from $1 billion a year to $5 billion, and we don't do big acquisitions. The only way to get that kind of growth is to get more and better products out the door faster.

I'm convinced that's a big reason Raychem grew so explosively in the early days. When we started the company, we didn't know what products we were going to make. We knew the first electron-beam machines were coming to market from General Electric, and we knew there were potential industrial applications for the technology. So we bought a machine. And pretty soon we started running out of money. We were under enormous pressure to find successful products—and we did. We came up with lots of good ideas because we had to. People need a fair amount of pressure to have creative ideas.

How do you maintain pressure in a successful global company?

Everyone has heard the cliché, "management by walking around." Well, you can't walk around 30 plants in 12 countries, which is what Raychem has right now, without dropping from exhaustion. But you can practice what I refer to as "management by calling about." Almost every day I use the telephone to contact Raychem people somewhere in the world. "How did your experiment go last night? What results do you have this morning? What are your ideas for a new approach? Why don't you fax me your product plan?" If you keep the pressure on in a constructive way, if you demonstrate genuine curiosity about what's happening in the labs, it stimulates people to keep the creative process going.

Why do organizations need such pressure and prodding? Isn't innovation the most exhilarating part of being in business?

What separates the winners and losers in innovation is who masters the drudgery. The creative process usually starts with a brilliant idea. Next you determine whether, if the brilliant idea worked, it would be worth doing from a business standpoint. That's the exhilarating part. It may be the most stimulating intellectually, but it's also the easiest.

Then comes the real work—reducing the idea to practice. That's the drudgery part of innovation, and that's where people need the most pressure and encouragement. You can draw a chart of how the original excitement of a new idea creates all kinds of energy, but then people go into the pits for a long time as they try to turn that idea into products that are reproducibly manufacturable. That's when you use the phone and the fax machine. That's when you have review meetings between the technical people and senior management. That's when, as CEO, you show the entire organization that you are just as interested in new product and process development as you are in manufacturing costs, sales, or quality.

We don't often hear the words "innovation" and "drudgery" together.

Too many people still think innovation is about one brilliant technologist coming up with one breakthrough idea. It's not. When we started Raychem, we began to learn what radiation chemistry could do. Within three or four years, we had generated virtually every idea behind the products we're selling today, and we're still working on that original inventory of ideas. Ten years ago, after we began work on conductive polymers, we identified a market for all the manifestations of the technology that totaled $747 million a year. We made our "747 list" and began working through it. At the time, it was a $5 or $10 million business. Today we're up to $150 million a year. So we still have a long way to go.

Or think about semiconductors. I can make a case that the semiconductor world hasn't had a really new idea for 15 or 20 years. Those companies have essentially been practicing the same technology. They've learned more about it, they've penetrated it throughout the economy, but the core technologies haven't changed that much. The pioneers of the semiconductor industry could recite within the first few years all that could be done with the technology. The winners have been the companies that reduced the technology to practice most quickly.

Does that explain some of our competitive slide against the Japanese?

This is where the Japanese are eating us alive. They're making us look like amateurs in product development. American technologists are still without peer in terms of the imagination they bring to problems. No one can question our technical brilliance. The Japanese don't pioneer the brilliant solutions, but they find the brilliant solutions. Then they bring them over to Japan and master the drudgery to reduce them to practice. Japan may not have the Nobel laureates yet, but I'm not sure it needs them to flourish. And if it wants them, all it has to do is create the right environment and that will happen too.

What's frightening to me is the thoroughness with which the Japanese scan the world for important technologies, learn them, know the patent literature, know the technical literature, and turn over every stone. We've been working on shape-memory alloys for almost 25 years. The Japanese keep knocking on our doors; they want a license from us. They are the only companies in the world besides Raychem that see the potential for this technology. In fact, whenever we find technologies that we consider powerful, for which we have great expectations, it isn't long before the Japanese show up and say, "How about a license?" or "How about a joint venture?" We seldom get chased by American or European companies.

Can a company teach its people to be innovative?

No. Innovation is an emotional experience. You can train people technically, but you can't teach them curiosity. The desire to innovate comes partly from the genes; you're born with it. It also comes from your early life, your education, the kind of encouragement you got to be creative and original. Innovative people come in all shapes and sizes and in all personality types. Some people are happiest when they're wrestling with a problem; I'm one of those. Others go into a green funk. They're miserable and depressed until they have the answer. But you can't have a good technologist who's not emotionally involved in the work. You can't have a good technologist who doesn't wake up in the middle of the night searching for answers. You can't have a good technologist who doesn't come into the lab eager to see the results of last night's experiment.

So before you hire people, you ask about their childhood?

You bet. One of my most important jobs is finding the right people to add to the Raychem environment—people who genuinely want to serve the customer, who want to build new products that are superior to anything that's come before, who are willing to stick their necks out to do new things. That means learning how their minds work, what they think about, what excites them, how they approach problems.

The top management of this company spends a huge amount of time—I probably spend 20% of my time—recruiting, interviewing, and training. It's not unusual for a technologist candidate to go through ten in-depth interviews. Now some people do better in interviews than others. But by keeping the evaluation process broad, we usually get broad agreement on candidates. I can't think of anyone who's been a great success at Raychem who wasn't a big success in the interviews.

How do you motivate people over the long haul to keep them focused on innovation?

The most important factor is individual recognition—more important than salaries, bonuses, or promotions. Most people, whether they're engineers, business managers, or machine operators, want to be creative. They want to identify with the success of their profession and their organization. They want to contribute to giving society more comfort, better health, more excitement. And their greatest reward is receiving acknowledgment that they did contribute to making something meaningful happen. So the most important thing we do is build an organization—a culture, if you'll pardon the word—that encourages teamwork, that encourages fun and excitement, that encourages everyone to do things differently and better—and that acknowledges and rewards people who excel.

Of course, people do use financial yardsticks to measure how they're doing. So you have to pay well. We pay our people above average, but only slightly above average—sixtieth percentile or so. Bonuses give them an opportunity to move up a fair amount based on overall corporate results and individual performance. Every person in the company earns a cash bonus each quarter based on after-tax profits as a percentage of sales. Ten percent of our people are in a second bonus pool. The size of a pool reflects the performance of the group or division; the distribution of the pool reflects individual performance.

Some companies spread bonuses quite evenly among group members. We have a different approach. Typically within a division there are significant differentials based on performance. Having a big spread causes some unhappiness. But it also creates drive, because I think people respect how we evaluate their contribution. We don't just reward success; we reward intelligent effort. We've paid sizable bonuses to people who have worked day and night, with remarkable proficiency, on a year-long project—only to find the market had disappeared.

We must be doing something right, by the way. Our attrition rate is very low, and the number of people who have left to start businesses to compete with us is virtually nil. That's pretty unusual when you consider what happens in the rest of Silicon Valley.

Let's talk about technology. Increasingly, companies are trying to close the innovation gap by working with other companies— often their competitors—in strategic alliances, joint ventures, and research partnerships. Does this worry you?

Yes. No company can do everything, and we use partnerships on a selective basis. We're working with Nippon Sheet Glass on switchable windows and with Furukawa Electric in shape-memory alloys. But those and a few other alliances are the exceptions. I've always believed that truly innovative companies must build an intellectual and technical infrastructure around core technologies. At Raychem, those core technologies are radiation chemistry, conductive polymers, shape-memory alloys, cross-linked gels, liquid-crystal displays, and a few others. Companies need a single-minded commitment to their core technologies, a commitment to knowing more about them than anyone else in the world. No partnership or joint venture can substitute for technology leadership.

• You also have to make sure your company has the very brightest people in your core technologies. Some who know the analytical part of the technology, some who know the molecular part, some who know the physics, some who know the chemistry. You make sure those people talk to each other, that there is regular and intensive interchange between all those disciplines. They have to work together, communicate, sweat, swear, and do whatever it takes to extract from the core technology every product possibility. The fax machine has been absolutely magnificent in that regard. Our technologists are using it to share sketches and plans, annotate them, and feed them back. The fax machine is much more important than videoconferencing as a tool for technical interaction.

Still, effective communication doesn't come easy. One of the problems with people at the cutting edge of their field is that they don't think anyone can teach them anything. That's why we recently started a "Not Invented Here" award at Raychem. We celebrate people who steal ideas from other parts of the company and apply them to their work. We give the person who adopts a new idea a trophy and a certificate that says, "I stole somebody else's idea, and I'm using it." The person on the other side, the person who had the idea, also gets an award. His certificate says, "I had a great idea, and so and so is using it." We hope to give out hundreds of these awards.

How does being committed to core technologies differ from how most companies manage technology?

Too many American companies are only immersed in their markets. They bring along whatever technology they think is necessary to satisfy a market need. Then they fall flat on their faces because the technology they deliver isn't sophisticated enough or because they don't know what alternatives the competition can deliver.

We think about our business differently. Raychem's mission is to creatively interpret our core technologies to serve the marketplace. That means we don't want to be innovators in all technologies. We restrict our charter to the world of material science, and within material science, to niches that can sponsor huge growth over a long period of time and in which we can be pioneers, the first and best in the world. And I mean *the* first. That means we can't just go to universities and find trained people; we have to train them ourselves. We usually can't use technologies from university and government labs, although we stay abreast of what's happening. After all, if we're a pioneer in a technology, how can we go to a university and learn about it?

Then we draw on those core technologies to proliferate thousands of products in which we have a powerful competitive advantage and for which our customers are willing to pay lots of money relative to what it costs us to make them. Think about that. If you can pioneer a technology, use it to make thousands of products, sell those products at high price-to-cost relationships to tens of thousands of customers around the world, none of which individually is that important to you, you wind up with an incredibly strong market position. That philosophy hasn't changed for 33 years. Our challenge has been to apply it to a bigger and bigger organization.

Why don't more companies follow this model?

Because it's a harder way to do business. Most companies say, "Let's pick markets in which we can be big players and move as fast as we can to do the simple things." More companies today want to be dominant players in big markets—you know, number one or number two in the world—or they get out. Jack Welch, General Electric's chairman, has followed that strategy very successfully for years. That's not our strategy at all.

A different, and I think more powerful, way to compete is to avoid competition altogether. The best way to avoid competition is to sell products that rivals can't touch. When we started Raychem, the last thing we wanted to do was make products that giants like GE or Du Pont would also be interested in making. We made sure to select products that would not be of interest to large companies. We selected products that could be customized, that we could make in many varieties—different sizes, different thicknesses, different colors. We wanted products that were more, not less, complicated to design and build. We wanted products with small potential annual revenues compared with the total size of the company, and we wanted lots of them.

After 33 successful years, I still have trouble pushing that vision inside Raychem; people struggle against it all the time. It takes a lot of confidence to believe that you can go out and master a technology, stay ahead of everybody else in the world, capture markets based on that technology, obtain broad patent coverage, and then end up with a strong gross profit margin in a protected business. People argue that it would be much easier, that we would grow more quickly, if we put less inventive content in our products and went for bigger markets. That's not my idea of a smart way to grow a business.

So innovation is primarily about pushing technology out the door?

Not quite. What we're really talking about is economically disciplined innovation. Sure, you have to know your core technologies better than anyone else. But you also have to know your marketplace better than anyone else. You have to understand your customers' needs. You have to understand whether or not your product is reproducibly manufacturable, which isn't easy when you're pioneering new technologies. You have to understand the competition's ability to respond to your innovation. You have to understand whether the product can generate a gross profit margin big enough to fund the new investments you need to keep pioneering and to allow for some mistakes along the way. For us, that means a gross profit margin of at least 50%. Unless you can figure ways to save your customers lots of money, to be economically important to them, and to beat the hell out of the competition with products for which they have no alternatives, and to do all that cost-effectively enough to earn big margins, you won't have economically successful innovation.

Don't all companies try to understand their markets and their customers?

But how do they do it? They go out and ask customers what they want. That's not nearly enough. I'm not talking about lip service. There are a whole series of questions that we have to answer before launching a new product. Will it save customers a little money or a lot of money? Will it make marginal improvements in the performance or efficiency of the customers' products or will it make major advances? What does it cost customers to use this new product beyond what we charge them? What are their overhead rates? What are the hourly rates for the people doing the installation? I could go on. That's why Raychem probably has more MBAs per capita than any other technology company in the United States. We have to know our customers' business problems and economics as well as we know our technology.

We also have to ask one last question: Will the customer accept a sole-source relationship with us? After all, we're in the business of delivering pioneering, proprietary products. An oil company can't decide to use one of our couplings for a pipeline in the desert and then bring in two other suppliers for the same product. We're the only supplier in the world. So we have to understand the customer deeply enough—and the customer has to know we understand him—that he has the confidence to establish a sole-source relationship with us for a new and novel product.

So companies aren't just selling innovation, they're selling confidence that they will stand behind the innovation?

Absolutely. Many customers have stuck their necks out to buy products from us that they have never seen before. That means we get into trouble from time to time. But I can't remember one case where this organization didn't rally day and night, as long as it took, to solve the problem. In fact, when you have those experiences, customers always wind up more friendly, more favorably disposed toward the next innovation. That's not the way we intend to do business, but it's part of the territory.

Customer responsiveness and trust can also lead to tremendous business opportunities. Cross-linked gels are now one of our core technologies. That business grew out of a very specific problem we had to solve for a customer. A hurricane hit Corpus Christi, Texas, and knocked out a bunch of telephones. We sent down a task force at the request of Southwestern Bell and discovered that most of the shorting out occurred in certain terminal boxes. At the time we had a tiny research effort in the area of cross-linked gels, and we thought we could use the technology to solve the problem. It worked, even though we didn't understand all the principles behind it. So we plugged gels into research to explore what fundamental technologies were involved. We discovered all kinds of fascinating things and expanded the research effort. Today we probably have 100 people throughout the company working on gels. It's a profitable, fast-growing business.

How do you develop an in-depth understanding of markets?

You can't understand the market unless you get your technologists to the customer in a deep and sustained way. Your sales force, the traditional link to the customer, only gets you part of the way. It can open doors and find opportunities, but it can't really solve the customer's problems. And you can't pass the details of what the customer needs through the filter of the salesperson. You can't expect salespeople to have the imagination and expertise to know what can be accomplished through manipulating the technology.

We have technologists at Raychem who are superb in the labs. We have salespeople and marketers, most with technical training, who are superb at understanding customer needs. The person who can combine deep knowledge of the technology with deep knowledge of the customer is the rarest person of all—and the most important person in the process of innovation. We don't have very many of those people at Raychem, but those we do have are all technologists. We have never come up with an important product that hasn't been primarily the work of a technologist. That's because doing something truly important in our field requires knowing all the things that have gone before. You have to have the technology in your bones.

It's easier to teach a technologist economics than it is to teach an economist technology. And our technologists enjoy learning about the business. Whenever they go out to visit customers, they absolutely love it. It stimulates them. It excites them. It teaches them all kinds of things they wouldn't know if they stayed in the labs. It's a very important part of the innovation process here. That doesn't mean we do enough of it; nobody does.

What are the biggest obstacles to innovation?

For an organization to remain innovative, it has to be willing—even eager—to "obsolete" itself as fast as it can. So one of the biggest obstacles to successful innovation is success itself. All too often a company will develop an important new product and spend years asking itself the same questions—how can we make it a little better, a little cheaper, a little more sophisticated? Those are all important questions; there's always room for incremental improvement. But you can't let the entire innovative thrust revolve around making products faster, better, cheaper. A truly innovative company never stops asking more fundamental questions about its most successful products. Are there whole new ways to solve the problem—ways that might cut costs in half or double or triple performance?

So Raychem is working to "obsolete" its own products?

Every day. Right now we are in the process of "obsoleting" one of our best products, a system for sealing splices in telephone cables. That product generates $125 million of revenue per year, more than 10% of our total sales. We introduced the original splice closure, which was based on our heat-shrinkable technology, about 20 years ago. It absolutely took over the market. Our customers, the operating telephone companies of the world, have been thrilled with it. We also do pretty well on it financially—gross profits are well above average.

Now we could have kept on improving that product for years to come. Instead, we've developed a radically new splice-closure technology that improves performance tremendously, and we're working very hard to cannibalize the earlier generation. We introduced this new technology, which we call SuperSleeve, in the last few years. Today we're about halfway through the conversion process; 50% of our splice-closure revenues this year will be from the new technology, 50% from the old. By the end of next year, we want virtually 100% of these revenues to be from the SuperSleeve technology. In fact, we recently closed our only U.S. manufacturing line for the old technology.

How's that different from what any good company does—once an old product runs out of steam, you introduce a new product?

That's precisely my point—our old product *wasn't* running out of steam. Our customers had virtually no complaints about it. But because we knew the product and its applications even better than our customers did, we were able to upgrade its performance significantly by using a new technology. Our margins on the new technology, at least until we get manufacturing costs down, are lower than our margins on the old product. We had to do an aggressive selling job and take a short-term financial hit—to persuade customers to adopt the new product.

Why are we doing it? Because we understand that if we don't "obsolete" ourselves, the world will become more competitive. We'd spend most of our time and energy reducing costs and outmaneuvering the competition that springs up. And for all that, we'd wind up with products that are only incrementally better, not fundamentally better.

Remember, we want products for which there is no competition. Even if we could have maintained our margins on the old product—and we probably could have by reducing manufacturing costs to keep pace with declining prices—we don't want to play that game. So today we're capable of delivering a demonstrably better product at the same price. And we're trying to persuade our telecommunications customers to write new specifications that require performance as good as what SuperSleeve can deliver. That's the game we want to play. And it's one of the hardest games any organization can play.

Are there other obstacles?

Size is the enemy of innovation. You can't get effective innovation in environments of more than a few hundred people. That's why as we continue to grow, we want Raychem to feel and function less like a giant corporation than a collection of small groups, each of which has its own technical people, marketing people, engineering people, manufacturing people. Sure we want to get big. But we must stay innovative.

Innovation happens in pockets, and the location of those pockets changes over time. So we play musical chairs with people and make extensive use of skunk works and project teams. Using small groups also allows us to make sure that a technologist is at the head of the group making the decisions. I prefer to put development decisions on the backs of technologists rather than on businesspeople. I don't want our new product teams automatically going after the biggest markets. I want them going after the best way to develop the technology along proprietary lines so long as growing and profitable markets exist. Once the product succeeds and your problems become cost, quality, and efficiency, then you can think about putting different managers in charge.

I'm surprised you haven't mentioned money as an obstacle.

Innovation takes patient capital. American companies just aren't spending enough on R&D. If companies increased their R&D spending by 2% of sales, and therefore lowered profits by 2% of sales, they'd be much better off in the long run—and so would the United States. Normally, we spend 6% or 7% of sales on R&D. This year we'll spend more than 11% of sales on R&D, even though revenues are flat and margins down a bit, because we're working on several technologies that are going to materialize into really good businesses. That's an extraordinary commitment for us to make during a disappointing period, but it's the kind of commitment more companies are going to have to start making.

Let me give you a specific example. About 25 years ago, we learned that the Naval Ordnance Laboratories were experimenting with metals that shrunk with incredibly high force when heated. We were in heat-shrinkable plastics, so we thought this was something we should know about. We started some research. We developed a metal coupling to join hydraulic lines for the F-14 fighter, and the Navy bought it in the second year we had the technology. So we continued the research and made major investments. We kept pushing to get manufacturing costs down. We searched for markets in which these shape-memory alloys could have explosive growth.

Last year, for the first time, we made money on that technology. We stayed with it for more than two decades. We are without question the world's pioneer. We have patents coming out of our ears. After 25 years, shape-memory alloys are on the verge of becoming a big and profitable business. And believe me, we are going to stick with that technology.

But you know the corporate lament: Wall Street won't let us make the investments we know we have to make to stay competitive.

Wall Street does apply pressure; Raychem's market value dropped by 10% in one day last year when we reported disappointing quarterly results. But the analysts aren't totally unreasonable. Our fiber-optics subsidiary, which is one of the most exciting new ventures in the company, is a good example. We started exploring the fiber-optics area more than ten years ago. After we worked with the technology for a few years and made some technical discoveries, we began to see what was possible. We concluded it would take several hundred million dollars to bring the technology to market and make it profitable. So far it's taken $150 million to get Raynet on its feet, and we haven't made the first sale yet.

Wall Street was shocked when we told the analysts about Raynet. We had been secretly working on the technology for years so the competition couldn't find out. Wall Street is still nervous. But the more it learns about our system and the potential markets, the more comfortable it gets. We've also tried to be smart about the financing. We brought in BellSouth as a partner to share some of the costs. And we break out Raynet's financials so the analysts can evaluate our existing businesses on a stand-alone basis.

Sure, it takes some courage to tell Wall Street, "Dammit, I'm going to spend a couple more percentage points of revenues on R&D and let my profits go down. But I'm going to show you how over a period of time that investment is going to pay off." That's not an easy story to sell. But it is sellable—especially if you have a track record of effective technology innovation.

Based on our conversation, we might identify the following principles of innovation: necessity is the mother of invention. Invention is 1% inspiration and 99% perspiration. Possession is nine-tenths of the law. Is the secret to innovation rediscovering old truths we somehow forgot?

Not quite. There are at least three new forces today. First, intellectual property is absolutely key. We are always driving for an ironclad proprietary position in all our products around the world. The ability of companies from other countries to copy important developments has increased so much that there's no way for this society, with our high standard of living, to compete against societies with lower standards of living unless we have protected, proprietary positions. So we make aggressive use of intellectual property laws and work as hard as we can to get the rest of the world to adopt effective protections.

Second, technology is becoming more complex and interdependent. To practice pioneering innovation, you must develop a critical mass of many different skills. If you're a small company, you better restrict yourself to one core technology in which you can do this. If you're a big company, you better take advantage of your technology scale and scope. You can't make that assumption anymore. You have to use your leadership position to push the frontiers of the technology, or you won't be a leader for long.

What's the third difference?

Innovation is a global game—both on the supply side and on the demand side. Raychem's most innovative lab is our telecommunications lab in

Belgium. It's a relatively small facility, but it's a melting pot of scientists and engineers from Belgium, America, England, France, and Germany. I can predict with a good deal of accuracy how a technologist brought up in the Flemish region of Belgium will approach a particular problem. I can tell you how a French engineer might approach that same problem. You have to create an organization that can mix and match all of its skills around the globe.

On the demand side, you can't leave a technology window open in another geographical marketplace. You have to fight foreign competition before it starts. Twenty years ago, MITI [Japan's Ministry of International Trade and Industry] targeted radiation chemistry as one of its industries of the future. MITI supported a lab in Osaka and tried to get the technology off the ground. Today there are 30 Japanese companies with radiation-processing technology, but together they probably have only 20% of our business. Why? Because we took the threat seriously; we refused to license our technology. We also built a business in Japan so that Japanese companies couldn't get a safe haven in which to charge high prices, grow their businesses, and then give us trouble around the world. If you want to lead with a new technology, you have to lead everywhere.

Can any company be innovative?

Every company *is* innovative or else it isn't successful. It's just a question of degree. The essence of innovation is discovering what your organization is uniquely good at—what special capabilities you possess—and taking advantage of those capabilities to build products or deliver services that are better than anyone else's. Every company has unique strengths. Success comes from leveraging those strengths in the market.

Copyright © 1990; revised 1991.

▬▬ DISCUSSION QUESTIONS

1. "The Japanese don't pioneer the brilliant solutions," states Paul Cook, "but they find the brilliant solutions." Based on what you have read about Raychem's strategy and practices, how would you distinguish between pioneering and innovating? What conditions in U.S. companies tend to encourage pioneering at the expense of innovation?

2. Cook calls size "the enemy of innovation." Do you agree? Or are there ways that size can contribute toward innovation? Cite examples from the interview and your own experience to support your view.

3. Aspiring entrepreneurs are constantly advised to "know what the customer wants." Many companies rely on their sales force to relay customer preferences to line managers and product development

teams. What, in Cook's view, are the weaknesses of this approach? How does his approach to understanding the market differ?

4. How do Raychem's hiring and compensation practices promote an innovative company culture?

5. "I prefer to put development decisions on the backs of technologists rather than businesspeople," Cook states, thereby blurring the traditional distinctions between line and staff. What are the benefits and risks of placing decision-making power in the hands of technologists?

The Joys of Keeping the Company Small: An Interview with Fritz Maytag

DAVID E. GUMPERT

You have very few employees—fourteen full-timers and seven part-timers—for a brewery that's gotten so much national attention. What's behind that?

Fritz Maytag: I've always wanted to keep my staff as small as possible. When we started 20 years ago, we would hire one or two people when we bottled. The bottling line consisted of five people, and the five included my secretary, the driver, and me, along with two part-timers. We would close the door, put up a sign saying "Closed for Bottling Today," and then the five of us would run the bottling line. In San Francisco we could find terrific people who really didn't want to work full-time but who loved the idea of working hard for a few hours a week and making good money.

The part-timers presumably also reduced your fixed expenses.

Yes, but I was also enchanted with the idea of having an artist or a teacher or some other interesting person working hard for us one day a week or so, making good money, and going back to painting. It was almost like providing a service to the community to offer very part-time, very well-paying, very hard physical—but not nasty—work. We had a kind of stable of part-timers. Right now, those we call part-timers are really almost full-time, and they have become a second category of employees. But because I've always wanted my company to be small, I tend to overemphasize the fact that we only have 14 full-time employees.

What's the idea of staying small when everyone else seems to want to be big?

I've always thought that it was more fun and satisfying to have all chiefs and no Indians. That was one of my ideas—to have a small group of people, where everyone knows they're all interrelated and where, as far as possible, everybody is in charge and nobody is looking over anyone's shoulder and there are no time clocks.

Actually, that's the way my father raised our family, from the earliest moment. Lots of responsibility. "We're counting on you. We trust you. And if you screw up, just tell us about it; don't worry about it. We're not encouraging you to screw up, but for heaven's sake, if you do, don't worry. We're all in this together, and we don't know what we're doing either, so come on and join in." And I always liked the idea of a small number of people. I just don't like what happens in large groups.

What's that?

Well, can a big group or a big company do something really well, so that employees enjoy knowing that they're doing it well? Sometimes I argue against myself. I'll laugh and say, "Well, the Maytag Company does pretty well with 3,000 employees, and I happen to know about that." Still, I've always enjoyed the idea that we have a small number of people.

I've made many decisions to invest capital in equipment and in efficiency so that we can make more beer with no more people. It's not just that I wanted to be efficient; mostly I wanted to avoid having a lot of people. The atmosphere changes when there are more people. I don't know how many is too many. We ask ourselves often, do we have too many people?

I know of companies with 200 employees where the head knows all their names. I've heard of companies with 1,000 people that work. I'm not very good at names. For me, maybe 20 or 30 employees is about right. I've often thought that too many people can hurt quality. We designed this brewery to operate on a normal work shift—eight hours a day, five days a week. Somebody comes in early on days when we brew. If we occasionally make three brews, somebody stays a little late. But the basic brewery is set up on one shift.

I'm sure this directly relates to quality. You can never come in and look at your tools and say, "Ugh, look what the night shift has done. Where's the hammer? Look, those jerks spilled something." Here, it's all us. Everybody who works here can go home and say, "I made the beer." And when they go to a restaurant somewhere and see a bottle, they know they produced it. And I think that kind of pride tends to improve quality. Real quality control takes place every minute. It has to be done right now, not later. A smaller group tends to be more quality oriented. There's an enthusiasm here, a spirit of being on the leading edge of beers and brewing styles. There's a feeling of creativity. Partly that comes from being small, a little team where we all know what's going on.

You talk about smallness and product quality. Can you elaborate?

Smallness has helped us to develop and stick to a theme. When Winston Churchill was asked at a dinner party what he thought of the dessert, he said, "Madam, it's a pudding without a theme."

We have a theme. No other beer in the world, and certainly no group of beers, have anything like the theme we have. It is that we make everything as simply as we can with as few shortcuts, adjuncts, and additives as possible, and in a pure, traditional manner. Just as an example, all of our beers are made with malt. We don't use corn or rice or sugars or sugar syrups or other grains.

How do other brewers compare in using these ingredients?

Almost all other brewers in this country and many overseas use them. For example, almost every beer and ale in England now has sugar. There's nothing wrong with it. It's not cheating. It's not evil. It's very common these days. There are a lot of advantages, especially in terms of cost and in ease of production. There's really nothing wrong with it. But we prefer to go back to the old way of making ale, the way it was done for thousands of years—with malted barley.

That's just one part of our theme. We also use nothing but whole hops—the little hop flowers. Traditionally, you pick these, dry them with warm air, pack them in a bag or a bale, and take them to the brewery to put in copper kettles. Our brew kettles are copper, of course. Nowadays, most new breweries don't have copper kettles. They use stainless steel. We wouldn't dream of having stainless.

Ask me why, and I can't really tell you. Copper looks good, it feels good. The old brewers say that it affects the flavor. I don't want to find out. The same with air-dried hops. We could use extract, which is what most brewers all over the world do now. Shipping and storing efficiency would be infinitely greater. Many breweries around the world also use a special treatment on the hops; it's something like packing the molecule, a way of getting more yield out of a pound of hops. Almost doubles the yield. A little chemical trick. We wouldn't dream of doing that.

And there's more. We ferment all of our beers in very strange, old-fashioned fermenters that are very shallow, very large. And we cool the fermenting room with filtered San Francisco air. Of course, if it gets hot, we can cool the air and if it gets too cold, we can warm up the air. But most of the time, we just bring San Francisco air in from outside and cool our fermenting room with it. We don't have coils in the tanks. This apparently is the way beer was made in the old days on the West Coast before they had ice. They just used the cool night air.

So here we are with these unusual fermenters and with the air cooled by San Francisco air. Does it make the beer different? I don't want to know. I hope so. Why do we do it? Because it feels good. Why is Chateau La Tour of any given year more fun to drink than XYZ co-op wine? I enjoy drinking Chateau La Tour because I know that it comes from one vineyard and that one wine maker does his best, given the weather and the soil and the conditions. Part of the joy of Anchor Steam beer is that it comes from this funny old way of fermenting.

Every beer we make is carbonated entirely naturally by fermentation under pressure. We don't inject any carbon dioxide. All of our ales use another process called dry hopping, which entails putting a special bag with fresh hops in the aging tank. Those little hops give it a little aromatic boost. Other people have done it, I'm sure, but when you add all this up, you see we've left everyone else behind.

How do you keep employees focused on quality?

I don't go around saying, "Here's a list of the five things that all of our employees should be doing to improve quality and here's the company song." In fact, my style is the opposite—to pretend that nothing is going on. Of course, I've always tried to involve everyone with a certain attitude toward work and toward what we're doing. All full-time employees eventually go off to special brewing courses—one- or two-week seminars and so forth. I'm sure we have the highest attendance per employee of any brewery in the United States. In the old days, we never mentioned this around the industry. Maybe when someone from the Anchor Brewing Company in San Francisco, some guy with a beard perhaps, showed up at a University of Wisconsin brewing course, he was the class joke. But when classmates—people from the big brewers—got to talking to him, he knew more about the big picture of what happens than anyone in the course.

What else do you do to get people involved?

A few months ago, we all went out and picked barley near Tule Lake, right on the Oregon border. We arranged to have the best farmer up there commit a field of his to barley. We all rode in the combine. We had 14 people, and everybody got on the combine and rode through this big rectangular field. We could hear the grain coming in there—whoosh—up in the back and into the truck. And then we took the farmer and the truck driver and everybody out to dinner that night—had some Anchor Steam beer and steaks and stuff and everybody came along. It was great.

If you're going to make rubber tires, you should go to Malaya and see the damn rubber trees. For the last four or five years, I've taken my top three people along with one or two other employees to Europe. We've gone to England twice for about ten days—just visiting little breweries, getting ideas, and looking and smelling and things like that. This year we made a trip to Germany because we were brewing wheat beer, and we wanted to do it more seriously than we had been doing before and do it just right. So we visited all kinds of little wheat beer breweries.

So that's a perk. But it's also valuable. My employees know more about how beer is brewed around the world in similar small breweries than employees of any other brewery, I would guess.

How does that benefit the company?

They know what dry hopping is. When we put the sack into the tank and it's upside down, they think to themselves, "That's not right." There's a process to dry hopping. If the tank's not clean, they think, "Gee, I wouldn't want to be like that little brewery we saw in Europe last year that was filthy dirty."

If they're bottling and the beer isn't foaming properly, they're going to say, "Gee, I don't want to be like those breweries in Europe that have oxidized beer that we all laughed about." It seems very obvious to me. Some of our employees even visit breweries on their vacations.

Because you come from a famous and wealthy family, people might wonder how important it is to you to earn a profit. Are you running this company for fun or for profit or for both?

People often ask me whether I do this for pleasure or for profit. There's usually a hidden agenda in that question, though. What they're really saying is: "You were born with a silver spoon in your mouth. Isn't this possibly just a hobby?"

I wouldn't do this just for pleasure or just for profit. The ideal is being able to do it for both. But to address the underlying question, it's terribly important to me that the business is profitable. It's not the total profit, but the return on investment that is important to me. If I wanted a lot of profit I'd be in a different business—a big business. I measure success in terms of the company's health and the return on investment. Without providing details, which I won't do, I'm very proud of both at Anchor Brewing.

Lots of brewers are now trying to do what you're doing—make premium quality beer. Does that concern you?

What does a little company do when it's been quietly trying to beat the heck out of a lazy, bored industry and just knock 'em dead in a tiny way and suddenly they figure out what you've been up to? Sell, I suppose. But I don't want to sell. I want to take 'em on again.

It took me 15 years to build a modern, superb, flexible little brewery. There's nothing like it in the world. We can brew wheat beer on Monday, barley wine on Tuesday, ale on Wednesday, steam beer on Thursday, Anchor porter on Friday, and Christmas ale on the weekend. Every one of them is completely different—different formulas, different hops, different yeast.

I've thought for years that we should have a range of products so that our company isn't known for just one product. It would be healthier to have a spread. The company should be known as a traditional brewery that makes many fine beers rather than just for the one funny name. And we should have a national presence. We should be in Boston. We should be in Dallas.

So how do you compete most effectively?

I've been thinking about that a great deal. I have two basic positions on the subject. First we have to decide what part of our activity has led to our success. For 20 years, we tried to hide from the industry. We didn't want it to catch on to us.

Now everyone has figured out what we're doing. Some breweries have invested a lot of time making good brew. The point is, everyone is either doing what we were doing or faking it. We can't assume we can stay the way we've been and keep up

That brings me to the second point. Once we've figured out what has led to our success, we have to concentrate on doing that and doing it better. Let them catch us.

We know a few things about our competitors that lead us to believe they haven't figured out all the things that are necessary to produce the kind of quality we produce. It's more than just putting a pretty label on the bottle. In many cases, competitors are copying us, but they're catching the superficial details, without the substance.

Having a small, loyal work force, it seems to me, is key to building on our theme of unusually high quality.

How do you identify these loyal and involved employees?

First we test people on the bottling line. And word spreads through the company right away when you get a new good guy down there. Gee, Ed is really working out. And there's a kind of biological reaction—you know how an organism will just close off if it gets a splinter? It just kind of gets around and pushes the splinter out. Something happens down in the plant at the bottling-line level. Ed isn't working out. And Ed just goes away. Joe is really working out. Joe works himself up. We rarely fire people now. Ed knows he's not working out. Ed's not happy. Ed quits. There's a nice sense that all of the employees have an interest in the new guy and want to see a new employee be our kind of guy. . . or woman. And I think again that's one of the advantages of being small.

It sounds like a family.

You know, I'm embarrassed by that. I'm proud of it, and I like it, but I'm also reluctant to say that I want to be the daddy to the family. But yes, there's a strong sense of camaraderie, or family. We usually have a party or two each year where everybody comes—kids and wives and husbands. And we try several times a year to do something just for the employees. Having spouses and kids and stuff is great, but there's also something different about that. We want to be sure that we have some things without spouses, just the 14 full-timers. So we try to have a mix. Linda and Dennis got married a year or so ago. Some of the employees get into little business deals together. We've had several people in the company make investments together or do little projects together. I love it.

One of my pleasures is having an employee come in and start to make a good salary and get married and have a child and then buy a house. I like to see that the company can get families going, and I'm still young enough or naive enough to be thrilled by the idea that our company can provide enough earnings to have a guy or a woman get married and raise kids, based on their hopes for the job.

I don't want to carry the family analogy too far. But what is your role as leader?

Originally, I was totally involved in everything, including production—building the brewery, designing the tanks, threading the pipes, brewing the beer, delivering it, and all the rest of it. But in recent years, I've built up a staff of people who really do everything, so I delegate enormous amounts. Now I think my role is to make sure that everybody here gets the idea that we have a theme and to remind people what we're up to and to set standards.

I sit here and talk to people. I go out and walk around the brewery and find out what's happening. And I think up new ideas, like wheat beer and barley harvesting and labels. I'm actually a little embarrassed to talk about what I do because I love it so much and it's such a sort of a selfish, quixotic kind of existence that I have. But life is short and if I thought we were being silly and the beer was a joke and it was all a con job, then I'd really be embarrassed about what I do. But I have so much fun and do such amazing things, I'm beginning to relax and enjoy it. Because I'm persuaded that the beer is so damn good.

Do you try to involve employees financially by, say, making stock available?

We never have. I've thought much about that, of course. In the early years, I thought about some kind of profit sharing or something. But the business was so risky. I was writing a check every Friday to make the payroll. Now how are you going to have a profit-sharing or stock plan if the company is losing money? I was never able to reconcile the situation.

I said to the original employees, "Look, we can't pay you very much now. But if we're right, we'll do well. And if you'll hang in there, we'll make it up to you." And we did. I'd hope the people who've been here for a long time would say I did make it up to them. And that it was worth it.

How about bonuses?

We used to have bonuses. We still give them occasionally. You know, the thing about a bonus is that if you pay it two years in a row, it's built in and the wives or husbands have already spent it. Then if you don't pay it, everyone gets upset. So we stopped paying bonuses, and we explained our reasoning to the employees. And after that had sunk in, we paid a bonus real quick. And then we didn't for a long time. It's a game. I've concluded that the best approach is to pay people well and on a rational basis. And then to do things like the barley harvest and the trips to Europe and the courses and the dinners and the ball games and the company van that you can borrow over the weekend if you're moving. Those things form a package that's a little vague but that's clearly there for you to count on. And if your mother-in-law arrives unexpectedly, and you want to tell us that you can't come in, that's fine. And if you're sick, there's no policy about how many days you can get sick and all that sort of thing. The fewer written rules, the better.

I confess that I have worried about how to share profit, ownership, whatever. But I have a dread of the co-op mentality. I think when you get a co-op mentality you almost always have deep problems of some other kind. I think that the best of all possible management situations is one with an authoritarian, almost mysterious overseeing manager combined with a very open atmosphere of knowledge and cooperation and information.

You seem to be advocating a combination of openness and executive privilege or control.

I favor a very democratic, open, egalitarian atmosphere combined with a slightly mysterious, quite powerful, benevolent authority—you never know when he might strike, change the rules, get angry, lose his temper.

I'm reluctant to be too precise about it. There are three or four people here who essentially make up senior management. And I think people sense that it's perfectly okay to go and talk to those people. I think they're a little scared to come and talk to me. But they will do it. I also think that the power is hard to pin down around here. And I like that. I like things to be a little vague and mysterious. Again, there's that combination of freedom and toughness. On the one hand, do anything you want. On the other hand, don't go goofing off or fiddling around.

Do people have titles in this scheme you have described?

Yes, but I've always said you can have any title you want. Except brewmaster. I'm the brewmaster—which is pretty much all title at this point. But in so many small breweries I've seen, the owner or the president is terrified of the brewmaster and of the production and of brewing itself. He doesn't know much about brewing. He comes home from a conference with a bright idea and wants to make an ale or a wheat beer or something. He goes out to talk to Otto, and Otto tyrannizes him.

You know how that goes in any business. You go out to the machine shop, and the foreman says your idea for a new product can't be carried through. And if you've never run a lathe, you're not going to argue with him. Ultimately, if you think he's wrong, the only way to prove it is to say, "Well, I'm sorry but we can and here is how we're going to do it and I'll show you. Watch me turn on the lathe, Otto." Right?

If you can't do that, you're in trouble. I've seen many small breweries that I thought could be more creative and successful if the owner knew more about brewing. So I've always thought I would remain the brewmaster and in that way I could go out there and say, "Guess what we're going to do now?"

Everybody knows who's in charge around here, but there are slightly vague ideas of exactly who's in charge of exactly what. That may not be a good idea, but that's the way we've done it. Of course, what really exists may be quite different from my perceptions. But that's what I'd like to think exists.

Do you have any feeling for what works best to motivate people? Is it one single thing or a combination of things?

I think it's a combination. I really believe the theory that says if you ask people confidentially what they want most in their job—if they're paid anything decent at all—they will say they want a greater sense of self-worth. I really believe that. And I think this giving of responsibility and respect and authority is one of the things that motivates people.

How would you summarize your management philosophy, then?

Actually, I'm quite uncomfortable talking about all this, pinning it down, because I think it's all very mysterious. I think there's a certain amount of magic to all this, and the more you understand it, or think you do, the more you may lose it. Good management in a small company involves a certain freshness and responsiveness and natural feeling that is by definition partly unspoken, unarticulated, undefined.

——— DISCUSSION QUESTIONS

1. Many readers might argue that Maytag's management priorities—avoiding growth, emphasizing tradition and continuity, playing the role of benevolent leader—are uncharacteristic of the entrepreneur. In your view, does Fritz Maytag promote an entrepreneurial culture within Anchor Brewing Company?
2. Maytag offers his employees an unusual combination of benefits and rewards in addition to salary—trips to European breweries, barley picking expeditions, company parties. What is the relationship between these activities and the company's goals?
3. "The fewer written rules, the better," says Maytag. Do you agree? In what areas of a small business should the rules be documented? In what areas is informality more desirable?
4. Maytag compares a small business to a family. In your view, is this analogy valid and useful? What are the benefits and risks of viewing a company as a family?
5. Maytag states: "I've always thought that it was more fun and satisfying to have all chiefs and no Indians." Is this an accurate description of Anchor Brewing Company? Is it a flat organization, or does hierarchy play a role in helping the company achieve its goals? Cite examples from the interview to support your view.

Entrepreneurship Reconsidered: The Team as Hero

4

ROBERT B. REICH

In novel after novel, nineteenth-century author Horatio Alger celebrated the virtues of the lone entrepreneur—the plucky individual who relies on his own wits, energy, and daring to rise in the world. A century after Alger produced his bestsellers, Americans continue to admire the rugged individualist, the inspired maverick. Yet, argues Robert Reich, in a world of global competition, this model of entrepreneurship offers little hope for our economy. If America is to compete effectively and enjoy a rising standard of living, it must uphold a new and different ideal—companies that draw on the talents and creativity of employees at all levels of the organization.

Emphasizing the power of images to shape our attitudes and mobilize us to action, Reich contrasts individual and collective entrepreneurship and explains how new competitive realities require us to discard long-held values and aspirations. By delineating the features of the entrepreneurial organization and using product histories to demonstrate the benefits of collaborative innovation, Reich sets forth an alternative ideal to guide the ways people work together to meet the challenge of global competition.

"Wake up there, youngster," said a rough voice.

Ragged Dick opened his eyes slowly and stared stupidly in the face of the speaker, but did not offer to get up.

"Wake up, you young vagabond!" said the man a little impatiently; "I suppose you'd lay there all day, if I hadn't called you."

So begins the story of *Ragged Dick, or Street Life in New York*, Horatio Alger's first book—the first of 135 tales written in the late 1800s that together sold close to 20 million copies. Like all the books that followed, *Ragged Dick* told the story of a young man who, by pluck and luck, rises from his lowly station to earn a respectable job and the promise of a better life.

Nearly a century later, another best-selling American business story offered a different concept of heroism and a different description of the route to success. This story begins:

All the way to the horizon in the last light, the sea was just degrees of gray, rolling and frothy on the surface. From the cockpit of a small white sloop—she was 35 feet long—the waves looked like hills coming up from behind, and most of the crew preferred not to glance at them. . . . Running under shortened sails in front of the northeaster, the boat rocked one way, gave a thump, and then it rolled the other. The pots and pans in the galley clanged. A six-pack of beer, which someone had forgotten to stow away, slid back and forth across the cabin floor, over and over again. Sometime late that night, one of the crew raised a voice against the wind and asked, "What are we trying to prove?"

The book is Tracy Kidder's *The Soul of a New Machine*, a 1981 tale of how a team—a crew—of hardworking inventors built a computer by pooling their efforts. The opening scene is a metaphor for the team's treacherous journey.

Separated by 100 years, totally different in their explanations of what propels the American economy, these two stories symbolize the choice that Americans will face in the 1990s; each celebrates a fundamentally different version of American entrepreneurship. Which version we choose to embrace will help determine how quickly and how well the United States adapts to the challenge of global competition.

Horatio Alger's notion of success is the traditional one: the familiar tale of triumphant individuals, of enterprising heroes who win riches and rewards through a combination of Dale Carnegie-esque self-improvement, Norman Vincent Peale-esque faith, Sylvester Stallone-esque assertiveness, and plain old-fashioned good luck. Tracy Kidder's story, by contrast, teaches that economic success comes through the talent, energy, and commitment of a team—through *collective* entrepreneurship.

Stories like these do more than merely entertain or divert us. Like ancient myths that captured and contained an essential truth, they shape how we see and understand our lives, how we make sense of our experience. Stories can mobilize us to action and affect our behavior—more powerfully than simple and straightforward information ever can.

To the extent that we continue to celebrate the traditional myth of the entrepreneurial hero, we will slow the progress of change and adaptation that is essential to our economic success. If we are to compete effectively in today's world, we must begin to celebrate collective entrepreneurship, endeavors in which the whole of the effort is greater than the sum of individual contributions. We need to honor our teams more, our aggressive leaders and maverick geniuses less.

—— HEROES AND DRONES

The older and still dominant American myth involves two kinds of actors: entrepreneurial heroes and industrial drones—the inspired and the perspired.

In this myth, entrepreneurial heroes personify freedom and creativity. They come up with the Big Ideas and build the organizations—the Big

Machines—that turn them into reality. They take the initiative, come up with technological and organizational innovations, devise new solutions to old problems. They are the men and women who start vibrant new companies, turn around failing companies, and shake up staid ones. To all endeavors they apply daring and imagination.

The myth of the entrepreneurial hero is as old as America and has served us well in a number of ways. We like to see ourselves as born mavericks and fixers. Our entrepreneurial drive has long been our distinguishing trait. Generations of inventors and investors have kept us on the technological frontier. In a world of naysayers and traditionalists, the American character has always stood out—cheerfully optimistic, willing to run risks, ready to try anything. During World War II, it was the rough-and-ready American GI who could fix the stalled jeep in Normandy while the French regiment only looked on.

Horatio Alger captured this spirit in hundreds of stories. With titles like *Bound to Rise, Luck and Pluck,* and *Sink or Swim,* they inspired millions of readers with a gloriously simple message: in America you can go from rags to riches. The plots were essentially the same; like any successful entrepreneur, Alger knew when he was onto a good thing. A fatherless, penniless boy—possessed of great determination, faith, and courage—seeks his fortune. All manner of villain tries to tempt him, divert him, or separate him from his small savings. But in the end, our hero prevails—not just through pluck; luck plays a part too—and by the end of the story he is launched on his way to fame and fortune.

At the turn of the century, Americans saw fiction and reality sometimes converging. Edward Harriman began as a $5-a-week office boy and came to head a mighty railroad empire. John D. Rockefeller rose from a clerk in a commission merchant's house to become one of the world's richest men. Andrew Carnegie started as a $1.20-a-week bobbin boy in a Pittsburgh cotton mill and became the nation's foremost steel magnate. In the early 1900s, when boys were still reading the Alger tales, Henry Ford made his fortune mass-producing the Model T, and in the process became both a national folk hero and a potential presidential candidate.

Alger's stories gave the country a noble ideal—a society in which imagination and effort summoned their just reward. The key virtue was self-reliance; the admirable man was the self-made man; the goal was to be your own boss. Andrew Carnegie articulated the prevailing view: "Is any would-be businessman . . . content in forecasting his future, to figure himself as labouring all his life for a fixed salary? Not one, I am sure. In this you have the dividing line between business and non-business; the one is master and depends on profits, the other is servant and depends on salary."[1]

The entrepreneurial hero still captures the American imagination. Inspired by the words of his immigrant father, who told him, "You could be anything you want to be, if you wanted it bad enough and were willing to work

---

1. Andrew Carnegie, *The Business of Empire* (New York: Doubleday, Page, 1902), 192.

for it," Lido Iacocca worked his way up to the presidency of Ford Motor Company, from which he was abruptly fired by Henry Ford II, only to go on to rescue Chrysler from bankruptcy, thumb his nose at Ford in a best-selling autobiography, renovate the Statue of Liberty, and gain mention as a possible presidential candidate.[2] Could Horatio Alger's heroes have done any better?

Peter Ueberroth, son of a traveling aluminum salesman, worked his way through college, single-handedly built a $300-million business, went on to organize the 1984 Olympics, became *Time* magazine's Man of the Year and the commissioner of baseball. Steven Jobs built his own computer company from scratch and became a multimillionaire before his thirtieth birthday. Stories of entrepreneurial heroism come from across the economy and across the country: professors who create whole new industries and become instant millionaires when their inventions go from the laboratory to the marketplace; youthful engineers who quit their jobs, strike out on their own, and strike it rich.

In the American economic mythology, these heroes occupy center stage: "Fighters, fanatics, men with a lust for contest, a gleam of creation, and a drive to justify their break from the mother company."[3] Prosperity for all depends on the entrepreneurial vision of a few rugged individuals.

If the entrepreneurial heroes hold center stage in this drama, the rest of the vast work force plays a supporting role—supporting and unheralded. Average workers in this myth are drones—cogs in the Big Machines, so many interchangeable parts, unable to perform without direction from above. They are put to work for their hands, not for their minds or imaginations. Their jobs typically appear by the dozens in the help-wanted sections of daily newspapers. Their routines are unvaried. They have little opportunity to use judgment or creativity. To the entrepreneurial hero belongs all the inspiration; the drones are governed by the rules and valued for their reliability and pliability.

These average workers are no villains—but they are certainly no heroes. Uninteresting and uninterested, goes the myth, they lack creative spark and entrepreneurial vision. These are, for example, the nameless and faceless workers who lined up for work in response to Henry Ford's visionary offer of a $5-per-day paycheck. At best, they put in a decent effort in executing the entrepreneurial hero's grand design. At worst, they demand more wages and benefits for less work, do the minimum expected of them, or function as bland bureaucrats mired in standard operating procedures.

The entrepreneurial hero and the worker drone together personify the mythic version of how the American economic system works. The system needs both types. But rewards and treatment for the two are as different as the roles themselves: the entrepreneurs should be rewarded with fame and fortune; drones should be disciplined through clear rules and punishments. Considering the overwhelming importance attached to the entrepreneur in this paradigm,

---

2. See Lee Iacocca and William Novak, *Iacocca: An Autobiography* (New York: Bantam Books, 1984).

3. George Gilder, *The Spirit of Enterprise* (New York: Simon and Schuster, 1984), 213.

the difference seems appropriate. For, as George Gilder has written, "All of us are dependent for our livelihood and progress not on a vast and predictable machine, but on the creativity and courage of the particular men who accept the risks which generate our riches."[4]

—— WHY HORATIO ALGER CAN'T HELP US ANYMORE

There is just one fatal problem with this dominant myth: it is obsolete. The economy that it describes no longer exists. By clinging to the myth, we subscribe to an outmoded view of how to win economic success—a view that, on a number of counts, endangers our economic future:

- In today's global economy, the Big Ideas pioneered by American entrepreneurs travel quickly to foreign lands. In the hands of global competitors, these ideas can undergo continuous adaptation and improvement and reemerge as new Big Ideas or as a series of incrementally improved small ideas.
- The machines that American entrepreneurs have always set up so efficiently to execute their Big Ideas are equally footloose. Process technology moves around the globe to find the cheapest labor and the friendliest markets. As ideas migrate overseas, the economic and technological resources needed to implement the ideas migrate too.
- Workers in other parts of the world are apt to be cheaper or more productive—or both—than workers in the United States. Around the globe, millions of potential workers are ready to underbid American labor.
- Some competitor nations—Japan, in particular— have created relationships among engineers, managers, production workers, and marketing and sales people that do away with the old distinction between entrepreneurs and drones. The dynamic result is yet another basis for challenging American assumptions about what leads to competitive success.

Because of these global changes, the United States is now susceptible to competitive challenge on two grounds. First, by borrowing the Big Ideas and process technology that come from the United States and providing the hardworking, low-paid workers, developing nations can achieve competitive advantage. Second, by embracing collective entrepreneurship, the Japanese especially have found a different way to achieve competitive advantage while maintaining high real wages.

Americans continue to lead the world in breakthroughs and cutting-edge scientific discoveries. But the Big Ideas that start in this country now quickly travel abroad, where they not only get produced at high speed, at low cost, and with great efficiency, but also undergo continuous development and

---

4. Ibid., 147.

improvement. And all too often, American companies get bogged down somewhere between invention and production.

Several product histories make the point. Americans invented the solid-state transistor in 1947. Then in 1953, Western Electric licensed the technology to Sony for $25,000—and the rest is history. A few years later, RCA licensed several Japanese companies to make color televisions—and that was the beginning of the end of color-television production in the United States. Routine assembly of color televisions eventually shifted to Taiwan and Mexico. At the same time, Sony and other Japanese companies pushed the technology in new directions, continuously refining it into a stream of consumer products.

In 1968, Unimation licensed Kawasaki Heavy Industries to make industrial robots. The Japanese took the initial technology and kept moving it forward. The pattern has been the same for one Big Idea after another. Americans came up with the Big Ideas for videocassette recorders, basic oxygen furnaces, continuous casters for making steel, microwave ovens, automobile stamping machines, computerized machine tools, integrated circuits. But these Big Ideas—and many, many others—quickly found their way into production in foreign countries: routine, standardized production in developing nations or continuous refinement and complex applications in Japan. Either way, the United States has lost ground.

Older industrial economies, like our own, have two options: they can try to match the low wages and discipline under which workers elsewhere in the world are willing to labor, or they can compete on the basis of how quickly and how well they transform ideas into incrementally better products. The second option is, in fact, the only one that offers the possibility of high real incomes in America. But here's the catch: a handful of lone entrepreneurs producing a few industry-making Big Ideas can't execute this second option. Innovation must become both continuous and collective. And that requires embracing a new ideal: collective entrepreneurship.

——— THE NEW ECONOMIC PARADIGM

If America is to win in the new global competition, we need to begin telling one another a new story in which companies compete by drawing on the talent and creativity of all their employees, not just a few maverick inventors and dynamic CEOs. Competitive advantage today comes from continuous, incremental innovation and refinement of a variety of ideas that spread throughout the organization. The entrepreneurial organization is both experience-based and decentralized, so that every advance builds on every previous advance, and everyone in the company has the opportunity and capacity to participate.

While this story represents a departure from tradition, it already exists, in fact, to a greater or lesser extent in every well-run American and Japanese corporation. The difference is that we don't recognize and celebrate this story—and the Japanese do.

Consider just a few of the evolutionary paths that collective entrepreneurship can take: vacuum-tube radios become transistorized radios, then stereo pocket radios audible through earphones, then compact discs and compact disc players, and then optical-disc computer memories. Color televisions evolve into digital televisions capable of showing several pictures simultaneously; videocassette recorders into camcorders. A single strand of technological evolution connects electronic sewing machines, electronic typewriters, and flexible electronic workstations. Basic steel gives way to high-strength and corrosion-resistant steels, then to new materials composed of steel mixed with silicon and custom-made polymers. Basic chemicals evolve into high-performance ceramics, to single-crystal silicon and high-grade crystal glass. Copper wire gives way to copper cables, then to fiber-optic cables.

These patterns reveal no clear life cycles with beginnings, middles, and ends. Unlike Big Ideas that beget standardized commodities, these products undergo a continuous process of incremental change and adaptation. Workers at all levels add value not solely or even mostly by tending machines and carrying out routines, but by continuously discovering opportunities for improvement in product and process.

In this context, it makes no sense to speak of an "industry" like steel or automobiles or televisions or even banking. There are no clear borders around any of these clusters of goods or services. When products and processes are so protean, companies grow or decline not with the market for some specific good, but with the creative and adaptive capacity of their workers.

Workers in such organizations constantly reinvent the company; one idea leads to another. Producing the latest generation of automobiles involves making electronic circuits that govern fuel consumption and monitor engine performance; developments in these devices lead to improved sensing equipment and software for monitoring heartbeats and moisture in the air. Producing cars also involves making flexible robots for assembling parts and linking them by computer; steady improvements in these technologies, in turn, lead to expert production systems that can be applied anywhere. What is considered the "automobile industry" thus becomes a wide variety of technologies evolving toward all sorts of applications that flow from the same strand of technological development toward different markets.

In this paradigm, entrepreneurship isn't the sole province of the company's founder or its top managers. Rather, it is a capability and attitude that is diffused throughout the company. Experimentation and development go on all the time as the company searches for new ways to capture and build on the knowledge already accumulated by its workers.

Distinctions between innovation and production, between top managers and production workers blur. Because production is a continuous process of reinvention, entrepreneurial efforts are focused on many thousands of small ideas rather than on just a few big ones. And because valuable information and expertise are dispersed throughout the organization, top management does not solve problems; it creates an environment in which people can identify and solve problems themselves.

Most of the training for working in this fashion takes place on the job. Formal education may prepare people to absorb and integrate experience, but it does not supply the experience. No one can anticipate the precise skills that workers will need to succeed on the job when information processing, know-how, and creativity are the value added. Any job that could be fully prepared for in advance is, by definition, a job that could be exported to a low-wage country or programmed into robots and computers; a routine job is a job destined to disappear.

In collective entrepreneurship, individual skills are integrated into a group; this collective capacity to innovate becomes something greater than the sum of its parts. Over time, as group members work through various problems and approaches, they learn about each others' abilities. They learn how they can help one another perform better, what each can contribute to a particular project, how they can best take advantage of one another's experience. Each participant is constantly on the lookout for small adjustments that will speed and smooth the evolution of the whole. The net result of many such small-scale adaptations, effected throughout the organization, is to propel the enterprise forward.

Collective entrepreneurship thus entails close working relationships among people at all stages of the process. If customers' needs are to be recognized and met, designers and engineers must be familiar with sales and marketing. Salespeople must also have a complete understanding of the enterprise's capacity to design and deliver specialized products. The company's ability to adapt to new opportunities and capitalize on them depends on its capacity to share information and involve everyone in the organization in a systemwide search for ways to improve, adjust, adapt, and upgrade.

Collective entrepreneurship also entails a different organizational structure. Under the old paradigm, companies are organized into a series of hierarchical tiers so that supervisors at each level can make sure that subordinates act according to plan. It is a structure designed to control. But enterprises designed for continuous innovation and incremental improvement use a structure designed to spur innovation at all levels. Gaining insight into improvement of products and processes is more important than rigidly following rules. Coordination and communication replace command and control. Consequently, there are few middle-level managers and only modest differences in the status and income of senior managers and junior employees.

Simple accounting systems are no longer adequate or appropriate for monitoring and evaluating job performance: tasks are intertwined and interdependent, and the quality of work is often more important than the quantity of work. In a system where each worker depends on many others—and where the success of the company depends on all—the only appropriate measurement of accomplishment is a collective one. At the same time, the reward system reflects this new approach: profit sharing, gain sharing, and performance bonuses all demonstrate that the success of the company comes from the broadest contribution of all the company's employees, not just those at the top.

Finally, under collective entrepreneurship, workers do not fear technology and automation as a threat to their jobs. When workers add value through judgment and knowledge, computers become tools that expand their discretion. Computer-generated information can give workers rich feedback about their own efforts, how they affect others in the production process, and how the entire process can be improved. One of the key lessons to come out of the General Motors–Toyota joint venture in California is that the Japanese automaker does not rely on automation and technology to replace workers in the plant. In fact, human workers still occupy the most critical jobs—those where judgment and evaluation are essential. Instead, Toyota uses technology to allow workers to focus on those important tasks where choices have to be made. Under this approach, technology gives workers the chance to use their imagination and their insight on behalf of the company.

——— THE TEAM AS HERO

In 1986, one of America's largest and oldest enterprises announced that it was changing the way it assigned its personnel: the U.S. Army discarded a system that assigned soldiers to their units individually in favor of a system that keeps teams of soldiers together for their entire tours of duty. An Army spokesperson explained, "We discovered that individuals perform better when they are part of a stable group. They are more reliable. They also take responsibility for the success of the overall operation."

In one of its recent advertisements, BellSouth captures the new story. "BellSouth is not a bunch of individuals out for themselves," the ad proclaimed. "We're a team."

Collective entrepreneurship is already here. It shows up in the way our best-run companies now organize their work, regard their workers, design their enterprises. Yet the old myth of the entrepreneurial hero remains powerful. Many Americans would prefer to think that Lee Iacocca single-handedly saved Chrysler from bankruptcy than to accept the real story: a large team of people with diverse backgrounds and interests joined together to rescue the ailing company.

Bookstores bulge with new volumes paying homage to American CEOs. It is a familiar story; it is an engaging story. And no doubt, when seen through the eyes of the CEO, it accurately portrays how that individual experienced the company's success. But what gets left out time after time are the experiences of the rest of the team—the men and women at every level of the company whose contributions to the company created the success that the CEO so eagerly claims. Where are the books that celebrate their stories?

You can also find inspirational management texts designed to tell top executives how to be kinder to employees, treat them with respect, listen to them, and make them feel appreciated. By reading these books, executives can learn how to search for excellence, create excellence, achieve excellence, or become impassioned about excellence—preferably within one minute. Managers are supposed to walk around, touch employees, get directly involved, effervesce with praise and encouragement, stage celebrations, and indulge in hoopla.

Some of this is sound; some of it is hogwash. But most of it, even the best, is superficial. Lacking any real context, unattached to any larger understanding of why relationships between managers and workers matter, the prescriptions often remain shallow and are treated as such. The effervescent executive is likely to be gone in a few years, many of the employees will be gone, and the owners may be different as well. Too often the company is assumed to be a collection of assets, available to the highest bidder. When times require it, employees will be sacked. Everybody responds accordingly. Underneath the veneer of participatory management, it is business as usual—and business as usual represents a threat to America's long-term capacity to compete.

If the United States is to compete effectively in the world in a way designed to enhance the real incomes of Americans, we must bring collective entrepreneurship to the forefront of the economy. That will require us to change our attitudes, to downplay the myth of the entrepreneurial hero, and to celebrate our creative teams.

First, we will need to look for and promote new kinds of stories. In modern-day America, stories of collective entrepreneurship typically appear in the sports pages of the daily newspaper; time after time, in accounts of winning efforts we learn that the team with the best blend of talent won—the team that emphasized teamwork—not the team with the best individual athlete. The cultural challenge is to move these stories from the sports page to the business page. We need to shift the limelight from maverick founders and shake-'em-up CEOs to groups of engineers, production workers, and marketers who successfully innovate new products and services. We need to look for opportunities to tell stories about American business from the perspective of all the workers who make up the team, rather than solely from the perspective of top managers. The stories are there—we need only change our focus, alter our frame of reference, in order to find them.

Second, we will need to understand that the most powerful stories get told, not in books and newspapers, but in the everyday world of work. Whether managers know it or not, every decision they make suggests a story to the rest of the enterprise. Decisions to award generous executive bonuses or to provide plush executive dining rooms and executive parking places tell the old story of entrepreneurial heroism. A decision to lay off 10% of the work force tells the old story of the drone worker. Several years ago, when General Motors reached agreement on a contract with the United Auto Workers that called for a new relationship based on cooperation and shared sacrifice, and then, on the same day, announced a new formula for generous executive bonuses, long-time union members simply nodded to themselves. The actions told the whole story. It is not enough to acknowledge the importance of collective entrepreneurship; clear and consistent signals must reinforce the new story.

Collective entrepreneurship represents the path toward an economic future that is promising for both managers and workers. For managers, this path means continually retraining employees for more complex tasks; automating in ways that cut routine tasks and enhance worker flexibility and creativity; diffusing responsibility for innovation; taking seriously labor's concern for job security; and giving workers a stake in improved productivity through profit-linked bonuses and stock plans.

For workers, this path means accepting flexible job classifications and work rules; agreeing to wage rates linked to profits and productivity improvements; and generally taking greater responsibility for the soundness and efficiency of the enterprise. This path also involves a closer and more permanent relationship with other parties that have a stake in the company's performance—suppliers, dealers, creditors, even the towns and cities in which the company resides.

Under collective entrepreneurship, all those associated with the company become partners in its future. The distinction between entrepreneurs and drones breaks down. Each member of the enterprise participates in its evolution. All have a commitment to the company's continued success. It is the one approach that can maintain and improve America's competitive performance—and America's standard of living—over the long haul.

Copyright © 1987; revised 1991.

▬▬ DISCUSSION QUESTIONS

1. Name some people—from business, sports, fiction, movies, politics, or your own personal experience—who have inspired you and shaped your professional ambitions. In considering the qualities you admire in these people, do you agree with Reich's assertion that we celebrate the virtues of individual heroes at the expense of team players?

2. Reich points out that foreign competitors quickly capitalize on American technological breakthroughs. "All too often," he observes, "American companies get bogged down somewhere between invention and production." What conditions in U.S. companies—structural, managerial, financial, technological, or otherwise—account for our failure to reap the full benefits of our own ideas?

3. According to the reading, heroes are admired for their boldness and creativity, and drones are valued for their "reliability and pliability." What are the qualities of an effective team player? What incentives can an organization create to foster these qualities?

4. To compete effectively, says Reich, we need a new kind of workplace and new kinds of work relationships. Does Reich's vision strike you as a realistic blueprint or as an unworkable ideal? What assumptions, attitudes, and practices would have to change for this vision to be realized?

5. Given the magnitude of the changes needed, can the current generation of American managers and workers learn to think and behave in new ways? What other social institutions might need to change in order to foster the attitudes and behavior that Reich advocates?

PART TWO

LAUNCHING THE NEW VENTURE

ASSESSING: WHAT ARE THE OPPORTUNITIES AND RISKS?

The Big Power of Little Ideas

5

PETER F. DRUCKER

Why do some ideas have a lasting impact on business practice and products, while others are momentarily raised and quickly forgotten? Are the most enduring ideas those that spring from the minds of geniuses and visionaries? According to Peter Drucker, the greatest achievements in business result from small ideas—small ideas shaped by an entrepreneurial perspective. Through diverse examples, Drucker identifies the distinctive features of entrepreneurial ideas and offers insights into the ways of thinking and acting that bring these ideas to life.

- Is long-range planning for the big company only?
- Does LRP mean predicting what the future will hold and adapting company actions to the anticipated trends?

Many executives, judging by their actions, would answer *yes* to both questions. But they are wrong. The correct answer to both is a resounding *no!*

The future cannot be known. The only thing certain about it is that it will be different from, rather than a continuation of, today. But the future is as yet unborn, unformed, undetermined. It can be shaped by purposeful action. And the one thing that can effectively motivate such action is an idea—an idea of a different economy, a different technology, or a different market exploited by a different business.

But ideas always start small. That is why long-range planning is not just for the large company. That is why the small business may actually have an advantage in attempting to shape the future today.

The new, the different, when judged in dollars, always looks so small and insignificant that it tends to be dwarfed by the sheer volume of the existing business in the large company. The few million dollars in sales that a new idea might produce in the next few years, even if wildly successful, look so puny compared to the hundreds of millions the existing businesses of the large company produce that these dollars are sometimes disregarded.

And yet the new requires a great deal of effort. So much so that the small company is often far more willing to tackle the job. This is why there is good reason for the large company to organize special long-range planning effort; otherwise it may never get around to anything but today's work.

But, of course, the small company that does a good job of shaping the future today will not remain a "small business" very long. Every successful large business in existence was once a small business based on an idea of what the future should be.

This "idea," however, has to be an entrepreneurial one—with potential and capacity for producing wealth—expressed in a going, working, producing business, and effective through business actions and business behavior. Underlying the entrepreneurial idea is always the question: "What major change in economy, market, or knowledge would enable our company to conduct business the way we really would *like* to do it, the way we would really obtain the best economic results?" The dominant question should not be: "What should future society look like?" This is the question of the social reformer, the revolutionary, or the philosopher—not the entrepreneur.

Because this seems so limited, so self-centered an approach, historians have tended to overlook it. They have tended to be oblivious of the impact of the innovating businessman. The *great* philosophical idea has had, of course, much more profound effects. But, on the other hand, very few philosophical ideas have had any effect at all. And while each business idea is much more limited, larger proportions of them are effective. As a result, innovating businesspeople as a group have had a good deal more impact on society than historians realize.

The very fact that theirs are not "big ideas"—ones that encompass all of society or all of knowledge, but "little ideas" that affect just one narrow area—makes the ideas of the entrepreneur much more viable. The people who possess such ideas may be wrong about everything else in the future economy or society. But what does it matter so long as they are approximately right in respect to their own, narrow business focus? All that they need to be successful is just *one* small, specific development. It is true that a few—a very few—big philosophical ideas do become footnotes in history books; however, a great many small entrepreneurial ideas become stock market listings.

Let us turn to history for some little ideas that have led to large results. First, let us note some ideas from which whole industries grew. (Afterward we will look at some ideas from which great corporations have sprung.)

———— COMMERCIAL BANKING

The entrepreneurial innovation that has had the greatest impact was that which converted the theoretical proposition of the French social philosopher, Claude Henri Saint Simon, into a bank a century ago. Saint Simon had started with the concept of the entrepreneur as developed earlier by his compatriot, the economist J. B. Say, to develop a philosophical system around the creative role of capital.

Saint Simon's idea became effective through a banking business: the famous Crédit Mobilier, which his disciples, the brothers Pereire, founded in Paris during the middle of the nineteenth century. The Crédit Mobilier was to be the conscious developer of industry through the direction of the liquid resources of the community. It came to be the prototype for the entire banking system of the then "underdeveloped" continent of Europe of the Pereires' days—beginning with France, the Netherlands, and Belgium. The Pereires' imitators then founded the business banks of Germany, Switzerland, Austria, Scandinavia, and Italy, which became the main agents for the industrial development of these countries.

After our Civil War the idea crossed the Atlantic. The U.S. bankers who developed U.S. industry—from Jay Cooke and the American Crédit Mobilier, which financed the transcontinental railroad, to J. P. Morgan—were all imitators of the Pereires, whether they knew it or not. So were the Japanese Zaibatsu—the great banker-industrialists who built the foundations for the economy of modern Japan.

The most faithful disciple of the Pereires, however, has been Soviet Russia. The idea of planning through controlled allocation of capital has been taken directly from the Pereires. There is nothing of this in Marx, above all no planning. All the Soviets actually did was to substitute the state for the individual banker. This was actually a step taken by an Austrian, Rudolf Hilferding, who started out in Vienna as a banker in the business bank tradition and ended as the leading theoretician of German democratic socialism. Hilferding's book, *Finance Capital* (1910), was acknowledged by Lenin to have been the source of his planning and industrialization concepts.

Every single "development bank" started in an underdeveloped country is a direct descendant of the original Crédit Mobilier. But the point about the Credit Mobilier is not that it has had tremendous worldwide impact. The point is that the Pereires started a business—a bank with the intention of making money.

—— CHEMICAL INDUSTRY

By all odds, the modern chemical industry should have arisen in England. In the mid-nineteenth century, England, with its highly developed textile industry, was the major market for chemicals. It was also the home of the scientific leaders of the time—Michael Faraday and Charles Darwin.

The modern chemical industry did actually start with an English discovery: Perkin's discovery of aniline dyes in 1856. Yet 20 years after Perkin's discovery (around 1875) leadership in the new industry had clearly passed to Germany. German businessmen contributed the entrepreneurial idea that was lacking in England: the results of scientific inquiry, organic chemistry in this case, can be directly converted into marketable applications.

—— MODERN MERCHANDISING

The most powerful private business in history was probably managed by the Japanese House of Mitsui, which before its dissolution after World War

II was estimated by American occupation authorities to have employed one million people throughout the world. Its origin was the world's first department store, developed in Tokyo during the mid-seventeenth century by an early Mitsui.

The entrepreneurial idea underlying this business was that of the merchant as a principal of economic life, not as a mere middleman. This meant fixed prices to the customer. And it also meant that the Mitsuis no longer acted as agents in dealing with craftsmen and manufacturers. They would buy for their own account and give orders for standardized merchandise to be made according to their specifications. In overseas trade the merchant had acted as principal all along. However, by 1650 overseas trade had been suppressed in Japan, and the Mitsuis promptly took the overseas-trade concepts and built a domestic merchant-business on them.

—— MASS DISTRIBUTION

Great imagination is not necessary to make an entrepreneurial idea successful. All that may be needed is systematic work that will make effective in the future something that has already occurred. Typically, for instance, new developments in the economy and market will run well ahead of distribution. Organizing the distribution, however, may make the change effective—and thereby create a true growth business.

A Canadian, Willard Garfield Weston, saw, for instance, that while the English housewives had come, by the end of World War II, to demand packaged, sliced bread, there was no adequate distribution system to supply them with what they wanted to buy where they wanted to buy it. Because of this small idea one of the largest food-marketing companies in Great Britain was established in a few years.

—— DISCOUNT CHAINS

The rise of the discount house began in the late 1940s with the application of an idea developed by Sears, Roebuck and Co. almost 20 years earlier. Sears, Roebuck became our leading appliance seller in the 1930s when it began to use a sample of each appliance on the store floor solely to demonstrate the merchandise. The appliance purchased by the customer was delivered straight from the warehouse—which realized savings in costs of uncrating, recrating, and shipping of up to 20% of retail price. Sears, Roebuck made no secret of this; yet there were few imitators of this idea. After World War II there was one small Chicago appliance merchant who adapted the idea to other makers' products. Today Saul Polk is credited with creating the first and largest and one of the most profitable discount chains in existence.

Little ideas have frequently been the seeds from which giant corporations have grown. Here are a few instances.

—— IBM

Thomas J. Watson, Jr., who founded and built IBM, did not see the coming development of business technology. But he had the idea of data processing as a unifying concept on which to build a business. IBM was, for a long time, fairly small and confined itself to such mundane work as keeping accounting ledgers and time records. But it was ready to jump when the technology came in—from totally unrelated war-time work—which made data processing by electronic computers actually possible.

While Watson built a small and unspectacular business during the 1920s by designing, selling, and installing punch-card equipment, the logical positivists (e.g. Perry Bridgman in the United States, Rudolph Carnap in Austria) talked and wrote on the systematic methodology of "quantification" and "universal measurements." It is most unlikely that they ever heard of the young, struggling IBM company and certain that they did not connect their ideas with it. Yet it was Watson's IBM and not their philosophical ideas that became operational when the new technology emerged during World War II.

—— SEARS, ROEBUCK

The men who built Sears, Roebuck and Co.—Richard Sears, Julius Rosenwald, Albert Loeb, and finally General Robert E. Wood—had active social concerns and lively social imaginations. But not one of them thought of remaking the economy. I doubt that even the idea of a *mass market*—as opposed to the traditional *class market*—occurred to them until long after 1930. From its early beginning, the founders of Sears, Roebuck had the idea that the poor person's money could be made to have the same purchasing power as the rich person's.

But this was not a particularly new idea. Social reformers and economists had bandied it around for decades. The cooperative movement in Europe grew mainly out of it. Sears, Roebuck was, however, the first business in the United States built on this idea. It started with the question: "What would make the farmer a customer for a retail business?" The answer was simple: "A farmer needs to be sure of getting goods of the same dependable quality as do city people but at a low price." In 1900 or even 1920 this was an idea of considerable audacity.

—— BATA

The basic entrepreneurial idea may be merely an imitation of something that works well in another country or in another industry. For example, when

Tomas Bata, the Slovakian shoemaker, returned to Europe from the United States after World War I, he had the idea that everybody in Czechoslovakia and the Balkans could have shoes to wear as did everybody in the United States. "The peasant goes barefoot," he is reported to have said, "not because he is too poor, but because there are no shoes." What was needed to make this vision of a shod peasant come true was someone supplying him with cheap, standardized, but well-designed and durable footwear as was done in the United States.

On the basis of this analogy with America, Bata began without capital in a rented shack and in a few years built pre-Nazi Europe's largest shoe business and one of Europe's most successful companies. Yet to apply U.S. mass-production methods to European consumer goods was hardly a very original idea in the 1920s when Henry Ford and his assembly line were all the rage in Europe. The only original thing was willingness to act on the idea.

To make the future happen requires work rather than "genius." The individual with a creative imagination will have more imaginative ideas, to be sure. But whether the more imaginative ideas will actually turn out to be more successful is by no means certain.

Creativity, which looms so large in present discussions of innovation, is not the real problem. There are usually more ideas in any organization, including businesses, than can possibly be put to use. Ask any company—including seemingly moribund ones—this question: "What in our economy, or our society, or our state of knowledge would give our business its greatest opportunity if only we could make it happen?" Dozens of responses will burst from management's lips. As a rule we are not lacking *ideas*—not even good, serviceable ideas. What is lacking is management's *willingness to welcome ideas*, in fact, solicit them, rather than just products or processes. Products and processes, after all, are only the vehicles through which the ideas become effective. The specific future products and processes often cannot even be imagined.

For example, when Du Pont started the work on polymer chemistry out of which nylon eventually evolved, it did not know that synthetic fibers would be the end-product. Du Pont acted on the assumption that any gain in the ability to manipulate the structure of large, organic molecules—a scientific skill at that time in its infancy—would lead to commercially important results of some kind. It was only after six or seven years of research work that synthetic fibers first appeared as a possible major result area.

Indeed, as the IBM experience shows, the specific products and processes that make an idea truly successful often come out of entirely different and unrelated work.

But there must always be a willingness to think in terms of the general rather than the specific, in terms of a business, the contributions it makes, the satisfactions it supplies, the market and economy it serves. This is the entrepreneurial point of view. And it is accessible to the average businessperson.

Also, the manager must have the courage to commit resources—and in particular first-rate people—to work on making the future happen. The staffs for this work should be small. But they should contain the very best people available; otherwise, nothing will happen.

The businessperson needs a touchstone of validity and practicality for entrepreneurial, future-making ideas. Indeed, the reason some businesses fail to innovate is not that they shy away from ideas. It is that they engage in hopelessly romantic ones—at great cost in people and money. An idea must meet rigorous tests of practicality if it is to be capable of making a business successful in the future.

It must first have operational validity. Can we take action on this idea? Or can we only talk about it? Can we really do something right away to bring about the kind of future we desire? Sears, Roebuck, with its idea of bringing the market to the isolated U.S. farmer, could show immediate results. In contrast, Du Pont with its idea of polymer chemistry could only organize research work on a very small scale. It could only underwrite the research of one first-rate man. But both companies could *do* something right away.

To be able to spend money on research is not enough. It must be research directed toward the realization of the idea. The knowledge sought may be general—as was that of Du Pont's project. But it must be reasonably clear, at least, that, if available, the knowledge gained will be applicable to operations.

The idea must have economic validity. If it could be put to work immediately, it would have to be able to produce economic results. We may not be able to do *all* that we would like to see done—not for a long time, and perhaps never. But if we could do something right away, the resulting products, processes, or services would find a customer, a market, an end use, and would be capable of being sold profitably. In short, they should satisfy want and need.

Finally, the idea must meet the test of personal commitment. Do we really believe in the idea? Do we really want to be that kind of people, do that kind of work, run that kind of business?

To make the future demands courage. It demands work. But it also demands faith. To commit oneself to the expedient is simply not practical. It will not suffice for the trials ahead. For no such idea is foolproof—nor should it be.

The one idea about the future that *must* fail is the apparently sure thing, the riskless idea, that is believed to be incapable of failure. The ideas on which tomorrow's business is to be built *must* be uncertain; no one can really say, as yet, what they will look like if and when they become reality. They *must* be risky; they have a probability of success, of course, but also a probability of failure. If they are not both uncertain and risky, they are simply not practical ideas for the future.

───── CONCLUSION

It is not absolutely necessary for every business to search for the idea that will make the future and to start work on its realization. Indeed, a good many managements do not even make their present business effective—and yet their company somehow survives for a while. Big businesses, in particular, seem able to coast a long time on the courage, work, and vision of earlier executives before they erode and run down.

But the future always does come, sooner or later. And it is always different. Even the mightiest company will be in trouble if it does not work toward the future. It will lose distinction and leadership. All that will be left is big-company overhead. It will neither control nor understand what is happening.

By not daring to take the risk of making the new happen, management takes, by default, the greater risk of being surprised by what will happen. This is a risk that even the largest and richest company cannot afford to take. And it is a risk that not even the smallest company need take.

—— DISCUSSION QUESTIONS

1. In any business, tradition, routine, and daily pressures favor the preservation of the status quo. Think of a product or service innovation that would meet customer needs and promote the interests of a company for which you have worked. How would you make a case for your idea to a group of skeptical managers?

2. Drucker argues that management must be more willing to embrace new ideas, but in a practical way. Suppose you are one of the skeptical managers mentioned in Question 1. What questions would you ask about the innovation being proposed?

3. What are the qualities that distinguish entrepreneurial thinking, according to this reading? Does the limited, self-centered approach Drucker describes fit your conception of entrepreneurship? Do entrepreneurs have a responsibility to think about the social as well as the financial consequences of their decisions?

4. Try to build on the foundation that Drucker lays in this reading by naming some significant entrepreneurial innovations of the past 10–15 years. What were the "small ideas" that made these innovations succeed?

5. "To commit oneself to the expedient is simply not practical," Drucker states. Does this reading clearly distinguish between an idea that is merely expedient and one that is small but significant? How would you make that distinction?

New-Venture Ideas:
Do Not Overlook Experience Factor

6

KARL H. VESPER

All new ventures start with an idea, and stories of brilliant successes and crushing failures are legion. How do prospective entrepreneurs land on an idea that will eventually prove to be profitable? Popular advice books for would-be entrepreneurs all too often either ignore the subject altogether or suggest that ideas arise largely through a mysterious combination of daydreaming and inspiration.

To discover if a more promising path exists, Karl Vesper studied the histories of 100 successful entrepreneurs and found that new venture ideas were usually a natural outgrowth of an individual's education, work experience, and hobbies. Drawing on diverse case examples, Vesper removes the mystique surrounding new-venture ideas and shows that, like other business activities, idea creation can be approached deliberately and systematically.

Discovering workable new-venture ideas is no easy feat. Many would-be entrepreneurs have unsuccessfully gambled huge sums testing seemingly profitable concepts.

Even a man as creative as Mark Twain came up a consistent loser when he bet on new business ideas. In his autobiography, he recalled the first in a series of failures he encountered backing the invention of a friend:

> At last, when I had lost $42,000 on that patent I gave it away to a man whom I had long detested and whose family I desired to ruin. Then I looked around for other adventures. That same friend was ready with another patent. I spent $10,000 on it in eight months. Then I tried to give that patent to the man whose family I was after. He was very grateful but he was also experienced by this time and was getting suspicious of benefactors. He wouldn't take it and I had to let it lapse.
>
> Meantime, another old friend arrived with a wonderful invention. It was an engine or a furnace or something of the kind. . . .

The best of Twain's business attempts was an invention of his that he patented and characterized as "the only rational scrapbook the world has ever seen." On that enterprise, he invested $5,000 and managed to recover $2,000.

Unfortunately, sound guidance on where to find profitable venture ideas is nearly as sparse today as it was in Mark Twain's day. And the guidance that has been available is of questionable quality because systematic research on the subject is almost nonexistent.

Many books on entrepreneurship have completely neglected the subject of new-venture ideas. In a widely used text in entrepreneurship courses, New Ventures and the Entrepreneur, Patrick R. Liles devoted eight chapters to various aspects of entrepreneurship but failed to examine the origination of venture ideas.[1]

A book by Charles B. Swayne and William R. Tucker, The Effective Entrepreneur, offered a "road map by means of which any venture can be formed" but did not indicate how to formulate venture ideas.[2] Robert S. Morrison's 558-page Handbook for Manufacturing Entrepreneurs presented guidance on whether to start a company, who should start one, and how to "select" a product but failed to offer advice on how to find alternatives from which to do the selecting.[3]

More popularized books on entrepreneurship typically recommend various mental exercises. In How to Think Like a Millionaire and Get Rich, Howard Hill recommended dreaming up ways to "add color or a new twist to commonplace products and services."[4] Russell Williams, author of How to Wheel and Deal Your Way to a Fast Fortune, advised the reader to "pick a product in your home and ask yourself, how is it marketed? How is it manufactured? Could you introduce a competitor?"[5]

In The Poor Man's Road to Riches, Duane Newcomb told the reader, "Ideas are everywhere. . . . To find them, you generally decide on an area of interest like the restaurant business . . . then as you go about your daily business you simply let anything that comes close to your interest area trigger your imagination."[6]

A composite list of recommended venture idea sources from these and other books on entrepreneurship appears in the Exhibit. Of course, most items on the list are categories that could be further subdivided into many other lines of action. Thus it is clear that the number of possible activities for seeking venture ideas is enormous and could consume nearly endless amounts of time.

Is there a better way of formulating new-venture ideas? A study of the histories of approximately 100 highly successful entrepreneurs suggests that there is. The cases were drawn primarily from five books about entrepreneurship as well as from magazine articles and interviews with successful

---

1. Homewood, Ill.: Irwin, 1974.
2. Morristown, N.J.: General Learning Press, 1973.
3. Cleveland, Ohio: Western Reserve Press, 1973.
4. West Nyack, N.Y.: Parker Publishing Co., 1968.
5. Parker, 1977.
6. Parker, 1976.

EXHIBIT
Idea Sources Advocated in Entrepreneurship Books

MENTAL GYMNASTICS	PERSONAL CONTACTS WITH	VISITS TO	READING OF	OBSERVATION OF TRENDS
Brainstorming	Potential customers	Trade shows	Trade publications	Materials shortages
Observation	Potential suppliers	Libraries	Trade directives	
Seeking new twists	Business brokers	Museums	Bankruptcy announcements	Energy shortage
	Business owners	Plants		Waste disposal
	Successful entrepreneurs	Invention expositions	Business opportunities classified	New technology
	Property owners	Universities	Old books and magazines	Recreation
	Professors	Research institutes		Nostalgia
	Graduate students		*Commerce Business Daily*	Fads
	Patent attorneys		Other commerce department publications	Legal changes
	Product brokers			Pollution problems
	Former employees			Health
	Prospective partners		NASA's *Tech Briefs Patents and Patent Gazette*	Self-development
	Bankers			Personal security
	Venture capitalists		New product publications	Foreign trade
	Chambers of commerce			Social movements
	Plastic molders		Doctoral dissertations	
	Corporate licensing departments		Idea books and newsletters	
	Editors		Bestseller lists	
	Management consultants		New technology publications	
	Technology transfer agencies		Licensing information services	
	Regional development agencies			

entrepreneurs.[7] The objective was not so much to obtain a scientifically representative sampling as to discover the range of sources prospective entrepreneurs can draw on to find promising venture ideas.

One key finding was that instead of searching randomly, as many popular entrepreneurship books seem to suggest, the entrepreneur should closely examine his or her own education, work experience, and hobbies as idea

7. The five books were : Orvis Collins and David G. Moore, *The Organization Makers* (New York: Appleton-Century-Crofts, 1970); Richard Lynn, *The Entrepreneur* (London: George Allen and Unwin, 1974); Harry Miller, *The Way of Enterprise* (London: Andre Deutsch, 1963);Lawrence A. Armour, *The Young Millionaires* (Chicago: Playboy Press, 1973); and Gene Bylinsky, *The Innovative Millionaires* (New York: Charles Scribner's Sons, 1976).

sources. The large majority of the entrepreneurs studied primarily used their own expertise rather than that of others.

The pattern of close connection between prior work and new-venture ideas was common to a large majority of the successful start-ups—between 60% and 90%, depending on the industry—the correlation being highest in advanced technology areas like computers and medical instruments and lowest in enterprises of a relatively unspecialized nature, such as nursing homes, fast food franchises, and other consumer-oriented businesses.

——— VARIATIONS IN BACKGROUND

Not surprisingly, the entrepreneurs differed in how they acquired their expertise. Nearly all entrepreneurs involved in starting successful advanced technology companies had earned one or more college degrees and had had substantial work experience in scientific research or engineering design before formulating their venture concepts. Entrepreneurs who conceived successful machining businesses, however, usually had not attended college but had put in five years or more working for other people on shop floors.

A spectacular, fairly typical example of an advanced technology start-up was that of Intel Corporation. Robert N. Noyce, an M.I.T. physics Ph.D., and Gordon E. Moore, a Cal Tech chemistry Ph.D., had worked for Fairchild Semiconductor since its inception in 1956. By 1968, Noyce was general manager, Moore was director of research, and Fairchild's annual sales had grown to $150 million.

At about that time, the two men became aware of a promising related area of semiconductors that had been neglected by big companies. Their observation coincided with their own growing frustration with long commuting times and the difficulties of working within a corporate bureaucracy. They convinced a venture capitalist to invest $300,000 and raised another $2.2 million through private placements.

The entrepreneurs used the money to start a new semiconductor memory company with Noyce as president and Moore as executive vice president. Seven years after the company's inception, sales had grown to $134 million and profits to $19.8 million.

Although it involved exceptionally large seed capital, this venture was not unusual for advanced technology start-ups. A team of technical specialists employed a clear product concept and sought fast growth—a classic pattern carried out, albeit on a smaller scale, by many such companies.

In contrast, consider the following more conventional manufacturing start-up. In 1961, Al Richards was fired as a machinist for a small cutting-tool company. The dismissal was a shock, made more painful by the fact that he had only meager savings. He was not unaccustomed to adversity, though, for he had been raised in orphanages, employed in a shipyard at age 16 by falsifying his age, and battle-tested in the Seabees. Because he had worked in several machine shops while he was taking related evening courses, he was confident of his knowledge of the cutting-tool business.

Against the advice of his lawyer, he sold his boat, car, and guns and took a second mortgage on his house to raise the $18,000 necessary to start his own shop. With rented space and used machinery, he began soliciting orders. He also moonlighted to cover his business and personal expenses. Orders came in slowly, and the company, after losing money the first year, moved into the black the second year. Eight years after start-up, the company's sales had reached an annual level of about $300,000.

——— SIMILARITIES STAND OUT

Though different conditions inspired creation of these two ventures—Noyce and Moore were motivated by dissatisfaction with secure jobs and Richards by unexpected discharge from a job he liked—a basic similarity stands out. Both enterprises represented activities similar to those performed for years in the entrepreneurs' prior jobs.

Working for Fairchild had given Noyce and Moore very special know-how, both in dealing with a particular advanced technology and in identifying and exploiting the technical frontier. The leap to the new-venture idea thus appears not to have been particularly difficult or surprising but rather a natural outgrowth of their work. Richards similarly did not have to search far for his new-venture idea.

Another important source of venture ideas can be hobbies, as the following example illustrates. Bill Nicolai dropped out of college in the late 1960s and hitchhiked to Yosemite to climb mountains. For several years he worked sporadically, supplementing his income with food stamps and spending much of his time climbing mountains in Yosemite and elsewhere.

Then one night a mountain blizzard blew his tent apart, bringing death too close for comfort and setting Nicolai to thinking about alternative tent constructions. He designed a tent made from a tube of fabric held open by circular metal hoops and borrowed a sewing machine to make it a reality. It worked, and he began to imagine an enterprise to fabricate and sell a product he would call "the omni-potent."

He then rented a booth at an annual Seattle street fair and put several tents on display. "I don't think we actually sold any at the fair," he recalled, "but we did sell a few a short while later after people had had a chance to look the flyer over." Sales began to drift in, and Nicolai moved the fledgling business from a friend's basement to a storefront with manufacturing space in the back. After two years, he was employing four of his friends, and annual sales were $60,000. "It wasn't much of a living," he said, "but we were surviving and enjoying the work."

At this point, we might note the source of the business idea and where it led. Nicolai used his substantial hobby experience to conceive his product and enterprise. In a sense, his hobby had been his job because it had been a relatively full-time commitment for several years. It had given him knowledge of the market and available technology. The tent collapse revealed a need, which in turn led to discovery of a product and creation of a business. Again, the moral for successful venture discovery seems to be to work from what one is familiar with—from a hobby if not from one's occupation.

——— IMPORTANCE OF SUBSEQUENT EVENTS

Nicolai's venture was not particularly successful at this point. The meager $60,000 gross sales did not allow him to escape food stamps. By the usual standards for wages and profits, the business was, after two years, a loser with no salvation in sight.

Then things changed. A salesman tried to interest Nicolai in using a new tent fabric that boasted the unique property of venting vapor without leaking water, so that breath moisture could escape the tent but rain could not enter. Producers of the new fabric "went to all the big companies first, because we were nobody," Nicolai recalled, "but each big company assumed the material was no good because none of the other big companies used it."

Seeing little to lose, Nicolai introduced a tent made of the new material and threw all his resources into advertising it. Within a month, sales leaped from $5,000 a month to $6,000 a day. Over the next three years, sales rose to $2 million annually, at substantial margins.

This shift from a modest enterprise with little promise to a fast-growing, highly profitable business was another important characteristic common to a large proportion of other extremely successful ventures. Except for the advanced technology enterprises, which virtually all started with high expectations, roughly 40% of the ventures studied began as relatively small-time enterprises. Some event occurred later that induced fast growth. Thus another reasonable conclusion to draw from the cases studied is that highly successful venture ideas can easily emerge from apparently small-time businesses as entrepreneurs gain experience, expertise, and business exposure.

The successful entrepreneurs' experience thus contrasts sharply with advice offered in the how-to-succeed books. Jobs, the main idea source, are not stressed at all. Though some of the books suggest hobbies, they neglect to emphasize the importance of accompanying experience. What the books mostly suggest—daydreaming, visiting museums, browsing in libraries, and studying world trends—produced few ideas used to start the businesses studied.

This is not to say that following the advice in the popular books is likely to cause failure. It is just difficult to find examples of successful entrepreneurs who have systematically used those approaches. While it seems plausible to expect that hopeful entrepreneurs who deliberately use such advice should achieve some success, this question might benefit from academic research.

—— OTHER IDEA SOURCES

Occasionally, winning ideas are discovered the way popularized entrepreneurship books say they should be. Ole Evinrude thought up the outboard motor when ice cream melted in a boat he was rowing to a summer picnic. King Gillette conceived the safety razor when his straight razor dulled. Such incidents are extremely rare, however, and nobody has demonstrated that a skill for creating them can be deliberately learned.

But there are some systematic approaches besides background and experience that sometimes work, as the following three examples illustrate:

- E. Joseph Cossman, author of *How I Made a Million Dollars in Mail Order*, tells of finding unexploited products by visiting trade shows, reading classified advertisements, and seeking unused tooling from products previously judged unsuccessful at plastic-moldng companies.[8]
- One entrepreneur adopted a strategy of calling or visiting at least one person daily who might be able to help him find an opportunity, any opportunity. After a year, he had located a partner. After two years, they had a product—a blood-testing device produced under a licensing agreement. And after three years, their company was profitable and nearing $1 million in annual sales.
- A prospective electronics manufacturer discovered a successful product by asking purchasing agents what items they were having trouble obtaining. He identified the need for a certain sophisticated electronic component, got it designed and into production, and wound up with a multi-million-dollar publicly held company.

Each of these entrepreneurs unearthed a venture opportunity through someone else. Cossman bought products other people had developed and then applied his merchandising talents to sell them. The medical-product manufacturer obtained a license (some entrepreneurs form partnerships with inventors). The electronics maker obtained information about a need and then developed a product.

But they all made use of others who had the specific idea they needed. Thus the idea search was largely one of making personal contacts until one paid off in a usable concept. For the prospective entrepreneur in search of a venture concept, the message is to seek new contacts for ideas. A further possibility is to look to others not only for venture concepts but also for complete on-going ventures—that is, for acquisitions. This approach comprised about one-fifth of the cases examined in this study. What is striking about this approach is that more than half of those who used it had no prior experience in the business areas they suddenly adopted through acquisitions. Yet all emerged extremely successful.

---

8. Englewood Cliffs, N.J.: Prentice-Hall, 1963.

Thus the acquisition approach seems well suited to those who either cannot or prefer not to find new-venture ideas based on their own work or hobby experience and who are not content to wait and hope someone else will come to them with a venture proposition.

Where do these findings leave the generalist manager? Does the view widely held among business schools that a good manager can manage any type of business also hold for entrepreneurs? Or can only a specialist start a particular type of business? No general answer has been demonstrated, but it can be observed that technical expertise must be brought into the new enterprise somehow, whether by the entrepreneur or by those he or she recruits.

One way to recruit needed talent is to buy a going concern in which the specialists are already employed. Another is to buy a franchise that comes with the opportunity for special training and guidance. A third is to hire or become partners with someone who has the needed special know-how.

In conclusion, it seems significant that none of the entrepreneurs in the cases examined discovered winning ideas through random mental reflection or even concentrated brainstorming. Those who scouted ideas out applied action, not just thinking, to find them. Hence, some final advice for the person desiring a venture who has not yet identified a suitable concept: don't just sit and think; move around, contact people, and act.

——— DISCUSSION QUESTIONS

1. Are new venture ideas really new?
2. How do the examples cited in this reading of successful entrepreneurs and the origins of their ideas influence your conception of entrepreneurship?
3. What experiences and interests inspired you to start thinking about starting your own venture?
4. Does this reading challenge the image of the entrepreneur as being a bold and brilliant visionary? Should this image be debunked?
5. Can technical expertise and a broad experience base be a liability to an entrepreneur? What other attributes should an entrepreneur bring to the task of discovering and evaluating new venture ideas?

The Start-Up Process   7

JOHN R. VAN SLYKE, HOWARD H. STEVENSON,
AND MICHAEL J. ROBERTS

"Entrepreneurs are finders and exploiters of opportunity," say these authors. As pathmakers, founders of business must be comfortable dealing with uncertainty. At the same time, because they have to justify the venture to many interested parties and are entirely accountable for its fate, they must develop a thorough understanding of the risks and rewards before the first step toward start-up is taken. They will first need to define the opportunity and its potential, determine the resources needed to exploit it, and set a strategy for realizing it—tasks that cannot be delegated to technical experts.

To help entrepreneurs conduct this analysis, this reading traces the stages of the start-up process—from evaluating the opportunity to harvesting the venture—and presents a series of key questions to raise at each stage. How thoroughly these questions are answered at the outset of the journey will inevitably determine its long-term direction.

Entrepreneurship is the process of pulling together a unique package of resources in pursuit of a particular opportunity. Because no entrepreneur controls all the necessary resources, pursuing an opportunity requires "bridging the resource gap." It is a task that involves making a series of choices in a manner that is both internally consistent and externally appropriate to the environmental context.

This reading describes both the elements of the entrepreneurial process and the analysis required for each step of the process. Thinking about these critical issues before actually starting a business is analogous to gauging the depth of the water before taking the plunge. The dominant goals of the "pre-start" analysis are

- To understand the dimensions of the opportunity and decide whether it is attractive or unattractive;
- To estimate the magnitude and key elements of the effort required to exploit the opportunity;
- To identify a strategy for weaving a path through the obstacles and risks inherent in any venture.

The end product of this phase of analysis is a business plan or a decision that the idea does not present an attractive opportunity.

The stages of the pre-start analysis correspond to the process of starting a business: evaluating the opportunity, developing the business concept, assessing required resources, acquiring necessary resources, managing the venture, and harvesting and distributing value. Yet, a thorough analysis for one stage requires an understanding of all the other elements. For example, a necessary dimension of the opportunity evaluation stage involves estimating potential financial returns, which is difficult to do without first developing the business concept, assessing the resources required to execute it, and looking down the road to see what kinds of returns the providers of resources will require at harvest. Thus, a thorough pre-start analysis requires an examination of all elements of the process before taking the first step.

—— EVALUATING THE OPPORTUNITY

An attractive, well-defined opportunity is the cornerstone of all successful ventures, but the way an opportunity is defined shapes how clearly it is understood. Several questions can help to evaluate an opportunity adequately.

WHAT ARE THE DIMENSIONS OF THE "WINDOW OF OPPORTUNITY?"

Any opportunity has several critical dimensions: its raw size, the time span over which it is projected to exist, and the rate at which it is expected to grow.

The raw size of the market is naturally a critical dimension, because it has a direct bearing on potential sales volume and, thus, financial returns. All things being equal, of course, bigger is better. But, things are not always equal. Large markets often attract large, powerful competitors, making smaller niches more hospitable to the entrepreneur.

Growth rate is also related to size, and new ventures often thrive in rapid-growth environments. By gaining—and holding onto—a piece of a small market and growing with that market, small ventures can become big businesses.

Every opportunity exists only for a finite period of time, which varies greatly depending on the nature of the business. For example, in the popular music business, the opportunity for a new hit tune is usually only a few months long. In real estate, by contrast, opportunities for profiting from a single property may span several decades. It is therefore important to understand both the time period and the economic life over which the opportunity will exist, and the time available for analyzing the opportunity. The two are not always the same.

The risk and reward potential of any given opportunity is also likely to vary over time. At certain points in its economic life an opportunity may have greater potential than at others, and a careful analysis of the timing and magnitude of opportunities for harvesting may place time limits on analysis and plans. Using real estate as an example again, we note that syndication of tax shelters typically exploits only part of the total economic opportunity of an income-producing property over only a fraction of its total economic life. In other businesses too it may be advantageous to pursue an underlying opportunity for only part of its total existence.

A key to exploiting an opportunity is understanding the forces that are creating it. Technological change, government regulation (or its relaxation), and shifts in consumer preferences and market demand can all create opportunity. By spotting patterns early, entrepreneurs can seize the initiative by creating ventures to exploit such changes. To do so they must identify the best period over which to pursue an opportunity and match their concepts of how value can be created with analyses of their own goals, skills, and time frame.

IS THE PROFIT POTENTIAL ADEQUATE TO PROVIDE A SATISFACTORY RETURN?

An opportunity must earn a sufficient return to justify taking an entrepreneurial risk. "Adequate" is a relative term and depends on the amount of capital invested, the time frame required to earn the return, the risks assumed in the process, and existing alternatives for both capital and time.

Opportunities that demand substantial capital, require long periods of time to mature, and have large risks usually make little sense unless enormous value is being created. In all too many cases, such opportunities create considerable value, but not for the original entrepreneurs. The numerous rounds of financing reduce the founders' percentage of ownership to such an extent that, ultimately, there is little recompense for the effort and risk.

Adequacy of return also depends on alternatives and opportunity costs, which vary with individuals, time, and circumstances. What may be attractive for one person may be unrealistic for another, due to the availability of better alternatives. Nonetheless, good opportunities are likely to display the following financial characteristics:

- Steady and rapid growth in sales during the first five to seven years in some well-defined market niche
- A high percentage of recurring revenue; that is, once sold, customers become recurring sources of revenue
- High potential for operating leverage with increased experience and scale of operations
- Internally generated funds to finance and sustain growth
- Growing capacity for debt supported by build-up of hard assets as collateral and/or increase in earnings and cash flow to service debt
- Relatively short time frame during which significant value can be created and sustained—usually three to five years
- Real harvest options to turn equity into after-tax cash or equivalents
- Rate of return on investment of 40% or more (after taxes).

DOES THE OPPORTUNITY OPEN UP ADDITIONAL OPTIONS FOR EXPANSION, DIVERSIFICATION, OR INTEGRATION?

Good opportunities create additional options in a variety of different ways. Since the future is usually unknown, it is critical not to be locked into a single, unvarying course. Good opportunities allow for mid-course corrections; poorer opportunities foreclose or limit future options. Opportunities that consume resources, eliminate alliances, or narrow technological options are inferior to those with built-in flexibility.

WILL THE PROFIT STREAM BE DURABLE IN THE FACE OF PROBABLE OBSTACLES?

One thing is certain: circumstances will change over time, particularly if the venture is successful. Success creates all sorts of pressures on performance, including imitative competitors, product substitutions, changing technology, shifts in customer preferences, personnel turnover, and changing relationships with both suppliers and buyers. It is absolutely essential, therefore, to evaluate whether the venture may become vulnerable to erosion of its profit stream. This requires identifying and combating potentially fatal vulnerabilities, recognizing that some, such as personnel turnover, are internal to the venture, while others, such as competitive reactions, are external.

DOES THE PRODUCT OR SERVICE MEET A REAL NEED?

The provision of real value is fundamental to any new venture. Successful products meet a real need in terms of functionality, price, distribution, durability, and/or perceived quality. Except in pure trading or promotion activities, the creation of value ultimately depends on the ability to convince potential customers of the need and the benefits of its products and services in a reasonable period of time and at an affordable marketing and selling cost.

Entrepreneurs surprisingly often fail to understand whether their products and services meet a customer's real needs and generally underestimate the time and marketing expense required to achieve high-volume distribution, particularly at the national level.

—— DEVELOPING THE BUSINESS CONCEPT

Having undertaken an analysis of the opportunity, it is necessary to develop a business concept—or strategy—that fully exploits the opportunity. The forces that drive the development of the business strategy include both external-market focus and the economics of various approaches to serving that market. For instance, if we believed that there existed an extraordinary opportunity in the retailing of freshly baked breads, we would still need a strategy to address a maze of choices:

- Franchising versus company-owned stores;
- Mall versus free-standing sites;
- On-premise preparation and baking versus central preparation and frequent delivery; and
- Specific geographic region versus national rollout.

Investigation of the following issues would help us clarify some of these strategic, choices.

CAN BARRIERS TO ENTRY BE CREATED?

Barriers to entry help sustain superior returns and can be created based on cost, distribution power, patents, trade secrets, and product differentiation. Given a good idea, a real advantage, and success, a venture will, in fact, have only a finite lead time. Competition will always emerge. Frequently, the first competitors will enter the market with a "copy and cut" strategy for products and pricing. We must, therefore, anticipate competitive threats and devise measures to protect our lead time and competitive advantages. An often fatal error of new firms is the failure to plan for competitive reactions and, therefore, for the renewal through new products or services that must occur if advantages are to be durable.

ARE CUSTOMERS IDENTIFIABLE, REACHABLE, AND OPEN TO CHANGE?

Opportunities that postulate the existence of a generalized market are almost always less successful than those based on knowledge of specific customers and how to reach them. Effective distribution planning requires the entrepreneur to identify specific groups of potential customers within markets and compare the benefits they receive with the products and services offered to them.

Customers must not only be identifiable and reachable, they must be willing to abandon investments they have made in other firms' people, procedures, facilities, or equipment. A new venture's success may depend on the ability to sell change to the customers. This typically requires the latter to change spending patterns and, perhaps, the way they do business.

Becoming integrated into the customers' procedures in this way is often the most effective barrier to the entry of competition. Unfortunately, it is also the major resistance a new product or process must overcome. It is essential, therefore, that the change being sold (1) be affordable to the customer, and (2) yield a clearly visible benefit.

WILL SUPPLIERS CONTROL CRITICAL RESOURCES AND CAPTURE INNOVATIVE RENTS OR PROFITS?

As a result of make-or-buy analyses and the desire to be "lean and mean," new companies frequently delay investment in facilities or technology on which their venture depends. In such cases, the new firm may become dependent on its suppliers, who could be in a position to squeeze extra profits from the venture through control of critical resources. Often relationships, either contractual or personal, are used to mitigate these risks.

WILL BUYERS BE SO STRONG AS TO DEMAND UNECONOMIC CONCESSIONS?

This area is a potential mine field, particularly in established markets. It is often the problem when a new, small business attempts to break into a market by selling to large corporations. The buyers enjoy such great advantages in purchasing (e.g., in terms of delivery, price, credit terms, quality standards, etc.) that they can wring concessions from the smaller business, sometimes rendering the transaction uneconomic or excessively risky.

——— ASSESSING REQUIRED RESOURCES

Entrepreneurs are people who find ways to bridge the gap between what they have in the way of skills and resources and what is actually needed to pursue an opportunity. Those who already have the skills and resources under personal control are more like investors than entrepreneurs.

Many entrepreneurial failures occur because there is too great a mismatch between the resources controlled by the entrepreneur and those required to pursue the opportunity successfully. Every venture depends on having the ability to control a minimum set of critical skills, resources, and relationships and to gain, as necessary, any required approvals. The key question is: What is the minimum resource set required, and how can the entrepreneur get and maintain control over it? In answering this question, it is useful to ask very specific questions that test the ability to assemble this minimum package.

WHAT SKILLS, RESOURCES, AND RELATIONSHIPS DOES THE ENTREPRENEURIAL GROUP ALREADY POSSESS?

The creation of real and lasting value depends on the ability to bring something new to the table. The less one brings, the more fragile and vulnerable the venture will be; the more one brings that can be protected and sustained, the more unique and potentially durable the venture will be.

Rarely does an individual entrepreneur possess or even substantially control all the skills, resources, and relationships required to pursue an opportunity over the longer term. It is therefore important to distinguish clearly between what is and is not controlled by the venture and to understand the resulting advantages and vulnerabilities of the mix.

WHO ARE THE LIKELY SUPPLIERS OF MISSING RESOURCES?

The full set of resources required for any venture will include expertise in law, finance, marketing and sales, technology, production, product development, human resources, general management, and systems planning.

The resourcefulness of many entrepreneurs shows most clearly in their ability to "bridge the gap"—that is, to understand where and how these needed resources can be obtained—and in their talent to "make do." Finding ways to get hold of and use—not necessarily to own—resources is a survival skill. In-depth knowledge of the industry and market is particularly useful in meeting this challenge. Such personal experience also improves an entrepreneur's credibility and increases the desire of potential resource suppliers to participate in a venture.

WHAT SKILLS AND RESOURCES MUST BE A PART OF THE INTERNAL ORGANIZATION?

First, to achieve critical economies of scale, a certain critical mass must be obtained. The soundest companies include and control, as part of their internal organization, the elements and resources that will yield distinctive competitive advantages as experience level and scale of operations increase.

Next, if possible, competitors should be preempted from controlling critical resources. This is a particularly important strategic issue for small companies seeking to compete against large established players offering similar products or services. Human resources can often be preempted by start-up ventures. To do so, however, requires careful attention early on to the venture's legal and economic structure by, for example, providing long-term incentives or so-called golden handcuffs.

Finally, for resources that require continued coordination through direct management, internal control is critical. Of course, some resources can be managed through indirect contractual relationships that are essentially self-enforcing (e.g., suppliers making product to specification).

Attractive price, quality, and delivery standards can often be achieved without direct authority over all processes. In other cases, however, direct contractual or other relations of authority must be established. For example, in the early stages of marketing a product or service, needs for technical and customer feedback, flexible definition of the marketing function, and "missionary" selling that has no immediate economic return probably require direct marketing authority. Later, as the marketing process becomes more routine and systematic, expansion can often be achieved without expanding employment.

WHAT AMOUNT OF EACH RESOURCE OR SKILL IS REQUIRED?

The entrepreneur must establish how much of a given resource is optimal versus the absolute minimal requirement. A bare-bones plan usually has lower costs but higher levels of operating risk. On the other hand, the assumption that more resources provide less risk is clearly incorrect; obtaining excess resources usually means higher cost but not necessarily lower operating risk.

Somewhere in the middle, there is usually an acceptable level of risk, which varies with the individual. Some entrepreneurs believe that their particular skills, knowledge, or experience allow them to assume risks others believe to be unwise, but for which they see minimal downside. The entrepreneur who understands both the resource needs of the venture and what causes increased risks will be able to devise an effective strategy to mitigate the risks assumed.

WHAT IS UNIQUE ABOUT THE PROPOSED BUSINESS CONCEPT?

An entrepreneur can build a long-term competitive advantage on numerous bases: cost structure, technology, product features or quality (including augmented product definitions), marketing and sales channels, financial resources, focus, and people.

Whichever choice is made, the entrepreneur must have (1) a clear strategy; (2) a thorough understanding of how it relates to the competition in both the short and long terms; and (3) most essential, control of the resources that generate the unique features of the approach. Without the latter, a venture's long-term advantage is vulnerable to exploitation by suppliers, customers, or innovative competitors.

WHAT QUALITY TRADE-OFFS CAN BE MADE AMONG THE REQUIRED SKILLS AND RESOURCES?

It is rarely necessary to have a uniform level of quality in every required resource. Many fine businesses have been built on the utilization of used equipment. In these cases management valued quality in the output more highly than the appearance of the manufacturing floor.

WHAT ARE THE MAJOR REQUIREMENTS FOR REGULATORY COMPLIANCE?

Compliance with governmental and other regulatory constraints is a critical but often overlooked step in the new venture analysis. Key aspects include:

- Licenses
- Operating procedures
- Product approvals and testing
- Insurance and bonding.

It is a telling mark of inexperience and naivete to pursue an opportunity without ensuring full compliance with the extensive laws, regulations, and standards of business practice. We live in a complex domestic and international environment in which we may need to obtain formal approval, licenses, or other sanctions just to begin conducting business.

Some required sanctions and approvals can be obtained by simply complying with known laws and/or regulations issued by federal, state, and local governments. Others, such as Underwriters' Laboratory approval of the safety of certain kinds of consumer and industrial products, are obtained through lengthy and frequently expensive application, testing, and approval processes. Still other cases—such as in commercial building construction and many government and large private-sector contracts—require legally enforceable bonding of suppliers and/or contractors by insurance companies.

WHAT CRITICAL CHECKPOINTS WILL MARK THE LOWERING OF RISKS?

As a venture develops, it typically becomes more viable. Many entrepreneurs think of major long-term objectives as broken down into achievable intermediate milestones. Planning to achieve these checkpoints and plateaus helps them understand how the risk of a venture can or will decrease over time. The plateaus also act as useful benchmarks in the acquisition of additional resources and may mark times when new players can be induced to play, new types of financing will become available, or new suppliers and subcontractors will choose to enter the picture as specific risk stages are passed. Entrepreneurs who are aware of these checkpoints and base their strategy on attaining them can often maintain a higher percentage of ownership.

ARE RESOURCES ADEQUATE TO SURMOUNT POTENTIAL VARIATIONS FROM THE PLAN?

Things will go wrong, and at the worst possible time. There is an old rule of thumb that new ventures can have variances of three and two: they will need three times as much time and twice as much money, or vice versa. In times of financial distress the "golden rule" takes effect—the party with the gold (i.e., cash) rules. Refinancing in times of financial distress is most often done on a confiscatory basis. In the venture capital industry, this is called "down and dirty" financing.

The bargaining disadvantage of an entrepreneur experiencing a major financial crisis provides a predatory opportunity for those with cash to exact concessions from those with money already trapped in the deal. Rarely does new money agree to buy (bail) old money out; the rule is last-in, first-out. To make matters worse, new money frequently demands not only that old money stay in the deal, but also that it retreat in terms of legal priority, control over the affairs of the venture, and future opportunities to exit.

Given this possibility, knowledgeable investors, suppliers, customers, and employees will want to know what will be done in a crisis and how it will affect their own expectations and rewards from the venture. A plan without contingency schemes and reserves is no plan at all.

Obviously, however, it is not feasible to have enough resources available up front to surmount every potential contingency. On the other hand, the plan must deal with the likely ones; the entrepreneur must have a back-up vision of the future that will ensure survival if misfortunes occur.

—— ACQUIRING NECESSARY RESOURCES

It is always necessary to structure some kind of legal vehicle and organization for conducting the affairs of the venture and for controlling the skills and resources that must be assembled. The ability to do so in a creative manner is one of the hallmarks of a successful entrepreneur.

Having determined the resources that are critical to the venture, it is time to acquire them. As noted earlier, *acquire* does not, necessarily, translate into *own*. One of the most valuable techniques of leverage is to obtain the desired measure of control without owning—through rents, royalties, and other incentives to owners of resources.

WHAT MECHANISMS FOR CONTROL OF EACH CRITICAL SKILL OR RESOURCE ARE AVAILABLE?

In addition to the classic approach of ownership and direct control, there are several alternatives for controlling resources, including:

- Contractual agreement
- Long-term noncontractual supply arrangements
- Ad hoc need fulfillment.

The analysis that determines the best control mechanism to use focuses on (1) understanding the critical factors required for success in the business, and (2) evaluating how feasible it is to achieve the required level of performance from each resource under each of the alternative control mechanisms. In general, direct ownership and administrative control of a resource—hiring people, buying plant and equipment—is the most expensive approach and should be followed only for the most critical resources.

WHAT ARE THE CRITICAL MOTIVATIONS OF POTENTIAL PROVIDERS OF REQUIRED RESOURCES AND SKILLS?

Potential providers have complex needs that must be fulfilled in order to persuade them to allow access to their resources. One of the keys to unlocking someone else's resources on favorable terms is knowing what the other person or organization values most. In addition to financial return, these needs may include:

- Professional advancement
- Operating integration
- Risk avoidance
- Social status
- Political response to an outside constituency.

CAN INCENTIVES BE STRUCTURED TO MEET THESE MOTIVATIONS?

It is possible to establish and maintain control over resources by providing incentives for the resource provider to cooperate. Where such incentives are inadequate, wise entrepreneurs will enhance them to motivate others to work actively on their behalf. This typically requires some kind of concession on the entrepreneur's part.

WILL THE OPPORTUNITY PRODUCE A RETURN ADEQUATE TO MEET RESOURCE PROVIDERS' NEEDS AND PROVIDE THE ENTREPRENEURIAL REWARD?

New business ventures are bounded in many ways and can support only so many players. However, there are many different types of returns in any venture, including noncash returns such as enhanced technical position, prestige, franchises on market segments, and so on. Skilled entrepreneurs know how to allocate all the important financial and noneconomic returns among the key players. The problem comes in "thin deals" where returns are insufficient to meet the expectations of the key players.

——— MANAGING THE VENTURE

Once the critical resources have been assembled, it is time to deploy them and actually start the business. The early days will be hectic, as the entrepreneur, management team, and employees begin to learn the business and their jobs. Everything that happens will be happening for the first time, and each time someone will have to make a decision about how a problem or procedure should be handled. This raises a number of issues.

DOES THE MANAGEMENT CONCEPT INCLUDE BOTH THE CRITICAL INTERNAL AND EXTERNAL ELEMENTS OF THE ORGANIZATION?

Somehow, the entrepreneur must devise and apply a formal or informal system of management that considers both what is internal to the venture (e.g., people, production processes, etc.) and what is outside the organization (e.g., key suppliers or distributors with whom the venture may have contracts and agreements).

Often the successful entrepreneurial venture is distinguished by the control it exerts over resources it does not legally own or employ. This control and influence can only be purposefully exercised within a managerial relationship that is neither hierarchical nor purely market oriented. To endure it must provide for continuity and clear mechanisms for feedback and evaluation and be mutually beneficial over the long term.

HOW WILL EMPLOYEES BE ATTRACTED AND SELECTED?

The task of recruiting employees for the venture is complicated, given both the resource scarcity of the early days and lack of certainty about what skills will be required. Most entrepreneurs respond to this dilemma by hiring eager young men and women who can be retained relatively inexpensively and seem willing to perform a wide variety of tasks. Occasionally these individuals can be groomed to become good managers within a short time. More often the entrepreneur must bring in some seasoned professionals as the firm matures and is financially able to afford their services.

It is therefore important at the start for the entrepreneur to have a picture of what managerial resources will be needed over the course of the venture and to begin training them. When this approach fails, the entrepreneur must be willing to reach outside the firm for new talent.

HOW WILL THE ENTREPRENEUR'S ROLE EVOLVE?

The entrepreneurial role will inevitably evolve as the business grows and matures. An expanded scope of activity for the firm will give the entrepreneur little choice but to delegate responsibility to a layer of middle managers. This action, in turn, will create a new function for the entrepreneur as a manager of managers, and he or she will need new skills to fulfill this role successfully.

The management of a growing venture is a challenging task, demanding skills that differ dramatically from those required to start the business. The ability to surmount these challenges depends on the entrepreneur's recognition that they call for often-difficult changes in behavior and management style.

—— HARVESTING AND DISTRIBUTING VALUE

If the business is successful, significant value will be created. The issue then becomes one of harvesting and distributing that value. The desire of outside investors to turn their initial investment back into cash will be one source of pressure. The personal wishes of the entrepreneur and key employees may also argue for some form of harvest. This stage of a venture raises a number of issues.

IS THERE A SPECIFIC MECHANISM FOR HARVESTING?

Not all ventures offer the same opportunities for harvesting; some cannot be harvested at all and must simply be operated for the income they generate. Personal service businesses often fall into this category. On the other hand, businesses that create assets are often harvestable even when the owner remains active in the business.

Business ventures that have no realistic prospects for a harvest represent mainly investments made to provide jobs for the entrepreneur, partners, and employees. However, for businesses that can be harvested, a range of options may be available. These include:

- Acquisition by a larger company
- Public offering of stock via Initial Public Offering (IPO). Typically new shares are issued by the company and sold to raise more financing and establish the market value of the stock.
- Secondary Offerings. Shares held by principals and early investors are sold to the public or new investors (may be part of IPO).
- Sale of the company to a third party or to the management and employees
- Liquidation and distribution of proceeds.

Of these mechanisms, acquisitions, mergers, and public offerings are most frequently used in venture capital situations. However, timing and market conditions are critical to the harvest. Public offerings are often the most elusive form of harvest; on becoming paper millionaires, many founders find themselves the last to realize after-tax cash gains. Acquisitions and mergers too often provide only illusory harvesting mechanisms. Entrepreneurs who substitute their own undiversified holdings for undiversified holdings in another firm often lose both control and wealth.

It is thus critical to understand both the goals and the detailed mechanisms of an efficient harvesting strategy.

HAS THE VENTURE BEEN STRUCTURED FINANCIALLY AND LEGALLY TO MAXIMIZE THE AFTER-TAX YIELD FROM HARVEST?

Here the devil is in the details and foresight is essential. The IRS has been as aggressive in collecting as taxpayers have been creative in attempting to retain the harvest. Substantial and frequently extensive legal and tax-related planning is always required, for some issues have lead times extending over several years. For example, achieving capital gains treatment of a partial liquidation and discontinuance of a line of business requires a corporate vehicle that meets certain conditions in periods prior to and after the liquidation.

WHAT CONDITIONS SHOULD TRIGGER A HARVEST?

Timing is everything. Many factors could determine when it is time to cash in, including:

- Need for large amounts of capital to press on to a major stage of growth;
- Peaking of profit potential;
- Changes in tax laws;
- Changes in debt or public equity markets;
- Economic cycles;
- Age, health, and interests of principals and founders.

WHAT CONDITIONS COULD PRECLUDE A HARVEST?

Depending on the nature of the venture, from time to time certain factors may work against harvesting or prevent it altogether. Among the more important external factors are

- Economic and market cycles;
- Tax law changes;
- Competition;
- Changes in laws and regulations.

The most important internal factors include:

- Major management or operating problems;
- Loss of trade secrets.

HOW WILL RESPONSIBILITIES TO OTHER PARTICIPANTS BE FULFILLED AT HARVEST?

All creditors, investors, partners, and key employees have or develop expectations about what they will gain from the venture. If the entrepreneur intends to do business with them again after the harvest transaction, he or she will plan ahead to ensure that they come away from the experience reasonably happy.

The harvest is a bittersweet experience for many entrepreneurs. While it represents a culmination of a long effort to build financial value, it can also represent the end of rewarding managerial experience. Yet, the fear of "giving up the baby" should not be allowed to interfere with sound financial planning. Moreover, many entrepreneurs have the special ability to build a business but are less adept at managing it over the long term. They should recognize where their strengths lie and focus on applying them in the appropriate situations.

—— CONCLUSION

Founding a business is a complex activity. It entails foresight and careful planning of all the details required to manage and eventually to harvest the venture. In addition it demands a special attitude toward general management and the unique role of the entrepreneur. Unlike other managers, who may be responsible for particular functions, entrepreneurs are ultimately accountable for the entire venture. It is this extremely close identity with the business that makes success so rewarding and failure so devastating. This unique role breeds a certain set of behaviors:

- *An action orientation.* Entrepreneurs cannot afford merely to elucidate the dimensions of the problem; they must act to carry out the solutions.
- *Attention to detail.* Because entrepreneurs are ultimately accountable, they cannot afford to delegate final responsibility for details to others, even trained professionals. Entrepreneurs must be familiar with all the legal, financial, and tax data that can significantly affect the business.

One of the most common, and often fatal, mistakes many first-time entrepreneurs make is believing that most of the responsibility for the pre-start phase can be delegated to technical experts like lawyers and accountants; they forget that from the very beginning accountability for results rests with lead entrepreneurs and their team.

Indeed, the process of entrepreneurship involves far more than the problem solving usually associated with management. Entrepreneurs are finders and exploiters of opportunities. It is an inescapable fact that any omissions made and any risk not assessed in the pre-start phase will automatically become—however unwelcome—part of the venture. On the other hand, early identification and management of risk factors can present opportunities for profit.

Although entrepreneurs need not know everything at the beginning, they must start with the realization that it is their responsibility to know the answers and to respond adequately to those steel-hearted outsiders who ask the hard questions. And they will ask them.

Finally, in spite of its potential difficulty and complexity, the pre-start analysis should induce a strong predisposition to decisiveness, timeliness, and go–no-go actions. The entrepreneur must not get bogged down in "analysis paralysis."

———— DISCUSSION QUESTIONS

1. Like a general manager, an entrepreneur must understand the relationships among all parts of a business. Compare and contrast the
   roles of a general manager in an established company and an
   entrepreneur planning a start-up. What new patterns of thought
   and behavior would a general manager aspiring to become an
   entrepreneur have to adopt?

2. The authors mention "technological change, government regulation (or its relaxation), and shifts in consumer preferences and
   market demand" as forces that create opportunities. What opportunities could these forces be shaping today? Try to project their
   market size and time horizon.

3. "The provision of real value is fundamental to any new venture,"
   say the authors. Cite some examples of entrepreneurial successes
   of the past ten years. How did these products or services create
   value for customers?

4. The authors emphasize the importance of effective resource management. Using the opportunity you came up with in Question 2,
   list the minimum essential resourrces you would need to assemble
   to pursue the opportunity you have chosen.

5. What new skills and attitudes must entrepreneurs adopt as they
   enter the managing and harvesting phases of the new venture cycle?

8 Purchasing a Business: The Search Process

ENNIS J. WALTON AND MICHAEL J. ROBERTS

There are several advantages to purchasing an existing company. The buyer need not create a new product or service; all that is needed is sufficient operating capital. Even when the purchase price exceeds start-up costs, a buyer typically incurs a lower risk than the founder of a business. Moreover, once the deal is closed, the new owner can focus more quickly than the founder on building and adding value to the business.

There are difficulties as well. Few written rules govern the search, and there is no established marketplace. The buyer must be prepared to assume responsibility for an enterprise that bears another's imprint.

This reading provides a framework for negotiating an inevitably unpredictable process. It covers such essentials as assessing your own personal motives and expectations, establishing selection criteria, locating deal sources, gathering resources, planning and negotiating the deal, and adding new value to the enterprise. The authors stress that although ideal acquisition candidates are rare, a realistic personal assessment and sound search and negotiation techniques can significantly improve the buyer's chance for success.

Buying a business is an informal process. No one has yet successfully defined the correct steps and alternatives for every situation. Success in the process often depends on serendipity—being the right person in the right place at the right time. It is a mistake, however, to depend on good luck rather than good work; there is no substitute for personal commitment, good business sense, and a cautiously optimistic exploration of every opportunity.

This reading provides a framework outlining the steps necessary to identify, evaluate, and negotiate a successful buyout. However, the framework is not exhaustive; rather, it provides a starting point that can be tailored to suit particular searches. The areas discussed are:

- *Self-Assessment.* Understanding your own motives, expectations, risk profile, and financial and professional resources; determining the strength of your commitment to the search.
- *Deal Criteria.* Clarifying the dimensions and characteristics of the project you find attractive.

- *Deal Sources.* Differentiating among various deal sources to find one that best fits your needs and criteria.
- *Resources.* Evaluating and gathering the additional cash, credibility, personal and professional contacts, and information necessary to begin the deal process.
- *The Deal Process.* Recognizing the sequential, often random, search process; establishing a timing schedule and work plan allowing for evaluation of deals that do not occur in parallel; understanding how to start the process, keep it moving, and establish initial contact with prospective sellers; assessing sellers' motives, weaknesses, strengths, and nonfinancial requirements.
- *The Evaluation Process.* Understanding various analytical methods used by sellers; requesting or obtaining key financial data; analyzing important financial dimensions of the deal.
- *Negotiating the Deal.* Identifying potential obstacles to a successful negotiation; learning from the collapsed deal; pursuing attractive deals.
- *Adding Value.* Adding new value to the business; understanding important harvesting options for the new enterprise.

——— SELF-ASSESSMENT

The first step in buying an existing business is a personal assessment. This crucial step will help to identify, articulate, and evaluate your hidden motives, expectations, risk profile, and, ultimately, the seriousness of your search. Without a good sense of personal values, the search process can become unfocused and unrewarding, and can waste time, resources, and energy.

The problems that could materialize in the absence of a thorough self-evaluation are intensified when two or more individuals are attempting to purchase a company. In such cases, it is essential that all parties understand and agree on motives and goals. Proceeding without a clear sense of those aspirations will probably lead to disagreements that impact the efficiency and effectiveness of the group during the later stages of the search process.

A good self-assessment will probably place you in one of three broad categories: serious, casual, or unrealistic. The serious, and realistic, search is characterized by

- A high level of commitment to the search;
- An ambitious set of expectations consistent with the degree of effort and commitment;
- A willingness to
  —risk at least some personal wealth/security
  —deeply research the target industry
  —be patient and wait for the right opportunity
  —move quickly and decisively as needed
  —pursue the search full time if necessary.

The casual, and still realistic, search involves:

- A set of expectations consistent with a lessened degree of commitment and effort;
- Less willingness to move quickly or decisively;
- No specified time horizon;
- Not being overly hungry to control one's own firm.

The unrealistic search involves:

- Objectives that are inconsistent with the level of commitment;
- Waiting for a "great deal" to fall in place;
- Looking for bargains and shortcuts.

While there is nothing wrong with either of the second two categories, the number and quality of opportunities discovered is proportional to the intensity of the search. Although one may find excellent deals by shopping the market casually, the process may take quite a while.

Another aspect of self-assessment many people disregard is the listing of business or personal relationships that can be called upon for assistance. Because the search process is lengthy and filled with important decision points, it is important to have advisers whose opinion you trust.

The most important reason for the self-assessment, however, is tactical. Throughout the search process you will have to deal with sellers or their intermediaries, and these individuals are often reluctant to invest time in individuals who do not exhibit a clear and convincing sense of what they are looking for. The better you have assessed yourself, the easier it will be to persuade others to take you seriously and work on your behalf.

——— DEAL CRITERIA

A consistent and thorough screening method is essential for successful completion of the acquisition process. Consistent criteria will make analyses performed on one company more readily comparable with those of other candidates; thoroughness will ensure that all relevant aspects of a potential acquisition are identified and analyzed. The screening method should have a clear focus and be fairly simple. At a minimum, one should consider such dimensions as:

- Size of deal (purchase price) desired;
- Preferred industry;
- Key factors for success: logistics, marketing, technology;
- Type of customer base (e.g., industrial vs. consumer, national vs. regional, etc.);
- Geographic preference;
- Profile of current ownership (e.g., how many, willingness to sell, reputation).

These criteria will establish a preliminary profile for identifying potential target companies. The screening process must then distinguish good deals from bad deals. Although several intangible and intuitive issues are involved in this process, as a rule, an ideal buyout target should include:

- Potential for improving earnings and sales;
- Predictable cash flow;
- Minimum existing debt;
- An asset base sufficient to support substantial new borrowings.

Buyout candidates will probably not fit in nice, neat little boxes, so that flexibility is important. One must constantly rethink and reassess the criteria. Do they fit? Are they appropriate? Is this the best way to examine this company? Will the criteria help to achieve the objectives in mind?

——— DEAL SOURCES

Initiating and sustaining a flow of potential deals is one of the most challenging tasks in buying a business. In general, expect to look at dozens of deals for every one that appears worth pursuing. A seemingly endless amount of groundwork is often necessary to initiate a deal, and a targeted effort is far more likely to result in a high percentage of attractive candidates than a random search. Thus, one of the first orders of business when starting out is knowing where to look.

Depending on the size deal sought, there are a number of potential deal sources, each with its own approach to acquisitions. Business brokers are the most readily available resource; they are listed individually in the Yellow Pages of most phone directories and advertise in the business sections of many newspapers. Brokers work on behalf of sellers to find appropriate buyers for their clients' businesses and are compensated by the seller at a given percentage of the price. Occasionally, a broker will work for a buyer in return for a retainer and/or a percentage of the ultimate purchase price. It should be emphasized, however, that brokers' interests lie in closing a transaction; they should not be considered impartial consultants.

Business brokers obtain listings through cold calls and advertising. Because these listings are actively marketed, it is safe to assume that you are not the first prospective buyer to see a business. More reputable brokers tend to regulate how "shopped" a business becomes in order to preserve its value, and some refuse to list properties sellers have already tried to market on their own.

At your initial meeting with the broker, you should be prepared to describe your financial constraints and industry preference. It is also valuable to indicate that you have a well-defined time horizon for a search and some knowledge of the target industry. You may want to touch base occasionally with each broker you meet, but it is a safe bet that you will be notified of interesting opportunities if you are a qualified buyer.

Independent brokers, which are almost entirely unregulated, are often the first place people turn to generate a deal flow. Because no license is required and anyone can claim to be one, it is essential to check a broker's references and reputation with intermediaries and past clients; in most states anyone with a telephone can claim to be a business broker. One can find a seemingly endless supply of one-person brokerage services in most any city. Typically, the deals they offer are small—less than $500,000 in sales—and are owned by entrepreneurs who have an unrealistic impression of the value of their businesses, an impression often fueled by the brokers themselves.

Professional brokers are business firms—rather than simply individuals—who specialize in the sale of companies. These organizations usually operate on a more professional basis than the independents, but they too represent the seller. Their interest is in obtaining a high price for the company, thereby ensuring themselves high commission fees (usually around 10%–12% at closing). However, most brokers are more interested in closing the deal than they are in squeezing out the last dollar in purchase price. Also, note that deals coming through professional brokers are very likely to be highly "shopped." The legitimacy of deals carried by professional brokers are often prescreened but usually carry a premium price.

Venture capital firms are often looking for liquidity on investments they made three to five years earlier. Venture-backed companies that have reached this stage are generally beyond many of the risks associated with start-ups and may offer a solid acquisition opportunity. Several points should be noted, however. First, venture capitalists are highly sophisticated investors and will probably extract the highest possible price for the company. Second, they want liquidity for their investment and will be less interested in earn-outs and other creative financing than in a deal financed primarily with cash. In addition, existing management will most likely be highly entrepreneurial and wary of controls introduced by new owners. Finally, as venture firms are often motivated to sell their problem companies, it is critical to understand the firm's situation thoroughly.

Leveraged-buyout funds in some situations pose competition to the buy-out effort. As a potential deal source, however, they may present opportunities to take over deals that are of no interest to the LBO fund. Such deals may be attractive candidates that simply did not match the particular focus of the LBO fund. LBO firms may also sell portions of acquired businesses to generate cash to pay back debt, and these, too, can be attractive deals.

Personal contacts, although often overlooked, may be a helpful source of deals; and contacts with people who have successfully completed the search process for their own businesses may provide both information and moral support. They may even be able to suggest contacts and strategies or allow you to tap their network; they may point out some of the pitfalls they encountered and suggest useful rules of thumb. You can locate these resources through your business and personal network or by tracking recently completed deals.

On occasion, *business periodicals* will help you identify opportunities. Indications that a company will be spinning off subsidiary operations are frequently mentioned, and the *Wall Street Journal, INC.,* and *Venture* routinely list business opportunities. On the local or regional level, there are business journals, franchise fairs, classified ads, and notices of bankruptcies and deaths. Newspapers, and the offices of the county clerk and court clerks, are good sources of leads, as are computer databases (usually available on a time-sharing basis) that provide lists of prospective buyers and sellers of businesses. Academic and commercial institutions in some communities sponsor industry forums or trade association meetings. Industry and phone directories (Yellow Pages, Dun & Bradstreet, *Million Dollar Directory,* Thomas' *Register of American Manufacturers*) may be useful for a cold call or letterwriting campaign and as a possible screen for industry, size, and location. In addition, you can run this process in reverse by placing your own advertisement in newspapers or journals, stating your needs and criteria for purchasing a business.

Local banks represent a broad range of local businesses and have in-depth knowledge of their finances and managerial situations. Like business brokers, the mergers and acquisitions-type departments of banks are primarily interested in closing transactions. Their inventory of deals may include both banking clients that are for sale and other firms that have engaged them to find a suitable buyer. A bank may also be amenable to helping you conduct a search on a success-fee basis. A good banker will be instrumental in structuring the financial arrangements of the newly acquired business and, often, will expect to become the new firm's principal banker.

Trust departments of banks are often the executors of estates, and, where there is a need to dispose of a business, may serve the same role as an estate lawyer. While the trust officer has a fiduciary responsibility to seek the highest price for the business, he or she has an equally important interest in keeping the transaction clean, fast, and, if possible, in cash.

Bank work-out departments are another potential source of bargain opportunities. Although the bank has a strong interest in not disclosing credit problems, it may serve as a confidential go-between for a potential buyer and the owners of a deeply troubled business. However, because of pressures within the bank to reschedule debt and the willingness of many owners to collateralize additional loans personally, most troubled loans are in fact worked out.

Traditional, mainline *investment banks* pose both a problem and an opportunity for buyers seeking a mid-sized deal. The problem is that investment banks are rarely interested in deals below, say, $20 million. Attracting their attention can be troublesome, and getting them to spend time moving on a small deal requires patience and tenacity. The opportunity exists because small deals carried by the investment banks are unlikely to have been widely shopped. Thus owners who rely exclusively on an investment bank to market their company will probably not receive extraordinary service, and a buyer who works this route may find a responsive seller on the other end of this inattentive pipeline.

No matter what the source of the deal, there will be a seller. Whether a single individual, a group of investors, or the shareholders of a small public company, one will have to evaluate the sellers' motivations. Issues of timing, types of financing, credibility, and desire to remain with the company after acquisition are all relevant considerations to keep in mind. Fairly early on, conversations should focus on sellers' motives for selling the business and their expectations about the value and form of the deal. A cautious investor can use this opportunity to gauge the character and integrity of the seller—traits that have probably affected the business in the past.

━━━ RESOURCES

Aside from tireless energy and a wealth of patience, the resources critical to the buyout project are cash, credibility, and contacts. These three factors, more than any others, govern the success of the effort. How much of each will be required is simply a question of deal size. Purchasing a $300,000 business certainly requires fewer resources than putting together a $20 million buyout. In larger deals the competition is more sophisticated, and sellers will demand that potential buyers possess the credentials necessary to put a complex deal together. Without such resources potential buyers may not even be able to set up an initial meeting with the seller. To get further than the first phone call about large deals, one should be prepared to respond satisfactorily to such inquiries as:

- How much cash do you have available?
- Who are your backers?
- What other deals have you done?
- What kind of management talent do you bring?
- What do you plan to do with the company?

Sellers value their time as much as the prospective buyer does; neither wants to expend fruitless energy when there is an obvious mismatch between what the buyer brings to the table and what the target company requires. No amount of debt leverage will compensate for a lack of the necessary equity capital and demonstrated personal experience. Only taking stock of the resources available for the buyout project and then targeting deals that can be reasonably snared with the available resources will ensure the buyer's credibility.

If backers are involved, purchasers must realize the extent to which they are dependent on them and gauge the backers' commitment; all the backers' cash and contacts are useless if they are unwilling to pursue a deal vigorously. Evaluate the backers' incentives: How important is the project to them? How much time have they agreed to set aside? Do their timing considerations match those of the buyers? Some backers are quite willing to employ the free efforts of a buyout group, simply hoping they will luck into a treasure chest. Be cautious of working like a neglected employee rather than a respected partner. Such characteristics may prove difficult to evaluate when early enthusiasm for a project runs high. Nonetheless, a skeptical assessment of backers' sincerity, interest, and ability to follow through on their part of the bargain is essential before relying on them for resources critical to success.

Another essential resource for the prudent buyer is an experienced lawyer. An attorney's review of documents to protect the client should ensure adequate contractual conditions, proper disclosure, and legal and regulatory compliance. He or she can also provide tax advice and may be able to identify potential risks and liabilities in a transaction. Experienced lawyers almost always turn out to be cheaper because they know the appropriate safeguards and can create good standard documents without extensive research. In addition, as established members of a local professional community, attorneys may have a wide network of contacts on the boards of local businesses and in the target industry. While tapping into this network might not generate a deal, it may provide buyers with opportunities to learn about the target industry and thus gain credibility with sellers. Large law firms occasionally keep an inventory of acquisition opportunities. Usually the buyer must compensate the lawyer, and if the deal is successful he or she generally expects to become the newly acquired firm's corporate counsel.

In selecting a business lawyer, buyers must consider issues of conflict of interest, reputation, and suitability. Although no reputable attorney would pursue an engagement while there is a potential conflict of interest (e.g., if he or she is representing the seller), it is up to you to determine whether a conflict might arise. It is also wise to do some checks of the reputation of individual attorneys and firms. Finally, the choice of lawyer should reflect perceived legal and other professional needs at various stages of the search and deal process. For example, a lawyer with the technical knowledge to structure the deal from a tax perspective may not be the most skilled negotiator.

━━━ THE DEAL PROCESS

Once you have established the target company profile, understood the best ways to generate deal flow, and gathered the necessary resources, you should prepare to enter the deal market. At this phase, it is important to recognize and prepare for the random nature of the process and two important timing issues.

First, the sequential nature of the search process makes it difficult to consider two deals within a timeframe allowing for a comparative evaluation. It is important to realize that if you let one deal pass, you will probably encounter another in the near future. An analytical framework for screening businesses (see *Exhibit*) will assist you in comparing and tracking various deals as you interface with sellers, deal sources, and other active parties throughout the deal process.

EXHIBIT
Business Screening Analyses

1. *GENERAL*

   Company, business strategy, age and history, trends

2. *PRODUCT*

   Description/technical specifications, function, volumes, prices, value added/commodity, patents

3. *MANAGEMENT TEAM*

   Key employees: names, positions, education, track record, skills

   Organization chart

   Is management team complete? Efforts/ability to hire new management?

   Willingness to remain after purchase?

   Characterization of management team (i.e., aggressive/passive, young/old, etc.)

4. *MARKET POSITION*

   Market size ($, units)

   Market growth and growth drivers

   Segmentation of the market (geographic, functional)

   Identification of customer: Who? How? Why does the buyer buy?

   Relationship with customers: number, loyalty, concentration

   Distribution channels: types, support/training required, advertisement strategy

   Market share of major players

   Company's major differentiating factors: price, quality, service, features, brand identity

5. *COMPETITIVE ANALYSIS*

   Barriers to entry/exit: economies of scale, proprietary technology, switching cost, capital requirements, access to distribution, cost advantages, government policy, expected retaliation, brand identity, exit cost

   Competitive factors: number, strength, characterization, product differences, concentration, diversity, management, industry capacity, competitive advantages, corporate stakes

   Substitution threat: relative price/performance of substitutes, switching cost, buyers' propensity to substitute

   Suppliers' power: relationship, concentration, manufacturing/marketing process, presence of substitute inputs, importance of volume to supplier, switching cost of supplier, cost relative to total purchases, impact of inputs on cost or differentiation, threat of forward integration, supplier profitability

   Buyers' power: bargaining leverage, buying patterns, concentration, volume, switching cost, ability to backyard integrate, substitute products, price sensitivity, price/total purchases, product differences, brand identity, impact on quality/performance, buyer profitability, decision-making units' incentives and complexity

   Trends: technology, economic, changes in tax law

EXHIBIT
Business Screening Analyses (Continued)

6. OPERATIONS

Work force: size, union/nonunion, work rules, contract expiration, age and skill level, match with developing technology, attrition, attitude, manufacturing engineering staff competence

Manufacturing flow and scheduling: job shop/batch continuous, systems, process flow, material handling, multiplant strategy/logistics, cost accounting, work discipline, work-order tracking, % dead time

Capacity: % of total capacity, bottlenecks (current and projected)

Purchasing: opportunities for redesign, fewer parts, add/subtract vendors, larger discounts, incoming material sampling, outsourcing policies

Quality control: attitude/priority, problem areas, methodology.

Capital equipment: age/maintenance, sophistication, general *vs.* special purpose, level of automation, trends

R&D: as % of sales compared to industry, type, technical strengths/weaknesses, organization, importance, trends

Information systems: importance, competitive advantage, level of sophistication, systems under development

7. FINANCIALS

Sales/Profitability: income statement, historical and 2, 3, 5-year pro formas, growth (sales, costs, profits, EPS, sustainable growth rates), quality of earnings (accounting, pension funding, depreciation, write-offs, earnings segments, earnings patterns, earnings sensitivity), ratio analysis (compared to competitors and industry averages, gross margins, ROS, ROE, P/E comparables)

Leverage and liquidity: balance sheet, historical and pro formas, examination of equity and debt composition, ratio analysis (current and quick ratios, debt as percentage of total capitalization, assets/equity, days receivable, days payable, days inventory)

Funds flow: statement of changes, historical and pro formas, analysis of sources and uses of cash

Assets: composition and type, quality, bankability, book and market values, obsolescence, age

8. VALUATION

Terminal value: FCF perpetuity/annuity, book value, liquidation value, P/E value

Components of value (i.e., investment tax credits, depreciation, energy cost savings, etc.)

Sensitivity analysis

Expected returns analysis

9. RISK/REALITY CHECK

Industry

Technology

Financial

Product/company liability

Employee/supplier/customer response

Seller's desire to do the deal

Is value appropriate?

Prohibitive terms?

Value to be added

The second critical issue concerns the timing of the approach to a given company: before it hits the market, as soon as it hits the market, or after it has been shopped. There are advantages and disadvantages to each stage. Being the first person to see a deal may give you the inside track. Yet, at this early stage, the seller may not have developed a realistic perspective on the asking price, terms, provision of desired information, willingness to part with the business, and so on. Discussions may be futile, or you may end up paying a high price. At a later stage, the seller may be more eager to sell, but you will need to be wary of a business that has been on the market for a long time.

Once you understand these basic timing issues, you can prepare a schedule and work plan and begin the search by setting up an introductory meeting with potential members of your search team. A persuasive presentation at this first meeting might include a demonstration of your industry research or experience, a well-thought-out preliminary business plan, a realistic assessment of your financial resources, and businesslike dress and demeanor. Academic credentials and referrals from mutual acquaintances will help you make these initial contacts. You may want to meet with many attorneys, CPAs, bankers, or other resource people before committing yourself to work with particular individuals. You might also schedule screening sessions with some of the professionals before meeting with your highest priority contacts.

At the preliminary meeting resources will be interested in qualifying you as a realistic potential buyer and as someone they want to work with. You should attempt to determine their expertise, willingness to help, any conditions they may place on the relationship, and their likely fee. The basis of fees ranges from hourly rates to contingent fees and may vary substantially from one lawyer to another—another reason to meet with many professionals before arranging to work exclusively with any one in particular.

The issue of exactly what cards to show often arises during preliminary discussions. While this is a personal decision, it is probably best to be frank about your financial resources and backing, level of commitment, and objectives. You may want to be more vague if you are dealing with an intermediary representing a potential seller or if you have reservations about the person you are meeting. Backers' insistence on remaining anonymous may also induce you to be somewhat guarded. It is always prudent to check out the reputations of such individuals before divulging any private information.

The average time required to find the right business runs about one year—significantly longer if the search is more casual or if the target is more elusive. Depending on your degree of commitment, financial flexibility, and time schedule, you may elect to manage your own search and call on search resources only periodically; or, conversely, you may choose to retain an individual or firm to conduct the search for you. Attorneys, for example, could make cold calls and write letters to industry sources on your behalf, and their personal and professional contacts *may* unearth your dream business. On the other hand, you could easily do much of the research you pay them for from industry directories and Yellow Pages. Thus, if time permits or your budget requires, and you are sophisticated about basic business and legal issues, you may choose to undertake much of the basic research. This has the additional advantage of providing firsthand contact with the marketplace. The industry-specific knowledge you pick up may be invaluable to you later on, when you need to demonstrate expertise and commitment to financing sources or a seller.

In some industries, acquisition opportunities rarely reach the market-place because the industry is essentially closed. To enter such an area, you must network your way in—meeting owners or executives of firms in the industry socially, attending industry-association meetings or trade conferences, and in general becoming more of an insider.

You will want to touch base with individuals in your new network periodically to see if they have any ideas for you and to reiterate your interest. A brief phone call every three or four weeks is appropriate, but more frequent contact may be annoying. You should also keep them informed about your progress. Keep in mind that people are more likely to pass on information or leads if you share your ideas and findings with them.

Once underway, you may come across a potential acquisition candidate and need to do some preliminary research. Dun & Bradstreet reports contain financial and operating information on the company and biographical back-grounds of owners or officers. The information, however, is provided by the company and is not independently verified.

When meeting the owner(s) and visiting the business it is important to evaluate the seller's psychology—his or her financial or psychological needs as they pertain to the business. A few owners have no real attachment to a business and are simply open to the highest bid. More often, especially in small opera-tions, much of the seller's life is tied up in the firm and there is a high degree of emotional involvement. Such factors as the seller's age, marital situation, health, or family situation may also need to be reflected in the form and terms of the deal. In such cases you may need to "sell" the seller.

Such selling includes more than a generous financial package (e.g., insurance, provision for the family, etc.); it may require you to demonstrate commitment to the original character, quality, and spirit of the enterprise. Occasionally an owner may indicate a willingness to sell but balk when it comes to actually closing the deal and transferring control. Understanding the owner's psyche early on may help avoid such an outcome by structuring a more mutually satisfying deal.

Your professional resource people may be able to provide valuable insight and advice if they know the seller or have dealt with similar situations in the past. In some cases you may want to have your agent handle the negotiations in order to preserve your own rapport with the seller, neutralize personality clashes, and retain decision options.

———— THE EVALUATION PROCESS

If after preliminary research and meetings with the seller, you decide to pursue the opportunity, you will need to review confidential operating and financial statements and interview key employees and customers. But "getting the numbers" is often difficult. Many small business owners are reluctant to share operating and financial data with outsiders for tax and competitive reasons. Most buyers receive no meaningful financial details until after signing a purchase agreement and putting down a deposit, although a good understanding of the industry may give you increased credibility and leverage with the seller. The owner of a distressed business may be willing to provide numbers earlier in the process; in the case of bankrupt firms, the numbers may be in the public domain. Confidentiality agreements are usually signed before the prospective buyer is allowed to review financials.

At this point you are well advised to retain counsel to ensure that you are protected and are covering all legal bases, especially if you are signing documents or agreements. An accountant may also be useful, especially in a complex situation, in analyzing financial reports, tax returns, inventory records, and so on; other experts can investigate leases and contracts.

It is often useful before performing any detailed analysis to collect information together into a thumbnail sketch of the deal's financial attractiveness. This preliminary check can screen the candidate for company size, profitability, and attractiveness of the balance sheet. Some deals may be thrown out at this point, while others will merit a more thorough examination of the numbers.

There are several ways to estimate the value of a company, and it is most often useful to employ more than one method. Different types of analysis will be needed to determine how much to pay, how much debt will be assumed and from what sources, and potential harvest values. Each will play an important role in the overall assessment of the opportunity at hand. Three types of analysis useful for establishing price estimate are:

Method used	What the results indicate
Discounted Cash Flow	Underlying operating value of the business and ability to service debt
Asset Valuation	Liquidation value and/or adjusted book value of assets
Multiples	Multiples of cash flow, P/E ratios, sales, or EBIT help establish some sense for market value relative to other firms in the same industry and offer an indication of harvest potential. Each type of multiple has its own merit, but must be consistently applied.

Both cash flow analysis and multiples analysis estimate value based on future events, either operating results or market reaction to public offering. Thus they require a multitude of assumptions; for example:

- *Level of risk.* How volatile are the company's cash flows?
- *Competition.* How fiercely contested is the market for the company's products?
- *Industry trends.* Is this a growing or declining industry? What are the profitability trends?
- *Organizational stability.* How well established is this company in its line of business?
- *Management.* Is a competent and complete team in place?
- *Company growth.* Historically has the company been growing or shrinking, and how fast?
- *General desirability.* To what degree does the marketplace find this line of business attractive?

A cautionary note on valuations: many deal proposals are put together on the basis of "recast" financial statements. In theory such a practice is legitimate and may reflect realistic operating results. In reality, however, assumptions implicit in the recast statement are not always attainable, and they can be downright misleading. Always ask whether or not the financials shown have been recast and if they have, make sure you understand all the adjustments made. No assumption should be left unchallenged. This is particularly true for smaller companies whose owners will often operate with numerous adjustments in order to minimize the tax burden.

Once a general idea of price is established, the deal will have to be structured to provide attractive returns to equity investment. There are two fundamental considerations in this regard. First is the overall financeability of the deal, including: (1) assets to secure bank financing; (2) cash flow to support further debt instruments (i.e., company-issued debentures); and (3) personal collateral, if any.

Second, one must consider (possibly in conjunction with the preceding analysis) the actual structure of the financing. An ideal structure caters to the interest of all parties involved. The buyer might, for example, establish financing "strips" of debt and equity to provide the investor both secured fixed income and participation in potential capital appreciation. Tax losses may be scrutinized and sold to investors.

——— NEGOTIATING THE DEAL

When you discover a company that is financially feasible and meets your other criteria, negotiate carefully. Don't let the wave of enthusiasm over having finally found a company cloud your judgment. Often during negotiations new information will begin to trickle out—a lawsuit that isn't quite settled, a previous industrial accident, receivables that may be less collectible than they appear. It is important to reevaluate information constantly in an objective fashion.

The seller can get cold feet as well or develop second thoughts about selling at a particular price. It will help to develop a sense of momentum by turning documents around quickly and dealing personally with the seller. Don't let lawyers become intermediaries in the transaction—manage the process yourself.

Obstacles need not get in the way of a deal, but you should be prepared to greet them if they do appear. Indeed, you may have to walk away from your share of deals. Although giving up on a business you wanted can be disappointing, it should teach you important lessons. You should become a better judge of character and business situations, knowledge that will be invaluable as you continue the search process. Moreover, the firsthand experience and knowledge of the industry you gain in the collapsed deal may enhance your future credibility with sellers or their intermediaries.

ADDING VALUE

Even before you purchase a company, you can begin to formulate plans for improving its performance. Indeed, such plans are a vital component of understanding a business's potential and being willing to pay a given price. Adding value to a new firm can be accomplished in many ways.

You may decide to make operational changes, perhaps to take advantage of an opportunity to broaden distribution, open new markets, or otherwise boost sales and/or margins. In evaluating such possibilities, be both realistic and creative; chances are the easy things have already been tried. Such operating improvements require an assessment of the management team and personnel in place. Are they reliable, competent, honest, and suited to the new challenge?

In many small businesses, the company can be vastly improved by modifying the underlying financial structure. For example, negotiating a longer payment schedule with creditors, creating incentives for customers to pay bills sooner, and obtaining lines of credit from commercial banks can change the dynamics of the business and improve cash flow.

CONCLUSION

Searching for a small business to buy can be difficult. Not only is there no established marketplace for these firms, but you are purchasing an entity created and cultivated by another person and attempting to meld it with your own style, character, and interests. The process can be extremely time consuming, expensive, and frustrating. But, although available research indicates the good acquisition candidates are few and far between, sound search techniques and a realistic personal assessment can significantly improve your chances of success and help achieve a measure of control over some elements of the process.

Finally, remember that the process is also an investment decision. Even a superb company is of little value to an investor if nobody else is willing to pay for it. Identifying an appropriate exit strategy to make one's investment liquid— whether running the company in perpetuity, getting out in a secondary public offering, liquidating the assets, or selling out—will help define the project's monetary returns.

──── DISCUSSION QUESTIONS

1. Suppose you have made a decision to purchase a business. In assessing your motives and goals, what questions would you ask yourself?

2. What are the advantages of purchasing rather than founding a business? What special skills and attributes should a purchaser bring to the enterprise?

3. What are the advantages and disadvantages of working with business brokers? With venture capitalists? With banks?

4. Think of a type of business you would be interested in purchasing and imagine you are entering your first meeting with a prospective seller. What questions are you going to ask?

5. The authors mention two ways in which a buyer can add value to an existing business: making operational changes and changing the financial structure. Using your example from Question 4, in what additional ways could you add value to your new company?

9   Valuation Techniques

MICHAEL J. ROBERTS

Whether preparing to start, buy, or harvest a business, entrepreneurs need a way to project its value. How attractive is the opportunity? What is the worth of the company as a whole, and how much of that worth can the entrepreneurial investor eventually realize? Though many methods of determining the value of a large public company are available, appraising a small, privately held firm requires more ingenuity.

In this reading, Roberts offers several tools for measuring value and considers some of their strengths and limitations, reminding readers that no single approach captures the true value of any firm. Ultimately, the decision to invest time and resources in an enterprise is a subjective one, influenced by many factors besides dollars and cents. Although the techniques Roberts describes will not yield one "right" answer, they will help entrepreneurs develop a realistic understanding of the potential outcomes, both good and bad, of pursuing a given opportunity.

Financial theorists have developed many techniques for evaluating a going concern. Of course, for a large public company, one can simply accept the market value of the equity. For an established business with a long history of audited financials it is possible to project earnings and cash flows accurately. But the valuation of a small, privately held business is difficult and uncertain at best.

In this reading I outline briefly three of the more widely used valuation approaches: asset valuations; earnings valuations; and cash flow valuations.

ASSET VALUATIONS

One approach to valuations is to look at the underlying worth of the business's assets as a measure of the investor's exposure to risk. If the company holds assets whose market value approximates the price of the company plus its liabilities, the immediate downside risk is low. In some instances, increase in the value of assets represents a major portion of the investor's anticipated return. There are various approaches to valuing a company's assets.

BOOK VALUE

The most obvious asset value that a prospective purchaser can examine is the book value. In a situation with many variables and unknowns it provides a tangible starting point. It is only a beginning, however; the company's accounting practices, as well as other factors, can significantly affect book value. For example, if the reserve for losses on accounts receivable is too low for the business it will inflate book value, and vice versa. Similarly, treatment of asset accounts such as research and development costs, patents, organization expenses, and so on, can vary widely. Nevertheless, book value provides a good point of departure.

ADJUSTED BOOK VALUE

An obvious refinement of stated book value is a value adjusted for large discrepancies between the stated book and actual market value of tangible assets such as buildings and equipment, which may have depreciated far below their market value, or land, which may well have appreciated substantially above a book value that stands at the original cost. An adjustment would probably also reduce the book value of intangible assets to zero unless they, like the tangible assets, also have a market value. A figure resulting from these adjustments should represent the value of the company's assets more accurately than stated book value.

LIQUIDATION VALUE

One step beyond adjusted book value is considering the net amount that would be realized if the assets of the company were disposed of in a quick sale and all liabilities were paid off or otherwise settled. This value would take into account that many assets, especially inventory and real estate, would not realize as much as they would if the company continued in operation or was sold more deliberately. This calculation would also allow for the various costs connected to carrying out a liquidation sale.

The liquidation value, it should be noted, is an indication only of what might be realized if the firm were liquidated immediately. Should the company continue in operation and encounter difficulties, a subsequent liquidation would be most likely to yield significantly less than the liquidation value calculated for the company in its current condition.

The liquidation value of a company is not usually important to a buyer interested in maintaining a going concern. However, this value might represent some kind of a floor price below which the seller would be unwilling to go.

REPLACEMENT VALUE

The current cost of reproducing the tangible assets of a business can be a significant consideration in that starting a new company may present an alternative means of getting into the business. Sometimes the market value of existing facilities is considerably less than the cost of building a plant and purchasing equivalent equipment from other sources. In most instances, however, this replacement value represents more of a reference point than a serious possibility.

───── EARNINGS VALUATIONS

A second common approach to an investor's valuation of a company is to capitalize earnings. This involves multiplying earnings by a capitalization factor or price/earnings (P/E) ratio. This immediately raises two questions: (1) Which earnings? and (2) What factor?

EARNINGS FIGURE

There are three basic kinds of earnings.

Historical Earnings   The assumption behind looking at historical earnings is that they can be used to project the company's future performance. However, there is no logical reason to evaluate a company on the basis of past earnings. They can rarely be used directly, and an extrapolation of these figures to obtain a picture of the future must be considered a rough, and frequently poor, approximation. Nonetheless, historical earnings can be a general guide to the future; they provide a concrete supplement to what would otherwise be just a series of best guesses. Some benefit from the financial history of past operations can be gained by studying each of the cost and income components, their interrelations, and their changes over time.

To do so, random and nonrecurring items should be factored out and an effort made to distinguish normal from extraordinary operating expenses and cash flows. Extraordinary costs or gains—or their absence—may be very important. For example, inordinately low figures for maintenance and repairs over a period of years may mean that extraordinary expenses will be incurred in the future for deferred maintenance. Similarly, nonrecurring windfall sales will distort the normal earnings picture.

In a small, closely held company, particular attention should be paid to the salaries of owner-managers and their family members. If these salaries have been unreasonably high or low for the type and size of the business or the duties performed, paying more normal salaries will result in an adjustment in earnings. An assessment should also be made of depreciation rates to determine their validity and to estimate the need for future earnings adjustments. The amount of federal and state income taxes paid in the past may also influence future earnings because of carryover and carryback provisions in the tax laws.

Future Earnings Under Present Ownership   How much and in what ways income and costs are calculated for future operations depends to a large degree on the operating policies and strategies of management. Both present and future owners' approaches will be influenced by management ability, economic and noneconomic objectives, and so on. In calculating future earnings for a company, these factors must be considered and weighed.

A calculation of value based on future earnings can provide a good indication of the current economic value of the company to the current owner. To an investor, including the present owner, this figure provides an economic basis for continued activity and investment. However, to an investor who anticipates a change in management with his investment, an evaluation based on earnings from the current owner's management is *not* an adequate assessment of the value of the company.

Future Earnings Under New Ownership   These earnings figures are relevant to someone investing in the turnaround of a dying company or the reinvigoration of a stagnant one. The basis for the figures—assumptions, relationships between costs and income, and so on—will probably show significant variance from the company's past performance. Plans may call for substantial change in the nature and operation of the business and involve large capital investments beyond the purchase price.

The projected future earnings of the new operation will determine the value of the company to the entrepreneur by influencing the return on investment (ROI). Because these projections will contain large elements of uncertainty, it will be helpful to consider high, low, and most likely outcomes for financial performance.

In addition to deciding on whether to focus on historical or future earnings periods, the entrepreneur will need to decide the issue of "what earnings?"—that is, profit before tax, profit after tax, operating income, or earnings before interest and taxes (EBIT). Most valuations look at earnings after tax (but before extraordinary items). Of course, the most important rule is to be consistent: don't base a multiple on earnings after tax and then apply that multiple to EBIT. Beyond this, it is essential to consider precisely what is being measured in the valuation. A strong argument can be made for using EBIT, which measures the actual earning power and underlying value of the business, free from the effects of financing. This is a particularly valuable approach if the entrepreneur is contemplating changing the financial structure of the business in the future.

PRICE-EARNINGS MULTIPLE (P/E)

The next issue is choice of multiple. The investor who expects the primary return to result from sale of the owner's stock at some future date should ask these questions: Given the anticipated pattern of earnings, the nature of the industry, the likely state of the stock market, and so on, what price will individuals or some acquisitive conglomerate be willing to pay me for my holdings? In terms of some multiple of earnings, what prices are paid for stock with similar records and histories? The difficulty of estimating with any degree of confidence the future multiple of a small company—that is, estimating both a small company's future earnings and future market conditions for the stock— in part explains why required returns on investment for new ventures are so high. Perhaps the best way to reduce this great uncertainty is to work with a range of values. In any case, consistency is critical: always derive the multiple as a function of the same base you wish to apply it to (profit after tax, EBIT, etc.).

To this point, we have been discussing methods of arriving at a value for the business as a whole. While entrepreneurs are naturally interested in this information, they should also attempt to estimate the value of their own potential equity. Residual pricing addresses this issue. It involves:

- Determining the future value of a company in year n through one of the methods described above;
- Applying a target rate of return to the amount of money raised via the initial sale of equity; and
- Using this information to develop a perspective on how much equity entrepreneurs must give up in order to get the needed equity financing.
- The residual, or remaining equity, can be retained by individual entrepreneurs as their return.

For example, if a company is projected to have earnings of $100,000 in year 5, and if after analysis, it seems that the appropriate P/E for the company is 10, we can assume the company will be worth $1,000,000 in year 5. Now if we know that the entrepreneur needs to raise $50,000 from a venture capital firm (in equity) to start the business, and if the venture firm requires a 50% annual return on that money, that $50,000 needs to be worth $50,000 x $(1 + 50\%)^5$ or $380,000. So in theory at least, the entrepreneur would have to give 38% of the equity to the venture firm to raise that sum.

———— CASH FLOW VALUATIONS

Traditional approaches to evaluating a company have placed the principal emphasis on earnings. Assuming that the company will continue in operation, the earnings method posits that a company is worth what it can be expected to earn.

But this approach is only partially useful for individuals' decisions on whether or not to invest in a business. As in residual pricing, entrepreneurs must distinguish between the value of the business as a whole and the portion of that value that can be appropriated for themselves; this value, in turn, will be determined by the need to give up a portion of the business to attract resources. Besides subjective reasons, the entrepreneur's chief criterion for the acquisition will be return on investment. But because an entrepreneur's dollar investment is sometimes very small, it may be useful to think in terms of a return on time rather than on dollar investment. To calculate this return, the prospective entrepreneur must estimate the individual or personal cash flow from the business, rather than the return inherent in the business itself. Several different types of cash flow can accrue to the entrepreneur.

OPERATING CASH FLOWS

Cash or value that flows out of the business during its operations includes:

Perquisites   These benefits are not literally cash but can be considered cash equivalents. Business-related expenses charged to the company, such as company cars and country club memberships, are received by the individual and are not taxed at either the corporate or personal level. Their disadvantage is that they are limited in absolute dollar terms.

Return of Capital Through Debt Repayment   This form of cash flow is also tax-free at both the corporate and personal levels. Its additional advantage is that it can occur while the entrepreneur maintains equity interest in the company. Its disadvantage is, of course, that it requires the entrepreneur to make the original investment.

Interest and Salary   Both these items constitute personal income and are taxed at the personal level; no tax is imposed on them at the corporate level.

Dividends   As a means of getting cash from a venture, dividends are the least desirable, as the resulting cash flow has undergone the greatest net shrinkage. Dividends incur taxes first at the corporate level (at the 15% or 34% rate as income accrues to the corporation) and then again at the personal level (at the personal income tax rate). At the maximum corporate income tax rate of 34% and the maximum personal income tax rate of 28%, this double taxation can reduce $1.00 of pretax corporate profit to $.48 after-tax cash flow to the individual.

TERMINAL VALUE

Another source of cash is the money the entrepreneur pulls out of the business when the venture is harvested. Again, there are several elements to this aspect of return.

Return of Capital Via Sale   When the owner/manager sells all or part of the business, the cash received, up to the amount of the cost basis, is tax-free at both the corporate and personal levels. Because a sale of interest is involved, however, it is evident that, unlike a return of capital via debt repayment, the entrepreneur does not maintain a continuous equity interest in the concern. As in the case of a cash flow based on debt retirement, an original investment is necessary.

Capital Gain Via Sale   When capital gains are realized in addition to the return of capital, no tax is imposed at the corporate level, and the tax rate at the personal level is less than that for regular income.

TAX BENEFITS

While not precisely cash flow, tax benefits can enhance cash flow from other sources. For example, if a start-up has operating losses for several years, and if these losses can be passed through to the individual, they create value by sheltering other income. Because entrepreneurs are often in a low-income phase when starting a business, these tax benefits may be of limited value to them. However, if properly structured, they can provide substantial value to investors. In a situation where the structure and form of the organization (i.e., a corporation) does not permit losses to flow to individuals, they can be used to offset corporate income in prior or future years.

NEGATIVE CASH FLOWS

Entrepreneurs must also take into account their negative cash flows, of which three types are particularly important: (1) cash portion of the purchase price, (2) deficient salary, and (3) additional equity capital.

Frequently the most critical aspect of the cash portion of the purchase price is that entrepreneurs must be able to pay it in the first place. Often a seller finances the purchase of a company by taking part of the purchase price in the form of a note, receiving cash from later earnings or from company assets. Of course, the less cash the entrepreneur must put up the more is available for other uses and the greater the opportunities to produce a high ROI. On the other hand, too much initial debt may hamstring a company from the start, thereby hurting the venture's subsequent financial performance and the entrepreneur's principal source of return—be it the income derived from the business or the funds received from its eventual sale.

The immediate significance to the entrepreneur of a negative cash flow based on a deficient salary is clear: a personal income lower than could be obtained elsewhere. In addition, early negative flows and the need for additional working capital or fixed assets may force the owner/manager to seek outside investors, thereby diluting his or her equity in the business and introducing the possibility of divergent financial and operational goals.

PRESENT VALUE OF CASH FLOW

At this point in the evaluation process it may appear obvious to some that the next step for the entrepreneur is finding the present value of the cash flow predicted for the venture, that is, discounting the value of future cash flows to arrive at a present cash value of the business. We shall see, however, that this approach raises more questions than it answers and that its usefulness to the analysis is questionable at best.

The essence of the problem is that present value is basically an investment concept utilizing ROI to determine the allocation of a limited supply of funds among alternatives; the entrepreneur, however, is faced with a personal situation in which return on both investment and time are key. In addition, the entrepreneur may have made a considerable investment in generating the particular option, and it is difficult to weigh this tangible opportunity against unknown alternatives. Unless the entrepreneur has a portfolio of well-defined opportunities to choose from, he or she needs to define some standard of comparison. This is typically the salary that could be obtained by working.

In an investment analysis utilizing present value, the discount rate is selected to reflect the uncertainty associated with cash flows; the higher the uncertainty, the higher the discount rate and, consequently, the lower the present value of the cash flows. In the corporate context the usual minimal ROI for noncritical investments must be at least higher than the firm's cost of capital. For the individual entrepreneur, however, the decision to buy or to start a company is fundamentally a subjective one. Return on investment and time for this kind of decision is measured not only in dollars, but also in choices about the work, one's associates, the time and energy expended, and resulting life-style. Different kinds of ventures present different kinds of return on time. Because cash is an important enabling factor for some of the things the entrepreneur is seeking, it is important to calculate what these cash flows might be and when they can be expected. However, because decisions affecting cash flow also affect the other returns to the entrepreneur, and because these other returns may be at least as important as the financial returns, a present value calculation often is not the most important measure.

In thinking about the attractiveness of a particular opportunity, an entrepreneur rarely has two similar and simultaneous alternatives to compare.

Most often the decision is either to go ahead with a venture or to keep looking. Perhaps the most useful way to think of this situation is to imagine an individual looking down a corridor that provides a range of subcorridors—opportunities to achieve different levels of financial and other rewards—each with its own accompanying set of risks and sacrifices. Financial theorists have recently begun to study investments in this way, in terms of their ability to generate a future stream of growth opportunities.

The preceding discussion has outlined a variety of approaches to the valuation of a firm. It is important to remember that no single approach will ever provide the "right" answer. To a large extent, the appropriateness of any method depends on the perspective of the evaluator. Nonetheless, some time in the course of the evaluation process one must come to a decision about the worth of a firm, no matter how scant the data. Even if the value is only a preliminary one, it will permit the individual to delve deeper into the issues at hand; for the purpose of the analysis is not to arrive at the one "true" answer but to:

- Identify critical assumptions;
- Evaluate the interrelations among elements of the situation to determine which aspects are crucial;
- Develop realistic scenarios, not a best case–worst case analysis;
- Surface and understand potential outcomes and consequences, both good and bad; and
- Examine the manner in which the business's value is being carved up to satisfy the needs of prospective resource suppliers.

No single valuation can capture the true value of any firm. Rather, its value is a function of the individual's perception of opportunity and risk, the nature of financial resources available to the purchaser, the prospective operating strategy, the time horizon for analysis, alternatives available given the time and money invested, and the potential methods of harvesting. Price and value are not equivalent; if entrepreneurs pay what the business is worth, they have not appropriated any value for themselves. The difference between the two will be determined by information, market behavior, pressures forcing either purchase or sale, and negotiating skills.

—— DISCUSSION QUESTIONS

1. The author points out that price and value are not the same thing. What is the difference?
2. This reading offers a number of techniques for measuring value but emphasizes that none will yield a right answer. What, then, is the proper role for these techniques? How are they useful? What important questions do they not answer?
3. Traditional valuation techniques, the author points out, stress the importance of earnings. By focusing only on what the company can be expected to earn in the future, what is the entrepreneur not thinking about and not finding out?
4. Value encompasses financial as well as nonfinancial dimensions. What are some of the important financial measures of value? If you were about to start or purchase a business, what other considerations would determine value for you? What rewards, financial or otherwise, would you be willing to defer or sacrifice in order to attain success as you define it?
5. The author proposes that entrepreneuers view investments in terms of time as well as money. What else, besides time and money, can investment in a business entail? Does broadening your definition of investment change your conception of return on investment?

PLANNING: TURNING IDEAS INTO VENTURES

How to Write a Winning Business Plan

10

STANLEY R. RICH AND DAVID E. GUMPERT

Many entrepreneurs continue to believe that if they build a better mousetrap, the world will beat a path to their door. A good product or service is important, but it is only part of the challenge. Equally important is writing a business plan that will address the concerns of the constituencies that give the venture its financial viability—marketers and investors. Marketers want to see evidence of strong customer interest in the product or service. Investors want to know how good the financial projections are and when they can realize a return. Pointing out that creating a business plan is more art than science, Rich and Gumpert provide valuable guidelines for writing a plan that looks outward to key constituencies, demonstrates what is unique about the enterprise, and wins the necessary investment and support.

A comprehensive, carefully thought-out business plan is essential to the success of entrepreneurs and corporate managers. Whether you are starting up a new business, seeking additional capital for existing product lines, or proposing a new activity in a corporate division, you will never face a more challenging writing assignment than the preparation of a business plan.

Only a well-conceived and well-packaged plan can win the necessary investment and support for your idea. It must describe the company or proposed project accurately and attractively. Even though its subject is a moving target, the plan must detail the company's or the project's present status, current needs, and expected future. You must present and justify ongoing and changing resource requirements, marketing decisions, financial projections, production demands, and personnel needs in logical and convincing fashion.

Because they struggle so hard to assemble, organize, describe, and document so much, it is not surprising that managers sometimes overlook the fundamentals. We have found that the most important one is the accurate reflection of the viewpoints of three constituencies.

1. The market, including both existing and prospective clients, customers, and users of the planned product or service.
2. The investors, whether of financial or other resources.
3. The producer, whether the entrepreneur or the inventor.

Too many business plans are written solely from the viewpoint of the third constituency—the producer. They describe the underlying technology or creativity of the proposed product or service in glowing terms and at great length. They neglect the constituencies that give the venture its financial viability—the market and the investor.

Take the case of five executives seeking financing to establish their own engineering consulting firm. In their business plan, they listed a dozen types of specialized engineering services and estimated their annual sales and profit growth at 20%. But the executives did not determine which of the proposed dozen services their potential clients really needed and which would be most profitable. By neglecting to examine these issues closely, they ignored the possibility that the marketplace might want some services not among the dozen listed.

Moreover, they failed to indicate the price of new shares or the percentage available to investors. Dealing with the investor's perspective was important because—for a new venture, at least—backers seek a return of 40% to 60% on their capital, compounded annually. The expected sales and profit growth rates of 20% could not provide the necessary return unless the founders gave up a substantial share of the company.

In fact, the executives had only considered their own perspective—including the new company's services, organization, and projected results. Because they had not convincingly demonstrated why potential customers would buy the services or how investors would make an adequate return (or when and how they could cash out), their business plan lacked the credibility necessary for raising the investment funds needed.

We have had experience in both evaluating business plans and organizing and observing presentations and investor responses at sessions of the MIT Enterprise Forum. We believe that business plans must deal convincingly with marketing and investor considerations. This reading identifies and evaluates those considerations and explains how business plans can be written to satisfy them.

━━━ EMPHASIZE THE MARKET

Investors want to put their money into market-driven rather than technology-driven or service-driven companies. The potential of the product's markets, sales, and profit is far more important than its attractiveness or technical features.

You can make a convincing case for the existence of a good market by demonstrating user benefit, identifying marketplace interest, and documenting market claims.

SHOW THE USER'S BENEFIT

It's easy even for experts to overlook this basic notion. At an MIT Enterprise Forum[1] session an entrepreneur spent the bulk of his 20-minute presentation period extolling the virtues of his company's product—an instrument to control certain aspects of the production process in the textile industry. He concluded with some financial projections looking five years down the road.

The first panelist to react to the business plan—a partner in a venture capital firm—was completely negative about the company's prospects for obtaining investment funds because, he stated, its market was in a depressed industry.

Another panelist asked, "How long does it take your product to pay for itself in decreased production costs?" The presenter immediately responded, "Six months." The second panelist replied, "That's the most important thing you've said tonight."

The venture capitalist quickly reversed his original opinion. He said he would back a company in almost any industry if it could prove such an important user benefit—and emphasize it in its sales approach. After all, if it paid back the customer's cost in six months, the product would after that time essentially "print money."

The venture capitalist knew that instruments, machinery, and services that pay for themselves in less than one year are mandatory purchases for many potential customers. If this payback period is less than two years, it is a probable purchase; beyond three years, they do not back the product.

The panel advised the entrepreneur to recast his business plan so that it emphasized the short payback period and played down the self-serving discussion about product innovation. The executive took the advice and rewrote the plan in easily understandable terms. His company is doing very well and has made the transition from a technology-driven to a market-driven company.

FIND OUT THE MARKET'S INTEREST

Calculating the user's benefit is only the first step. An entrepreneur must also give evidence that customers are intrigued with the user's benefit claims and that they like the product or service. The business plan must reflect

---

1. Organized under the auspices of the Massachusetts Institute of Technology Alumni Association in 1978, the MIT Enterprise Forum offers businesses at a critical stage of development an opportunity to obtain counsel from a panel of experts. In addition to Cambridge, Massachusetts, chapters are located in 16 cities throughout North America. Two affiliate organizations are located in Stockholm, Sweden, and Berlin, Germany.

clear positive responses of customer prospects to the question "Having heard our pitch, will you buy?" Without them, an investment usually won't be made.

How can start-up businesses—some of which may have only a proto-type product or an idea for a service—appropriately gauge market reaction? One executive of a smaller company had put together a prototype of a device that enables personal computers to handle telephone messages. He needed to demonstrate that customers would buy the product, but the company had exhausted its cash resources and was thus unable to build and sell the item in quantity.

The executives wondered how to get around the problem. The panel offered two possible responses. First, the founders might allow a few customers to use the prototype and obtain written evaluations of the product and the extent of their interest when it became available.

Second, the founders might offer the product to a few potential custom-ers at a substantial price discount if they paid part of the cost—say one-third—up front so that the company could build it. The company could not only find out whether potential buyers existed but also demonstrate the product to potential investors in real-life installations.

In the same way, an entrepreneur might offer a proposed new service at a discount to initial customers as a prototype if the customers agreed to serve as references in marketing the service to others.

For a new product, nothing succeeds as well as letters of support and appreciation from some significant potential customers, along with "reference installations." You can use such third-party statements—from would-be cus-tomers to whom you have demonstrated the product, initial users, sales repre-sentatives, or distributors—to show that you have indeed discovered a sound market that needs your product or service.

You can obtain letters from users even if the product is only in prototype form. You can install it experimentally with a potential user to whom you will sell it at or below cost in return for information on its benefits and an agreement to talk to sales prospects or investors. In an appendix to the business plan or in a separate volume, you can include letters attesting to the value of the product from experimental customers.

DOCUMENT YOUR CLAIMS

Having established a market interest, you must use carefully analyzed data to support your assertions about the market and the growth rate of sales and profits. Too often, executives think "If we're smart, we'll be able to get about 10% of the market" and "Even if we only get 1% of such a huge market, we'll be in good shape."

Investors know that there's no guarantee a new company will get any business, regardless of market size. Even if the company makes such claims based on fact—as borne out, for example, by evidence of customer interest—

they can quickly crumble if the company does not carefully gather and analyze supporting data.

One example of this danger surfaced in a business plan that came before the MIT Enterprise Forum. An entrepreneur wanted to sell a service to small businesses. He reasoned that he could have 170,000 customers if he penetrated even 1% of the market of 17 million small enterprises in the United States. The panel pointed out that anywhere from 11 million to 14 million of such so-called small businesses were really sole proprietorships or part-time businesses. The total number of full-time small businesses with employees was actually between 3 million and 6 million and represented a real potential market far beneath the company's original projections—and prospects.

Similarly, in a business plan relating to the sale of certain equipment to apple growers, you must have U.S. Department of Agriculture statistics to discover the number of growers who could use the equipment. If your equipment is useful only to growers with 50 acres or more, then you need to determine how many growers have farms of that size, that is, how many are minor producers with only an acre or two of apple trees.

A realistic business plan needs to specify the number of potential customers, the size of their businesses, and which size is most appropriate to the offered products or services. Sometimes bigger is not better. For example, a saving of $10,000 per year in chemical use may be significant to a modest company but unimportant to a Du Pont or a Monsanto.

Such marketing research should also show the nature of the industry. Few industries are more conservative than banking and public utilities. The number of potential customers is relatively small, and industry acceptance of new products or services is painfully slow, no matter how good the products and services have proven to be. Even so, most of the customers are well known and while they may act slowly, they have the buying power that makes the wait worthwhile.

At the other end of the industrial spectrum are extremely fast-growing and fast-changing operations such as franchised weight-loss clinics and computer software companies. Here the problem is reversed. While some companies have achieved multi-million-dollar sales in just a few years, they are vulnerable to declines of similar proportions from competitors. These companies must innovate constantly so that potential competitors will be discouraged from entering the marketplace.

You must convincingly project the rate of acceptance for the product or service—and the rate at which it is likely to be sold. From this marketing research data, you can begin assembling a credible sales plan and projecting your plant and staff needs.

ADDRESS INVESTORS' NEEDS

The marketing issues are tied to the satisfaction of investors. Once executives make a convincing case for their market penetration, they can make the financial projections that help determine whether investors will be interested in evaluating the venture and how much they will commit and at what price.

Before considering investors' concerns in evaluating business plans, you will find it worth your while to gauge who your potential investors might be. Most of us know that for new and growing private companies, investors may be professional venture capitalists and wealthy individuals. For corporate ventures, they are the corporation itself. When a company offers shares to the public, individuals of all means become investors along with various institutions.

But one part of the investor constituency is often overlooked in the planning process—the founders of new and growing enterprises. By deciding to start and manage a business, they are committed to years of hard work and personal sacrifice. They must try to stand back and evaluate their own businesses in order to decide whether the opportunity for reward some years down the road truly justifies the risk early on.

When an entrepreneur looks at an idea objectively rather than through rose-colored glasses, the decision whether to invest may change. One entrepreneur who believed in the promise of his scientific-instruments company faced difficult marketing problems because the product was highly specialized and had, at best, few customers. Because of the entrepreneur's heavy debt, the venture's chance of eventual success and financial return was quite slim.

The panelists concluded that the entrepreneur would earn only as much financial return as he would have had holding a job during the next three to seven years. On the downside, he might wind up with much less in exchange for larger headaches. When he viewed the project in such dispassionate terms, the entrepreneur finally agreed and gave it up.

CASHING OUT

Entrepreneurs frequently do not understand why investors have a short attention span. Many who see their ventures in terms of a lifetime commitment expect that anyone else who gets involved will feel the same. When investors evaluate a business plan, they consider not only whether to get in but also how and when to get out.

Because small, fast-growing companies have little cash available for dividends, the main way investors can profit is from the sale of their holdings, either when the company goes public or is sold to another business. (Large corporations that invest in new enterprises may not sell their holdings if they're committed to integrating the venture into their organizations and realizing long-term gains from income.)

Venture capital firms usually wish to liquidate their investments in small companies in three to seven years so as to pay gains while they generate funds for investment in new ventures. The professional investor wants to cash out with a large capital appreciation.

Investors want to know that entrepreneurs have thought about how to comply with this desire. Do they expect to go public, sell the company, or buy the investors out in three to seven years? Will the proceeds provide investors with a return on invested capital commensurate with the investment risk—in the range of 35% to 60%, compounded and adjusted for inflation?

Business plans often do not show when and how investors may liquidate their holdings. For example, one entrepreneur's software company sought $1.5 million to expand. But a panelist calculated that, to satisfy their goals, the investors "would need to own the entire company and then some."

MAKING SOUND PROJECTIONS

Five-year forecasts of profitability help lay the groundwork for negotiating the amount investors will receive in return for their money. Investors see such financial forecasts as yardsticks against which to judge future performance.

Too often, entrepreneurs go to extremes with their numbers. In some cases, they don't do enough work on their financials and rely on figures that are so skimpy or overoptimistic that anyone who has read more than a dozen business plans quickly sees through them.

In one MIT Enterprise Forum presentation, a management team proposing to manufacture and market scientific instruments forecast a net income after taxes of 25% of sales during the fourth and fifth years following investment. While a few industries such as computer software average such high profits, the scientific instruments business is so competitive, panelists noted, that expecting such margins is unrealistic.

In fact, the managers had grossly—and carelessly—understated some important costs. The panelists advised them to take their financial estimates back to the drawing board and before approaching investors to consult financial professionals.

Some entrepreneurs think that the financials are the business plan. They may cover the plan with a smog of numbers. Such "spreadsheet merchants," with their pages of computer printouts covering every business variation possible and analyzing product sensitivity, completely turn off many investors.

Investors are wary even when financial projections are solidly based on realistic marketing data because fledgling companies nearly always fail to achieve their rosy profit forecasts. Officials of five major venture capital firms we surveyed said they are satisfied when new ventures reach 50% of their financial goals. They agreed that the negotiations that determine the percentage of the company purchased by the investment dollars are affected by this "projection discount factor."

THE DEVELOPMENT STAGE

All investors wish to reduce their risk. In evaluating the risk of a new and growing venture, they assess the status of the product and the management team. The farther along an enterprise is in each area, the lower the risk.

At one extreme is a single entrepreneur with an unproven idea. Unless the founder has a magnificent track record, such a venture has little chance of obtaining investment funds.

At the more desirable extreme is a venture that has an accepted product in a proven market and a competent and fully staffed management team. This business is most likely to win investment funds at the lowest costs.

Entrepreneurs who become aware of their status with investors and think it inadequate can improve it. Take the case of a young MIT engineering graduate who appeared at an MIT Enterprise Forum session with written schematics for the improvement of semiconductor-equipment production. He had documented interest by several producers and was looking for money to complete development and begin production.

The panelists advised him to concentrate first on making a prototype and assembling a management team with marketing and financial know-how to complement his product-development expertise. They explained that because he had never before started a company, he needed to show a great deal of visible progress in building his venture to allay investors' concern about his inexperience.

THE PRICE

Once investors understand a company qualitatively, they can begin to do some quantitative analysis. One customary way is to calculate the company's value on the basis of the results expected in the fifth year following investment. Because risk and reward are closely related, investors believe companies with fully developed products and proven management teams should yield between 35% and 40% on their investment, while those with incomplete products and management teams are expected to bring in 60% annual compounded returns.

Investors calculate the potential worth of a company after five years to determine what percentage they must own to realize their return. Take the hypothetical case of a well-developed company expected to yield 35% annually. Investors would want to earn 4.5 times their original investment, before inflation, over a five-year period.

After allowing for the projection discount factor, investors may postulate that a company will have $20 million annual revenues after five years and a net profit of $1.5 million. Based on a conventional multiple for acquisitions of ten times earnings, the company would be worth $15 million in five years.

If the company wants $1 million of financing, it should grow to $4.5 million after five years to satisfy investors. To realize that return from a company worth $15 million, the investors would need to own a bit less than one-third. If inflation is expected to average 7.5% a year during the five-year period, however, investors would look for a value of $6.46 million as a reasonable return over five years, or 43% of the company.

For a less mature venture—from which investors would be seeking 60% annually, net of inflation—a $1 million investment would have to bring in close to $15 million in five years, with inflation figured at 7.5% annually. But few businesses can make a convincing case for such a rich return if they do not already have a product in the hands of some representative customers.

The final percentage of the company acquired by the investors is, of course, subject to some negotiation, depending on projected earnings and expected inflation.

——— MAKE IT HAPPEN

The only way to tend to your needs is to satisfy those of the market and the investors—unless you are wealthy enough to furnish your own capital to finance the venture and test out the pet product or service.

Of course, you must confront other issues before you can convince investors that the enterprise will succeed. For example, what proprietary aspects are there to the product or service? How will you provide quality control? Have you focused the venture toward a particular market segment, or are you trying to do too much? If this is answered in the context of the market and investors, the result will be more effective than if you deal with them in terms of your own wishes.

An example helps illustrate the potential conflicts. An entrepreneur at an MIT Enterprise Forum session projected R&D spending of about half of gross sales revenues for his specialty chemical venture. A panelist who had analyzed comparable organic chemical suppliers asked why the company's R&D spending was so much higher than the industry average of 5% of gross revenues.

The entrepreneur explained that he wanted to continually develop new products in his field. While admitting his purpose was admirable, the panel unanimously advised him to bring his spending into line with the industry's. The presenter ignored the advice; he failed to obtain the needed financing and eventually went out of business.

Once you accept the idea that you should satisfy the market and the investors, you face the challenge of organizing your data into a convincing document so that you can sell your venture to investors and customers. We have provided some presentation guidelines in the *Exhibit*.

Even though we might wish it were not so, writing effective business plans is as much an art as it is a science. The idea of a master document whose blanks executives can merely fill in—much in the way lawyers use sample wills or real estate agreements—is appealing but unrealistic.

EXHIBIT
Packaging Is Important

A business plan gives financiers their first impressions of a company and its principals.

Potential investors expect the plan to look good, but not too good; to be the right length; to clearly and concisely explain early on all aspects of the company's business; and not to contain bad grammar and typographical or spelling errors.

Investors are looking for evidence that the principals treat their own property with care—and will likewise treat the investment carefully. In other words, form as well as content is important, and investors know that good form reflects good content and vice versa.

Among the format issues we think most important are the following:

Appearance

The binding and printing must not be sloppy; neither should the presentation be too lavish. A stapled compilation of photocopied pages usually looks amateurish, while bookbinding with typeset pages may arouse concern about excessive and inappropriate spending. A plastic spiral binding holding together a pair of cover sheets of a single color provides both a neat appearance and sufficient strength to withstand the handling of a number of people without damage.

Length

A business plan should be no more than 40 pages long. The first draft will likely exceed that, but editing should produce a final version that fits within the 40-page ideal. Adherence to this length forces entrepreneurs to sharpen their ideas and results in a document likely to hold investors' attention.

Background details can be included in an additional volume. Entrepreneurs can make this material available to investors during the investigative period after the initial expression of interest.

Cover and Title Page

The cover should bear the name of the company, its address and phone number, and the month and year in which the plan is issued. Surprisingly, a large number of business plans are submitted to potential investors without return addresses or phone numbers. An interested investor wants to be able to contact a company easily and to request further information or express an interest, either in the company or in some aspect of the plan.

Inside the front cover should be a well-designed title page on which the cover information is repeated and, in an upper or a lower corner, the legend "Copy number__" provided. Besides helping entrepreneurs keep track of plans in circulation, holding down the number of copies outstanding—usually to no more than 20—has a psychological advantage. After all, no investor likes to think that the prospective investment is shopworn.

Executive Summary

The two pages immediately following the title page should concisely explain the company's current status, its products or services, the benefits to customers, the financial forecasts, the venture's objectives in three to seven years, the amount of financing needed, and how investors will benefit.

This is a tall order for a two-page summary, but it will either sell investors on reading the rest of the plan or convince them to forget the whole thing.

Table of Contents

After the executive summary, include a well-designed table of contents. List each of the business plan's sections and mark the pages for each section.

Businesses differ in key marketing, production, and financial issues. Their plans must reflect such differences and must emphasize appropriate areas and deemphasize minor issues. Remember that investors view a plan as a distillation of the objectives and character of the business and its executives. A cookie-cutter, fill-in-the-blanks plan or, worse yet, a computer-generated package, will turn them off.

Write your business plans by looking outward to your key constituencies rather than by looking inward at what suits you best. You will save valuable time and energy this way and improve your chances of winning investors and customers.

——— DISCUSSION QUESTIONS

1. "Too many business plans are written from the viewpoint of the third constituency—the producer," state the authors. How can entrepreneurs or producers leave their imprint on the business plan while addressing the concerns of the market and the investors?
2. To write a persuasive business plan, an entrepreneur must be able to look at the product or service from the customer's point of view. Think of a product or service that you value and purchase regularly. If you were writing a business plan for this product or service, how would you describe its benefits?
3. Consider some of the important topics covered in a business plan— the product or service itself, resource requirements, user benefit and market interest, financial projections, management team, and so on. What aspects of these topics would be of particular concern to the following constituencies—bankers, venture capitalists, customers, suppliers, employees?
4. The main purpose of a business plan is to win investment and support for a new enterprise. In what other ways can writing a business plan benefit an entrepreneur?
5. Can you think of any additional features not mentioned in the reading that would enhance effectiveness of a business plan?

11 Milestones for Successful Venture Planning

ZENAS BLOCK AND IAN C. MACMILLAN

How can founders of new companies or corporate ventures plan effectively for the many unknowns they will encounter? Identifying milestones over the project's life enables planners to learn from experience and make adjustments in strategy and goals as necessary. The authors describe ten typical milestones that new businesses pass, including concept and product testing, first financing, market testing, production start-up, and competitive reactions. At each stage, executives must match their assumptions with actual outcomes and determine whether, and how, to proceed to the next milestone.

Starting a new business is essentially an experiment. Implicit in the experiment are a number of hypotheses (commonly called assumptions) that can be tested only by experience. The entrepreneur launches the enterprise and works to establish it while simultaneously validating or invalidating the assumptions. Because some will be dead wrong and others partially wrong, an important goal of the business plan must be to continually produce and build on new knowledge. Managers must justify moving to each new stage or milestone in the plan on the basis of information learned in the previous stage.

Learning in an evolutionary way is valuable not only for venture managers but also for investors, senior corporate managers, and directors. It can help them make informed decisions about whether to fund each stage, as indications of the business's potential unfold. They can use our milestone approach to measure management performance by examining what has been learned and how effectively the venture planners have modified plans to respond to new information—rather than using projections versus performance as the measure.

Milestone planning is hardly new. Traditionally, though, such forethought relies on predetermined dates set for reviews or project completions. The problem with date milestones is that they are totally unreliable for new ventures. Therefore, we suggest that managers make financing decisions instead as events are completed, using what they have just learned to make go, no-go, or redirection decisions. Obviously, new enterprises may need some deadlines and constraints. For instance, a recent proposal for a health and indoor tennis center included a completion date that would allow the club to open for the coming winter season. Every milestone was linked to meeting this deadline.

For most ventures, however, significant events—not dates—should determine milestones. The only hard dates in the plan should be externally imposed, for example, by factors like contract agreements or competitive pressures.

This approach to milestone planning has three advantages for enterprises.

1. It helps avoid costly mistiming errors.
2. It gives logical and practical milestones for learning and for reevaluating the entire venture.
3. It offers a methodology for "replanning" based on a growing body of ever-harder information.

——— WRITING THE PLAN

To give an event milestone maximum learning value, the business plan must define the event's completion so that managers can test any assumptions they make. For example, a plan would not read: "Milestone—completion of product development." A better, more specific statement would be:

> Milestone—completion of product development. Completion of a prototype machine that costs no more than $150,000; that can be manufactured for a direct cost of $12,000; that can produce 40 widgets per minute at 30 cents per widget; that the FCC will approve; and that high school graduates can operate with three days of training.

As planners reach each milestone, they can compare results with the detailed specifications to ascertain whether their original assumptions still hold. Then they can use their experience to make decisions about the next steps.

As an example, suppose you are managing the project we have just described and you learn after completion of product development that the assumptions appear well founded, except that the direct cost will be $30,000 instead of $12,000. You know that you need to find out how you can change the price. Is there still a market at another price? Do you continue the project, redirect it, or abort it? How does the new target market differ from the one you originally projected? Does the prototype have any other features—negative or positive—you had not anticipated? How will you go about changing your plan? What will the changes teach you?

Few entrepreneurs use such planning for their new ventures, explicitly mapping out a sequence of events. More common are the horrifying consequences of not planning thoroughly: the attendant mistimings, heightened cash-flow "burn rates," and the accumulation of losses.

Obviously, all enterprises are different, and while every event in a product's history can teach something, our experience suggests several important milestones that are likely to be most significant. We describe them in this reading, and for each important event, we ask appropriate questions and offer lessons based on actual cases.

MILESTONE 1. COMPLETION OF CONCEPT AND PRODUCT TESTING

This stage has a very low cost relative to future steps and precedes complete product development; indeed, it often comes before any product development at all. This phase's purpose is to determine whether to proceed with any further development. At this point, planners consider whether a real market need exists for the product as they have conceived it or the model they have developed, or whether it has a potentially fatal flaw. At this milestone, entrepreneurs may have discovered a different opportunity as the result of testing their original concept and changing it.

The concept testing challenges assumptions made about desired product characteristics, target markets, pricing range, and perception of need. Planners need to ask themselves the following questions:

- Have we confirmed that an opportunity exists with sufficient up-side gain to warrant the necessary risks and costs?
- What has this test taught us that modifies our assumptions and therefore, possibly, product-development objectives and target markets?

Concept and product model testing are probably the least expensive ways of avoiding costly failure if planners link product-development decisions to results. While some actual product development, production, and test marketing may appear cheap enough to warrant eliminating this stage, it has tremendous value as a safeguard against self-delusion and as a source of alternative-opportunity identification in every situation.

For example, long before starting development work, entrepreneurs in a word processor venture in the 1970s identified through interviews with potential users highly desirable characteristics for the processor. They then looked at important target markets with special programming needs in law firms and government agencies. Long before they initiated expensive micro-programming efforts, the founders radically revised the initial product concept, based on the research results, to be a software product rather than a combined hardware-software product.

MILESTONE 2. COMPLETION OF PROTOTYPE

Entrepreneurs can obtain much useful information from carefully analyzing prototype development. They must look carefully at what caused road-blocks and disappointments and how they overcame them; the seeds of significant, hidden opportunities lie in the creative solutions to these frustrations.

For example, the software programmer in one venture to develop a specialized, interactive information retrieval service eventually had to work out some radically new programming procedures to overcome a serious data-searching bottleneck. When the entrepreneurs looked for lessons in the situation, they realized they had an important invention on their hands and they patented it. The invention's profit potential is ten times greater than that of the original business and was developed at a fraction of the cost.

To apply lessons from prototype completion, entrepreneurs must answer the following questions:

- What assumptions did we make about development time and costs and how have they changed? Why?
- What impact have those changes had on our plans and timing with respect to new hires, plant construction, marketing, and so forth?
- How do they affect financial needs and timing?
- What have we learned about labor, material, and equipment availability and costs and how does this affect our pricing plans?
- Do our observations and assumptions about our target markets still hold? If not, how have they changed, and how will the changes affect our plans—objectives, timing, and resource utilization—for each succeeding event?
- Do the product's characteristics fit with the original concept and plan? Does this create any new opportunities? How should we modify our actions as a consequence?
- Are our assumptions regarding significant competitors and competitive product characteristics still valid?
- How should we revise our investment requirements?
- Are our projections about important suppliers and service distributors still valid?

If planners expect product-development time to be lengthy, they may find it useful to divide development activities into submilestones for review.

MILESTONE 3. FIRST FINANCING

Whether the first outside financing is for seed money to test the concept's potential, start-up financing for product development and market testing, or first-stage financing to initiate manufacturing or sales, the entrepreneur must understand how investors perceive the venture.

Businesses must compete in the capital as well as product markets to survive. Entrepreneurs should view securing financing as an opportunity to learn about their ventures' acceptable financial and expense structure in view of the highly competitive financial market.

For example, a publisher seeking funds for a new magazine soon learned that investors objected to her plan because she had budgeted for the purchase of a large piece of capital equipment. In a revised plan, she budgeted for leasing the equipment at conventional rates; once again she encountered resistance. Eventually, she persuaded a supplier to lend her the equipment for the first nine months of operations. This favorable assist to cash-flow projections, along with her determination, enabled her to secure the funding she needed. What was important in this case was that she treated each rejection as an opportunity to ask why the plan had been turned down, and she learned what investors considered to be an acceptable financial structure.

MILESTONE 4. COMPLETION OF INITIAL PLANT TESTS

Entrepreneurs should use plant tests (or pilot operation for a service venture) to challenge or change their assumptions and to produce information about the following:

- Material suitability and costs
- Processing costs and skills
- Investment prerequisites
- Training needs for production personnel, reject percentages and costs, and quality control requirements
- Material uniformity from suppliers
- Processing specifications, run time, and maintenance

Early data about these factors will improve performance and cost estimates during full-scale operations. In one case, entrepreneurs who were pilot testing a new process to be licensed for the manufacture of a frozen food product aimed at the traditional market for such products—the food-service market—discovered that the product was physically more durable than anyone had thought it would be. By making a point of asking themselves what new opportunity this difference created, the founders identified the possibility of consumer marketing. Because the product was robust enough, they could automatically produce it in small packages and give it high product visibility—something that had never been achieved before in this product category. The planners had assumed that the new product, like the old, would be fragile and would require exorbitantly expensive manual packaging. Company executives revised the marketing plan to include consumer as well as food-service marketing.

Fortunately, the executives had also decided not to enter any licensing agreements until they had learned all they could from the pilot studies. Now they could raise projected royalties without potential clients accusing them of reneging on prior agreements.

MILESTONE 5. MARKET TESTING

The first truly demanding challenges of the venture's basic market assumptions occur at this milestone. The questions managers ask themselves now are:

- Have customers demonstrated that they'll buy the product? Why are they buying it? Why are they not buying it?

- Is it really different from and superior to the competition?
- Are the pricing assumptions still valid, considering emerging information about costs?
- Does the product perform well in varying field applications? Where do the problems lie and why?
- How should we modify estimates of achievable market share and size and target markets?
- Are our servicing-requirement assumptions accurate?
- What impact does this information have on plans and timing?

A group of people who had developed a new electronic device for amateur band musicians decided they could build a worthwhile small business. The first step was to produce a few hundred units for market testing. The entrepreneurs decided to make no commitment to fixed costs until they had learned from market tests at what volumes the product would sell. So they subcontracted all tasks and proceeded to test market with virtually no overhead. Test market results showed the business potential to be marginal, and the inventors dropped the project with a negligible loss.

MILESTONE 6. PRODUCTION START-UP

The first successful production run tests the revised assumptions generated from pilot operations. The first runs are likely to reveal a host of problems that need solving. Most important, project planners will learn the true costs of producing a steady flow of the product and of meeting the quality requirements. Unfortunately, entrepreneurs consistently miscalculate the time this process takes and its impact on the timing for future events—especially plans for expanding the marketing effort and financing requirements.

Selling and making delivery commitments in anticipation of plan production can lead to extreme pressure to get the product out. Attempting to squeeze product out of a plant that is running into start-up problems can result in compromises in product quality along with production at enormous rejection rates, both of which give rise to customer dissatisfaction and waste huge amounts of resources. This vicious circle can destroy a new venture.

In the start-up of a baked-food business, a new plant scaled up from a pilot operation ran into quality problems from trying to produce too much too soon. Because the owners had already made significant delivery commitments to customers, many of whom had in turn employed sales forces to sell the product, the new business found itself operating at full scale with rejects at 20 times the planned level. The owners needed months to solve the problems and years to recover from the losses.

Planners can best manage production start-ups by making up a separate critical-path milestone plan for them and by providing for inventory accumulation before shipments begin.

MILESTONE 7. BELLWETHER SALE

In the industrial market, this is the first substantial sale to an expected major account. In the consumer business, this is the first important sale to a significant distributor. Achieving this sale is likely to give the new business a big push forward; failure to achieve it can become a stumbling block to sales growth. Entrepreneurs learn the following from this milestone.

- How their product compares with the competition in the real world rather than on a limited test basis.
- Whether the product is functional.
- Whether to continue or alter the initial selling method.
- Information about service requirements on a continuing basis.
- Additional data regarding quality controls and specifications.

Ideally, the bellwether sale will be to an important prospect who has been in contact with the owners during the entire development of the new business and whose needs the owners have considered along the way. New opportunities may present themselves as well.

Federal Express's experience with IBM as an early large customer illustrates the learning opportunities this milestone offers. Instead of congratulating itself on its good fortune, Federal Express investigated why IBM was so strong a customer and learned that the company was using its service to reduce inventories of very expensive parts that IBM service bureaus held to support customer service. Federal Express then modified its marketing effort and targeted a significant portion of its promotion on the particular needs of its industrial customers rather than only promoting package delivery service. The company thus rapidly identified and secured a much larger industrial business than it had expected.

MILESTONE 8. FIRST COMPETITIVE ACTION

It is obviously impossible for entrepreneurs to know in advance how competitors will respond to a new product or service. It is possible, however, to plan alternative responses to possible moves and study these moves to learn what rivals' true competitive position is.

Consider the case of an instrument company that in early 1984 developed a highly innovative microprocessor-based device. Its entire marketing campaign depended on how close a significant competitor was to coming out with an equivalent product. The top executives reasoned that if the competitor were close, the response to the new product would be to cut the prices of its existing products to reduce inventories. On the other hand, the competitor would probably first attempt to defend share by increasing its sales promotion, advertising, and other marketing efforts if it were not ready with a similar new product. When the competition did not cut prices, the instrument company moved aggressively into the market, and by late 1984 it still had the market to itself.

In another instance, a leading travel wholesaler introduced a series of tours to the Middle East but hoped to discourage its biggest competitor's standard follow-the-leader reaction. The wholesaler deliberately held off from its largest advertising and promotion activities until the competitor acted. The wholesaler figured that if the competitor entered the market in a tentative manner by offering only one or two tours, that would signify only half-hearted commitment. If it entered on a grander scale, it meant business. When the competitor offered only one tour, the wholesaler responded with a blockbuster marketing campaign, which scared the competition away.

MILESTONE 9. FIRST REDESIGN OR REDIRECTION

Entrepreneurs may discover at any point on the milestone path a need to redesign the product or alter the target market. This redirection may recast prospects for the entire venture or, at the other extreme, create whole new areas of opportunity by defining follow-on product or market needs. At this point, entrepreneurs learn the differences between what they have offered and what the market needs.

The redesign or redirection decision is a time for reexamining all the basic assumptions concerning market size, segments, investment requirements, pricing, and financing (both needs and availability). A dramatic example is the design and marketing of Apple Computer's Lisa to combat the IBM PC with enhanced features and capability. Although greatly admired for its technical aspects, Lisa sales lagged, and Apple discontinued it. The company did notice, however, a potential market in the personal computer arena for many of Lisa's features. Apple incorporated several of them into its Macintosh at a much lower price and reached a mass market.

Another case involves Thermo-Fax, which failed when 3M introduced it for researchers in copying library documents. The company redesigned the product for the office market and it became highly profitable.

MILESTONE 10. FIRST SIGNIFICANT PRICE CHANGE

New venture planners must base all their pro forma activities on assumptions regarding prices, costs, and competition, but the true value of a product or service is difficult to know until the company launches it in a competitive environment. Changes in competition, technology, and costs may force a large price revision, which, because of its direct effect on the bottom line, can make this milestone the most important in determining whether to abandon a project or redirect it. Entrepreneurs need to ask themselves at this stage:

- Will the price change be permanent or temporary?
- Is the business viable if this change is permanent?
- If not, what can we do to restructure fixed and variable costs to make it viable?
- Can we isolate the price change to a particular market segment?

In one case, the managers of an electronics business wanted to supply digital switching gear to the telecommunications field, but they encountered strong price resistance from telecommunications companies when they offered the equipment for sale as a unit. The price assumptions had been wrong because an insufficient incentive existed for replacing the existing product. Management offered to install the equipment and charge on a per usage basis but still had no success. Their price assumptions were still wrong because the new charge would be too high for the companies' clients. Finally, management unbundled the services and offered standard switching at a low per usage cost for the direct customers and specialized switching options (such as automatic disaster or other emergency signals) for the customers' clients on a monthly rental basis. This approach succeeded.

—— MILESTONES, MILLSTONES, OR TOMBSTONES?

Milestone reviews are pointless unless managers use them for making decisions. The decisions help planners determine what they can do to ensure success or reduce the cost of failure.

Each new venture has its own set of milestones. Descriptions of these important events should include a statement of the significant questions that managers need to ask to test their assumptions at each stage. Such a design forces planners to learn as well as to replan on the basis of what they have learned. The milestone approach satisfies the dual need for planning and flexibility and makes obvious the hazards of neglecting linkages between certain events.

Decision choices at each milestone are not limited to either pouring more money in to make the highly improbable occur or aborting the project altogether. Equally feasible possibilities include slowing down, speeding up, trying something to learn more, redirecting, changing scale, or postponing or resequencing certain actions. The point is that milestone planning takes entrepreneurs at the lowest possible cost to the next important stage, where they can make informed decisions rather than blunder along adhering to a fixed plan that out of ignorance they have based on faulty projections.

In summary, we recommend that new venture managers adopt the following procedure when developing a business plan:

1. Identify the most important events or actions that must occur to achieve your objectives.
2. Determine which events are prerequisites to others, that is, the necessary sequential links between events.
3. Develop a critical-path milestone chart that graphically displays the sequence.
4. Identify the significant assumptions on which the venture's success depends.
5. Ask if an event on the milestone chart will test each assumption. If not, design such a step and insert it. Specify what information will replace the assumption and how you will obtain it.
6. As each event occurs and replaces assumptions with information, review the planned future events. Where necessary, change their sequence and nature. Evaluate the business based on evolving and changing projections. Ask yourself along the way: Do the upside gain, downside risk, and feasibility assessment still justify moving ahead?
7. Establish a review schedule that relates to event completion as well as time factors. Evaluate performance based on what you have learned and what you can apply.
8. Rather than argue about whether results met projections, design financing rewards—and resource allocations and rewards—based on the results achieved.

Copyright © 1985; revised 1991.

▬▬ DISCUSSION QUESTIONS

1. Compare the milestone approach to planning with an approach that sets annual targets for implementing a predetermined goal. What assumptions about new business development underlie each approach?
2. As Robert Reich points out in "Entrepreneurship Reconsidered: The Team as Hero," Americans like to think that entrepreneurs come up with Big Ideas and, through their genius, turn them into reality. What do the examples in this reading tell you about the ways ideas originate and evolve?
3. Choose a product that you would like to develop and promote, and write a statement summarizing your goals for Milestone 1—completion of concept and product testing. What assumptions have you based your concept on? What would be the most cost-effective way of testing these assumptions?
4. Imagine an obstacle presents itself—an investor turns down your request for funding, production time is proving to be much longer

than you had anticipated, potential customers say the product doesn't meet their needs. Can a different opportunity emerge from the setback? What questions would you ask in order to determine what your options are?

5. Choose two milestones from the reading. What steps must you take and in what sequence to advance your product from one milestone to the next?

Attracting Stakeholders 12

AMAR BHIDE AND HOWARD H. STEVENSON

Every new enterprise needs employees, customers, suppliers, and financiers who are willing to risk time and money. Attracting stakeholders and inspiring their confidence in a new and untried venture is particularly challenging. This reading spells out the tasks involved in enlisting stakeholder commitment: designing the enterprise to minimize stakeholder exposure, selecting stakeholders who are most willing and able to bear the risk, and convincing stakeholders to participate in the enterprise. Acquiring resources is a basic entrepreneurial task requiring preparation and skill; done carefully, it is the key to turning an opportunity into a business operation.

Acquiring resources—or, put more broadly—attracting stakeholders, is a basic entrepreneurial task. In this reading, we use the hypothetical example of a young man seeking to launch a revolutionary new computer to address the issues and challenges of attracting stakeholders. The principles described are generally applicable to any new enterprise.

Many participants are at risk in an enterprise. Those most obviously so are the financial stakeholders: the venture capital firms, institutional and individual investors, bond holders, or banks that provide entrepreneurs with the funds needed for research and development, machinery, new product promotion, and growth in inventory and receivables. Much of this investment is irreversible; if the enterprise fails, liquidation of its tangible and intangible assets will rarely make financial stakeholders whole, especially when their opportunity costs are taken into account. This is true, the record shows, even for the lenders whose investment is supposedly secured by assets.

Employees, customers, and suppliers have equally important, if less obvious, stakes in the success of the enterprise. The individual who leaves IBM to head up marketing for our entrepreneur's new computer project may be as much at risk as the venture capitalists who fund it. If the enterprise fails, the marketing manager is unlikely to be repaid for the time and effort she has invested. IBM will not take her back in her old position, and she may have to eat into savings while looking for a new job.

Failure of the enterprise may similarly wipe out suppliers' and customers' investments. Suppliers may not recover the costs of designing and producing special components for the new computer nor collect on their receivables.

Customers may find that they have invested time and money on hardware that cannot easily be serviced and upgraded.

Moreover, the process of attracting the stakeholders needed to launch a new computer is much more of a challenge for an individual entrepreneur than it is for a large corporation like IBM. Since IBM's managers effectively control the corporation, they can mandate investment of shareholder funds for a new product. In addition, because IBM has a well-established, profitable franchise in mainframe computers, as well as a long-standing reputation for fair dealing, employees, suppliers, and customers have confidence that they will not be left in the lurch if the new product fails.

If our computer entrepreneur cannot inspire such confidence he may face employees, suppliers, customers, and financiers whose perceptions of the downside risk cause them to demand conditions of exchange that cannot be met if the enterprise is to be viable. Suppliers may refuse to dedicate a production run without a cash advance that a fledgling enterprise cannot provide; and demands for ownership stakes by venture capitalists and key employees may exceed the total equity pie. Worst of all, players may refuse to participate altogether: for example, conservative purchasing agents may reject an innovative computer even though it offers outstanding price and performance advantages.

—— MINIMIZING STAKEHOLDER EXPOSURE

The extent to which stakeholders are at risk in a venture depends upon the irreversibility of their investment. Although entrepreneurs cannot make the investment required by their ventures fully reversible, there are a number of ways to hold the required "sunkenness" to a minimum and thus overcome stakeholders' reluctance.

REUSABLE, OFF-THE-SHELF INPUTS

Financiers', suppliers', and employees' risks may be reduced by using components, capital equipment, and other factors of production that can be easily put to alternative uses; if possible such elements should be available off the shelf. Stakeholders need not commit substantial resources, and the resources they do commit can be easily recovered if the enterprise fails.

Using standard fungible inputs affects several strategic choices. For our computer entrepreneur these might include:

- Hardware design that relies on off-the-shelf processors and sub-systems;
- A product differentiated along easily comprehensible performance dimensions or on price so that salespeople (or distributors) do not need to acquire special skills or knowledge to sell it;

- Software based on an industry standard operating system such as UNIX or MS-DOS;
- An assembly line restricted to elementary capital goods such as a conveyor belt and screwdrivers; use of general-purpose machine tools, ovens, and CAD-CAM tools instead of special designs;
- A Silicon Valley, Route 128, or Research Triangle site so that key employees need not invest in relocating and can more easily find alternative employment;
- Modest volume or market-share goals so that suppliers do not have to dedicate special production runs or build new capacity;
- A marketing plan that seeks product awareness through a few influential opinion makers rather than through advertising or missionary selling.

Even seemingly trivial decisions matter. For example, using an industry standard accounting or word processing package reduces the training required for accounting and typing staff, enhances their marketability in the eyes of other employers, and thus reduces their risk in joining a new venture.

CUSTOMER INVESTMENT

Many of the product design decisions that help reduce other stakeholders' investment in an enterprise will reduce customers' risks as well. For example, the use of industry standard components in a computer reduces the buyer's risk of being stuck without spare parts should the vendor go out of business. The adoption of an industry standard operating system likewise eliminates the investment a customer might otherwise have to make in adapting existing software to a new supplier's hardware. At the simplest level, products that can be easily purchased due to some simple cost or performance advantages do not require the customer to sink much time and money in the purchase decision and in employee education.

Other product decisions may directly reduce a customer's investments in learning, search, and adaptation. For example, a new computer may be designed to slot easily into customers' existing hardware network. In the software arena, adoption of "open system architecture" allowing for easy modification or upgrading of the product without the assistance of the original vendor may reduce customers' stake in the start-up.

TRADE-OFFS

Unfortunately, there is no free lunch. Securing the participation of stakeholders by reducing the sunkenness of their investment may also reduce the profitability and long-run sustainability of the enterprise. In the case of the computer start-up:

- Industry standard, off-the-shelf components may lead to higher variable costs and rapid knock-offs by competitors.
- Flexible capital equipment designed to have high salvage value may be more expensive.
- A Silicon Valley, Route 128, or Research Triangle location may entail high real estate and labor costs.
- A plug-compatible, me-too product with low switching costs for the customer may be vulnerable to competitors offering marginally better prices or features.

The entrepreneur may thus be squeezed between being unable to get the enterprise off the ground at all because risks to stakeholders are too high or launching a marginally profitable, short-lived venture.

One way to resolve this dilemma lies in undertaking irreversible investment only in areas where the greatest leverage is expected in terms of profitability or sustainability or when a stakeholder is prepared to make the investment for idiosyncratic reasons. For example, a computer start-up may seek irreversible stakeholder investment in the one element—a proprietary microprocessor, unique architecture, a low-cost, out-of-the-way location, or an innovative distribution channel—in which stakeholder investment seems most readily available and/or where the investment will provide the greatest sustainable advantage. This same company will forcefully adhere to industry standards in all other areas. Asking the question: "Is this uniqueness really the key to a major competitive edge?" is often a good starting place.

Another resolution to the viability/sustainability dilemma can lie in phased investment. The enterprise may be launched with very low irreversible investment and gradually build to higher levels as stakeholder confidence rises. Apple Computer is a case in point. In its early years its products were based on an industry standard operating system (CP/M), were promoted virtually without any advertising, and were manufactured in plants whose capital equipment consisted largely of conveyor belts and screwdrivers. As the company earned the confidence of stakeholders, however, new products used a proprietary operating system, were assembled in highly automated state-of-the-art plants, and were launched with multimillion dollar advertising budgets.

———— SELECTING STAKEHOLDERS

Since irreversible investment required by an enterprise cannot be entirely eliminated, a critical entrepreneurial task is selecting stakeholders who are the most willing to and capable of bearing the risk. All other things being equal, the most desirable stakeholders have one or more of the following characteristics: they are diversified, experienced in the type of risks they are expected to bear, have excess capacity, and are risk seekers. Let us consider these in turn.

DIVERSIFICATION

Diversified stakeholders are more capable of bearing the risks of investing in an enterprise than those with undiversified holdings or interests. Thus, in the case of a computer start-up:

- The venture capitalist with a large diversified portfolio of investments will probably be better able to provide risk capital than an individual with no other start-up investments.
- The distributor who handles the products of a number of vendors will be less concerned about dedicating 10% of the time of 10 salespersons to the new machine than any one salesperson considering full-time employment. In general we may note that employees in a single business start-up will not be able to diversify their risks to the same extent as "outside" subcontractors serving many businesses.
- The buyer for a firm with an installed base of computers from a variety of manufacturers will be more likely to try out a new vendor than a buyer whose company has standardized on just one system.

EXPERIENCE AND SPECIALIZATION

The risk a particular individual or firm sees in investing in an enterprise depends as much on the investor's past experience and knowledge as on the objective dangers. Therefore an entrepreneur should, when possible, seek the participation of stakeholders who are experienced in bearing the required risks. Our computer entrepreneur may, for example, seek to establish relationships with:

- Customers who have bought (and, preferably, successfully used) computers from start-ups in the past rather than customers who have never strayed from name brand vendors;
- Law and accounting firms that specialize in new ventures and recognize that an up-front investment in helping a start-up can pay off in the long term;
- Employees who have worked for an unsuccessful start-up and realize that being laid off is a setback but not the end of the world (rather than people who have been employed, for example, at IBM for their entire working lives, who may grossly overestimate the risks of not finding a new job);
- Lenders who have dealt with the industry and its products and are comfortable about the downside and have experience with the upside that makes them more adventurous.

Experienced and specialized participants may not only be easier to sign on, they may help bring in other stakeholders. Participants in a venture need reassurance about each others' competence and reliability: the customer for a new computer has to be confident that the vendor's service staff is capable, and the key software engineer needs reassurance that the venture capitalists backing the project are solid. Targeting an experienced team of stakeholders can go a long way toward building the necessary mutual confidence.

"Bell cows"—individuals or organizations with established reputations as leaders and savvy predictors of the future—are especially valuable. If our entrepreneur can get Arthur Rock, the doyen of high-tech venture capitalists, or Steve Wozniak, designer of the first Apple, to sign on, a number of other investors, employees, suppliers, and customers will participate too. The perception will be that if Rock or Wozniak are players, the venture must be solid.

Bell cows cannot only open doors and induce timely commitment to the entrepreneur, they usually also often stand at the nexus of important information and influence networks. Entrepreneurs have two problems: finding them and convincing them. Finding them requires industry knowledge, or at least access to it. The fledgling entrepreneur acquires it by investing time and effort and having knowledge to exchange. It helps to know who is doing what; it helps to read the industry trade papers; and it helps to have made friends.

Accessing industry knowledge beyond your own depends on building an effective team of insiders and such service providers as lawyers, accountants, advertising and public relations firms, and consultants. The entrepreneur's reputation for reciprocity and follow-through is even more critical.

EXCESS CAPACITY

The risks of participation are lower for stakeholders with excess capacity who are not required to make new investments or incur significant opportunity costs. They may even be under pressure to use existing resources. Our hypothetical computer entrepreneur, therefore, might target:

- Customers with a well-staffed technology-evaluation department for whom the time required to assess a new product is free, and who may also be under organizational pressure to make new product recommendations (in preference to customers with a small, overworked purchasing department);
- Venture capitalists (or banks) with a large, unused quota of technology investments (or loans);
- Writers of technical manuals and product literature who are not kept fully occupied by their employers or who may work part time for personal reasons;
- Young professionals in an accounting firm who are under pressure to build a client base in order to make partner;
- Distributors with a hole in their product line but good customer coverage;

· Assemblers and other suppliers with unused capacity, especially those who have recently undergone aggressive capacity-expansion programs.

Capitalizing on excess capacity requires a thorough understanding of the cost structure and organizational dynamics of the target stakeholder. Obviously for this criterion of selection to be useful, stakeholders' unused capacity must be greater than the enterprise's needs; in this situation, staged growth and volume goals are a great help in attracting stakeholders.

RISK SEEKING

Rather than targeting stakeholders whose participation in an enterprise involves the least risk to them, the entrepreneur may instead cultivate risk seekers—individuals or firms who by temperament or circumstance are willing to take on projects that have a negative expected value. For example, the entrepreneur in our computer start-up might seek:

· "Leading-edge" customers, for whom the publicity and thrill of being the first user of a new technology far outweighs the economic downside;
· Cultist programmers who derive satisfaction from working for Mission Impossible-type enterprises;
· Wealthy individuals for whom an investment in the venture is like the casual purchase of a lottery ticket or a contribution to the local theater company.

There are, however, risks in seeking the participation of risk seekers. They may be fickle. The wealthy individual who invests with our entrepreneur on a lark may not be as prepared to invest in future rounds as a professional, level-headed venture capitalist. Moreover, the participation of risk seekers may scare away other more conservative players. The reputation of your stakeholders has the potential for creating both a halo effect and a negative aura for the venture.

───── CONVINCING STAKEHOLDERS

Assume that our computer entrepreneur has formulated a plan that minimizes risk for stakeholders and has identified the ideal participants for the computer venture. The most formidable task—a challenging mix of analysis and action—remains. He must sell the project, converting participants' expressions of interest and encouragement into firm commitments. This requires him to possess particular attributes and a good reputation, to go through a process we call "ham and egging" and to master basic closing techniques.

ENTREPRENEURIAL ATTRIBUTES

A prerequisite for gaining stakeholder commitment is the entrepreneur's enthusiasm and belief in the project. Because the immediate payoff for stakeholders in an entrepreneurial project is almost always low, their participation is based on expectations of substantial long-term reward. The entrepreneur's strong inner conviction that the project can and will succeed must create this expectation. In addition, the entrepreneur must have a reputation for complete reliability. A track record for success is helpful but not absolutely necessary. What participants look for is evidence that in the past the entrepreneur has (1) honored implicit as well as explicit promises and fairly shared rewards with stakeholders; and (2) has not abandoned ventures in midstream when things have gone badly.

HAM AND EGGING

Besides these attributes and reputation (which an entrepreneur either has or has not) there are a number of techniques for securing commitment that can be learned. One of the most important is "ham and egging."

The need for this technique arises from the desire of each participant to hold off a commitment until others have signed on. Customers are reluctant to spend the time to evaluate, much less place an order for a new computer until the entrepreneur can actually deliver a product; employees are hesitant to commit to a job until the financing is in place; and investors are unwilling to step forward unless customers have shown a willingness to buy.

The ultimate ham-and-egging solution is for the entrepreneur to simultaneously convince each participant that everyone else is on board or almost on board. Not all entrepreneurs have the ability to pull off this feat or even feel comfortable trying it. The alternative is to ask for a small increment of commitment from a participant, to parlay that commitment into another increment of commitment from the next participant, and to repeat the cycle for as many times as is necessary.

Our computer entrepreneur might, for example, first get customers to spend a little time talking about the general features they would like to see in a new machine. He could then use these customer reactions to raise money to build a prototype and to persuade an engineer to work part time on the prototype in exchange for cash or equity. At this point, he might want to demonstrate the prototype to the customer and ask for more detailed feedback. The same process of sequential ham and egging would be extended to potential investors and suppliers. Of course, it works particularly well if one or more of the participants is a bell cow.

BASIC SALES CLOSING SKILLS

In addition to ham and egging—a process unique to launching a new venture—the entrepreneur needs to employ techniques that are basic to closing any kind of sale: developing a schedule, knowing what the venture needs, anticipating objections, managing advisers, and handling problems that arise after the close.

Developing a Schedule   Entrepreneurship is like driving fast on an icy road. It requires anticipation. Early in the process all participants should agree on a schedule so that progress can be monitored and commitment tested. Intermediate checkpoints can help distinguish between a serious stakeholder and one who is just toying with the idea of participating. A schedule may minimize the effects of one of the most dangerous events—the withdrawal of a potential stakeholder on whom the deal depends. Such a departure destroys the ham and egging process, damages credibility, and leaves a critical resource gap. A schedule, however, exerts social pressure and gives the entrepreneur at least the appearance of control; if others do not meet the schedule, the entrepreneur can quickly initiate the search for a replacement.

Knowing the Venture's Needs   Of course, it is always nice to have more, but successful entrepreneurs know what degree of commitment is required at any given moment and ask only for that amount. Knowing the bottom-line requirements for both time and commitment is a great aid to effective negotiation.

Anticipating Objections   Stakeholders have both real and imaginary concerns. Getting to closing on a commitment requires addressing both kinds. Real objections need be met with both acknowledgement of their importance and contingency planning. The prospective market manager, for example, wants to know that the entrepreneur is aware of the real risk she is taking. Acknowledging that risk and discussing the "window of foresight"—the lead time that will be available before problems become serious—and even honestly discussing the "fume date"—when the company will run out of cash—may be all the reassurance she needs. Similarly, a customer worried about the risk of commitment to a new product can be reassured by understanding how service would be handled if the firm closes down.

Imaginary objections need be dealt with, too. Often the important thing is to discover why the issue is being raised so that underlying uncertainties can be addressed with realistic answers and well-thought-out contingency plans.

Handling Advisers   The entrepreneur's advisers and those of stakeholders are often roadblocks on the road to commitment. The motives of lawyers, accountants, and other staff are frequently different from those of the principals. Moreover, they often get no credit when things go right but bear the brunt of blame when a deal falls through. Agreeing on a schedule, anticipating objections, and conveying a sense of their importance to the team will often gain the adherence of advisers to the project. Often this means getting them to see the concluded agreement as the beginning and not the end of the relationship.

Following Up   Many agreements have been broken after the initial commitment is secured. In the hectic pace of the entrepreneurial life, maintaining the commitment may be difficult. New objections may arise as customers see the problems of implementation. New alternatives for prospective employees often open up when old employers are faced with the loss of valuable personnel. Details of covenants, warranties, and representations become points of contention, then points of honor, then irreconcilable differences in the process of negotiation. The entrepreneurial task becomes one of keeping the sale in place—which frequently can be achieved only by constant attention and follow-up.

—— DISCUSSION QUESTIONS

1. Choose a hypothetical product and identify the major production factors you will need. Which factors require an irreversible investment and why? In what ways can you minimize the resources committed to the others?
2. The authors of the reading emphasize the importance of securing the trust and confidence of stakeholders; entrepreneurs must sell themselves as much as the product or service. What personal qualities would financiers, customers, suppliers, and employees look for in an entrepreneur? In what ways, large and small, can entrepreneurs best demonstrate their credibility to potential stakeholders?
3. The entrepreneur must be a good judge of character. In addition to the criteria mentioned in the reading, by what standards would you assess the suitability of the financiers, customers, suppliers, and employees you plan to approach?
4. As this reading shows, the entrepreneur must, above all, be versatile; at different times, he or she will assume the roles of product expert, market analyst, politician, salesperson, team builder, diplomat, negotiator, and so on. Which of these roles do you feel prepared to take on? How would you cultivate the skills needed to assume the other roles?

5. Suppose you are trying to persuade a marketing manager to quit a secure, prestigious, well-paying position to join your new venture. How would you convince this person that such a move would be worthwhile? What objections would he or she be likely to raise, and how would you respond to them?

13   The Politics of New Venture Management

IAN C. MACMILLAN

Entrepreneurs sometimes become so excited about a new venture that they forget what it looks like to the rest of the world. Potential lenders are concerned about whether their loans will be repaid. Potential suppliers worry about being paid for goods and services. Prospective customers wonder whether the venture can really deliver on its promises.

More often than not, none of these groups wants to be the first to commit itself to a new venture; each wants to see evidence of initial commitment from elsewhere. To overcome the resistance and reluctance of these parties, entrepreneurs must develop political skills. This reading outlines steps they can take to mobilize stakeholders: coalition building, bypassing resisting groups, developing networks, reducing stockholders' risks, and forging keystone alliances.

In setting up new ventures, entrepreneurs tend to focus on the technical, marketing, and financial feasibility of their endeavors. While all these aspects are necessary for a venture's success, they are not sufficient in themselves.

Entrepreneurs cannot neglect a separate and rarely considered component of success—management of the politics of the new venture. The entrepreneur must be able to mobilize all parties with a stake in the venture to commit themselves firmly to it. These parties are outsiders—bankers, investors, suppliers, and customers—as distinct from insiders, who would include partners and employees. Without the necessary political skills to overcome initial resistance, the greatest entrepreneurial ideas remain but dreams.

Political skills are especially necessary for ventures using low technology, of modest scale, or with limited protection from competitive imitation. These projects do not have the glamorous traits of high-technology ventures, including easy patent protection, spectacular growth potential, and large potential returns on investment, which many venture capital firms find so attractive.

—— WHERE RESISTANCE LIES

To identify the key political challenges that face entrepreneurs, I investigated eight new ventures from the stages of initial idea to final launch.

The first entrepreneur encountered several major political obstacles while attempting to launch a quality magazine. She found material and equipment suppliers reluctant to extend credit, distributors reluctant to pay in advance for copies of the magazine, banks unwilling to provide unsecured funds, and advertisers hesitant to make commitments until the magazine had built sufficient circulation. When these parties finally did develop some interest in the venture, each one insisted that someone else make the first commitment.

The second entrepreneur wanted to act as an agent for inventors seeking to sell their inventions to established companies. He encountered tremendous resistance from R&D departments, which viewed his service as a threat to their competence. Because one of the inventions he was attempting to broker threatened to render obsolete a large research project in a target client company, its R&D department fiercely resisted his services. He also found that many potential clients shrank from retaining him as an agent before he had a track record in delivering satisfactory inventions. Finally, because inventors were afraid their ideas might be stolen, they were reluctant to show the entrepreneur and his clients their inventions.

The third entrepreneur sought to start a consulting business to bring together clients wishing to transfer technology between the United States and foreign countries. He intended to handle the acquisition, purchase, licensing, or joint-venture arrangements to enable U.S. technology to be marketed abroad, or foreign technology to be marketed in the United States.

This entrepreneur encountered problems similar to those of the invention broker. Several R&D and engineering departments of target companies regarded his activities as a threat to their interests. One manufacturing division strongly resisted the technology he suggested; he later discovered it had recently installed equipment that could be made obsolete by a new technology that he was offering. He found potential clients reluctant to provide him with up-front funds to do the marketing research necessary to find suitable prospects for transactions. They also expressed concern about the risk of revealing their technologies to him and interested, but uncommitted, third parties.

The fourth entrepreneur wanted to start a haute cuisine catering service for private parties and business functions. This person found that potential clients were unwilling to risk their personal or professional reputations on an unknown catering service. It became increasingly obvious that he was in a Catch-22 situation: a prestigious client was necessary to attract other clients, but no prestigious clients would sign up until he had already landed a prestigious name. Moreover, a key partner hesitated to join the venture unless it appeared to have a strong chance of survival. Finally, the unwillingness of suppliers to extend credit until the venture proved viable threatened an enormous cash-flow strain on the business.

The fifth entrepreneur identified an application for synthetic filter cloth in an industrial market relying on cotton. For approximately twice the price, the synthetic filter had three to four times the life span of cotton filters and yielded better results. The entrepreneur wanted to purchase fiber in bulk, have it processed by an outside contractor, and then distribute the product to manufacturers.

He encountered resistance from a supplier whose marketing group thought it should have come up with the idea. Ignoring the fact that he was offering a new, different range of synthetics, manufacturing managers in target companies also resisted. They claimed that synthetics "had been tried before and had not worked." In addition, they claimed it wasn't worth keeping stocks of various synthetics for differing applications when all they needed was one type of cotton product. Finally, purchasing agents would not commit themselves until the feasibility of the fiber had been proved, and this could take up to nine months. He was short of funds but could not get banks to supply the financing or suppliers to provide the credit, which he needed to wait out the test period.

The sixth entrepreneur wanted to launch a wholesale travel business. His plan was to buy block bookings on an aircraft or ship, design a tour and arrange accommodations, and retail the package to, say, a company that would use the tour as an incentive for sales performance or as a conference location. His idea was to pick destinations and tailor tours to suit companies' particular needs. He encountered resistance in client companies from people responsible for creating incentive programs, who felt threatened by his plans. Carriers and potential clients alike hesitated to trust an unproven tour packager.

The seventh entrepreneur sought to build an advertising-copy service based on her ability to create catchy and intriguing ads for mundane products and services. (Owners of such products and services frequently encounter little enthusiasm from established advertising agencies.) She intended to specialize in brochures, pamphlets, product-line catalogs, and usage instructions, which, imaginatively done, can be a useful, inexpensive way of differentiating a company's products from those of competitors. To her surprise, she met intense resistance from people inside target organizations, who claimed that her suggestions, if implemented, would disrupt packaging inventories and distribution procedures in return for very little in the way of perceived benefits. Some insisted that it would be necessary, and costly, to scrap master plates or lithos for existing copy.

The eighth entrepreneur wanted to make a high-quality souvenir for the tourist business. However, distributors, fearing she would be unable to produce the souvenir with the required quality and deliver it on time, declined to take orders until they had seen a prototype. Potential lenders refused to supply development funds until orders had been placed, and designers insisted on substantial progress payments to work on the prototype. Meanwhile, she greatly feared that an existing company, which had started to investigate the potential market, would decide to produce the souvenir first.

In all these cases, despite the clear presence of markets for technically feasible products or services, these people encountered major political obstacles arising from doubts about their ability to deliver on their promises.

These experiences help identify several important political issues that an entrepreneur must resolve.

—— UNEXPECTED ENEMIES

Five of the eight entrepreneurs encountered groups or individuals other than competitors who had a vested interest in the failure of the new venture. Clearly, the invention broker, the technology-transfer consultant, the travel tour agent, and the copywriter threatened groups or individuals within potential client companies. It was a sobering experience for these entrepreneurs to discover that the most significant problems lay with active resistance from suppliers and customers. Entrepreneurs launching a business should anticipate such resistance, which saps vast amounts of valuable time and effort.

Before launching a venture, then, the entrepreneur is well advised to consider which groups or individuals in the chain of suppliers, distributors, and clients are likely to be somehow threatened by the new venture. If their resulting resistance could be effective, the entrepreneur must develop a coping strategy or risk the venture's failure.

Entrepreneurs can take three steps to overcome vested interest in failure.

Co-Opt the Obstructing Group   The technology consultant and the invention broker eventually won support from resisting R&D groups by making sure to acknowledge these groups' contributions, particularly to senior management.

The filter distributor achieved great success by arranging for a recalcitrant production manager of a target industrial manufacturer to be associated with the venture's success and dissociated from the venture's failure, thus making his commitment risk-free. He emphasized this arrangement by saying to the company president, in the manager's presence, that "with the kind of good advice Joe's given me and with all Joe's past experience, it certainly won't be Joe's fault if the filters don't work like dynamite." Thus publicly absolved of all risk, Joe became a staunch supporter of synthetic fiber products and a useful reference in securing other sales in the industry.

Build a Coalition   Three entrepreneurs forged alliances of sorts with groups or individuals in customer and supplier organizations. These served to counter attacks by those organization members who had an interest in the ventures' failure. The strategy helped get the ventures going, but it also created polarized groups within the target organizations. The resisters seized every possible reason to justify their contrary position, and every entrepreneur underestimated the time and effort needed to cope with the resulting strife.

The invention broker formed an alliance with the client organization's marketing department. This coalition supported his position that a key person in the R&D department was being obstructive and secured the removal of the obstructionist, thus resolving the problem. He subsequently preferred the strategy of co-opting his opponents, however, and only occasionally resorted to coalition building.

Bypass Resistance   This strategy focuses on an organizational level higher than the source of resistance. Four entrepreneurs tried at one time or another to persuade senior managers in customer and supplier organizations to force reluctant subordinates to accept their ventures.

Bypassing generally met with better success than coalition building. The entrepreneurs overcame the source of resistance without the resistant parties losing face. Sometimes, however, this "reluctant compliance" led to time-consuming implementation problems.

——— THE RISK FACTOR

In the absence of active resistance, reluctant stakeholders can prove to be a serious, if not fatal, stumbling block. Why should a supplier, banker, financier, or customer run the personal or professional risk of giving support to an embryonic venture when the status quo appears to be working well? Most new ventures are quite chancy; often the safest option for a potential stakeholder is to refuse support. All eight entrepreneurs that I studied seriously underestimated the time required to sell their ideas to reluctant stakeholders.

Simply recognizing this problem is important: several entrepreneurs encountered serious difficulties because they would not recognize the validity of stakeholders' concerns. Until they came to see the situation through the eyes of potential backers, they were either inclined to dismiss these reluctant stakeholders as stupid, fainthearted, or obstructive, or they tried to use irrelevant arguments and facts. It was only when the entrepreneurs realized that potential supporters were taking a real risk with their support that they focused on strategies to deal with this problem:

Reduce Stakeholders' Risks   One way to overcome initial reluctance in stakeholders is to devote attention to reducing their risk.

For instance, the filter-cloth manufacturer realized that potential customers were reluctant to pay double the usual amount—up front, in cash—for an untried product and then wait several months to see if their faith was justified. He decided that the only way to get the business started was to suggest to a large and prestigious client that payment could be made after a satisfactory trial period. Although the potential user was still reluctant because the synthetic filter might create production problems, the barrier of high initial purchase cost had disappeared.

In a similar vein, both the invention broker and the technology-transfer consultant made nondisclosure agreements with inventors and researchers as assurance that their ideas would not be stolen.

Develop an Influence Network   If an effective way of reducing the risk cannot be identified for the stakeholder, the entrepreneur is obliged to at least demonstrate credibility. One way of developing credibility is via a network of influential contacts.

In fact, in every case I studied, the entrepreneurs eventually developed groups of influential contacts. Two, with previous new venture experience—the quality-magazine publisher and the invention broker—spent time developing networks long before attempting to launch their ventures. The other six evolved contact networks as their businesses developed.

As all these businesses evolved, it became apparent that the old aphorism is correct: "whom you know" is as important as "what you know." Strengthening commitment at each round, entrepreneurs shuttled among various stakeholders until finally the ventures started to come together.

Establish Credibility   An entrepreneur's credibility as a business person is particularly important in building a network. All entrepreneurs found it especially helpful to develop a business plan that they could present to stakeholders. They also found it important to demonstrate a successful track record.

The three entrepreneurs who had the fewest difficulties getting started already had experience in the industries of their new ventures. Two others had expertise with their product and service but no business background. Three, with neither experience nor expertise, eventually convinced stakeholders of their credibility by using credible contacts as references. Apparently stakeholders interpreted the entrepreneurs' abilities to generate moral (if not material) support from influential references as proof that they had the necessary skills to pull the projects together.

Entrepreneurs seeking quick development of an effective network could benefit from some careful planning. My observations of network building indicate that the following procedures speed up the process:

1. Identifying people and organizations among existing connections who are close to potential stakeholders.
2. Seeking criticism, advice, and suggestions on the new venture from these people.
3. Asking them for advice about contacts (at least two) to approach in target organizations and getting permission to use their names when doing so.
4. Asking them what preparation is necessary before speaking with the target contacts and doing the necessary preparation.

5. Telling existing connections later how they have been particularly helpful, thus cementing useful relationships.
6. Repeating these steps for the new sets of contacts.

IMPORTANCE OF RAPPORT

Once new venture owners develop a network, they need to nurture it to obtain maximum benefits. This can be done initially by:

Stressing Commonality   All eight of the people I studied discovered they had interests in common with their contacts arising from such things as similar backgrounds, experiences, schooling, training, ethnic origins, families, religions, and friends. They devoted time to reinforcing these commonalities.

Seeking Advice   To develop rapport, four entrepreneurs often sought advice from their contacts. The contacts seemed to feel more favorably disposed toward owners who asked for their opinions. Individuals who followed up by letting the contacts know how their advice had been helpful solidified their relationships even further.

Providing Help   Some entrepreneurs took a reverse approach; they made a point of learning about each contact's difficulties or irritations. They then followed up with suggestions to solve these problems, either directly or by referring them to others who might provide solutions; this approach enabled the individuals I studied to demonstrate either their own expertise or their ability to draw on their own networks. Once again, the result was increased respect and improved rapport with the contact they were building.

The process of network building was very time consuming, often taking weeks of patient and determined effort. It eventually paid off for four of the ventures analyzed. The other entrepreneurs, however, found that even this effort resulted in insufficient support. An additional political skill was required to turn their ventures into reality.

FORGING KEYSTONE ALLIANCES

When all else fails, entrepreneurs may have to launch their ventures by securing the support of an outside party—a keystone ally—who develops a vested interest in the venture's success. In four of the cases I studied, the ventures came together only after the entrepreneurs had developed a strategy to secure support from such keystone allies.

The quality-magazine publisher finally succeeded in starting up by persuading an equipment manufacturer to supply expensive, sorely needed equipment on a trial basis. She enlisted the help of this keystone ally by convincing him that her venture could demonstrate the equipment's capability in a new market. The consequent favorable impact of this loan of the equipment on cash-flow requirements induced reluctant financial backers and her other suppliers to finally commit themselves to the venture.

The synthetic-fiber distributor persuaded a raw material supplier to provide a limited amount of stock on 270-day credit by arguing that he had a prestigious customer who would take the product on a nine-month trial but that the customer would guarantee payment only if the product performed to expectations. He used this stock to convince the customer to place an order. With this order in hand, the entrepreneur secured orders from other customers, but on 90-day credit, and was thus able to launch the entire venture.

The souvenir manufacturer could get no support for her venture until she could present a fully developed prototype that required expensive design work. She found a foreign designer looking for a chance to demonstrate his skills in the United States who was prepared to postpone payment for his services. Thus, the prototype was developed at little up-front cost. Other stakeholders, particularly distributors, then started to provide support, and the venture was finally launched.

Finally, the caterer persuaded the university that he had attended to enter into a contract for his services, appealing to the institution as his alma mater. This agreement guaranteed enough support to meet the initial fixed costs of the venture. More important, he then parlayed the account's prestige into several other influential accounts. These commitments convinced a key partner to join the operation.

In each of these latter cases, the owner was able to break an impasse by focusing on an important area where vested interests coincided and a keystone alliance could be forged. This provided the impetus needed to initiate the venture. The facility to pinpoint vested interests and to forge such a keystone alliance is an important component of an entrepreneur's repertoire of skills.

ANTICIPATING THE DIFFICULTIES

In summary, several lessons seem clear. First, to avoid delay and frustration in getting the venture off the ground, the entrepreneur must anticipate resistance from groups or individuals in the stakeholders' organizations.

Next, unless a clear and compelling benefit exists for all stakeholders, entrepreneurs are wise to anticipate reluctance from some stakeholders to risking their resources or reputations; and they should develop strategies to reduce this reluctance.

Finally, despite stakeholders' expressed interest in a venture, entrepreneurs may find themselves in a Catch-22 situation whereby stakeholders will not join in until commitments from other stakeholders are forthcoming. Here the challenge is to put together a keystone alliance with the key subset of stakeholders.

For those ventures that lack the allure of high-technology products, market and technical feasibility are necessary but not sufficient conditions for the launch and subsequent success of a new enterprise. A vital ingredient is political skill in managing new ventures.

──── DISCUSSION QUESTIONS

1. Many people dream of starting their own businesses and being their own boss. Can the hopes for freedom and flexibility that motivate many entrepreneurs blind them to the inevitable constraints on their actions? How can these entrepreneurs learn to temper their desire to do everything their own way?

2. Many entrepreneurs think of themselves as product and market experts, not politicians. What kinds of experiences can prepare the entrepreneur for the job of mobilizing recalcitrant stakeholders? How can the entrepreneur overcome a lack of experience in coalition building and networking?

3. "Several entrepreneurs encountered serious difficulties because they would not recognize the validity of stakeholders' concerns," the author points out. In reviewing the case examples, do you think the entrepreneurs should have anticipated the resistance they encountered? How can entrepreneurs learn to better anticipate and take seriously contrary points of view?

4. What concerns besides reducing risk and making money could motivate stakeholders in a new venture? How can the entrepreneur respond to these concerns?

5. Choose one of the eight case examples given in the reading and work out a detailed plan for resolving the problem and preventing similiar problems in the future. Use the approaches suggested in the reading as well as approaches of your own.

FINANCING: MARSHALING RESOURCES

Alternative Sources of Financing   14

MICHAEL J. ROBERTS AND HOWARD H. STEVENSON

The art of successful financing lies in answering a series of tricky questions: How much money does the business need? How much money is available? How, when, and from whom should the money be raised? Of course, a few factors are givens: investors expect something in return for financing the venture and will demand a higher return when they perceive a higher risk; the entrepreneur seeks to secure financing at the lowest possible cost. Understanding both the needs of the business and the needs of the financier will assist entrepreneurs in sorting through the maze of potential financing options. This reading helps them develop this understanding by providing an overview of the common sources of equity and debt capital and the conditions under which money is typically lent or invested.

As in most transactions, the owners of capital expect to be rewarded for financing a new venture. Providers of funds typically use some form of a risk/return model to evaluate potential opportunities; that is, they demand a higher return when they perceive a higher risk.

The entrepreneur's objective, of course, is to secure financing at the lowest possible cost. The art of successful financing, therefore, lies in getting providers of funds to view the investment as relatively less risky. The entrepreneur can do several things to structure the financing so it will be perceived as less risky. A few of the possible mechanisms are:

- Pledging personal or corporate assets against a loan;
- Promising to pay the money back in a short period of time, when the investors can judge the health of the business, rather than over the long term when its financial strength is less certain;
- Giving investors a measure of control over the business, through either loan covenants or participation in management (i.e., a seat on the board).

In this reading, after a brief discussion of start-up financing, we describe the three principal types of financing: outside equity capital, debt capital, and internally generated financing.

START-UP FINANCING

The first investment in a business will almost always be equity capital. In start-up financing the highest risk capital (and therefore the potentially highest return capital) appears at the bottom of the balance sheet as equity. Even when debt capital is available—perhaps secured by assets of the business, such as a building or equipment—some equity capital is usually required to get a business off the ground. Especially at this riskiest stage of a venture investors will perceive, and rightly so, that the individual entrepreneur will be more committed to the venture if she or he has a substantial portion of personal assets invested in it. This fact has led some to claim that: "You're better off trying to start a business with $5,000 than with $100,000 in personal resources. If you are relatively poor, you can demonstrate your commitment for a smaller sum." This statement presumes that you will be seeking capital from some outside source. If you were going to fund the venture by yourself, you would, of course, prefer to start with $100,000 instead of $5,000.

There is another, more practical reason why this start-up phase is usually financed with the entrepreneur's own funds. Raising money typically requires more than having an idea. The entrepreneur will need to invest some money initially—perhaps to build a prototype or do a market study—to convince potential investors that the idea has potential.

These funds need not be equity capital in the purest sense of the word but only equity from the point of view of potential investors in the business. The entrepreneur can obtain these "equity funds" by mortgaging personal assets like a house or a car, by borrowing from friends or relatives, or even through a personal bank loan or credit card advances. The important fact is that the money goes into the business as equity, not as debt to be repaid by the entrepreneur out of company earnings.

Although a few specialized firms do provide "seed capital," most venture capital firms require that a business move beyond the idea stage before they will consider financing it. Some businesses require a good deal of work (and money) to get from the concept phase to the point where they can obtain venture capital financing.

OUTSIDE EQUITY CAPITAL

Typically, the entrepreneur will exhaust his or her own funds before the business becomes a viable operation. At this point, it is usually still too early to obtain all the required financing in the form of debt. The entrepreneur must approach outside sources for equity capital.

PRIVATE INVESTORS

One popular source of equity capital, which presents both advantages and disadvantages, is private wealthy individuals. These investors range from family and friends with a few extra dollars up to millionaires; members of the medical professions, for example, are a significant source of private equity capital. Though some of these investors manage their own money, others are advised by accountants, lawyers, or other professionals with whom the entrepreneur must be prepared to deal.

The best way to find wealthy investors is through a network of friends, acquaintances, and advisers. A local lawyer or accountant who has helped prepare a business plan or offering document may know of wealthy people who invest in similar ventures.

Besides an introduction, you will usually need at least a business plan to approach a wealthy investor. A formal offering memorandum has the advantage of providing more legal protection for the entrepreneur in the form of disclaimers and legal language. However, it may strike potential investors as unduly negative in tone and, because it requires legal counsel, may be costly to prepare. Moreover, its distribution is limited by SEC rules to only 35 "offerees" (though some attorneys believe you can show the plan to more individuals and then formally "offer" it only to those who demonstrate a real interest).

At this point, it is worth reiterating the importance of following securities laws and obtaining legal advice. Wealthy individuals may be unsophisticated about business, and if the venture is unsuccessful they may (and often do) claim they were misled by the conniving entrepreneur. In this instance, having a carefully drawn offering document provides essential protection.

Even so, wealthy investors may be well suited to participate in equity financings that are too small for a venture capital firm to consider (usually those under $500,000). Individuals are typically considered a less expensive source of equity than venture capital firms. While this is generally true, they often present some drawbacks. They seldom, for example, possess either the expertise or the willingness to advise the entrepreneur on operations, and they are far less likely to come up with additional funds when required. Wealthy investors are also more likely to be a source of problems or frustration, particularly if there is a large number of them. Their frequent telephone calls or complaints when things are not going well can create headaches for even the best-intentioned and even-tempered entrepreneur.

VENTURE CAPITAL

Venture capital refers to a pool of equity capital that is professionally managed. Individuals invest in this fund as limited partners, and the general partners manage the pool in exchange for a fee and a percentage of the gain on investments. In order to compensate for the high risk of their investments, give their own investors a handsome return, and make a profit for themselves, venture firms seek a high rate of return. Target returns of 50% or 60% are not uncommon.

In exchange for this high return, venture firms often provide advice to their portfolio companies. These people have been through many times what the entrepreneur is usually experiencing for the first time. They can often provide useful counsel on the problems a company may experience in the start-up phase.

Venture firms differ along several dimensions. Some prefer to invest in certain kinds of companies. High-tech is popular with most, although definitions of what this is are imprecise. Some firms have a reputation for being very involved with the day-to-day operations of the business; others exhibit a hands-off policy.

Prior to investing, a venture capital firm will expend a good deal of effort investigating proposals. To capture the firm's interest, therefore, the entrepreneur needs a business plan. This document, which serves a far different purpose than it would in the case of wealthy individuals, should be concise and attempt to stimulate further interest rather than describe the business in exhaustive detail. Only the naive entrepreneur will propose the actual terms of the investment in the initial document. While the plan should spell out how much financing the entrepreneur is seeking, detailing the terms (e.g., "for 28% of the stock crashing. . . .") is premature in an initial presentation.

A topic of frequent concern to entrepreneurs is confidentiality. On the one hand, it seems wise to tell potential investors about your good ideas to get them interested; on the other, what if someone takes them? In general, venture capitalists are a professional group and will protect confidential information, though private investors may be less scrupulous. In either case, it is generally not a good idea to put proprietary material in the business plan, lest it accidentally falls into the wrong hands. A plan might, for example, describe the functions of a new product or service but should not include circuit designs, engineering drawings, nor other critical data.

Not all venture firms invest on a pure equity basis. Some may want a package of debt and equity, convertible debt (or convertible preferred). Each of these options has its advantages. A combined debt and equity package allows the venture firm to get some of its fund back in interest payments, which are deductible and result in tax savings. In addition, the venture firm will recover tax-free cash when the loan principal is repaid. Convertible debt (or preferred) gives the venture firm a liquidation preference. If the business should fail, the venture capitalist will have a priority claim on assets. Often too, the terms can force eventual repayment, even if the business never achieves public status.

A venture firm usually syndicates a large investment, getting other firms to take a piece of the action. This permits investment in a larger number of companies and spreads its risk. This practice proves particularly important for the entrepreneur on subsequent rounds of financing, when other venture firms will see the continuing investment of the original firm(s) as a sign of confidence in the company. If the existing, more knowledgeable investors are no longer interested in the company, why should a new venture firm step in?

PUBLIC EQUITY MARKETS

The largest source of equity capital remains the public equity markets: the New York, American, and over-the-counter stock exchanges. Typically, however, a firm must have a history of successful operation before it can raise money in this way. In "hot" markets, some smaller start-up companies have been able to raise public equity, but the process is lengthy, detailed, and expensive.

Whether the investors are wealthy individuals or a venture capital firm, terms will have to be negotiated. In exchange for their investment, investors will receive a security representing the terms of their ownership in the company. In the case of a public offering, the investment bank negotiates the terms on behalf of its clients.

——— DEBT CAPITAL

The other large category of capital is debt. Debt is presumed to be lower risk capital because principal and interest are repaid according to a set schedule.

In order to have a reasonable expectation of being paid according to this schedule, creditors lend against either assets or cash flow. Asset-based financing can be obtained for most hard assets that have a market value. A building, equipment, or soluble inventory are all assets against which a company could borrow. Lenders will also allow firms to borrow against their expected ability to generate the cash to repay the loan. Creditors attempt to check this ability through such measures as interest coverage (earnings before interest and taxes) [EBIT] ÷ interest payments) or debt/equity ratio. Obviously, a healthy business with little debt and high cash flow will have an easier time borrowing money than a new venture.

CASH FLOW FINANCING

Cash flow or unsecured financing is of several types and can come from a variety of sources.

Short-term Debt   Short-term unsecured financing is frequently available to cover seasonal working capital needs for periods of less than one year, usually 30 to 40 days.

Line-of-Credit Financing   A company can arrange for a line of credit, to be drawn upon as needed. Interest is paid on the outstanding principal, and a "commitment fee" is paid up front. Generally, a line of credit must be "paid-down" to an agreed-upon level at some point during the year.

Long-term Debt   Generally available to solid creditworthy companies, long-term debt may be available for up to 10 years. Such debt is usually repaid according to a fixed schedule of interest and principal.

Cash flow financing is most commonly available from commercial banks but can also be obtained from savings and loan institutions, finance companies, and such institutional lenders as insurance companies and pension funds. Because cash flow financing is generally riskier than asset-based financing, banks will frequently attempt to reduce their risk through *covenants*. These covenants place certain restrictions on a business wishing to maintain credit with the bank. Typical loan covenants concern:

- Limits on the company's debt/equity ratio,
- Minimum standards on interest coverage,
- Lower limits on working capital,
- Minimum cash balance,
- Restrictions on the company's ability to issue senior debt.

These and other covenants attempt to protect the lender from actions that would decrease its chances of being repaid.

ASSET-BASED FINANCING

Because cash flow financing usually requires an earnings history, new ventures are more often able to obtain asset-based financing. In an asset-based financing, the company pledges or gives the financier a first lien on the asset. In the event of a default on financing payments, the lender can repossess the asset.

Asset-based financing is available from commercial banks and other financial institutions. Insurance companies, pension funds, and commercial finance companies provide mortgages and other forms of asset-backed financing. Entrepreneurs themselves can also provide debt capital to a business once it has passed the risky start-up period. The following types of asset-financing are generally available:

- *Accounts receivable.* Usually up to 90% of the accounts receivable from creditworthy customers can be financed. The lender—usually a bank—conducts a thorough investigation to determine which accounts are eligible for this kind of financing. In some industries a "factor" buys approved receivables at a discount and collects the accounts.
- *Inventory.* Inventory is often financed if it consists of merchandise that can be sold easily. Typically 50% or more of a finished goods inventory can be financed.

- *Equipment.* Equipment can usually be financed for a period of 3 to 10 years. 50% to 80% of the value of the equipment can be financed, depending on its salability. Leasing is another form of equipment financing, in which the company never takes ownership of the equipment.
- *Real estate.* Mortgage financing is usually readily available to finance a company plant or buildings; 75% to 85% of the value of the building is a typical figure.
- *Personally secured loans.* A business can obtain virtually any amount of financing if one of its principals (or someone else) is willing to pledge a sufficient amount of personal assets to guarantee the loan.
- *Letter-of-credit financing.* A company can obtain a letter of credit, a bank guarantee, to enable it to purchase goods. A letter of credit functions almost like a credit card, allowing businesses to make commitments and purchases in places where the company does not have relationships with local banks.
- *Government-secured loans.* Certain government agencies (the Small Business Administration, the Farmers Home Administration, and others) guarantee loans to businesses that could not obtain them on their own.

—— INTERNALLY GENERATED FINANCING

A final category of financing is internally generated after the business is in operation. One method of increasing working capital utilizes credit from suppliers by paying bills in a less timely fashion. Some suppliers will charge interest for this practice, while others may simply stop deliveries—a severe risk in the case of a key resource supplier. The opposite strategy would generate financing through accounts receivable—that is, by collecting the company's own bills more quickly—or by reducing working capital for certain items (e.g., inventory, cash) to use for others. Perhaps the most drastic move, selling some of the company's assets, will also generate capital.

Each of these techniques represents an approach to generating funds internally without the help of a financial partner. Although the purely financial costs are low, the entrepreneur must be wary of attempting to run the business "too lean."

—— DISCUSSION QUESTIONS

1. The authors suggest that an initial investment of equity capital in a new venture sends a message to future investors. If you had $5,000 of your own to start, what areas of the business would you invest in to demonstrate your commitment and the worthiness of your idea?

2. Suppose you were going to approach a wealthy individual or a venture capitalist for financing. What questions would you ask these investors and ask others about them before deciding whether to do business with them?

3. The authors point out that business plans must be adapted for different audiences. What kinds of information would you emphasize in a business plan that you are presenting to a wealthy individual? To a venture capitalist? To a bank?

4. The reading lists three forms of cash financing: short-term debt, line-of-credit financing, and long-term debt. If a combination of such loans were available to you, for what purposes would you use each one?

5. If you were an investor projecting risk, how would you rank the alternatives of asset-based financing listed in the reading?

How Much Money Does Your New Venture Need?

15

JAMES MCNEILL STANCILL

"It is impossible to know exactly how much a new business will need in its first five years, but it is possible to come up with realistic estimates," says James McNeill Stancill. As he demonstrates in this reading, the entrepreneur can calculate the new venture's financial requirements by compiling a financial forecast consisting of an income statement, a balance sheet, and a cash flow statement. Stancill traces the steps involved in reaching a realistic figure, explaining how to construct each element of the forecast. Because forecasts are not foolproof, he cautions, entrepreneurs should forecast alternative scenarios: a most likely, a most pessimistic, and a most optimistic; in negotiating with financiers, they must be sure to obtain commitment for the entire amount of financing necessary to get the venture started successfully and through the hardest times expected.

Every entrepreneur planning a new venture faces the same dilemma: determining how much money is necessary to start the business. More often than not, entrepreneurs estimate on the low side. They may simply not allow for unexpected expenses and lower-than-predicted sales.

It is impossible to know exactly how much a new business will need during its first five years, but it is possible to come up with realistic estimates. These come from the financial forecast: the income statement, the balance sheet, and, most important, the cash flow statement.

This reading shows how to calculate the new venture's capital requirements through such financial forecasting. It also shows how financial forecasting provides the basis for determining equity investments.

Thanks to various computer spreadsheet programs, calculations associated with even the most detailed forecasting are fairly simple. What used to require days or weeks now takes only minutes or hours. Such programs enable entrepreneurs to use variables and test scenarios in ways that are impractical with conventional push-the-pencil methods. Such split-second calculating tools should not, of course, blind entrepreneurs to the logic of the numerical estimate and the cash flow model.

EXHIBIT 1
Sample Income Statement

Sales[1]	$XXX
Less cost of goods sold[2]	XXX
Gross profit margin	**XXX**
Less general and administrative expenses[3]	XXX
Less selling expenses[4]	XXX
Operating income or loss	**XXX**
Less interest expense	XXX
Income before taxes	**XXX**
Less income taxes[5]	XXX
Net income or loss	**XXX**

Notes to the Financial Statements:

1. The sales forecasts shown here are based on market research, details of which are provided separately.

2. See the separate cost accounting module for details of how the cost of goods was arrived at [not shown in this reading].

3. See *Exhibit 3*.

4. See *Exhibit 5*.

5. This includes federal and corporate income taxes.

——— BEGINNING THE PROCESS

Simplicity is a virtue in presenting financial statements. Show items in summary form, but reserve all the details for separate schedules or footnotes attached to the financial statements. And make certain the statements conform with generally accepted format practices; creativity is welcome in many areas of business planning but not in financial statements.

For most manufacturing and many other start-ups, the form of the income statement will be like that shown in *Exhibit 1*.

Each item has a footnote, which is included in "Notes to the financial statements." In these notes, you may refer the reader to another supporting schedule or you may simply explain the item. Each item has a separate footnote number. Having an explanation for each item is the most important aspect of an effective forecast. By explaining each item, you can defuse disputes about what value an item should have. If much uncertainty exists about an item, you can state in the footnote that the estimate is merely a guess but that the general order of magnitude is probably appropriate.

The financial forecast initially requires three estimates of sales for five years: a most likely, a most pessimistic, and a most optimistic estimate. Express this sales forecast in both number of items sold and dollars to account for factors that might affect the selling price. The sales forecasts should, of course, be accompanied by written justification of the sales estimates so that you can

EXHIBIT 2
Sample Balance Sheet

ASSETS		LIABILITIES	
Cash	$XXX	Accounts payable[11]	$XXX
Accounts receivable[6]	XXX	Accrued taxes[5]	XXX
Inventory[7]	XXX	Accrued expenses[12]	XXX
Other assets (prepaids)[8]	XXX	Current portion of long-term	
Total current assets	**$XXX**	debt	XXX
		Total current liabilities	**$XXX**
Plant, property, and equip-			
ment at cost[9]	XXX		
Less reserve for depreciation[10]	XXX	Long-term equipment loans[13]	XXX
Net plant, property, and		Equity	XXX
equipment	XXX	Retained earnings or loss	XXX
Total assets	**$XXX**	**Total liabilities and capital**	**$XXX**

Notes to the Financial Statements:

5. This includes federal and corporate income taxes.

6. See *Exhibit 5* for the aging schedule.

7. For details of the finished-goods inventory, see *Exhibit 7*.

8. For the changes in prepaid assets, see separate schedule [not shown in this reading].

9. See separate schedule [not shown in this reading].

10. Generally, straight-line depreciation was used for equipment.

11. See separate schedule for details of changes in accounts payable [not shown in this reading].

12. See separate schedule for details of changes in accrued expenses [not shown in this reading].

13. The face amount of the loans is $140,000, payable in monthly installments of $5,023 for 36 months at an interest rate of 15%.

---

begin to project the required financial statements—first the income statement, then the balance sheet, and finally the cash flow statement.

A pro forma five-year income statement is, of course, only tentative. It is based on the assumption that the proposed output is feasible and that the level of production can be financed.

Before putting together the income statement, the forecaster must project which assets and liabilities will support the forecast sales level. This projection leads to the balance sheet estimate. For most new ventures, the balance sheet form shown in *Exhibit 2* is appropriate.

At this preliminary stage, it is important to avoid structuring the balance sheet—and the terms of the financing—by putting in the entire amount of outside investments or loans. Unless the whole proposal is to be syndicated, leave the decision about the allocation of debt and equity to the financiers. Thus the cash account, even if negative, becomes the balancing item on the balance sheet.

Most new ventures should do projections for five years—a monthly forecast for the first two or three years and quarterly or yearly projections for the remaining years. The time period each statement covers should be the same.

That is, you shouldn't have monthly income statements and quarterly balance sheets for each period.

The monthly forecasts serve two purposes. First, they act as a form of budget, especially for general, administrative, and sales expenses. Second, they show the effect of quarterly tax payments on cash flow. The need to forecast for five years is dictated by the venture capitalist's desire to determine future earnings so as to arrive at a projected value for the business. This value, in turn, largely determines how much equity the venture capitalist will insist on for the capital investment.

——— GETTING TO COST OF GOODS SOLD

To illustrate the forecasting of capital requirements, I'll use the case of the McDonald Company, which was created to manufacture a water-purification unit for maritime and other uses. A colleague and I assumed that the company would start in January of year 1, would not produce any units in the first month, but would then produce 100 units a month in February through April and 300 a month for the next three months. It would then start dropping production in anticipation of seasonally lower sales and make a total of 2,100 units for the first year. The company did enough market research to warrant the sales forecast for the most-likely scenario. We assumed a selling price of $600 per unit, resulting in sales for year 1 of $1,020,000. We forecast that sales would rise in year 2 to $3 million and in year 3 to $3,780,000 and that the company would grow 25% in years 4 and 5.

After you have made the sales forecast, the next and most important item to estimate is the cost of goods sold. In service and wholesale businesses, making this estimate is not as complicated as in manufacturing. In service and wholesale, pricing, and thus sales, will probably be a function of labor or cost of materials; and a forecast of sales in units will easily produce a forecast of cost of goods sold.

For a manufacturing venture, simply using a percentage of sales, as you might when the business is reasonably well established, could lead to some serious errors. Unfortunately, the proper way is quite laborious and complicated, for it means using a separate forecast model. For the McDonald Company, we did an elaborate cost accounting module for all three scenarios, which turned out to be extraordinarily expensive in terms of time, even though we did it on a computer.

Remembering that the cost of goods sold consists of direct labor, cost of materials, and factory overhead, we handled the cost accounting model in the following way. Starting with a section on volume data, we forecast unit sales. Next, we made a decision on production, which began two months before sales were to commence. (This decision led to an ending inventory total that rose and fell as monthly sales went up and down.) In general, average wage rates and the time needed to assemble a unit were fairly easy to forecast.

Other components of the cost accounting model were raw materials, inventory, work-in-process inventory, finished-goods inventory, total inventory, factory overhead, work-in-process flow in units, and weighted-average cost per unit.

In some cases, estimating cost of goods sold as a percentage of sales, albeit a declining percentage, may be sufficient for the purpose at hand, particularly if you consider all the other variables. For example, after we made the cost accounting model for the McDonald Company, we calculated the cost of goods sold as a percentage of sales. Beginning at 53%, the percentage declined to about 40%. If it were possible to estimate the ratio of cost of goods sold to sales for, say, six-month intervals, the results would be approximately the same as what we got through the modeling. But for the shortcut approach, remember to have the necessary facts on hand to support the assumed percentages—such as efficiency of assembly, declining cost of raw materials because of increasing purchases, and spreading the factory overhead over the growing number of units purchased.

——— KEY EXPENSES

Estimate the depreciation expenses that are assumed to be included in the cost of goods sold so that this amount can be removed when you are compiling the cash flow statement. (To calculate taxable profit or loss, you must include the depreciation expense in the income statement; you can show it as a separate item.)

General and administrative expense (G&A) is the next income statement item to forecast. Since sales are increasing over the five-year planning horizon and G&A is mostly fixed, estimating this item as a percentage of sales is inappropriate. Instead, you must forecast a detailed schedule for all the items. Although the income statement shows only the total G&A expense, a footnote can refer the reader to the detailed schedule of G&A expenses.

The list of items in *Exhibit 3* is representative of what might be included. One item deserves special attention: officer's salaries. While entrepreneurs go into business to make lots of money, seeking one's fortune in a struggling new venture is foolish. Even if the entrepreneur is providing all the necessary start-up funds, the wisdom of taking a salary comparable to what might be expected in a more mature company is questionable, to say the least. Investors do not, however, expect the entrepreneur to live on a clerk's salary. Perhaps the best advice is to start off rather low and increase the salary as profits permit. McDonald assumed it would hire a second officer after the first year, so the total was the product of two, and later more, officers' salaries.

McDonald's other G&A expenses included such calculations as payroll taxes, predetermined items like rent and insurance, and items to be negotiated, such as lobbying in the state capital. Some items were mere guesses (nonsales travel and telephone), and some catchall attempts (start-up costs).

EXHIBIT 3
General and Administrative Expenses, Year 1, the McDonald Company

	JAN.	FEB.	MAR.	APR.	MAY	JUNE	JU
Consultant fees	$2,000	$2,000	$2,000	$2,000	$2,000	$2,000	
Depreciation	400	400	400	400	400	400	
Insurance	200	200	200	200	200	200	
Legal & acct.	500	500	500	500	500	500	50
Govt. lobbying	3,000	3,000	3,500	500	500	500	3,000
Office supplies	1,000	1,000	1,000	1,000	1,000	1,000	
Payroll taxes	840	1,060	1,260	1,260	1,260	1,260	
Rent	400	400	400	400	400	400	40
Office salaries	1,800	1,800	1,800	1,800	1,800	1,800	
Officer salaries	3,000	3,000	3,000	3,000	3,000	3,000	
Telephone	800	800	800	1,200	1,200	1,200	1,
Non-sales travel	2,000	2,000	2,000	2,000	1,400	1,400	1,000
Utilities	100	100	100	100	100	100	
Start-up expense	12,000	3,000	8,000	0	0	0	12,0
Bad debts	0	0	0	1,800	5,400	5,400	5,4
Totals	$28,040	$19,260	$24,960	$16,160	$19,160	$19,160	

Selling expenses can be treated the same as G&A. A company needs to develop a detailed schedule (see *Exhibit 4* for an example) to include the items relevant to the business at hand. For McDonald Company, we included salaries for two salespeople for the first month, three for the second, and four for the fourth month on through the rest of the first year. Travel expenses for the salespersons were estimated to be equal to salaries after the first few months. Interest expense on the equipment loan for the McDonald Company was $2,333 for the first month and declined thereafter as principal was paid.

The only other forecast item on the income statement is taxes. At first, there are no taxes, but even with the tax-loss carryforward (forward for 15 years, back for 3), taxes have to be included for the second year. Include state income taxes, if any, and use the percentage to be applied to net profit before tax. Estimating state income taxes is quite simple; the complication comes in forecasting the accrued taxes for the balance sheet. Once the income forecast is complete, you can turn to the balance sheet.

——— COMPLETING THE BALANCE SHEET

Keep the balance sheet as simple as you did the income statement. The first item on the balance sheet—cash—is the balancing item and is thus not forecast separately. Instead, it results from the computation of the cash flow statement.

EXHIBIT 4
Selling Expenses, Year 1, the McDonald Company, Most Likely Case

	JAN.	FEB.	MAR.	APR.	MAY	JUNE	JU
Advertising	$6,000	$6,000	$8,000	$4,000	$4,000	$4,000	
Travel	3,600	5,800	7,200	7,200	7,200	7,200	
Salaries	3,600	5,800	7,800	7,800	7,800	7,800	
Promo supplies	0	0	10,000	1,000	1,000	1,000	1,000
Commissions	0	0	0	0	0	0	
Totals	$13,200	$17,600	$33,000	$20,000	$20,000	$20,000	$20,

Accounts receivable may be forecast in two ways, each yielding different results. The more complicated way is to estimate what percentage of this month's sales the company will collect this month (for the McDonald Company, we assumed 5%), what percentage for the next month (we assumed 50%), and what percentage for the following two months (we assumed 30% and 15%). A separate schedule is necessary (for example, see *Exhibit 5*).

The standard way of forecasting accounts receivable is to use a turnover ratio (equal to monthly sales times 12 divided by the turnover figure—for example, 9). Because of the seasonality of sales, you would get dramatically different accounts receivable balances if you applied a constant turnover to each month.

In the first year for McDonald, the turnovers would have been those shown in *Exhibit 6,* Part A.

These turnovers make clear that the first procedure is advisable for monthly cash flow forecasting for a new venture, especially if sales are seasonal.

Inventory presents a more difficult problem than accounts receivable. Because of the pronounced seasonality in production and sales, using a constant turnover for cost of goods sold is not possible. For example, the inventory turnovers for the McDonald Company for the first year were as shown in *Exhibit 6,* Part B.

While the balance sheet shows inventory as one line, three types of inventory are actually on hand at any time: raw material, work in process, and finished goods. If you are using a cost accounting model, each month will produce these three totals. But because of the complexity of this model, you may wish to estimate (perhaps *guess* is the better term) what each of these inventory components will be, total them for each month, and use that number as the amount for inventory for the balance sheet. In the case of McDonald, we estimated unit production for the first year to be as shown in *Exhibit 7*.

By estimating the average cost of each finished unit, you can approximate the finished-goods component of inventory. With an eye to the production schedule, you can estimate how much raw material you will require. By spreading this raw material over the other months, you can get a crude estimate of the

EXHIBIT 5
Calculation of the McDonald Company's Monthly Accounts Receivable Balance, Year 1

	JAN.	FEB.	MAR.	APR.	MAY	JUNE
Beginning accounts receivable	$0	$0	$0	$0	$55,290	$192,060
Add sales (debits)[1]	0	0	0	58,200	174,600	174,600
Subtotal	0	0	0	58,200	229,890	366,660
Collections[2]						
Month's sales (5%)	0	0	0	2,910	8,730	8,730
1 month ago (50%)		0	0	0	29,100	87,300
2 months ago (30%)			0	0	0	17,460
3 months ago (15%)				0	0	0
Total collections	0	0	0	2,910	37,830	113,490
Ending accounts receivable	0	0	0	55,290	192,060	253,170
Change in accounts receivable	$0	$0	$0	$55,290	$136,770	$61,110

1. Assumes net of bad debts.
2. Representative collection figures assumed for years 4 and 5.

EXHIBIT 6
Turnover at the McDonald Company

A. TURNOVER OF ACCOUNTS RECEIVABLE

	MAY	JUNE	JULY	AUG.	SEPT.	OCT.	NOV.	DEC.
Turnover	39.1%	11.3%	8.5%	5.3%	1.7%	6.8%	12.6%	12.7%

B. TURNOVER OF INVENTORY

	MAY	JUNE	JULY	AUG.	SEPT.	OCT.	NOV.	DEC.
Turnover	3.6%	3.0%	3.7%	3.0%	0.1%	1.0%	1.6%	1.1%

raw material component. You estimate work in process by examining the production schedule and assuming an average cost for the units, say, when they are half completed.

Totaling these admittedly crude estimates (as in *Exhibit 8*) reveals a surprisingly close approximation of the needed inventory level required.

Other assets, which for a new venture include principally prepaid expenses, should be itemized and priced on a separate schedule and the total shown on the balance sheet. Do not show these items as a turnover or a percentage of sales.

EXHIBIT 7
Calculation of Finished-Goods Inventory, the McDonald Company

	JAN.	FEB.	MAR.	APR.	MAY	JUNE	JULY	AUG.	SEP.	OCT.	NOV.	DEC.
Number of units manufactured	0	100	100	100	300	300	300	200	100	200	200	200
Cumulative units manufactured	0	100	200	300	600	900	1,200	1,400	1,500	1,700	1,900	2,100
Less cumulative units sold	0	0	0	100	400	700	1,000	1,200	1,250	1,350	1,500	1,700
Finished-goods inventory	0	100	200	200	200	200	200	200	250	350	400	400

EXHIBIT 8
Estimated End-of-Month Inventory versus Actual Inventory, the McDonald Company
(in thousands of dollars, crudely estimated)

	JAN.	FEB.	MAR.	APR.	MAY	JUNE	JULY	AUG.	SEP.	OCT.	NOV.	DEC.
Raw material	$198	$100	$154	$150	$140	$132	$120	$110	$132	$120	$110	$330
Work in process	25	25	25	75	75	75	50	25	50	50	50	125
Finished goods	0	32	63	95	158	158	158	126	95	142	173	189
Estimated	$223	$157	$242	$320	$373	$365	$328	$261	$277	$312	$333	$644
Actual	$208	$219	$283	$378	$310	$375	$300	$248	$383	$370	$341	$652

Plant, property, and equipment must also be individually budgeted and not shown as a percentage of sales. If the vendor of the equipment or a third party offers financing, show it in the liabilities section of the balance sheet.

For the McDonald Company, the accounts payable amount included all raw material purchases except for the initial one and assumed payment in the following month. These purchases further assumed, of course, that once under way the business could get credit. For other companies, accounts payable might include items in addition to raw material purchases. For the McDonald Company, we put those items in a separate account—accrued expenses (not shown on the sample cash flow statement). For the accounts payable forecast, we simply let the raw materials purchased lag one month.

Accrued expenses for the McDonald Company included prepaid, selling, and G&A expenses less insurance, depreciation, and bad debts. We assumed most of these expenses would be paid in the following month and let them lag one month for balance sheet purposes. Payroll taxes we assumed would be paid quarterly.

Accrued taxes are the result of applying the tax rules to the income statement item for taxes. Taxes are payable on the fifteenth day of the fourth, sixth, ninth, and twelfth months, and estimates can be based on the prior year's taxes or the current year's earnings. (We used the prior year's for McDonald.)

How do you best handle the delicate problem of distinguishing between long-term debt and equity? My preference is to include in long-term debt only what I call "bring-along financing"—that is, financing that is offered almost as a matter of course on such purchases as equipment. (Real estate, too, might involve such financing, but buying land and buildings at the start of a new venture would be a strange use of precious funds. It's better to rent or lease until the business is well established.)

Structuring the debt/equity ratio of a new venture is quite acceptable if you are underwriting or syndicating the venture yourself. But if you have to go to one or two venture capital sources for the bulk of the financing, you will probably want to leave that decision to your outside investors. (I once lost the financing for a start-up venture when the institution took exception to my structuring the deal. It thought the debt/equity issue was its prerogative and rejected the deal rather than hassle over the matter.) Interest and principal payments will throw off the cash flow forecast, but you can correct this imbalance later.

In this model, the object is to forecast how much money will be needed to capitalize the venture. To avoid anticipating the decision of potential financiers, it's best not to consider how much of this to invest via debt instruments and how much by equity—common or preferred stock. When that decision is made and the capitalization known, the forecast can be revised to include this decision. An overdraft in the cash account can replace the required long-term debt and equity, at least initially.

—— AT LAST: THE CASH FLOW STATEMENT

Once you have completed the income statement and the balance sheet forecasts, you have the ingredients for the cash flow statement. Essentially a combination of the income statement and the balance sheet, it shows the changes that will occur in the cash balance.

Before considering the items on the cash flow statement, I must point out that for income statement items, the actual dollar amount is shown for the period in question. For example, if net sales for one month were $300,000, the amount would appear on the cash flow statement for that month. (See *Exhibit 9* for a sample cash flow statement.)

For balance sheet items, however, it is the period-to-period change that should be included in the cash flow statement, and whether the change is added or subtracted is indicated by the symbol $+\Delta$ or $-\Delta$, which should be read "plus a positive change" or "minus a positive change." Of course, if the change is

EXHIBIT 9
Sample Cash Flow Statement

CASH FLOW STATEMENT FOR THE PERIOD _____ TO _____

	Month			
Operating cash inflows				
+ Net sales	$	$	$	$
+ Other income				
−Δ Accounts receivable[1]				
1 Net operating cash inflows	$	$	$	$
Operating cash outflows				
+ Cost of goods sold less depreciation	$	$	$	$
+ General and administrative expenses				
+ Selling expenses				
+ Taxes				
−Δ Accrued taxes				
+Δ Inventory				
+Δ Prepaid expenses				
−Δ Accounts payable				
2 Total operating cash outflows	$	$	$	$
3 Net operating cash flow (item 1 less item 2)	$	$	$	$
Priority outflows				
+ Interest expenses	$	$	$	$
+ Current debt repayable				
+ Lease payments (not included above)				
4 Total priority outflows	$	$	$	$
Discretionary outflows				
+ Capital expenditures	$	$	$	$
+ Research and development expenses				
+ Preferred stock dividends				
+ Common stock dividends				
5 Total discretionary outflows	$	$	$	$
Financial flows				
+Δ Debt instruments (borrowings)	$	$	$	$
+Δ Stock securities (equity)				
+Δ Term loans				
6 Total financial flows	$	$	$	$
Net change in cash and marketable securities accounts				
+ Net operating cash flow (item 3)	$	$	$	$
− Priority outflows (item 4)				
− Discretionary outflows (item 5)				
+ Financial flows (item 6)				
7 Net change in cash and marketable securities	$	$	$	$
End-of-period cash balance	$	$	$	$

1. Δ = Period-to-period change in total dollar amount.

negative and the symbol is $-\Delta$, then algebraically this would be minus a minus, so the amount should be added.

The cash flow statement has seven parts. The first three deal with the basic operations of the company. Part one, net operating cash inflow, includes sales from the income statement minus a positive change in accounts receivable.

Later, after the venture is reasonably well established, you may want to pledge receivables and/or inventory as collateral for a working capital loan from a bank. In that case, you would add, under $-\Delta$ accounts receivable or $+\Delta$ bank borrowing, the increase or decrease in the loan amount. Including this item in this section, even though it is a financial rather than an operating matter, prevents the net operating cash flow (NOCF) from being negative much of the time.

It is true that if you start out using a receivables-based credit line, you will need less venture capital to start the business. But this type of financing may make it impossible to obtain extra financing later because the company will have no collateral left to offer. It is best instead to leave receivables-based financing as a contingency financing source in case it's really needed.

Even worse would be factoring, which is the sale of the receivable. I first formed this opinion in the course of assisting with the start-up of an ophthalmic laboratory. The entrepreneur's lawyer did his best to convince us that we should sell the receivables to the company for which he was counsel. We resisted, and well we did, for when the venture got into trouble, it was able to use the receivables as another source of capital.

The second part of the cash flow statement, total operating cash out-flows, includes cost of goods sold (excluding depreciation), G&A expenses, selling expenses, and taxes from the income statement. Next comes minus a positive change in accrued taxes, plus a positive change in inventory and prepaid expenses, and $-\Delta$ accounts payable. Subtract this second item, total operating cash outflows, from the first, net operating cash inflows, and the result is net operating cash flow. NOCF pinpoints how much cash was generated from the basic operations of the company. This is cash with which to grow the company.

The first use of NOCF is to pay the priority outflows, which consist of interest expense and debt repayment. Here you would also include a large lease payment—say for the premises the company occupies—in lieu of a mortgage payment. (Small lease payments go under cost of goods sold, G&A expense, or selling expense.)

The next section, discretionary outflows, includes a ranking of four discretionary expenditures. For example, in certain businesses—toys, for example—advertising expenses might be as much as or more than R&D or capital expenditures in other businesses. Even the sequence can be different. Use whatever sequence fits your business.

If you plan to buy equipment and have the manufacturer or other third party finance a portion of the price, you would, looking at *Exhibit 9,* record the transaction as follows: show the total price of the equipment in the "start" column for capital expenditures, the amount of the note in the start column as a debt instrument in the financial flows section, and periodic payments in their respective time period columns as priority outflow—interest expense and debt repayment.

In the initial financial cash flow forecast for the new venture, I suggest that no entry be made in the financial flows section except the bring-along financing I referred to previously.

The punch line of the cash flow statement is part seven, net change in cash and marketable securities. This is defined as part three (NOCF) minus part four (total priority outflows) minus part five (total discretionary outflows) plus or minus part six (total financial flows). For convenience, the end-of-period cash balance (the same as the balance sheet amount) is shown at the very bottom of the cash flow statement.

Since cash is the balancing item in the financial forecast, part seven would normally be negative for at least the first few months. This information helps answer the question on every entrepreneur's mind.

——— HOW MUCH CASH IS NEEDED?

The cash flow projection gives a reasonable estimate of the amount of cash needed to start the venture.

If net change in cash is –$57,833 in a month (as it was in February of year 1 for the McDonald Company), the business would have zero dollars at the end of the month if it started that month with $57,833 in its cash (checking) account. Not all monthly changes are negative, but if we algebraically add these changes to net change in cash, a running cash balance emerges for the end of the month.

Exhibit 10 shows a portion of the most likely scenario for the first two years of the cash flow statement for the McDonald Company. This projected negative cash balance keeps increasing until it reaches a maximum decrease in January of year 2 of –$846,063. From this time on, the cumulative cash balance rises, becomes a positive balance briefly in December of year 2, and falls back to a negative number for several more months until June of year 3, when it becomes positive consistently. This means that the company needs $846,063 in its bank account at the start to finance the most likely scenario of the financial forecast.

But what if the company does not meet these forecasts exactly? Surely it won't!

The solution is to forecast two other scenarios—a most pessimistic and a most optimistic situation. These forecasts are not as much trouble as they may seem since a number of items are the same for all these scenarios.

While these forecasts are not shown here, we did them for the McDonald Company and noted the largest decrease in the cash balance for each scenario.

EXHIBIT 10
Cash Flow Statement for the McDonald Company, Year 1; Jan.–Mar., Year 2

	JAN.	FEB.	MAR.	APR.	MAY	JUNE	JULY	AUG.	SEPT.	OCT.	NOV.	DEC.	JAN.	FEB.	MAR.
Operating cash inflows															
+ Net sales	$0	$0	$0	$60,000	$180,000	$180,000	$180,000	$120,000	$30,000	$60,000	$90,000	$120,000	$180,000	$300,000	$420,000
− Change in accounts receivable	0	0	0	55,290	136,770	61,110	17,460	(55,290)	(109,125)	(20,370)	27,645	45,105	74,460	143,085	173,640
(1) Net operating cash inflows	0	0	0	4,710	43,230	118,890	162,540	175,290	139,125	80,370	62,355	74,895	105,540	156,915	246,360
Operating cash outflows															
+ COGS (less depreciation)	27,640	18,860	24,560	32,013	94,165	93,227	93,077	62,498	15,629	31,245	46,845	62,074	92,284	153,179	213,731
+ G & A expense (less depreciation)	13,200	17,600	33,000	15,760	18,760	18,760	19,180	17,380	14,680	15,580	16,480	17,380	29,610	32,010	34,410
+ Selling expenses	0	0	0	20,000	20,000	20,000	20,000	20,000	20,000	20,000	20,000	20,000	41,000	43,400	45,800
+ Taxes	0	0	0	0	0	0	0	0	0	0	0	0	9,302	27,426	49,309
− Change in accrued taxes	0	0	0	0	0	0	0	0	0	0	0	0	9,302	27,426	49,309
+ Change in inventory	208,430	10,430	164,430	(5,723)	(67,875)	65,063	(74,717)	(52,068)	134,731	(12,885)	(28,485)	310,076	(50,134)	(111,029)	188,349
+ Change in prepaid expenses	2,200	(200)	(200)	(200)	(200)	(200)	(200)	(200)	(200)	(200)	(200)	(200)	2,750	(250)	(250)
− Change in accounts payable	43,040	(5,940)	173,000	(176,340)	660	129,480	(130,320)	1,380	129,240	(130,620)	1,380	327,240	(292,440)	1,960	349,280
(2) Net operating cash outflows	208,430	52,630	48,790	238,190	64,190	67,370	187,660	46,230	55,600	184,360	53,260	82,090	407,950	115,350	132,760
(3) Net operating cash flow	(208,430)	(52,630)	(48,790)	(233,480)	(20,960)	51,520	(25,120)	129,060	83,525	(103,990)	9,095	(7,195)	(302,410)	41,565	113,600
Priority outflows															
+ Interest expenses	2,333	2,286	2,237	2,187	2,137	2,086	2,034	1,981	1,928	1,873	1,818	1,761	1,704	1,645	1,586
+ Current debt repayable	2,870	2,917	2,966	3,015	3,066	3,117	3,169	3,222	3,275	3,330	3,385	3,442	3,499	3,557	3,617
(4) Total priority outflows	5,203	5,203	5,203	5,202	5,203	5,203	5,203	5,203	5,203	5,203	5,203	5,203	5,203	5,202	5,203

EXHIBIT 10

Cash Flow Statement for the McDonald Company, Year 1; Jan.–Mar., Year 2 (Continued)

	JAN.	FEB.	MAR.	APR.	MAY	JUNE	JULY	AUG.	SEPT.	OCT.	NOV.	DEC.	JAN.	FEB.	MAR.
Discretionary outflows															
+ Capital expenditures	200,000	0	0	0	0	0	0	0	0	0	0	0	0	0	0
(5) Total discretionary outflows	200,000	0	0	0	0	0	0	0	0	0	0	0	0	0	0
Financial flows															
+ Debt instruments (borrowings)	140,000	0	0	0	0	0	0	0	0	0	0	0	0	0	0
(6) Total financial flows	140,000	0	0	0	0	0	0	0	0	0	0	0	0	0	0
Net change in cash and marketable securities															
+ Net operating cash flow (item 3)	(208,430)	(52,630)	(48,790)	(233,480)	(20,960)	51,520	(25,120)	129,060	83,525	(103,990)	9,095	(7,195)	(302,410)	41,565	113,600
– Priority outflows (item 4)	5,203	5,203	5,203	5,202	5,203	5,203	5,203	5,203	5,203	5,203	5,203	5,203	5,203	5,202	5,203
– Discretionary outflows (item 5)	200,000	0	0	0	0	0	0	0	0	0	0	0	0	0	0
+ Financial flows (item 6)	140,000	0	0	0	0	0	0	0	0	0	0	0	0	0	0
(7) Net change in cash and marketable securities	($273,633)	($57,833)	($53,993)	($238,682)	($26,163)	$46,317	($30,323)	$123,857	$78,322	($109,193)	$3,892	($12,398)	($307,613)	$36,363	$108,397
Projected ending cash balance	($273,633)	($331,466)	($385,459)	($624,141)	($650,304)[1]	($603,987)	($634,310)	($510,453)	($432,131)	($541,324)	($537,432)	($549,830)	($857,443)	($821,080)	($712,683)

1. Maximum negative cash balance.

For the most optimistic scenario, the maximum negative cash balance was $1,052,289 (occurring in April of year 2). For the most pessimistic scenario, the comparable number for the first two years was $859,756 (occurring in April of year 2). It's not really surprising that the most optimistic scenario required more cash than the most pessimistic, as generating more sales meant heightening working capital requirements, especially accounts receivable and inventory.

If you take the larger difference between the maximum negative cash balance for the most likely scenario and either the most optimistic or the most pessimistic situation, you get an estimate of our contingency factor. In this case, the most pessimistic is only $13,693 more than the most likely scenario number, but the difference for the most optimistic projection is $194,846.

Surely, if you listed the capital required as $846,063 plus a contingency reserve of $194,846, your figures would have specious accuracy, which would not speak well for the forecaster. So round off the numbers and state that the business needs capital of $850,000 plus a contingency amount of $200,000, or a total of $1,050,000.

What if the entrepreneurs perceive that their track record will not support a request for the amount needed to finance the venture? They can go back to the income statement and balance sheet and make adjustments that might save money. Perhaps scaling back the sales forecast even more than the most pessimistic estimate might help. A company could save on working capital or buy used machinery instead of new or could subcontract production until the business was healthy. Whatever the alternatives, you can use the same model.

Now a potential venture capitalist might examine these forecasts and say, "Fine, but you don't need all this money now, at the start. Let's put up some of the required capital, and when you need the rest, ask for it."

Such a directive can be the kiss of death for a new venture because when the entrepreneur calls for more money, the venture capitalist can well say, "Sorry, but my funds are tied up right now. You'll have to wait awhile." (This was the response the first start-up venture on which I worked got. As a result, I formed my first law of entrepreneurship: if you want to fly to financial paradise, have enough gas to make the trip, as there are no service stations along the way!)

If the business attempts to raise venture capital once it has started and before it gets to a positive cash flow position (ready for second-stage financing), all it will have to show is a trail of red ink on its financial statements. True, the new business does not need all the required cash on day 1, but the cash should be available when needed.

One way to ensure that funds will be available is to arrange with a bank for a letter of credit. Then, if the venture capital source is temporarily short of funds, the bank can advance the funds based on the venture capitalist's credit.

The process for determining the capital requirements for a new venture really is not mysterious, only a bit complicated. The key to this determination (and to financial forecasting in general) is the cash flow statement. A two-step financial forecast is advisable, one to summarize the data and two to support the data with details in footnotes and schedules.

The cash flow statement is at the heart of the answer to the question, How much cash is needed to finance the venture? The negative cash balance line on the most likely scenario provides an estimate of the required venture capital. You can calculate the contingency amount of venture capital by comparing the maximum decreases in cash balance for the other two scenarios.

━━━ DISCUSSION QUESTIONS

1. The author advises the entrepreneur to forecast sales for five years. Choose a product or service and identify the factors, internal and external to your venture, that would affect sales over the next five years.

2. In forecasting sales, an entrepreneur must rely on more than intuition. Think of an event that could affect the sales of your product or service in the third year. How would you determine the degree to which this event is likely or unlikely to occur?

3. Set up a sample income statement for your product or service, as shown in *Exhibit 1*. Choose an item from the statement and in a separate footnote, show how you arrived at your estimated figure.

4. If the most likely scenario reflects the entrepreneur's best judgment, why are a most optimistic and a most pessimistic scenario necessary?

5. Suppose you have come up with a carefully thought out amount that an investor says is too high. Would you try to win the investor over with a convincing argument, or would you make adjustments to save money and decrease the amount you are requesting? If you choose the latter course, where would you make these adjustments?

16 Everything You (Don't) Want to Know about Raising Capital

JEFFRY A. TIMMONS AND DALE A. SANDER

Few entrepreneurs need to be persuaded to seek the money they need to grow their businesses. But most need to be reminded that the fund-raising process has many built-in problems and risks. While the challenge of winning over investors is exhilarating, the search for capital can ruin a business that isn't prepared for the harsh realities inherent in the process.

One of these realities is that raising money is costly and cumbersome; it cannot be done casually, nor can it be delegated. Another is that fund-raising drains managers' time and energy; and the business can suffer as a result. As the examples in this reading demonstrate, entrepreneurs must be prepared to undertake a thorough and careful search for capital and learn as much as they can about the process—including the things they are probably least interested in knowing.

Most entrepreneurs understand that if the fundamentals of a business idea—the management team, the market opportunities, the operating systems and controls—are sound, chances are there's money out there. The challenge of landing that capital to grow a company can be exhilarating. But as exciting as the money search may be, it is equally threatening. Built into the process are certain harsh realities that can seriously damage a business. Entrepreneurs cannot escape them but, by knowing what they are, can at least prepare for them.

After ten years of hard work and sleepless nights to get the company to $5 million in sales, the founder of Seattle Software (the disguised name of a real company) was convinced he could hit $11 million in the next three years. All he needed was cash. Ten banks refused to extend his credit line and advised him to get more equity. He met a lawyer at a seminar for entrepreneurs who said he would take the company public in Vancouver or London and raise $2.5 million fast. The founder was tempted to sign him on.

Texas Industrial (again, disguised) had grown from an idea to a $50-million-a-year leader in the industrial mowing-equipment business. The company wanted to keep growing and in 1987 decided it was time for an initial public offering. The underwriters agreed. They started the paperwork and scheduled a road show for early November.

The founders of both these companies thought they were prepared for the fund-raising process. They put together business plans and hired advisers. But that isn't enough. Every fund-raising strategy and every source of money implies certain out-of-pocket expenses and commitments of various kinds. Unless the entrepreneur has thought them through and decided how to handle them ahead of time, he or she may end up with a poorly structured deal or an inefficient search for capital.

Entrepreneurs should not be afraid to seek the money they need. Though they may be setting sail on dark waters and will always be at a disadvantage when negotiating with people who make deals every day, they can take steps to ensure that they get the capital they need, when they need it, on terms that do not sacrifice their future options. The first of those steps is knowing the downside of the fund-raising process.

—— RAISING MONEY COSTS A LOT

The lure of money leads founders to grossly underestimate the time, effort, and creative energy required to get the cash in the bank. This is perhaps the least appreciated aspect of raising money. In emerging companies, during the fund-raising cycle, managers commonly devote as much as half their time and most of their creative energy trying to raise outside capital. We have seen founders drop nearly everything else they were working on to find potential money sources and tell their story.

The process is stressful and can drag on for months as interested investors engage in "due diligence" examinations of the founder and the proposed business. Getting a yes can easily take six months; a no can take up to a year. All the while, the emotional and physical drain leaves little energy for running the business, and cash is flowing out rather than in. Young companies can go broke while the founders are trying to get capital to fund the next growth spurt.

Performance invariably suffers. Customers sense neglect, however subtle and unintended; employees and managers get less attention than they need and are accustomed to; small problems are overlooked. As a result, sales flatten or drop off, cash collections slow, and profits dwindle. And if the fund-raising effort ultimately fails, morale suffers and key people may even leave. The effects can cripple a struggling young business.

One start-up began its search for venture capital when, after nearly ten years of acquiring the relevant experience and developing a track record in their industry niche, the founders sensed an opportunity to launch a company in a field related to telecommunications. The three partners put up $100,000 of their own hard-earned cash as seed money to develop a business plan, and they set out to raise another $750,000. Eight months later, their seed money was spent, and every possible source of funding they could think of—including more than 25 venture capital firms and some investment bankers—had failed to deliver.

The would-be founders had quit their good jobs, invested their nest eggs, and worked night and day for a venture that was failing before it even had a chance to get started.

The entrepreneurs might have spent their time and money differently. We asked them what their sales would have been if they had spent the $100,000 seed money over the previous 12 months to generate their first customers. Their answer? One million dollars. The founders had not been prepared to divert so much of their attention away from getting the operations up and running. Raising money was actually less important to the company's viability than closing orders and collecting cash.

Even when the search for capital is successful, out-of-pocket costs can be surprisingly high. The costs of going public—fees to lawyers, underwriters, accountants, printers, and regulators— can run 15% to 20% of a smaller offering and can go as high as 35% in some instances. And a public company faces certain incremental costs after the issue, like administration costs and legal fees that increase with the need for more extensive reporting to comply with the SEC. In addition, there are directors' fees and liability insurance premiums that will also probably rise. These expenses often add up to $100,000 a year or more.

Similarly, bank loans over $1 million may require stringent audits and independent reviews to ensure that the values of inventory and receivables are bona fide. The recipient of the funds shoulders all these costs.

The demands on time and money are unavoidable. What entrepreneurs can avoid is the tendency to underestimate these costs and the failure to plan for them.

——— YOU HAVE NO PRIVACY

Convincing a financial backer to part with money takes a good sales job—and information. When seeking funds, you must be prepared to tell 5, 10, even 50 different people whether you are dependent on one brilliant technician or engineer, what management's capabilities and shortcomings are, how much of the company you own, how you're compensated, and what your marketing and competitive strategies are. And you will have to hand over your personal and corporate financial statements.

Revealing such guarded secrets makes entrepreneurs uneasy, and understandably so. Although most potential sources respect the venture's confidentiality, information sometimes leaks inadvertently—and with destructive consequences. In one instance, a start-up team in Britain had devised a new automatic coin-counting device for banks and large retailers. The product had a lot of promise, and the business plan was sound. When the lead investor was seeking coinvestors, he shared the business plan with a prospective investor who ultimately declined to participate. The deal came together anyway, but months later the entrepreneurs discovered that the investor, who had decided not to join, had shared the business plan with a competitor.

In another instance, an adviser was helping an entrepreneur sell his business to a Midwestern company. Sitting in the office of a senior bank officer who was considering financing the purchase, the seller asked for more information about the buyer's personal financial position. The bank officer called the buyer's bank a thousand miles away, got a low-level assistant on the line, and listened in amazement as the clerk said, "Yes, I've got his personal balance sheet right here," and proceeded to read it line by line.

The chance that information will get into the wrong hands is an inherent risk in the search for capital—and is one reason to make sure you really need the money and are getting it from highly reputable sources. While you cannot eliminate the risk, you can minimize it, by discussing the issue with the lead investor, avoiding some sources that are close to competitors, and talking to only reputable sources. You should in effect do your own "due diligence" on the sources by talking with entrepreneurs and reputable professional advisers who have dealt with them.

——— EXPERTS CAN BLOW IT

Decisions about how much money to raise, from what sources, in debt or equity, under what terms—all limit management in some way and create commitments that must be fulfilled. These commitments can cripple a growing business, yet managers are quick to delegate their fund-raising strategies to financial advisers. Unfortunately, not all advisers are equally skilled. And of course, it's the entrepreneur—not the outside expert—who must live or die by the consequences.

Opti-Com (the fictitious name of a real company) was a start-up spun off from a public company in the fiber optics industry. Though not considered superstars, the start-up managers were strong and credible. Their ambition was to take the company to $50 million in sales in five years (the "5-to-50 fantasy"), and they enlisted the help of a large, reputable accounting firm and a law firm to advise them, help prepare their business plan, and forge a fund-raising strategy. The resultant plan proposed to raise $750,000 for about 10% of the common stock.

The adviser urged Opti-Com's founders to submit the business plan to 16 blue-ribbon, mainstream venture capital firms in the Boston area; four months later, they had received 16 rejections. Next they were told to see venture capital firms of the same quality in New York, since— contrary to conventional money-raising wisdom—the others were "too close to home." A year later, the founders were still unsuccessful—and nearly out of money.

Opti-Com's problem was that the entrepreneurs blindly believed that the advisers knew the terrain and would get results. The fact is, the business proposal was not a mainstream venture capital deal, yet the search included none of the smaller, more specialized venture capital funds, private investors, or strategic partners that were more likely to fund that type of business.

Furthermore, the deal was overvalued by three to four times, which undoubtedly turned off investors.

Opti-Com eventually changed its adviser. Under different guidance, the company approached a small Massachusetts fund specifically created to provide risk capital to emerging companies not robust enough to attract conventional venture capital but important to the state's economic renewal. This was the right fit. Opti-Com raised the capital it needed and at a valuation more in line with the market for start-up deals: about 40% of the company instead of the 10% that the founders had offered.

The point is not to avoid using outside advisers but to be selective about them. One rule of thumb is to choose individuals who are actively involved in raising money for companies at your stage of growth, in your industry or area of technology, and with similar capital requirements.

——— MONEY ISN'T ALL THE SAME

Although money drives your fund-raising effort, it is not the only thing potential financial partners have to offer. If you overlook considerations such as whether the partner has experience in the industry, contacts with potential suppliers or customers, and a good reputation, you may shortchange yourself.

How fast the investor can respond is sometimes another crucial variable. One management group had four weeks to raise $150 million to buy a car phone business before it would be auctioned on the open market. It did not have enough time to put together a detailed business plan but presented a summary plan to five top venture capital and LBO firms.

One of the firms asked a revealing question: "How do you prevent these phones from being stolen? You can't penetrate the market unless you solve that problem." The founders soon concluded that this source was not worth pursuing. The firm obviously knew little about the business: at that time, car phones weren't stolen like CB radios because they couldn't be used until they'd gone through an authorized installation and activation. The entrepreneurs didn't have time to wait for the investor to get up to speed. They focused their efforts on two investors with experience in telecommunications and got a commitment expediently.

Yet another entrepreneur had a patented, innovative device for use by manufacturers of semiconductors. He was running out of cash from an earlier round of venture capital and needed more to get the product into production. His backers would not invest further since he was nearly two years behind his business plan.

When the well-known venture capital firms turned him down, he sought alternatives. He listed the device's most likely customers and approached the venture capital firms that backed those companies. The theory was that they would be able to recognize the technology's merit and the business opportunity. From a list of 12 active investors in the customer's industry, the entrepreneur landed three offers within three months, and the financing was closed soon thereafter.

THE SEARCH IS ENDLESS

After months of hard work and tough negotiations, cash hungry and unwary entrepreneurs are quick to conclude that the deal is closed with the handshake and letter-of-intent or executed-terms sheet. They relax the street-wise caution they have exercised so far and cut off discussions with alternative sources of funds. This can be a big mistake.

An entrepreneur and one of his vice presidents held simultaneous negotiations with several venture capitalists, three or four strategic partners, and the source of a bridge capital loan. After about six months, the company was down to 60 days of cash, and the prospective backer most interested in the deal knew it. It made a take-it-or-leave-it offer of a $10 million loan of 12% with warrants to acquire 10% of the company. The managers felt that while the deal was not cheap, it was less expensive than conventional venture capital, and they had few alternatives since none of the other negotiations had gotten that serious.

Yet the entrepreneurs were able to hide their bargaining weakness. Each time a round of negotiations was scheduled, the company founder made sure he scheduled another meeting that same afternoon several hours away. He created the effect of more intense discussion elsewhere than in fact existed. By saying that he had to get to Chicago to continue discussions with venture capitalist XYZ, the founder kept the investors wondering just how strong their position was.

The founder finally struck a deal with the one investor that was interested and on terms he was quite comfortable with. The company has since gone public and is a leader in its industry.

The lead entrepreneur understood what many others do not: you must assume the deal will never close and keep looking for investors even when one is seriously interested. While it is tempting to end the hard work of finding money, continuing the search not only saves time if the deal falls through but also strengthens your negotiating position.

LAWYERS CAN'T PROTECT YOU

Why should you have to get involved in the minutiae of legal and accounting documents when you pay professionals big fees to handle them? Because you are the one who has to live with them.

Deals are structured many different ways. The legal documentation spells out the terms, covenants, conditions, responsibilities, and rights of the parties in the transaction. The money sources make deals every day, so naturally they are more comfortable with the process than the entrepreneur who is going through it for the first or second time. Covenants can deprive a company of the flexibility it needs to respond to unexpected situations, and lawyers, however competent and conscientious, cannot know for sure what conditions and terms the business is unable to withstand.

Consider a small public company we'll call ComComp. After more than two months of tough negotiations with its bank to convert an unsecured demand bank note of over $1.5 million to a one-year term note, the final documentation arrived. Among the many covenants and conditions was one clause buried deep in the agreement: "Said loan will be due and payable on demand in the event there are any material events of any kind that could affect adversely the performance of the company."

The clause was so open to interpretation that it gave the bank, which was already adversarial, a loaded gun. Any unexpected event could be used to call the loan, thereby throwing an already troubled company into such turmoil that it probably would have been forced into bankruptcy. When the founders read the fine print, they knew instantly that the terms were unacceptable, and the agreement was then revised.

An infusion of capital—be it debt or equity, from private or institutional sources— can drive a company to new heights, or at least carry it through a trying period. Many financing alternatives exist for small enterprises, and entrepreneurs should not be afraid to use them.

They should however, be prepared to invest the time and money to do a thorough and careful search for capital. The very process of raising money is costly and cumbersome. It cannot be done casually, nor can it be delegated. And it has inherent risks.

Since no deal is perfect and since even the most savvy entrepreneurs are at a disadvantage in negotiating with people who strike deals for a living, there is strong incentive for entrepreneurs to learn as much as they can about the process — including the very things they are probably least interested in knowing.

—— DISCUSSION QUESTIONS

1. "The lure of money leads founders to grossly underestimate the time, effort, and creative energy required to get cash in the bank." For what reasons besides money might entrepreneurs blind themselves to the realities of fund raising?
2. The authors point out that business can suffer severely during a fund-raising campaign. What can entrepreneurs do to fortify operations while they are engaged in a search for funds?

3. What tasks might entrepreneurs be tempted to delegate to advisers that they should be performing for themselves? What can financial and legal advisers do and not do for entrepreneurs?

4. What steps should the founder of Seattle Software take before signing on the lawyer who has promised to raise $2.5 million fast?

5. Entrepreneurs should learn as much as possible about the fund-raising process, say the authors. In many of the examples given in the reading, the entrepreneurs learn their lessons the hard way, by making mistakes. What other means of learning are available?

17 You *Can* Negotiate with Venture Capitalists

HAROLD M. HOFFMAN AND JAMES BLAKEY

Venture capitalists are in the business of funding risky ventures and reaping a handsome return on their investment. They have much to offer the fledgling business—large sums of cash as well as useful counsel—but their resources come with strings attached. Some firms, for example, may demand an un-restricted right to decide when the company should be taken public and require that the public offering be undertaken at the company's expense. Or they may expect the business to forfeit stock to them if it fails to achieve revenue and profit goals.

Venture capitalists are tough negotiators, and the eager entrepreneur may be tempted to take their funds on any terms. But, say the authors, entrepreneurs have every right to protect their interests and do not have to agree without negotiation to each provision set forth by investors. This reading describes some common provisions—antidilution, performance/forfeiture, employment contracts, control, shareholder agreements, and disclosure—and suggests approaches for negotiating terms on each. The best strategy, it advises, is to fight provisions that would undermine effective management of the company or that are clearly unfair, while not wrestling too hard over the others.

If you are an entrepreneur looking for venture capital, you are probably well aware of the frustrations in finding loose purse strings in the financial markets. Your business is too new or your product is still too untried to qualify for conventional intermediate- or long-term debt financing. Or, although you know you might qualify for a loan, you do not want to take on the risk of more debt.

You have already used your savings and borrowed from relatives to get the seed capital you need. And you may have reached the point where you're generating healthy sales figures. But you still have a long way to go before you can think of a public offering, and you cannot finance the growth you want from retained earnings alone.

You need equity capital. If your management has a good track record and your business has the potential to generate a very high return on investment (ROI)—say 30% or 40% per year—professional venture capitalists may be prepared to fork over high-risk capital of $1 million or more to finance your growth. You do not have to have a high-tech company to qualify; venture capitalists will also invest in conventional businesses that offer high ROI potential. We have recently negotiated venture capital deals involving an oil-drilling-equipment manufacturer, a movie distributor, and a financial newsletter publisher, among others.

Because you have heard that money talks when a deal gets structured, you may worry that if you rock the boat by demanding too much, the venture capital firm will lose interest. That is an understandable attitude; venture capital is hard to get and if you have gotten as far as the negotiating process, you are already among the lucky few.

But that does not mean you have to roll over and play dead. A venture capital investment is a business deal that you may have to live with for a long time. Although you will have to give ground on many issues when you come to the bargaining table, there is always a point beyond which the deal no longer makes sense for you. You must draw a line and fight for the points that really count. The extent to which you can stand your ground will depend, of course, on the leverage you have in the negotiations. If your business already shows a profit or if you are selling a highly desirable service or product, you will have more bargaining power than if your company is burning up cash because sales are still several years down the road.

STRUCTURING THE INVESTMENT

Before you and the venture capitalists agree to a financing package, you have to settle two important issues: the worth of your business before the investors put their money in and the type of securities they will receive in exchange for their investment.

VALUATION

Although your company's tangible net worth (book value) may be low or negative, the fair market value may be higher because of proprietary technology, sales potential, or other factors. You can more easily defend the value you place on your company if your projections are prepared with the assistance of a reputable accounting firm. It also helps to bring to the negotiations valuation data for comparable business ventures.

It is important to negotiate hard for a reasonable valuation of your company because the amount of equity you give the venture capitalists (VCs) will depend largely on that calculation. Let us assume, for instance, that you and the venture capitalists agree that your business is now worth $4 million. Based on this valuation and the company's cash needs, you strike a deal whereby the VCs will invest $1 million. The company's worth accordingly rises to $5 million. Their $1 million should, therefore, buy the equivalent of 20% of the total post-investment equity outstanding.

CAPITAL STRUCTURE

When it comes to capital structure, venture capitalists like to have their cake and eat it too: they want equity because that will give them a big slice of the profits if your company succeeds; but they also want debt because debt holders get paid before equity holders if the company fails. So they usually invest in redeemable preferred stock or debentures. If things go well, VCs can convert preferred stock or debentures to common stock. If things go badly, however, they will get paid before you and other holders of common stock.

If you have a choice, try to get them to accept a capital structure that consists entirely of common stock, because it's simpler and keeps the balance sheet clean. Chances are, however, that you will not get them to agree to this unless your bargaining position is extremely strong.

In some deals, they ask for a debenture together with warrants that allow them to purchase common stock at a nominal price. Under this arrangement, the VCs really do get to eat their cake and have it too because they do not have to convert their debt to equity. They will regain 100% of their investment when the debt is repaid and still share in the equity appreciation of the company when they exercise their warrants.

Although the documents used to create debentures, preferred stock, and warrants are usually so much boilerplate, they must still be reviewed with care. One consideration is the legal structure of the investment, for the laws that govern what a corporation can do with its securities vary from state to state. Some states, New York for example, do not permit issuance of preferred stock that is redeemable at the holder's option. Antidilution and liquidation provisions, which are discussed in the next section, can have unexpected effects if not carefully crafted. Subordination provisions in debentures are also important, because your trade creditors and institutional lenders will expect clear-cut language placing the venture capitalists' claim to the company's assets behind their own.

PROTECTING THE INVESTMENT

Many venture capitalists seek to protect their investments by asking for antidilution, performance/forfeiture, and other protective provisions. Their concern over preserving the value of their capital is legitimate. At the same time, you should review these provisions carefully to make sure they are fair to you and any other founders.

ANTIDILUTION PROVISIONS

The VCs' preferred stock and debentures will be convertible, at their option, into common stock at a specified rate. Obviously, neither of you expect the value of your company's stock to drop, but you cannot control the value the market places on your business. If your company begins to do poorly and you need more money, you may have no choice but to sell off new equity more cheaply than in the past. Once they have bought in, the VCs will want to be sure that later stock issuances will not water down the value of their investment.

Antidilution protection does not mean that an investment must always be convertible into a fixed percentage ownership share of the company, without regard to intervening growth and investment. As long as any new common stock is sold at a price equal to or higher than the rate at which the VCs can convert into common stock, their investment will not be diluted economically. Although their slice of the pie will shrink, the pie itself will grow at least commensurately. But if new common stock is sold for less than that price, the pie will not expand as quickly as the VCs' slice shrinks—and their investment will, consequently, be diluted. To guard against this outcome, the conversion right usually includes an antidilution adjustment, or "ratchet."

There are two kinds of ratchets, full and weighted. With a full ratchet, the rate for converting the VCs' debentures or preferred stock into common is reduced to the lowest price at which any common is subsequently sold—a situation that can have drastic consequences for you and other founders. If the company sells a single share cheaply, *all* the VCs' securities suddenly become convertible into common at that lower rate. They can very quickly end up with the lion's share of the company.

Let's return to the situation in which a VC firm has invested $1 million and received a 20% share of your now $5 million company. On this basis, if your company started out with four million shares outstanding, the VCs' $1 million will be initially convertible at the rate of $1 per share into one million shares of stock (or 20% of the five million shares outstanding after conversion).

Under a full ratchet, if your company sells one share of common stock for 25 cents, the conversion rate of the VCs' securities will drop to that price. Their $1 million will now buy four million common shares. After conversion, the VCs will thus own four million out of eight million shares, or 50% rather than 20% of the company. So even though the sale of this single share would have no material dilutive effect on the venture capitalists' investment, under a full ratchet provision such a sale would severely reduce the value of the equity that you and any other founders hold.

The more common and equitable approach is to negotiate a weighted ratchet whereby the conversion rate for the VCs' shares is adjusted down to the weighted average price per share of all outstanding common after the issuance of cheaper stock. If only a few cheap shares are issued, the downward adjustment will be minor. The usual method is to treat all shares outstanding before the cheaper dilutive issuance as if they were floated at the initial conversion price.

Mechanics aside, negotiating the antidilution adjustment carefully is important because its purpose is to place any dilutive effect of a future stock issuance on you and the other founders, not on the VCs. You can, however, seek to moderate the effect of such a provision. For example, you can ask that any common shares issuable to the venture capitalists on conversion of their preferred stock or debentures be included in the number of outstanding shares used for calculating the adjustment. This will spread the impact of a dilutive issuance over a larger number of shares. You can also request that any common shares sold cheaply to officers, directors, employees, or consultants—a customary practice in start-up situations, and one that benefits all investors—will not trigger the antidilution adjustment.

The risk posed by an antidilution provision, especially one with a full ratchet, is that you and other founders can be squeezed out if the company runs into serious financial problems. If the company's market value falls far enough below the dollar value of the VCs' original investment, an antidilution adjustment will not only wipe out your equity but can actually prevent you from seeking new investors, unless you can get the VCs to waive their antidilution rights.

PERFORMANCE/FORFEITURE PROVISIONS

As a condition for investment, the VCs may subject your stock—including a stock you acquired years earlier—to a performance/forfeiture arrangement. Under this provision, if the company fails to meet certain earnings or other targets, you must forfeit some or all of your stock.

A performance/forfeiture provision serves several purposes. For one, it protects the VCs from paying for an overvalued company. The valuation of unseasoned companies usually relies heavily on speculative sales and earnings projections. If you overestimated operating results by a wide margin, the venture capitalists will have paid too much for their share of the company.

Because sales and earnings forecasts are only projections, not promises, the VCs cannot sue the company if management fails to perform as expected. But if you have agreed to a performance/forfeiture provision, they can compensate themselves by increasing their ownership interest at your expense.

Another reason the VCs may want this provision is that if the company does not do well, it will be free to reissue the forfeited stock to any new executives brought in without diluting the VCs' holdings. The performance/forfeiture provision also serves as a golden handcuff: it motivates you and any other founders to work hard and stick with the business.

If your company is in an early stage of development, you may have to place a large portion of your stock at risk of forfeiture because the company's future is still very uncertain. As time passes, your enterprise is more likely to gain in value and enjoy a more predictable future. Then you can legitimately refuse to agree to a forfeiture provision on the grounds that the company's valuation is realistic, based on past performance.

What should you negotiate for? If the VCs insist on including a forfeiture provision, you may be able to persuade them to include stock bonuses for performance that beats your sales and earnings projections. If you are expected to forfeit stock for failing to hit 80% of the sales or earnings targets in your business plan, for example, it stands to reason that you should get an equivalent bonus if you exceed those targets.

EMPLOYMENT CONTRACTS

The terms of the founders' employment are always part of the financing arrangement. The VCs will want an agreement covering your salary, bonuses, benefits, and the circumstances under which you can quit or be fired by the board.

It may come as a shock to realize that the VCs are making an investment in the company, not you. As companies grow, they often require professional management skills that you and the other founding entrepreneurs may lack. The time may come when the VCs think you are no longer competent to run the business and decide to terminate your employment.

If the venture capitalists are buying a controlling interest, you should seek an employment contract of reasonable duration—at least two to three years. If your business is well past the start-up stage, you may want to negotiate a longer term of at least five years.

There is, however, one potential drawback: a long-term contract may prevent you from leaving the company to do other things. If the company is doing poorly, the VCs may want you to stay and keep trying after you have decided to move on. Although they cannot prevent your departure, they may be able to sue you for breach of contract. Also, your contract may preclude your working in the same industry once you quit.

The grounds on which the board can terminate your employment should be fully spelled out and kept narrow in scope. Good examples of reasonable and narrow grounds include a felony conviction, theft of company property, or chronic failure to carry out reasonable instructions from the board despite repeated requests. If you are fired and you decide to sue for wrongful termination, you will find it easier to prove your case if specific grounds were written into your contract.

Here are some other provisions to check for in the employment agreement before signing the deal:

- Are you assured adequate advance notice of the board's decision not to renew your original contract or its decision to renew but on terms that are less beneficial to you?
- Are you getting an adequate severance package, including extended insurance coverage?
- If you are obligated not to compete with the company after termination, what is the scope and duration of your obligation? Are you only prohibited from hiring away employees and soliciting business from the company's established customers, or must you leave your line of business altogether?

- Is the company required to buy back any or all of your stock if you are terminated, or does it have the option of doing so? How will the price be determined? You should try to negotiate for an option to sell your stock back to the company according to a fixed formula (for instance, a certain multiple of earnings) in the event that you are fired. Many companies resist having to buy back equity, so you may have trouble cashing out unless you include this option in your contract.

You may, of course, persuade the venture capitalists to accept an employment agreement that does not permit the board to terminate you. Moreover, your postemployment rights and obligations may vary depending on whether you quit of your own accord, did something egregiously wrong, or were simply fired because the board was unhappy with your performance.

CONTROL

You will have to let the VCs share in running your company. In all likelihood you will be required to retain a nationally recognized accounting firm to certify your annual financial statements. You may also have to accept the addition of managers recommended by the VCs to cover areas of the business they think need improvement. They will usually place one, and possibly more, of their representatives on your board, depending on their ownership interest. Important decisions like whether to merge, liquidate assets, or sell stock will require their consent even if they have only a minority position.

Nevertheless, there is some room for negotiation when it comes to control provisions. If you and other founders agree to a deal that leaves you with a minority interest, ask for no less than the VCs would probably demand: that they guarantee you board representation and obtain your consent before making any major business decisions.

SHAREHOLDER AGREEMENTS

In almost all deals, the VCs will also want the company's founders to enter into a shareholders' agreement. Such an agreement may require the founders to vote for one or more directors of the VCs' choosing. It may also grant the VCs majority control of the board if the business runs into serious trouble, even if they have only a minority interest.

Shareholder agreements can also govern the sale of stock, including newly issued shares. Under most arrangements, the seller is required to offer the stock to the company or other parties to the agreement (insiders) before selling to outsiders. The VCs may also want to include a co-sale stipulation that would oblige any selling shareholder to arrange for the other insiders to participate in the sale to an extent proportionate to their holdings.

Usually the company is also bound to the shareholder agreement. Depending on the agreement, the company may have to offer stock to the VCs, to all parties to the agreement, or to all current shareholders (in proportion to their holdings) before issuing any new stock to a third party. Because this preemptive right to purchase additional shares allows investors to maintain an absolute percentage interest in the company, the VCs are almost certain to insist on having it. You should ask for no less for yourself. If the company issues more shares, you should have the same opportunity as the VCs to retain your current percentage of ownership.

DISCLOSURE

Before the VCs hand over the money, they will doubtless want extensive disclosure about your company. You will be asked to verify that the company is in good standing, has paid its taxes, and is in compliance with all laws. You must also establish that the company's financial statements are correct and that it has no agreements or contingent obligations other than those referred to in an attached disclosure schedule. You should seek, whenever possible, to narrow the scope of these representations and qualify them as being to the best of your knowledge at the time. Inclusion of any matter you think may apply will avoid later argument by the VCs that you failed to disclose relevant information.

It is a good idea to negotiate for a cushion in your favor, so that if there are omissions in your representations that later cost the company no more than, say, $50,000, the omissions will not be considered a breach of the representation. In addition, ask for a time limit on your representations about the company—they should not apply for more than six months to a year after the deal has been closed.

—— CASHING OUT THE INVESTMENT

In any venture capital deal, the investors will be looking ahead to the day when they can liquidate their investment in your company. They will probably want provisions written into the agreement that will give them the opportunity to cash out on favorable terms at a time of their choosing.

REGISTRATION RIGHTS

Federal securities laws (and the "blue sky" laws of many states) prohibit you from selling an interest in your company unless you have either filed a registration statement with the SEC or qualified for an exemption from registration. Registration is an expensive process, which most companies avoid by getting a "private placement" exemption. To qualify for this exemption, your company must approach no more than a small number of wealthy and sophisticated investors.

The securities laws also impose legal restrictions that generally will prevent the venture capitalists and other shareholders from reselling any stock acquired under a private placement exemption for at least two years, and may limit the amount that can be sold without a registration even after that period. Accordingly, the VCs will probably want the right to require the company to register their stock at the company's expense.

The VCs' registration rights may include either piggyback rights, which require the company to include the VCs' shares only if the company itself decides to file a registration statement, or demand rights, which allow the VCs to force the company to file a registration statement covering their shares. In granting piggyback rights to the VCs, check to make sure that the provision includes you and the other shareholders on an equal basis and that the company's ability to grant future piggyback rights is not limited.

Demand rights should be negotiated with even greater care. Because of the expense, try to limit the VCs to one request for demand registration, or they may keep the company in constant registration. Also, try to get them to agree to postpone exercising this right until after the company's first public offering. Without this restriction, the VCs may be able to force the company to go public before it can afford the heavy reporting and other burdens imposed on publicly held companies.

If you agree to registration rights, you should be sure to include yourself. As an insider, you will probably be subject to transfer limitations under the securities laws regardless of how long you have held your stock. If you do not have a contractual right to be included in a registration, you may find yourself squeezed out of a public offering by investors who do. Furthermore, be sure that the company is obliged to pay your registration expenses. If it is not, you will have to pay a proportionate share of what can be an enormous bill—for lawyers, accountants, printers, state securities filings, and underwriters' expenses. (Certain states will not permit the company to pay insiders' registration expenses; if your underwriter wants to offer stock in those states, you may have to waive your registration rights.)

LIQUIDATION AND MERGER PROVISIONS

Provisions governing the liquidation or merger of your business are important, yet they are often overlooked. If you are not careful, you may unwittingly agree to a provision that harms you or creates windfall gains for the venture capitalists in the event of a merger or other corporate combination.

If, for example, preferred shareholders are allowed to treat a merger like a liquidation, they can demand a cash payment at the time of the merger. This kind of provision makes the merger less appealing to a potential partner. It can kill a deal outright, or at least give the preferred shareholders leverage to extract other concessions—usually at your expense.

Clauses relating to liquidation preferences should also get careful scrutiny. Liquidation preferences specify the order in which holders of different classes of securities get paid and how much of the liquidation proceeds they can collect before other investors are repaid. Under some preference provisions, the VCs not only receive 100% of their investment back but also have the right to share in any remaining proceeds, as if the investment consisted of common stock.

One risk to you of such a provision is that the VCs may be better off if the company liquidates than if it remains in operation. While the company remains in business, the VCs can only participate as either holders of preferred stock or debt or holders of common stock. On liquidation, they can participate as both. Moreover, liquidation provisions do not apply just in cases of failure, when there is nothing left to distribute; companies are sometimes liquidated even when business is good. And the VCs may control the decision whether to liquidate.

MODIFYING RIGHTS

To avoid a situation in which a right given the VCs can block a transaction crucial to the company's survival, it's important to include a provision that allows the venture capitalists' rights to be changed. Their rights cannot be modified without their consent. Because you may have investments from a number of venture capital firms, and you may therefore not be able to get a unanimous decision, you should try to get them to agree in advance that a majority or two-thirds count of their combined interests can waive the VCs' rights on behalf of all.

The key to weathering the venture capital process is to put the transaction in perspective. When it is all over, your young and not particularly bankable company will have a large sum of cash to put to work. Although some venture capitalists' demands may seem ridiculous, burdensome, or even insulting, you cannot expect to get that amount of money without a lot of strings attached—and some of the things they make you do may even be good for you.

Remember that even though funding risky ventures is their business, venture capitalists will do all they can to avoid losing their capital. Expect them to be tough negotiators.

But this does not mean that you do not have the right to protect your interests in the deal. You will not get your way on every provision, but you should be able to persuade the VCs to see matters from your point of view on some. The best strategy is to try to fight any provisions that will keep you from running your company effectively or that are clearly unfair to you, and not wrestle too hard over the others.

Your negotiations should be guided by a spirit of fairness and respect for each other's legitimate interests. Properly handled, these negotiations can build a foundation of trust and cooperation from the very start—giving your business the best possible chance for success.

───── DISCUSSION QUESTIONS

1. The authors point out that while venture capital comes with strings attached, certain stipulations may actually be good for the growing company. Choose one of the stipulations described in the reading and identify its possible benefits for the entrepreneur.

2. Venture capital is not easily won and entails many costs. At what point in your company's growth would you feel confident enough to approach and negotiate with venture capitalists?

3. Do you agree that entrepreneurs should "not wrestle too hard" over most VC provisions? Besides winning funds, what are the benefits of cooperating on issues of lesser importance? Are there ways in which such a cooperative spirit could harm the entrepreneur?

4. Choose one of the provisions described in the reading and explain how the clauses serve the interests of the venture capitalists. Then distinguish between the clauses that you would be willing to live with and those you think would interfere with the effective management of your company.

5. Propose a compromise that you would present to the venture capitalist on a clause that you think is unreasonable. What arguments would you use to persuade the venture capitalist?

Strategy vs. Tactics from   18
a Venture Capitalist

ARTHUR ROCK

The preceding selection spelled out some strategies entrepreneurs can employ when bargaining with venture capitalists. The following reading looks at the entrepreneurial start-up from the venture capitalist's perspective. With more than 30 years' experience in evaluating new ventures, Arthur Rock has learned to pay more attention to the people who conceive and develop the company than to the details of the business plan. In this reading, he offers a range of insights on the personal qualities he looks for when deciding whether to back an aspiring entrepreneur: an ability to benefit from constructive criticism and persevere despite bad news and setbacks, skill in knowing when to take charge and when to delegate, an appreciation of the importance of sound and solid management—and, above all, a desire to build a great company.

As a venture capitalist, I am often asked for my views on why some entrepreneurs succeed and others fail. Obviously, there are no cut-and-dried answers to that question. Still, a few general observations about how I evaluate new businesses should shed some light on what I think it takes to make an entrepreneurial venture thrive and grow.

Over the past 30 years, I estimate that I've looked at an average of one business plan per day, or about 300 a year, in addition to the large numbers of phone calls and business plans that simply are not appropriate. Of the 300 likely plans, I may invest in only one or two a year; and even among those carefully chosen few, I'd say that a good half fail to perform up to expectations. The problem with those companies (and with the ventures I choose *not* to take part in) is rarely one of strategy. Good ideas and good products are a dime a dozen. Good execution and good management—in a word, good *people*—are rare.

To put it another way, strategy is easy, but tactics—the day-to-day and month-to-month decisions required to manage a business—are hard. That's why I generally pay more attention to the people who prepare a business plan than to the proposal itself.

Another venture capitalist I know says, somewhat in jest, that the first thing he looks at in a business plan is the financial projections. Frankly, how anyone can figure out what sales and earnings and returns are going to be five years from now is beyond me. The first place I look is the résumés, usually found at the back. To me, they are the essence of any plan. (Maybe no one reads the middle section!)

I see the plan as really an opportunity to evaluate the people. If I like what I see in there, I try to find out more by sitting down and talking with the would-be entrepreneurs. I usually spend a long time on this. (Unless their first question is "How much money am I going to get?" Then the interview is very short.) I don't talk much during these meetings; I'm there to listen. I want to hear what they've got to say and see how they think.

Some of the questions I ask have little to do directly with the particular business under discussion: Whom do they know, and whom do they admire? What's their track record? What mistakes have they made in the past, and what have they learned from them? What is their attitude toward me as a potential investor—do they view me as a partner or as a necessary evil? I also ask specific questions about the kind of company they want to develop—say, whom do they plan to recruit, and how are they going to do it?

I am especially interested in what kind of financial people they intend to recruit. So many entrepreneurial companies make mistakes in the accounting end of the business. Many start shipping products before confirming that the orders are good, or that the customers will take the product, or that the accounts are collectible. Such endeavors are more concerned about making a short-term sales quota than about maximizing the long-term revenue stream.

Granted, the pressure on new businesses to make sales quotas is strong. And that's precisely why the company needs a very, very tough accounting department. Otherwise, it will get into trouble. I always ask what kind of chief financial officer the entrepreneurs plan to bring on board. If they understand the need for someone who will scrutinize the operation closely and impose appropriate controls, they are more likely to be able to translate their strategy into a going concern.

This may go without saying, but I also look at a person's motivation, commitment, and energy. Hard work alone doesn't bring success, of course, but all the effective entrepreneurs I've known have worked long, hard hours. And there's something more than the number of hours: the intensity of the hours. I think of two software entrepreneurs I know who are going at 110 miles per hour, 18 hours per day, 7 days a week. And they have instilled their intensity and their belief in the business in all the people who work for them.

Belief in the business, clearly, is critical. If you're going to succeed, you must have a burning desire to develop your idea; you must believe so firmly in the idea that everything else pales in comparison. I usually can tell the difference between people who have that fire in their stomachs and those who see their ideas primarily as a way to get rich. Far too many people are interested in building a financial empire instead of a great company.

I want to build great companies. That's how I get my kicks. I look for people who want the same thing.

At a presentation I gave recently, the audience's questions were all along the same lines: "What are the secrets to writing a business plan?" "How do I get in touch with venture capitalists?" "What percentage of the equity do I have to give to them?" No one asked me how to build a business! And here's a question that both amused me and bothered me: "How do I get rid of the venture capitalists after they've made their investment?"

I'm looking for entrepreneurs who ask, "How can I make this business a success?"—not "How do I make a fortune?" And I prefer someone who *wants* me to play a role in the enterprise's decision making. Obviously, when they come to me entrepreneurs are interested in getting my money. Many have the attitude, "Uh oh, is this guy going to want to come to staff meetings and open his big mouth?" But they should realize that I can be a resource for them in more ways than one. I've been around for a long time; there just aren't many business problems that I haven't seen before. And most entrepreneurs can use all the help they can get in developing and implementing the tactics that will make them successful in the long run.

When I talk to entrepreneurs, I'm evaluating not only their motivation but also their character, fiber. And the issue I set the most store by is whether they are honest with themselves. It's essential to be totally, brutally honest about how well— or how badly—things are going. It's also very difficult.

Too many businesspeople delude themselves. They want so much to believe that they listen only to what they want to hear and see only what they want to see. A good example is a top executive in the parallel-processing industry; he believed his engineering people when they told him the product would be ready on time, and he believed his marketing people when they told him how much they could sell. So he developed a sales staff and doubled the size of the plant and built up inventories before he had a product to sell. The computer was late because of some last-minute bugs, and he was stuck with it all. The first 98% of designing a computer is easy; the bugs always come up in the last 2%. Fixing the problems took time, which ate up all kinds of overhead. And when he was finally ready, he couldn't meet the company's forecasts— which had been unrealistic from the beginning.

This story illustrates well my thesis that strategy is easy, execution is hard. The company's product was two years ahead of its competition. Execution of the idea, however, was terrible. That the strategy was good is obvious now; several other manufacturers have entered the field and are doing very well. But the company has lost the competitive advantage it would have enjoyed if its management had been better.

I can cite a similar example, also from the computer industry. The three people who started the company were the president, the manager of the software division, and the manager of the hardware division. The two managers kept telling the president that things were going swimmingly, and he wanted to believe what they said. Then one day, faced with an order the company couldn't fill, the software division manager called the president, who was out of town, and let forth a blast that in essence said, "We've been making a lot of mistakes we haven't told you about. We're at least a year behind."

Now, that's a ridiculous situation; the president should have known the status of product development. He had enough background in the field, and he knew the managers well enough that he shouldn't have been caught by surprise.

But he didn't look closely enough, and he didn't ask the right questions. In the meantime, the business had a rather large marketing and sales force. Then the question became whether to keep the sales force (which by this time was fully trained but doing nothing) or to let everyone go and wait for the software to be finished. If the latter, they'd have to hire and train a new sales force—a no-win situation either way.

Failure to be honest with yourself is a problem in any business, but it is especially disastrous in an entrepreneurial company, where the risk-reward stakes are so high. As an entrepreneur, you can't afford to make mistakes because you don't have the time and resources needed to recover. Big corporations can live with setbacks and delays in their "skunkworks"; in a start-up situation, you'd better be right the first time.

After being honest with yourself, the next most essential characteristic for the entrepreneur is to know whom to listen to and when to listen, and then which questions to ask. Sometimes CEOs listen only to what they want to hear because of fear of the truth; in other cases, it's because they are arrogant or have surrounded themselves with yes-men/women. A lot of managers simply will not accept criticism or suggestions from other people; they demand absolute loyalty from their subordinates and call disloyal anybody who tries to tell them something they don't want to hear.

It's usually easy to spot this trait by the way someone talks with outsiders about the organization. If an entrepreneur says, "This guy's lousy and that one doesn't know what she's doing, but I saved the company"— or if he or she explains how brilliantly he or she performed at his last job, in spite of being fired—I get wary. That kind of attitude is a red flag, like the statement, "I'll be honest with you": you know you're not getting the whole story.

To be sure, there's a thin line between refusing to accept criticism and sticking to your guns. Good entrepreneurs are committed to their ideas. In fact, I knew one company was in trouble when the CEO accepted almost everything I told him without argument or question. But some people have an almost perverse desire to prove to the world that their way is the right way—and the only way. I remember one CEO who had a great strategy—an idea for a unique computer architecture—but who refused to accept any advice on anything from anyone, including potential customers. He ended up with a product that had to be totally re-engineered and a weak staff. The company is now under new management and may be able to make something out of what is still a good idea, but the CEO's tunnel vision sure stalled it at the starting gate.

Another important quality—one that also has to do with taking a hard look at oneself and one's situation—is to know when to bring in skills from outside and what kind of skills.

As I see it, a company's growth has three stages. During the start-up, the entrepreneur does everything himself: he or she is involved in engineering the product, making sales calls, and so on. After a while, the company grows and others are hired to do these things—a vice president of sales, a vice president of engineering—but they report directly to him, and he or she still knows everything that's going on.

The company reaches the third stage when it hits, say $100 million to $200 million in sales. At that point, it's just too large for the president to be involved in all the doings. More management layers are in place and a fleet of executive vice presidents, and it now calls for entirely different skills to run the company than it did during its infancy. The president has to get work done by delegating it to other people and get information through two or more organizational layers.

The ideal would be a president who could manage a company at all three stages, starting the business from scratch and staying involved until retirement. Alfred Sloan at General Motors and Tom Watson at IBM were able to do just that, and the leaders of Teledyne and Intel have done it more recently.

But not all entrepreneurs can manage a large company. And many do not want to. Some people who relish business start-ups are simply not interested in running a formal, multi-tier organization. After Cray Computer grew to a fairly good size, for example, Seymour Cray wanted to get back to designing computers. Similarly, Apple Computer's Steve Wozniak and Steve Jobs (at least in the early stages) recognized that their genius was technical and promotional, not managerial, and that they needed experienced, professional managers to oversee their company's growth.

Other entrepreneurs have been less aware of their own limitations. Consider the experience of Diasonics and Daisy. Both flourished when they were small enough that their founders were able to control all aspects of the business. But they grew too fast, and the managers didn't realize that they now needed a different style of management and control. In both cases, a resounding initial success turned into an ignominious mess. As a result, both enterprises were reorganized.

Sometimes problems arise because the entrepreneur doesn't grasp the importance of strong management. I know of one young company that has already gone through two CEOs and is looking for a third. On the plus side, the men who founded the business acknowledged that they were engineers, not managers, and they went out and looked for a CEO. They considered their strategy so brilliant, though, that they figured anyone could carry if off. The first man they hired talked a good game but had been a disaster at two other corporations; eventually they had to let him go. He just couldn't manage the company. Then the directors hired another CEO who lasted only a few months. The company's product is still a good one, but without equally good leadership it may die in infancy.

The point of these examples is simple. If entrepreneurs do not have the skills required to manage the company, they should bring in an experienced professional. And they should never settle for someone mediocre by telling themselves that the business is such a winner that it doesn't need the management and controls that other companies do.

A great idea won't make it without great management. I am sometimes asked whether there is an "entrepreneurial personality." I suppose there are certain common qualities—a high energy level, strong commitment, and so on—but there are as many different personal styles as there are entrepreneurs. Henry Singleton of Teledyne, for example, reminds me of Charles de Gaulle. He has a singleness of purpose, a tenacity that is just overpowering. He gives you absolute confidence in his ability to accomplish whatever he says he is going to do. Yet he's rather aloof, operating more or less by himself and dreaming up ideas in his corner office.

Max Palevsky, formerly at Scientific Data Systems (SDS), is, by contrast, a very warm person. At SDS he'd joke around with his employees and cajole them into doing what needed to be done. His very informal style was evidenced by his open shirt and feet up on the desk.

The CEO's personality is extremely important because it permeates the company, but there's no one style that seems to work better than another. What *is* important is to *have* a style. An "average Joe" won't inspire others and lead a business to success.

I look for an entrepreneur who can manage. A conventional manager isn't risk oriented enough to succeed with a new venture, while an entrepreneur without managerial savvy is just another promoter.

Good entrepreneurs are tough-minded, with themselves and with their teams. They can make hard decisions. They have to be able to say, "No, that won't work" to colleagues who come to them with ideas, or to say, "That's a good idea but we can't do it because we have other priorities." To make such professional judgments, managers should ideally be well versed in the technology on which the company is based.

There are exceptions, of course. John Sculley at Apple Computer comes immediately to mind. When Apple was looking for someone to fill the top slot, it instructed the executive recruiter to find a CEO with a technical computer background. But the recruiter asked Apple to consider someone from left field (from the soft-drink industry), and I need not point out that the results were excellent. It was a lucky fit. In fact, as far as the "secrets of entrepreneurial success" go, it's important to recognize that a little bit of luck helps and a lot of luck is even better.

Another company I know, formed by two young, inexperienced men, benefited from a lucky break. Though very knowledgeable, they seriously underestimated how long it would take to write the 1,500,000 lines of software code they needed to launch their product. Consequently, they were two years late in bringing the product to market. But the market was also slow in developing. If the product had been ready on time, the company probably would have gone bankrupt trying to sell something for which the market wasn't ready. As it turned out, the market and the product were ready at the same time, and the company could exploit the product without competition. Many business success stories are due at least in part to simple good luck.

I emphasize people rather than products, and for good reason. The biggest problem in starting high-tech businesses is the shortage of superior managers. There is too much money chasing too few good managers.

I have always preferred to wait and have entrepreneurs come to me, to approach me because they have a great desire to build a business. Now with all the megafunds available, it's often the venture capitalist who goes out to start a company and looks for people who can head it up.

Those who call us "vulture capitalists" do have a point; some venture capitalists lure away a company's best people, thus hampering its growth. How can an enterprise develop and thrive when its top executives are always being pursued to start new companies? Unfortunately, in the high-tech industries, more and more businesses are being formed simply to make a buck. As for myself, though, I will continue to look for the best people, not the largest untapped market or the highest projected returns or the cleverest business strategy.

After all, a good idea, unless it's executed, remains only a good idea. Good managers, on the other hand, can't lose. If their strategy doesn't work, they can develop another one. If a competitor comes along, they can turn to something else. Great people make great companies, and that's the kind of company I want to be a part of.

Copyright © 1987; revised 1991.

──── DISCUSSION QUESTIONS

1. "Strategy is easy," the author says, "but tactics are hard." What are the qualities of a good strategist and a good tactician? What can go wrong if an entrepreneur performs well in only one of these roles?

2. Rock distinguishes between a financial empire and a great company. What else, besides high sales and profits, makes a company great in your view?

3. Rock places great importance on the entrepreneur's character and describes the qualities that he thinks matter most. Are these qualities innate or can they be cultivated? What qualities would you add to the list?

4. "I prefer someone who *wants* me to play a role in the enterprise's decision making. . . . most entrepreneurs can use all the help they can get in developing and implementing the tactics that will make them successful in the long run." Would you welcome or be wary of this attitude in a venture capitalist? What questions would you ask to ascertain in more detail how Rock conceives his roles and responsibilities?

5. "Belief in the business," Rock says, "is critical." How does having strong conviction serve the entrepreneur's interests? What dangers can it pose?

19   Aspects of Financial Contracting in Venture Capital

WILLIAM A. SAHLMAN

Once the entrepreneur has determined what resources the venture needs, identified the most likely avenues for pursuing them, and learned the ins and outs of fund raising, he or she must be prepared to enter negotiations with investors and make a deal.

All deals have certain elements in common. They take place in an uncertain environment. They require resolution of a few key questions: How are cash and risk allocated? What are the incentives for each of the partners in the deal? Beyond these basics, endless variations on a theme are possible. Through a series of examples illustrating transactions between an entrepreneur and a venture capitalist, this reading suggests the numerous possibilities for structuring deals and distinguishing between the characteristics of a sensible deal and a bad deal. As these examples demonstrate, financing terms can be crucial in determining the ultimate value of an investment—for both entrepreneur and venture capitalist.

The interaction of entrepreneur and venture capitalist has resulted in the evolution of a unique set of financial contracts. And in no other kind of transaction does the implied link between value and financial structure appear so strong and direct as in the typical venture capital deal. As I hope to show in this reading, an effective financial design may well be the difference between a flourishing and a failed (if not a still-born) enterprise.

—— FIRST PRINCIPLES

As is true of all financial transactions, structuring a venture capital deal involves the allocation of economic value. Value, in turn, is determined by the interaction of three major ingredients: cash, risk, and time.

My colleague Bill Fruhan argues that all financial transactions can be classified into three categories: those that create value, those that destroy value, and those that transfer value between two or more parties.[1] This taxonomy can

---

1. William E. Fruhan, Jr., *Financial Strategy: Studies in the Creation, Transfer, and Destruction of Shareholder Value* (Homewood, Ill.: Richard D. Irwin, Inc., 1979).

be readily transferred to venture capital because almost all venture capital deals either create, destroy, or transfer value. For example, a sound deal that provides appropriate incentives for an entrepreneur is likely to result in significantly higher value to be shared by entrepreneur and venture capitalist alike. The same deal, while increasing total value, may also have opposite effects on the value of two different claims on total value (for example, debt and equity), thus providing an example of a value transfer. Finally, a promising deal that is not well designed can result in a failed venture, the extreme case of value destruction.

A SIMPLE EXAMPLE

Before turning to the case of venture capital, let's begin by considering a very simple project with the following characteristics:

Investment required at time 0	$1000
Annual cash flow	$500
Total number of cash payments	5
Terminal value (end of year 5)	$1000

The resulting cash flows are put in *Exhibit 1*. Suppose also that the payment of these cash flows is guaranteed by the government and that the current appropriate (risk-free) discount rate is 10%.

In this case, the present value of the future cash flows is $2,516, and the net present value of the project is $1,516. If you owned the rights to this investment project, you would be indifferent between selling the rights to another person (with the same information) for $1,516 or keeping the project for yourself. Any offer above that value would induce you to sell. In this simple deal, the cash flows are known with certainty by both the buyer and the seller. Moreover, each agrees, or is likely to agree, on the appropriate discount rate to apply to convert future cash flows to the present. And, finally, the expected cash flows are not affected by any action by the buyer or the seller. Given these conditions, it is easy to describe the terms on which a deal such as this one will trade.

EXHIBIT 1

PERIOD	0	1	2	3	4	5
Investment	(1,000)					
Cash inflow		500	500	500	500	500
Terminal value						1,000
Net cash flow	(1,000)	500	500	500	500	1,500

DEALMAKING IN THE REAL WORLD

If the world consisted principally of investment projects like this one, then the study of deals would not be very important, or very interesting. In the real world, however, the following conditions are far more likely to apply:

- The future cash flows are unknown (both in amount and timing);
- The appropriate discount rate is unknown;
- Any two parties analyzing the same deal will disagree about the future cash flows, the appropriate discount rate to apply, or both;
- The sources of potential disagreement are many and range from simple disagreement based on common knowledge to the fact that the parties may be governed by different rules (for example, tax treatment) to the possibility that one party knows more than the other;
- There will be conflicts of interest: one or more of the dealmakers may be in a position to influence the outcome of the project so as to benefit at the expense of the other participants; and
- The terms that govern the allocation of the cash flows will themselves affect the nature (amount, timing, and risk) of the cash flow stream.

Now, take the same basic expected cash inflows and outflows from the example above, but introduce uncertainty. That is, the annual cash flow is *expected* to be $500 per year, but the actual number will only be known over time. In this case, it may be appropriate to apply a higher discount rate than before (especially if the new risk includes a systematic, or market-related, component).

Suppose the appropriate discount rate were 20% instead of 10%. In this case, the present value of the cash flows would be $1,897 (instead of $2,516), and thus the net present value would be $897 (instead of $1,516). If someone offered you $1,000 today for the right to exercise the option to invest in this project, then you would gladly sign it over. If you were to offer to sell for $800, then any investor would gladly buy.

In the preceding paragraph, I assumed that buyers and sellers could agree on the expected cash flows and on the discount rate. Obviously, Pandora's box could be opened further, and the introduction of differences and disagreements between dealmakers will reveal many other grounds on which to trade.

If, for example, the parties to the deal disagree about the magnitude or the nature of the risk inherent in the cash flow, then they will apply different discount rates in their analysis. This sort of disagreement may render impossible an agreement on an appropriate price. Or, it may expand the set of possible deal terms. For example, if the potential seller used a discount rate of 20% and the buyer thought 10% to be the correct figure, then there would be a wide range of prices (in this case, between $897 and $1,516) at which the seller would gladly sell and the buyer willingly buy the right to make the investment. Or, if the buyer thought the cash flows would rise at an annual rate of 5%, then even if the buyer and seller used the same discount rate (of 20%), they would both be willing to accept a price between $897 (the seller's minimum) and $1,026 (the buyer's maximum).

ALLOCATING CASH FLOW

Now the fun starts. Suppose this generic deal is now called a start-up venture, and the two parties negotiating are identified as the entrepreneur and the venture capitalist. The venture capitalist uses a discount rate of 40% for projects like the one under consideration. The question is, what proportion of the equity will the venture capitalist demand in order to justify investing the $1,000 capital required to get the project off the ground?

To answer this question, you must determine what proportion of each future cash flow figure would provide a 40% annual rate of return to the venture capitalist, given an initial investment of $1,000. One way to attack this problem is to calculate the present value of the gross future cash flows, using the venture capitalist's 40% required return. In so doing, we find that the present value is equal to $1,204.

This is the total "value pie" to be split between entrepreneur and venture capitalist. If the venture capitalist only needs to invest $1,000 to receive all of these cash flows, then he would increase his net present value by $204. If the venture capitalist owned only 83% ($1,000/$1,204) of the deal, however, then the present value of his share of the future cash flows would be $1,000, exactly equal to the cost of the investment. Therefore, the venture capitalist would willingly pay $1,000 to buy 83% of the equity in this hypothetical venture because the anticipated return would be 40% per year. The entrepreneur would be left with the remaining 17% of the equity, corresponding to $204 divided by $1,204.

ALLOCATING RISKS

The analytics described above are straightforward and are based on some simplifying assumptions. Suppose, however, that the venture capitalist and the entrepreneur are in the process of negotiating a deal and that the forecasts are those included in the company's business plan. The venture capitalist, having seen hundreds of unfulfilled "conservative" projections in the past, is skeptical about the numbers. Partly, his skepticism is already reflected in the higher discount rate applied to the estimates, a discount rate that is higher than the true expected return on the venture capital portfolio. Other than buying simple common equity, and thus implicitly agreeing to a proportional risk-reward sharing scheme, how else could the venture capitalist structure a deal with the entrepreneur to assuage his skepticism? (See *Exhibit 2*).

EXHIBIT 2

Common Stock (Proportional Sharing)	Venture Capitalist		Entrepreneur		Total	
Share of total stock		83%		17%		100%
Annual cash received: Bad scenario	$ 373	83	$ 77	17	$ 450	100
Annual cash received: Good scenario	456	83	94	17	550	100
Expected annual cash received	415	83	85	17	500	100
PV of cash received (incl. TV)	1,000	83	204	17	1,204	100
Net PV (incl. investment)	0		204		204	100
Std. dev'n of PV (and of NPV)	85	83	18	17	102	100

Preferred Stock	Venture Capitalist		Entrepreneur		Total	
Share of total stock		83%		17%		100%
Annual cash received: Bad scenario	$ 415	93	$ 35	7	$ 450	100
Annual cash received: Good scenario	415	73	135	27	550	100
Expected annual cash received	415	83	85	17	500	100
PV of cash received (incl. TV)	1,000	83	204	17	1,204	100
Net PV (incl. investment)	0		204		204	100
Std. dev'n of PV (and of NPV)	0	0	102	100	102	100

One possibility would be to invest in the form of preferred (or, more commonly, convertible preferred) stock.[2] In this alternative, the venture capitalist would have a prior claim on the earnings of the company and may also have a prior claim on the liquidation value of the company. Suppose, for example, that the venture capitalist asks for a preferred stock that entitles him to receive up to $415 in the form of dividends from the company each year before the entrepreneur receives anything. (Note that $415 is equal to 83% of the expected cash flow of $500.) Also assume that the two parties split the $1,000 return of capital in the final year according to the original 83%/17% rule. What has changed?

In this new situation, a great deal has changed; there has been a major shift in risk from the venture capitalist to the entrepreneur. This shift in risk occurs even though the expected return to each party remains the same. To explore this risk-shifting process, suppose there were really two different, but

---

2. Convertible preferred is the convention; we use straight preferred for purposes of simplicity in exposition.

equally likely scenarios for future cash flows. In the first, the actual cash flows turn out to be $450 per year. In the other, the cash flows are $550 per year. The terminal value is the same under either scenario.

Obviously, under both the proportional sharing rule and the new preferred stock arrangement, the expected total annual cash flow is $500, the expected total present value is $1,204, and the expected total net present value is $204. The standard deviation of the total expected present value is $102.

Under the straight equity deal, the venture capitalist and entrepreneur share proportionately (83%/17%) both the risk and the reward. That is, the venture capitalist has an expected present value of $1,000, an expected net present value of $0, and a standard deviation of expected present value of $85; the entrepreneur has an expected present value of $204, an expected net present value of $204, and a standard deviation of expected present value of $18. Note that the total risk in the project, as measured by the standard deviation, is split according to the 83%/17% rule.

Under the new preferred stock deal, however, the venture capitalist has managed to shift all of the risk to the entrepreneur. That is, given the narrow range of possible cash flow outcomes, the venture capitalist will always receive his $415 per annum cash flow. The entrepreneur, however, will no longer receive 17% of the cash flows regardless of the actual cash flow; instead, he will receive $35 per year in the bad scenario (7% of the expected value) and $135 in the favorable scenario (27%). The standard deviation of the venture capitalist's return is now zero, while the standard deviation of the entrepreneur's present value is $102.

The reader should ignore the fact that the example is contrived and slightly silly. No investor would demand a 40% return for a riskless project. Also, the lower and upper bound of possible annual cash flows are purely arbitrary and meant only to simplify the example to show how risk is shifted from one party to the other. In the real world, the lower bound would almost always be significantly lower than the expected value of the venture capitalist's share, thus forcing the venture capitalist to bear enough risk to justify use of a 40%-return requirement. And if the lower bound were below the expected value of the venture capitalist's share, then the expected present value would be lower than in the previous scenarios unless the entrepreneur were required to meet the shortfall in preferred stock dividends out of his own pocket, or the venture capitalist were entitled to receive a bonus payment during the favorable scenario.

Why would the venture capitalist suggest using preferred stock rather than straight equity? The obvious reason would be to try to improve his reward-to-risk ratio. But simply transferring risk to the entrepreneur by gaining liquidation preferences is probably not the primary motive for structuring venture capital deals this way. Two other possibilities come to mind: (1) by increasing the entrepreneur's risk, the venture capitalist is trying to "smoke out" the entrepreneur and get the entrepreneur to signal whether he really does believe the forecasts in the business plan; and (2) the venture capitalist is trying to provide the strongest possible incentives for the entrepreneur to do at least as well as projected. If the business exceeds plan, then the entrepreneur will share disproportionately in the benefits of doing so. Given the entrepreneur's strong incentives to beat the plan, structuring the deal this way may actually increase the probability that a more favorable outcome will occur.

SUMMING UP

Let's stop here for a moment and briefly review our progress to this point.

The process of financial contracting in venture capital focuses on a few very simple questions:

- How is cash allocated?
- How is risk allocated?
- What are the incentives for both parties in the deal?

In the examples above, we looked at two simple versions of common arrangements for sharing risk and reward. In the first example, a proportional sharing scheme was employed. In the second, a nonproportional scheme was introduced in which the venture capitalist demanded a fixed dollar return, regardless of the actual outcomes.

There are of course a myriad of possible variations on this theme. It is possible to combine proportional sharing schemes with fixed hurdles. Or, the timing of the hurdles can be altered. There are also many other mechanisms for affecting the allocation of value and the implicit incentives in a given deal. What is important to note, at this point, is that investors can infer information about the abilities and convictions of entrepreneurs by offering different deal terms and gauging the response. The ability to signal intentions credibly may enable some entrepreneurs to obtain funding that would not have been available were there no means for communicating true abilities or convictions.

STAGED CAPITAL COMMITMENT

Suppose you present an investment proposal to a venture capitalist that calls for an expenditure of $20 million to build a semiconductor fabrication facility. The $20 million will be required over a three-year period. How will the venture capitalist respond to your offer to sell him 75 percent ownership of the venture for $20 million?

After picking himself up off the floor, the venture capitalist will begin a process of trying to educate you about the real world. And, if he has not been too offended by your proposal, he will make a counter-proposal. The terms of

EXHIBIT 3

ROUND OF FINANCING	AMOUNT INVESTED THIS ROUND	% REC'D THIS ROUND	CUMULATIVE		IMPLIED VALUATION (POST MONEY)
			VC'S SHARE	FOUNDER'S SHARE	
First round	$ 1,000,000	50.0%	50.0%	50.0%	$ 2,000,000
Second round	4,000,000	33.3	66.7	33.3	12,000,000
Third round	15,000,000	25.0	75.0	25.0	60,000,000

the counter-offer will likely call for staged infusions of capital over time. In the first round, for example, the venture capitalist might offer to invest $1 million for the purpose of assembling the managerial team, writing a business plan, completing engineering specifications, conducting market research, and testing the feasibility of the process.

The $1 million capital would be expected to last about nine months. At that point, the venture would be expected to raise additional capital for the purpose of building a prototype manufacturing plant. That process might require $4 million in capital. Finally, there would be plans for a third round of financing for the purpose of building a full-scale manufacturing facility and beginning to market. The investment required at that point might be $15 million.

With respect to valuation at each stage of the process, it is entirely possible that the entrepreneur will end up owning the 25% share that he demanded in the initial negotiation. But the process by which that ownership is attained will be very different. One plausible scenario is described in *Exhibit 3*.

In this plan, the company raises the total of $20 million over three rounds. At each point new capital is infused into the company, the valuation increases. In the first round, for example, the venture capitalist demands 50% of the company for only $1 million. In the last round, however, the venture capitalist is content to receive only 25% of the company in return for $15 million, thus implying a post-money evaluation of $60 million.[3]

Why does the venture capitalist demand that capital be staged over time rather than committed up-front? Why would any self-respecting entrepreneur accept such a process? Remember that the venture is scheduled to run out of capital periodically; if it cannot raise capital at the second or third rounds, then it goes out of business and the entrepreneur is out of a job.

---

3. Note that, although the venture capitalist purchases a third of the company in this round, he only increases his cumulative share by a sixth (to 66.7%). When a company issues new shares of stock to raise capital, the resulting dilution is essentially charged proportionately to each existing shareholder. Thus, the venture capitalist's share increases only by that portion of the new equity he does not already hold. To compute the cumulative shares: *Second Round:* 50.0% + (33.3% x (1–50.0%))=66.7%; *Third Round:* 66.7% + (25.0% x (1–66.7%)) = 75.0%.

To begin to understand the reasons underlying this seemingly peculiar process, it is important to think about how the venture under consideration will evolve over time. In particular, what new information will the venture capitalist and the entrepreneur have at each point that the company goes back to raise capital?

Consider the point at which the company needs to raise $4 million. At this point, the venture capitalist and entrepreneur will know how the company has performed relative to its initial business plan. What is the management team like? How do they work together? Does the new business plan make sense? Has the company developed complete engineering specs? How has the perceived opportunity changed? Does the market research reveal adequate demand? What new competition exists? How have valuations in the capital market changed since the previous financing round? These are the types of questions that can be answered at the end of the first nine months of operation. If all goes well, the major risks outstanding at the time of the first round of financing—the "people risk" due to the lack of a complete management team, the technical risk from the lack of product specification, and the market risk due to the lack of market research—will have been greatly reduced. If so, the venture capitalist will be willing to buy shares at a much higher price, thus in effect accepting a lower expected rate of return.

If the company continues to proceed as hoped while approaching the third round of financing, there should be a similar reduction in perceived risk to the investor. Whereas, at the second round, consulting engineers could evaluate the product specifications for the venture capitalist, now there will be an actual product. Market research and initial marketing should by now have produced verifiable interest in the product, if not a backlog of orders. At this stage, then, the venture capitalist is evaluating an investment in a real product, within a known competitive context, on the eve of full-scale production and marketing. The increase in valuation at the third round reflects the further reduction of risk of investing at this point.

Suppose, however, that all does not go according to plan. At the time the $4 million is required, the company has not done well, and there are new competitors not previously anticipated. At this point, the venture capitalist can either abandon ship and allow the company to fail, or can strike a new price with the entrepreneur that reflects the less sanguine outlook. For example, the venture capitalist might demand as much as 50% of the company for his $4 million, implying a total valuation of only $8 million.

The point here is simple: by staging the commitment of capital the venture capitalist gains the options to abandon and to revalue the project as new information arrives. These are extremely valuable options, as will be demonstrated later.

But does this process make sense from the standpoint of the entrepreneur? Go back to the original proposal. Remember that the entrepreneur asked for $20 million in return for 75% of the shares. It seems likely that, even if the venture capitalist had been willing to consider the offer, he would have demanded a much higher share of the company than 75%, given the enormous risk as of the first round. This would likely have created a situation in which neither side would have found it sensible to proceed. The entrepreneur would have had too little incentive to risk his career, and the venture capitalist would have been worried about this loss of motivation. (As a general rule, if there does not appear to be enough room to provide sufficient incentives to management, then the deal probably won't get done.)

THE VALUE OF THE OPTION TO ABANDON

Why do the venture capitalist and the entrepreneur seem to end up better off under the alternative of staged capital commitment? To explore this issue, it will make sense to return to our simple example at the beginning. For a $1,000 initial investment, the projected cash flows were $500 per year for each of five years, followed by a $1,000 return of capital at the end of the fifth year. Suppose that instead of a simple $1,000 investment up-front, the investment can be made in two stages of $500 each. Suppose also that there is great uncertainty about the future annual cash flows to be received. There is a 50% chance they will be $50 per year and a 50% chance they will turn out to be $950 per year; and the expected value thus remains $500 per year.

We will now explore two different sets of rules governing this investment project. In the first, the venture capitalist has no choice but to invest the second $500 in the second year; that is, even if the actual annual cash flows turn out to be $50, the $500 will be spent. Under the second set of rules, the venture capitalist has the right, or option, to decide whether or not to invest the second $500. He can make this decision at the end of the first year, just after he has learned what the actual annual cash flows will be. If he decides not to invest (that is, to abandon the project) then he forfeits the right to receive any of the annual cash flows and receives a reduced share, $750, of the terminal payment of $1,000. The different possible sets of cash flows are provided in *Exhibit 4*.

What is the present value of the investment project under the different sets of rules? Evaluating the first is easy; the expected present value of the cash inflows and outflows is $846 and the expected net present value is $346. Note that the latter figure is higher than the $204 determined in the previous section because the venture capitalist is now allowed to defer investing $500 for one year.

Under the second set of rules, the venture capitalist must evaluate whether or not it makes sense to invest in the second year, after the actual cash flows are revealed. If the cash flows turn out to be $950 per year, then the venture capitalist would be crazy not to spend the $500 necessary to receive the annual cash flows. (An investment that required investing $500 to receive $950 immediately, not to mention $950 for four years and an additional $250 of terminal value, has an infinite internal rate of return.)

EXHIBIT 4

	0	1	2	3	4	5	PV @ 40%
Rule I: VC Must Invest in Both Years							
Good scenario		$950	$950	$950	$950	$950	$1,933
Bad scenario		50	50	50	50	50	$ 102
Expected Ann's cash		500	500	500	500	500	$1,018
Terminal value						1,000	$ 186
Expected cash in.		500	500	500	500	1,500	$1,204
Investment	($500)	(500)					($ 857)
Expected net cash	($500)	$ 0	$500	$500	$500	$1500	$ 346
	0	**1**	**2**	**3**	**4**	**5**	**PV @ 40%**
Rule II: VC Has Option to Abandon in Year One							
Good scenario							
Annual cash flow		$950	$950	$950	$950	$950	$1,933
Terminal value						1,000	$ 186
Investment	($500)	(500)					($ 857)
Net cash flow	($500)	$450	$950	$950	$950	$1,950	$1,262
Bad scenario							
Annual cash flow		$ 0				$ 0	
Terminal value						750	$ 139
Investment	($500)						($ 500)
Net cash flow	($500)	$ 0	$ 0	$ 0	$ 0	$750	($ 361)
Expected (or average) value of scenarios[1]							
Expected net cash	($500)	$225	$475	$475	$475	$1,225	$ 451

1. Expected value of option to abandon (Rule I – Rule II): $104

If, however, the cash flows turn out to be only $50 per year, then the venture capitalist has a tougher analysis. If he invests $500, he will receive $50 immediately and $50 a year for 4 years, as well as an additional $250 in terminal value. If he chooses not to invest, he will forfeit the $50 payment stream and the additional terminal value.

Given a discount rate of 40%, it turns out that he is much better off deciding not to invest. The net present value of the incremental investment from that point forward is –$292. By not investing, the venture capitalist raises the net present value of the project as a whole, as of year 1, from –$97 to $195, thus "creating" $292 in value.

After determining the optimal decision, conditional on the arrival of new information, the venture capitalist can then evaluate the entire project looking forward. Because he can cut off the investment process if the cash flows turn out to be low, the venture capitalist has an expected present value of $951 and an expected net present value of $451.

The new expected net present value of $451 can be compared to the $346 determined when the venture capitalist had no choice. Somehow, an extra $104 of value has been created simply by changing the rules a little bit. This difference is the value of the option to abandon. To gain this option, the venture capitalist would be willing to invest up to an additional $104 at the outset for a given level of ownership.

In this regard, the process of estimating the value of the option to abandon is usually far more complex than that described above. This is so because the number of possible scenarios is effectively infinite, as is the number of points in time at which the value of continuing the project must be evaluated. Despite the obvious complexity of the real world, financial economists have devised promising techniques for valuing such operating options by using an offshoot of option pricing theory called "contingent claims analysis."[4]

This analysis reveals, among other things, that the value of the option to abandon is higher under the following conditions:

- The greater the uncertainty about the future value of the venture;
- The greater the amount of time before the actual decision to abandon must be made; and
- The higher the ratio of the value of the abandoned project (the liquidation value) to the value of the project if pursued (present value of additional free cash flow less additional investment).

It is important to note that the traditional process of calculating expected net present values does not give the same answer as the process described above, in which each decision is evaluated at each point in time and the decision tree folded back to the present assuming optimal decisions are made at each intermediate point in time. In our example, to be sure, the difference in approaches does not change the basic fact that the project looks good. But it is very easy to imagine situations in which the value of the option to abandon might be sufficiently high to change the net present value from negative to positive. Such might be the case when there is great uncertainty and the investor has the option to stage the capital investment over time. But, this is exactly the case in most venture capital investments; and this is why one almost always sees staged capital commitment in these investments.

APPLICATION TO DEALMAKING

From the above analysis, it seems clear that a driving force behind staged capital commitment is the preservation of the option to abandon. This

---

4. *See* Volume 5, Number 1 of the *Midlands Corporate Finance Journal,* which is devoted almost entirely to the applications of contingent claims analysis in capital budgeting.

option has great value to the venture capitalist. And, indeed, the option is exercised relatively frequently in the real world.

But let's return once more to the view of the entrepreneur. Because the option to abandon is valuable to the venture capitalist doesn't necessarily mean, after all, that it adds value for the entrepreneur. Wouldn't the entrepreneur almost always be better off if the venture capitalist committed all the required capital up-front?

While generalizations are dangerous, staged capital commitment probably makes as much sense for the entrepreneur as for the venture capitalist. The reason, as I suggested earlier, is that the entrepreneur has a chance to minimize the dilution he suffers by bringing in outside capital. Because there is more value initially (precisely because of the option to abandon), the share of value awarded to the venture capitalist is lower, holding all other things constant.

In addition, staged capital commitment not only provides the venture capitalist with the option to abandon, but also gives the entrepreneur the option to raise capital at a higher valuation. The entrepreneur is betting that there will be positive results on which to base higher and higher valuations as the company grows, thus necessitating less dilution at each stage that new capital is required. And the willingness of the entrepreneur to bet on himself, as we have seen, sends a positive signal to the venture capitalist.

The entrepreneur, then, faces a conflict of motives in raising capital. On the one hand, he is tempted to raise only the minimum necessary amount of capital to avoid selling too much stock in early rounds at low prices, thus suffering great dilution. At the same time, however, he is also tempted to raise excessive amounts of capital early to preserve the option to continue operations through tough times. Some have described this problem confronting the entrepreneur as "the horse race between fear and greed"—that is, between the fear of running out of capital and the desire to retain maximum possible ownership (and I will return to this later).

Finally, there is an additional and powerful reason why the deal should be structured in stages. There is no more powerful motivator than the knowledge that the enterprise is scheduled to run out of cash in the relatively near future. In the parlance of entrepreneurial finance, the rate at which a company consumes cash is called the "burn rate." Given any level of initial cash and a burn rate, it is possible to calculate the "fume date"—the date on which the company will have exhausted its cash and will be operating solely on fumes. The existence of periodic "fume dates" focuses the energies of management on creating value from limited resources; and this process can accrue to the benefit of both entrepreneur and venture capitalist.[5]

---

5. The reader should also keep in mind the tension that exists in such situations between the entrepreneur and the venture capitalist. For the venture capitalist, a single venture is but one of many. For the entrepreneur, the venture is all they have. Abstract discussions of the option to abandon should be tempered with knowledge that people's careers and egos are at stake.

To summarize, then, a common technique used in financing new ventures is to infuse capital over time, retaining the option to abandon the venture at any point that the net present value, looking forward, is negative. This technique appeals to venture capitalist and entrepreneur alike. The venture capitalist preserves a valuable option and also creates the strongest possible incentives for management to create value and meet goals. The entrepreneur minimizes dilution and also benefits to the extent that his energies are appropriately focused on value creation.

But while the above example tends to suggest that the preservation of such financing options is an unequivocal boon, the reader should also always keep in mind the fact that the real world is more complicated and that providing such options to the venture capitalist may create its own problems. For example, having a periodic "fume date" will work in many situations as a motivating factor. In others, though, it may create incentives to aim for short-term success rather than long-term value creation. This may or may not be in the best interests of both parties. Also, the future cash flows will never be known with any degree of certainty. Because of the great uncertainty remaining at any stage of development, some ventures will be abandoned even though they actually have excellent prospects; and some will be funded when they should not be.

It is worth noting in passing, however, that many successful companies have gone through periods when they came very close to their "fume date." Many have also had to change their business plans dramatically as new information was revealed. These realities often make the staged capital commitment process not only valuable to entrepreneur and venture capitalist alike, but also a very trying experience for anyone involved.

THE OPTION TO REVALUE A PROJECT

In the preceding section, the focus was on achieving some understanding of the option to abandon a given project. There are also steps short of abandonment that warrant consideration. The process of staged capital commitment involves periodically evaluating whether to continue funding and investment and, if so, on what terms. The right to revalue a given project has value when compared to an alternative situation in which the future financing terms are decided irrevocably at the start of the venture.

Suppose a venture starts with a 50/50 split in equity ownership between the entrepreneur and the venture capitalist. One year after the venture starts, the company needs more capital. The question is: At what price will the new capital come in? If the original deal awarded the venture capitalist the right to invest in future rounds at a price to be negotiated later, the answer will depend on the progress the company has made since its last funding as well as the state of the economy and capital markets at the time. If the prospects are good, then the value will be relatively high; if not, value will be low. In the former case, the entrepreneur will suffer minor dilution; in the event of poor performance, the dilution factor will be much larger.

Now, suppose that instead of flexible pricing on the second round of financing, the venture capitalist was granted a fixed price option at the beginning to buy one million shares at a price of $10.00 per share at any point within two years. If the justifiable per share price at the end of two years is above $10.00, then the venture capitalist will exercise the option. If the price is below $10.00, the venture capitalist will walk away from the option, thereby truncating the lower side of the return distribution.

But if the company really needs the $10 million, and the justifiable price is below $10.00 per share, then the money will not necessarily be forthcoming. Moreover, another outside investor might find the existence of the call option (actually warrants in this case) problematic in terms of investing because of the potential for future dilution if the company does succeed in increasing value above $10.00 per share. If the money cannot be raised, then the venture will suffer and may even fail.

Flexibility in future pricing can make the difference between a venture succeeding and failing when performance is not as favorable as expected. The reader might argue that no venture capitalist will walk away from a venture with value simply because of some inflexible deal provisions. But the situation described above has occurred many times and a complex game of "chicken" develops between the entrepreneurial team and the venture capitalists, in which each tries to obtain the best deal. The result of such a game can be very detrimental to the economic vitality of the enterprise. Moreover, it should also be remembered that the venture capital fund has many companies in its portfolio, and the venture capitalist may well decide to walk away from one investment that is not performing up to expectations even if doing so seems not to make sense.

THE OPTION TO INCREASE CAPITAL COMMITTED

Another option to be considered is the right to increase funding to a company, particularly if the company is doing well. Consider a start-up venture in the specialty retailing area. The company's business plan calls for having 20 stores in the Northeast by the end of two years. Suppose after the first year, the company has 6 stores, each of which is performing well above expectations. It might make sense for the entrepreneur and venture capitalist to accelerate the rate at which new stores are introduced. To do so will entail raising additional capital. The venture capitalist will welcome the opportunity to invest more heavily in such a successful venture and would like to lock in the right to do so. The entrepreneur, however, would want to ensure that the price at which additional capital is raised reflects the superior past performance and prospects of the company.

In this example, the right to increase capital invested at some interme- diate point is very valuable. One unresolved issue, however, is who should "own" the right to invest more money. To whom does the benefit of superior performance belong?

One way in which venture capitalists gain the right to invest more, while still allowing the entrepreneur to benefit from success, is by asking for rights of first refusal on all subsequent financings. By doing so, they buy the option to invest later, but only on whatever terms are deemed appropriate by the capital market.

In sum, there are a variety of financing options—options to abandon, to re-value, and to increase capital committed—built into the financing contracts fashioned by the professional venture capital community. Over the life of any venture capital portfolio, there are likely to be some losers, some winners, and some intermediate performers. Successful funds generate high rates of return by cutting their losses early, not investing great amounts in early rounds, and letting their winners run by investing larger amounts of money in multiple rounds of financing. Phrased differently, they frequently exercise their options to abandon and their options to participate in later rounds of financing. You will also discover that some of the most successful companies in their portfolios had a distress round of financing in which the ability to re-value the investment was the difference between continued financing and bankruptcy. Prominent examples are Federal Express and MCI Communications.

—— ANTICIPATING THE CONSEQUENCES OF FINANCING DECISIONS

Managers and capital suppliers are making extraordinarily complex decisions in environments characterized by great uncertainty. More important, they must live with the consequences of those decisions. One way to approach the task of decision making is to ask three questions before making a decision:

- What can go wrong?
- What can go right?
- What decisions can be made today and in the future that will maxi- mize the reward-to-risk ratio?

These simple questions are designed to force the decision maker to confront uncertainty directly and to manage the uncertainty.

One of the most critical issues in venture capital financing, as we have seen, is the decision whether to raise capital in excess of expected requirements. A risk common to virtually every venture ever started is that all will not go as planned and that the introduction of a product or the sales response will fail to meet expectations. It is also often the case that the company will have to change the focus of its efforts dramatically as it gathers more information about the opportunity.

To raise capital in excess of anticipated needs is equivalent to buying an option to change strategy as required or to keep the company on sound financial footing until results do match expectations. Of course, in gaining that option, the venture capitalist is denied valuable options to re-value or to abandon. One compromise is not to raise excess capital, but nevertheless to retain the option to call on the investors for additional capital if needed, in return for which the current equity round would have to be sold at a lower price.

Maximizing the reward-to-risk ratio also requires examining the other side of the spectrum—what can go right—and ensuring that in the event of the venture's success, the value created can be fruitfully harvested. One means of harvest is for the venture to be acquired after a period of years. The question is: what decisions can management make that will increase the likelihood that such a rewarding end to the venture will take place? In this regard, management must carefully avoid introducing any form of "poison pill" into its capital structure that will preclude a buyout offer.

To illustrate, some start-up companies raise capital from a major participant in the industry. Although doing so may provide necessary capital and some expertise or marketing, it may also mean that no other large competitor of the original funder will even consider an offer later on. A start-up can thus lose the option to market the company to the highest bidder in the industry. In this situation, as when any option is being given up, this route should be pursued only if there are sufficient offsetting benefits.

Venture capitalists often ensure that they will profit in the event of success by gaining the right to force the company to go public or the right to sell stock jointly with the company's public offering. By structuring an investment in the form of preferred stock, a venture capitalist can also profit from a success that is too modest to permit a public offering—that is, by recovering capital through the redemption of preferred stock and the payout of accumulated dividends. Such a structure also permits the venture capitalist to receive some payout in the form of dividends in the event of a "sideways" scenario.

The process of anticipating good or bad news and making decisions that maximize the chance that the good will outweigh the bad is a critical element of good decision making. Moreover, it is not all that difficult to decide what events, good or bad, are likely to occur in any venture over time. These events will occur with respect to:

- The people (e.g., death, motivation);
- The individual company (e.g., production or marketing issues);
- The industry in question (e.g., competition, substitutes);
- The sociological environment (social rules/legal system); and,
- The state of the economy and capital markets (e.g., boom, recession, lower or higher stock prices).

Sensible deals will preserve options to react to and receive maximum benefit from good news and will also protect the company from going under when bad news arises. Sensible deals will also provide strong incentives to all parties to skew the outcome toward the good news side of the ledger.

AN EXAMPLE OF A BAD DEAL

Anyone familiar with start-up companies recognizes that a common problem is that the company consumes more cash than was projected when it raised capital. Frequently, the primary cause is a shortfall in revenues which may occur for many different reasons. And because running out of cash is not an uncommon occurrence, any deal terms that govern the relationship between the company and the suppliers of capital must reflect the likelihood that the company will require more capital.

Unfortunately, deals are very often designed that make it extremely difficult to raise capital when the company needs to. For example, in one case, the original capital suppliers to a start-up demanded the option to acquire up to 51% of the common stock that would be outstanding at any time in the following three years. The option could be exercised at a fixed price equal to the price paid in the first round of financing. The same group also got the right of first refusal on all subsequent financings, for a period lasting 60 days.

There were several problems that arose as time passed. First the company's progress was disappointing when compared against the business plan projections. The result was that the company needed a significant infusion of capital long before anticipated. The logical supplier of the new capital was the group owning the option. But, there was a problem: the financing group had very little incentive to exercise their option early. Doing so would sacrifice the value of being able to wait to learn more about the company. And that value was considerable because of the length of time left on the option and the high risk involved in the venture.

On the other hand, potential new capital suppliers were confronted with the problem that they might be diluted immediately after they invested because the original financing group could then acquire up to 51% of the *then outstanding* shares at a fixed price. Moreover, because the group had a 60-day right of first refusal, the new potential investors also faced the possibility that the investment of time and energy required to evaluate the deal might go for naught if the original investors exercised their right of first refusal. This was entirely possible because the very fact that the new investors were interested would signal that the company's prospects were attractive to a third party. A final problem was that the original financing group did not really have sufficient resources to exercise their options when the money was needed.

This example demonstrates precisely where the thought process described above is critical in designing deals. Neither management *nor* the investors should have signed this deal. Doing so was essentially a bet that everything would transpire exactly as outlined in the business plan, an outcome that probably has only a 10 percent chance of happening. The financial structure almost drove this company into bankruptcy, and only very intense negotiations to modify the deal saved the company.

Having stated boldly that this deal should never have been signed, we now ask if a different deal could have been structured to accomplish the same basic objectives. First, the investors were clearly interested in preserving three options: (1) the right to control the company (the "51%" option); (2) the right to invest more money at a fixed price for an extended period of time; and (3) the right to maintain their ownership position in the event a subsequent financing round was about to take place at an unfairly low valuation. Management was interested in raising enough capital to get the company off the ground. At the same time, however, it wanted to minimize the dilution from selling shares at a low valuation relative to that possible on future rounds if the company did well.

If both parties had anticipated the future by asking questions detailed at the beginning of this section, the deal they struck could have been quite different while still satisfying the implicit objectives of each party. To illustrate, both the investors and the management would probably have been far better off to raise additional capital in the first place. The company was already far behind the plan when this deal was made, and there was not sufficient new (positive) information on which to base a new capital infusion. The investors and management had raised too little capital for the company to get to the point where a new, better-informed decision about whether or not to proceed could be made.

Second, the investor group could have structured a deal in which they simply paid a lower initial price per share for the company, rather than acquiring the right to invest more money at a fixed price later. The investors purchased a package consisting of some common stock and some rights. On the surface, it would appear that they paid a relatively high price per share of stock. But when a portion of the original investment capital is attributed appropriately to these "ancillary" rights, then the actual economic price paid for the common stock turns out to be far lower. If the investor group had structured a simpler deal in which they paid the lower price, they would have been confronted with far less trouble later.

With respect to the right to invest more money later, this goal could have been accomplished by gaining proportional rights of first refusal, which would allow the investor to participate in later rounds of financing in proportion to the equity already held. Such rights, however, should not be structured so as to discourage another outside group from investing the time and resources required to decide whether or not to invest.

Also, the deal could have been structured with a "ratchet," enabling the original investors to be protected against subsequent financing rounds at lower prices. With a ratchet in place, the shares owned by the original investor would be retroactively adjusted so that the effective price per share paid would be no higher than the price paid by the subsequent round.

Finally, with respect to the control issue, the investor group was deluded into believing that 51% was a magical figure, and the only way to retain control in the situation. In reality, control vests in the hands of those who have capital when capital is needed. Control can also be attained by having a majority representation on the board of directors or through employment contracts with rigid performance specifications. The particular mechanisms by which this investor group sought to retain control—the rolling 51% option—almost brought the company to its knees.

——— CONCLUSION

We began this reading on venture capital by introducing a relatively simple example of a deal, one in which the entrepreneur sought capital from a venture capitalist. We saw that the terms negotiated affected the split of cash and the split of risk, and hence the split of value between the supplier and the user of capital. We then pointed out that alternative structures would affect the incentives of the entrepreneur such that the total amount of value at stake was affected by the terms negotiated.

We then took the relatively simple single-investment-type deal and expanded the terms to include the more realistic possibility that the investment would be made in several distinct stages over time. In so doing, we discovered that certain options provided venture capitalists, both explicit and implicit, are valuable to venture capitalist and entrepreneur alike, and thus improve the terms on which the entrepreneur is able to raise capital. Staging capital infusions into ventures, for example, enables the venture capitalist to retain the option to abandon a project if that makes sense. We also observed that the entrepreneur enters into such contracts willingly, though there are obvious possible scenarios in which having structured the deal that way will not have been in the best interests of the entrepreneur.

Similarly, both parties can gain from providing the other party the option to re-value a project or from the venture capitalist's option to increase capital committed if the project proves unexpectedly successful. Building such options into venture capital contracts also helps overcome initial differences of opinion between venture capitalist and entrepreneur as to, say, the probability of different outcomes. Such options also provide a signaling mechanism, if you will, by which entrepreneurs can credibly communicate to investors their confidence in the project and in their own abilities.

These options not only add to the total project value as of a first financing round, but also provide a structure for avoiding a financing impasse should things not work out as planned. The terms of financing must allow the company to obtain the capital necessary for survival in (temporary) bad-news scenarios, as well as providing for the exploitation of good-news scenarios. If the deal is structured such that it is almost impossible to raise additional capital (for example, there is an implicit "poison pill" built into the contract), then the financial structure of the deal will reduce instead of adding to the value of the project.

The message that seems to emerge most clearly, then, from this look at venture capital is this: The total value of an investment opportunity may depend critically on the financing terms governing the deal. By restructuring terms, the size of the total economic pie can be dramatically changed—for better or worse. The extent to which these insights into venture capital markets have a bearing on the financial practices of public corporations remains an open question, but one that surely merits further attention.

Copyright © 1988.

—— DISCUSSION QUESTIONS

1. Apply the author's approach to decision making to a significant decision in your life—where and what to study, changing jobs, leaving a job to return to school, for example. What risks and rewards are involved? What actions could you take at the time of the decision to promote the best possible outcome in the long run?

2. The author describes a scenario in which a skeptical venture capitalist shifts risk from himself to the entrepreneur by investing in convertible preferred stock. Would you agree to the arrangement, try to negotiate it, or reject it? Explain your reasoning.

3. A staged capital commitment is a mixed blessing for the entrepreneur. By seeking as much capital as possible up front, what signals is the entrepreneur sending to the venture capitalist? Alternatively, by agreeing to incremental infusions of cash, what is the entrepreneur communicating?

4. A fume date, the author says, "may create incentives to aim for short-term success rather than long-term value creation." Suppose after a third round of financing, you are building a manufacturing facility and undertaking a marketing campaign; cash is being consumed much more rapidly than you had anticipated. What actions would you take to protect the long-term interests of your company?

5. Do you think that venture capitalists and entrepreneurs are more like allies or more like adversaries? Is their relationship a zero-sum game—the bargains struck between the two parties represent victory for one and defeat for the other? What do you think are the hallmarks of a good deal?

PART THREE

MANAGING VENTURE GROWTH

BUILDING AN EFFECTIVE ORGANIZATION

The New Venture　　20

PETER F. DRUCKER

Every entrepreneur must eventually make the transition from founder to general manager. As the new venture begins operations, a host of new challenges and responsibilities arise: hiring managers and staff, designing personnel policies, marketing, financial planning, developing accounting systems. Success in initiating a business does not guarantee success in managing one. As Peter Drucker points out in this reading, even Thomas Edison, a brilliant inventor and business planner, failed as a company head in every venture he undertook.

Many entrepreneurs distrust the concept of "management," associating it with formality, stodginess, bureaucracy. Drucker challenges this bias, making a strong case for entrepreneurial management with an emphasis on management. For a new venture to survive and flourish, he says, new skills and approaches are needed; he delineates four essential ingredients of entrepreneurial management—a market focus, financial foresight, a strong top management team, and perspective on the founder's own future. In a discussion rich in historical example, this reading demonstrates the role of foresight and discipline in strengthening entrepreneurial spirit and ensuring lasting success.

For the existing enterprise, whether business or public-service institution, the controlling word in the term "entrepreneurial management" is "entrepreneurial." For the new venture, it is "management." In the existing business, it is the existing that is the main obstacle to entrepreneurship. In the new venture, it is its absence.

The new venture has an idea. It may have a product or a service. It may even have sales, and sometimes quite a substantial volume of them. It surely has costs. And it may have revenues and even profits. What it does not have is a "business," a viable, operating, organized "present" in which people know where they are going, what they are supposed to do, and what the results are or should be. But unless a new venture develops into a new business and makes sure of being "managed," it will not survive no matter how brilliant the entrepreneurial idea, how much money it attracts, how good its products, nor even how great the demand for them.

Refusal to accept these facts destroyed every single venture started by the nineteenth century's greatest inventor, Thomas Edison. Edison's ambition was to be a successful businessman and the head of a big company. He should have succeeded, for he was a superb business planner. He knew exactly how an electric power company had to be set up to exploit his invention of the light bulb. He knew exactly how to get all the money he could possibly need for his ventures. His products were immediate successes and the demand for them practically insatiable. But Edison remained an entrepreneur; or rather, he thought that "managing" meant being the boss. He refused to build a management team. And so every one of his four or five companies collapsed ignominiously once it got to middle size and was saved only by booting Edison himself out and replacing him with professional management.

Entrepreneurial management in the new venture has four requirements.

- It requires, first, a focus on the market.
- It requires, second, financial foresight, and especially planning for cash flow and capital needs ahead.
- It requires, third, building a top management team long before the new venture actually needs one and long before it can actually afford one.
- And finally, it requires of the founding entrepreneur a decision in respect to his or her own role, area of work, and relationships.

—— THE NEED FOR MARKET FOCUS

A common explanation for the failure of a new venture to live up to its promise or even to survive at all is: "We were doing fine until these other people came and took our market away from us. We don't really understand it. What they offered wasn't so very different from what we had." Or one hears: "We were doing all right, but these other people started selling to customers we'd never even heard of and all of a sudden they had the market."

When a new venture does succeed, more often than not it is in a market other than the one it was originally intended to serve, with products or services not quite those with which it had set out, bought in large part by customers it did not even think of when it started, and used for a host of purposes besides the ones for which the products were first designed. If a new venture does not anticipate this, organizing itself to take advantage of the unexpected and unseen markets; if it is not totally market-focused, if not market-driven, then it will succeed only in creating an opportunity for a competitor.

There are exceptions, to be sure. A product designed for one specific use, especially if scientific or technical, often stays with the market and the end use for which it was designed. But not always. Even a prescription drug designed for a specific ailment and tested for it sometimes ends up being used for some other quite different ailment. One example is a compound that is effectively used in the treatment of stomach ulcers. Or a drug designed primarily for the treatment of human beings may find its major market in veterinary medicine.

Anything genuinely new creates markets that nobody before even imagined. No one knew that he needed an office copier before the first Xerox machine came out around 1960; five years later no business could imagine doing without a copier. When the first jet planes started to fly, the best market research pointed out that there were not even enough passengers for all the transatlantic liners then in service or being built. Five years later the transatlantic jets were carrying fifty to one hundred times as many passengers each year as had ever before crossed the Atlantic.

The innovator has limited vision; in fact, he has tunnel vision. He sees the area with which he is familiar—to the exclusion of all other areas.

An example is DDT. Designed during World War II to protect American soldiers against tropical insects and parasites, it eventually found its greatest application in agriculture to protect livestock and crops against insects—to the point where it had to be banned for being too effective. Yet not one of the distinguished scientists who designed DDT during World War II envisaged these uses of DDT. Of course they knew that babies die from fly-borne, "summer" diarrhea. Of course they knew that livestock and crops are infested by insect parasites. But these things they knew as laymen. As experts, they were concerned with the tropical diseases of humans. It was the ordinary American soldier who then applied DDT to the areas in which he was the "expert," that is, to his home, his cows, his cotton patch.

Similarly, the 3M Company did not see that an adhesive tape it had developed for industry would find myriad uses in the household and in the office—becoming Scotch Tape. 3M had for many years been a supplier of abrasives and adhesives to industry, and moderately successful in industrial markets. It had never even thought of consumer markets. It was pure accident which led the engineer who had designed an industrial product no industrial user wanted to the realization that the stuff might be salable in the consumer market. As the story goes, he took some samples home when the company had already decided to abandon the product. To his surprise, his teenage daughters began to use it to hold their curls overnight. The only unusual thing about this story is that he and his bosses at 3M recognized that they had stumbled upon a new market.

A German chemist developed Novocain as the first local anesthetic in 1905. But he could not get the doctors to use it; they preferred total anesthesia (they only accepted Novocain during World War I). But totally unexpectedly, dentists began to use the stuff. Whereupon—or so the story goes—the chemist began to travel up and down Germany making speeches against Novocain's use in dentistry. He had not designed it for that purpose!

That reaction was somewhat extreme, I admit. Still, entrepreneurs *know* what their innovation is meant to do. And if some other use for it appears, they tend to resent it. They may not actually refuse to serve customers they have not "planned" for, but they are likely to make it clear that these customers are not welcome.

That is what happened with the computer. The company that had the first computer, Univac, knew that its magnificent machine was designed for scientific work. And so it did not even send a salesman out when a business showed interest in it; surely, it argued, these people could not possibly know what a computer was all about. IBM was equally convinced that the computer was an instrument for scientific work: their own computer had been designed specifically for astronomical calculations. But IBM was willing to take orders from businesses and to serve them. Ten years later, around 1960, Univac still had by far the most advanced and best machine. IBM had the computer market.

The textbook prescription for this problem is "market research." But it is the wrong prescription.

One cannot do market research for something genuinely new. One cannot do market research for something that is not yet on the market. Around 1950, Univac's market research concluded that, by the year 2000, about one thousand computers would be sold; the actual figure in 1984 was about one million. And yet this was the most "scientific," careful, rigorous market research ever done. There was only one thing wrong with it: it started out with the assumption, then shared by everyone, that computers were going to be used for advanced scientific work—and for that use, the number is indeed quite limited. Similarly, several companies who turned down the Xerox patents did so on the basis of thorough market research, which showed that printers had no use at all for a copier. Nobody had any inkling that businesses, schools, universities, colleges, and a host of private individuals would want to buy a copier.

The new venture therefore needs to start out with the assumption that its product or service may find customers in markets no one thought of, for uses no one envisaged when the product or service was designed, and that it will be bought by customers outside its field of vision and even unknown to the new venture.

If the new venture does not have such a market focus from the very beginning, all it is likely to create is the market for a competitor. A few years later "those people" will come in and take away "our market," or "those other people" who started "selling to customers we'd never even heard of" all of a sudden will indeed have preempted the market.

To build market focus into a new venture is not in fact particularly difficult. But what is required runs counter to the inclinations of the typical entrepreneur. It requires, first, that the new venture systematically hunt out both the unexpected success and the unexpected failure. Rather than dismiss the unexpected as an "exception," as entrepreneurs are inclined to do, they need to go out and look at it carefully and as a distinct opportunity.

Shortly after World War II, a small Indian engineering firm bought the license to produce a European-designed bicycle with an auxiliary light engine. It looked like an ideal product for India; yet it never did well. The owner of this small firm noticed, however, that substantial orders came in for the engines alone. At first he wanted to turn down those orders; what could anyone possibly do with such a small engine? It was curiosity alone that made him go to the actual area the orders came from. There he found farmers were taking the engines off the bicycles and using them to power irrigation pumps that hitherto had been hand-operated. This manufacturer is now the world's largest maker of small irrigation pumps, selling them by the millions. His pumps have revolutionized farming all over Southeast Asia.

To be market-driven also requires that the new venture be willing to experiment. If there is any interest in the new venture's product or service on the part of consumers or markets that were not in the original plan, one tries to find somebody in that new and unexpected area who might be willing to test the new product or service and find out what, if any, application it might have. One provides free samples to people in the "improbable" market to see what they can do with it, whether they can use the stuff at all, or what it would have to be like for them to become customers for it. One advertises in the trade papers of the industry whence indications of interest came, and so on.

The DuPont Company never thought of automobile tires as a major application for the new Nylon fiber it had developed. But when one of the Akron tire manufacturers showed interest in trying out Nylon, DuPont set up a plant. A few years later, tires had become Nylon's biggest and most profitable market.

It does not require a great deal of money to find out whether an unexpected interest from an unexpected market is an indication of genuine potential or a fluke. It requires sensitivity and a little systematic work.

Above all, the people who are running a new venture need to spend time outside: in the marketplace, with customers and with their own salesmen, looking and listening. The new venture needs to build in systematic practices to remind itself that a "product" or a "service" is defined by the customer, not by the producer. It needs to work continuously on challenging itself in respect to the utility and value that its products or services contribute to customers.

The greatest danger for the new venture is to "know better" than the customer what the product or service is or should be, how it should be bought, and what it should be used for. Above all, the new venture needs willingness to see the unexpected success as an opportunity rather than as an affront to its expertise. And it needs to accept that elementary axiom of marketing: Businesses are not paid to reform customers. They are paid to satisfy customers.

——— FINANCIAL FORESIGHT

Lack of market focus is typically a disease of the "neo-natal," the infant new venture. It is the most serious affliction of the new venture in its early stages—and one that can permanently stunt even those that survive.

The lack of adequate financial focus and of the right financial policies is, by contrast, the greatest threat to the new venture in the next stage of its growth. It is, above all, a threat to the rapidly growing new venture. The more successful a new venture is, the more dangerous the lack of financial foresight.

Suppose that a new venture has successfully launched its product or service and is growing fast. It reports "rapidly increasing profits" and issues rosy forecasts. The stock market then "discovers" the new venture, especially if it is high-tech or in a field otherwise currently fashionable. Predictions abound that the new venture's sales will reach a billion dollars within five years. Eighteen months later, the new venture collapses. It may not go out of existence or go bankrupt. But it is suddenly awash in red ink, lays off 180 of its 275 employees, fires the president, or is sold at a bargain price to a big company. The causes are always the same: lack of cash; inability to raise the capital needed for expansion; and loss of control, with expenses, inventories, and receivables in disarray. These three financial afflictions often hit together at the same time. Yet any one of them by itself endangers the health, if not the life, of the new venture.

Once this financial crisis has erupted, it can be cured only with great difficulty and considerable suffering. But it is eminently preventable.

Entrepreneurs starting new ventures are rarely unmindful of money; on the contrary, they tend to be greedy. They therefore focus on profits. But this is the wrong focus for a new venture, or rather, it comes last rather than first. Cash flow, capital, and controls come much earlier. Without them, the profit figures are fiction—good for twelve to eighteen months, perhaps, after which they evaporate.

Growth has to be fed. In financial terms this means that growth in a new venture demands adding financial resources rather than taking them out. Growth needs more cash and more capital. If the growing new venture shows a "profit," it is a fiction: a bookkeeping entry put in only to balance the accounts. And since taxes are payable on this fiction in most countries, it creates a liability and a cash drain rather than a "surplus." The healthier a new venture and the faster it grows, the more financial feeding it requires. The new ventures that are the darlings of the newspapers and the stock market letters, the new ventures that show rapid profit growth and "record profits," are those mostly likely to run into desperate trouble a couple of years later.

The new venture needs cash flow analysis, cash flow forecasts, and cash management. The fact that America's new ventures of the last few years (with the significant exception of high-tech companies) have been doing so much better than new ventures used to do is largely because the new entrepreneurs in the United States have learned that entrepreneurship demands financial management.

Cash management is fairly easy if there are reliable cash flow forecasts, with "reliable" meaning "worst case" assumptions rather than hopes. There is an old banker's rule of thumb, according to which in forecasting cash income and cash outlays one assumes that bills will have to be paid sixty days earlier than expected and receivables will come in sixty days later. If the forecast is overly conservative, the worst that can happen—it rarely does in a growing new venture—is a temporary cash surplus.

A growing new venture should know twelve months ahead of time how much cash it will need, when, and for what purposes. With a year's lead time, it is almost always possible to finance cash needs. But even if a new venture is doing well, raising cash in a hurry and in a "crisis" is never easy and always prohibitively expensive. Above all, it always sidetracks the key people in the company at the most critical time. For several months they then spend their time and energy running from one financial institution to another and cranking out one set of questionable financial projections after another. In the end, they usually have to mortgage the long-range future of the business to get through a ninety-day cash bind. When they finally are able again to devote time and thought to the business, they have irrevocably missed the major opportunities. For the new venture, almost by definition, is under cash pressure when the opportunities are greatest.

The successful new venture will also outgrow its capital structure. A rule of thumb with a good deal of empirical evidence to support it says that a new venture outgrows its capital base with every increase in sales (or billings) of the order of 40 to 50 percent. After such growth, a new venture also needs a new and different capital structure, as a rule. As the venture grows, private sources of funds, whether from the owners and their families or from outsiders, become inadequate. The company has to find access to much larger pools of money by going "public," by finding a partner or partners among established companies, or by raising money from insurance companies and pension funds. A new venture that had been financed by equity money now needs to shift to long-term debt, or vice versa. As the venture grows, the existing capital structure always becomes the wrong structure and an obstacle.

In some new ventures, capital planning is comparatively easy. When the business consists of uniform and entirely local units—restaurants in a chain, freestanding surgical centers or individual hospitals in different cities, home-builders with separate operations in a number of different metropolitan areas, specialty stores and the like—each unit can be financed as a separate business. One solution is franchising (which is, in essence, a way to finance rapid expansion). Another is setting up each local unit as a company, with separate and often local investors as "limited" partners. The capital needed for growth and expansion can thus be raised step by step, and the success of the preceding unit furnishes documentation and the incentive for the investors in the succeeding ones. But it only works when: (a) each unit breaks even fairly soon, at most perhaps within two or three years; (b) the operation can be made routine, so that people of limited managerial competence—the typical franchise holder, or the business manager of a local freestanding surgical center—can do a decent job without much supervision; and (c) the individual unit itself reaches fairly swiftly the optimum size beyond which it does not require further capital but produces cash surplus to help finance the start-up of additional units.

For new ventures other than those capable of being financed as separate units, capital planning is a survival necessity. If a growing new venture plans realistically—and that again means assuming the maximum rather than the minimum need—for its capital requirement and its capital structure three years ahead, it should normally have little difficulty in obtaining the kind of money it needs, when it needs it, and in the form in which it needs it. If it waits until it outgrows its capital base and its capital structure, it is putting its survival—and most assuredly its independence—on the block. At the very least, the founders will find that they have taken all the entrepreneurial risk and worked hard only to make other people the rich owners. From being owners, they will have become employees, with the new investors taking control.

Finally, the new venture needs to plan the financial system it requires to manage growth. Again and again, a growing new venture starts off with an excellent product, excellent standing in its market, and excellent growth prospects. Then suddenly everything goes out of control: receivables, inventory, manufacturing costs, administrative costs, service, distribution, everything. Once one area gets out of control, all of them do. The enterprise has outgrown its control structure. By the time control has been reestablished, markets have been lost, customers have become disgruntled if not hostile, distributors have lost their confidence in the company. Worst of all, employees have lost trust in management, and with good reason.

Fast growth always makes obsolete the existing controls. Again, a growth of 40 to 50 percent in volume seems to be the critical figure.

Once control has been lost, it is hard to recapture. Yet the loss of control can be prevented quite easily. What is needed is first to think through the critical areas in a given enterprise. In one, it may be product quality; in another, service; in a third, receivables and inventory; in a fourth, manufacturing costs. Rarely are there more than four or five critical areas in any given enterprise. (Managerial and administrative overhead should, however, always be included. A disproportionate and fast increase in the percentage of revenues absorbed by managerial and administrative overhead, which means that the enterprise hires managerial and administrative people faster than it actually grows, is usually the first sign that a business is getting out of control, that its management structure and practices are no longer adequate to the task.)

To live up to its growth expectations, a new venture must establish today the controls in these critical areas it will need three years hence. Elaborate controls are not necessary nor does it matter that the figures are only approximate. What matters is that the management of the new venture is aware of these critical areas, is being reminded of them, and can thus act fast if the need arises. Disarray normally does not appear if there is adequate attention to the key areas. Then the new venture will have the controls it needs when it needs them.

Financial foresight does not require a great deal of time. It does require a good deal of thought, however. The technical tools to do the job are easily available; they are spelled out in most texts on managerial accounting. But the work will have to be done by the enterprise itself.

———— BUILDING A TOP MANAGEMENT TEAM

The new venture has successfully established itself in the right market and has then successfully found the financial structure and the financial system it needs. Nonetheless, a few years later it is still prone to run into a serious crisis. Just when it appears to be on the threshold of becoming an "adult"—a successful, established, going concern—it gets into trouble nobody seems to understand. The products are first-rate, the prospects are excellent, and yet the business simply cannot grow. Neither profitability nor quality, nor any of the other major areas performs.

The reason is always the same: a lack of top management. The business has outgrown being managed by one person, or even two people, and it now needs a management team at the top. If it does not have one already in place at the time, it is very late—in fact, usually too late. The best one can then hope is that the business will survive. But it is likely to be permanently crippled or to suffer scars that will bleed for many years to come. Morale has been shattered and employees throughout the company are disillusioned and cynical. And the people who founded the business and built it almost always end up on the outside, embittered and disenchanted.

The remedy is simple: To build a top management team *before* the venture reaches the point where it must have one. Teams cannot be formed overnight. They require long periods before they can function. Teams are based on mutual trust and mutual understanding, and this takes years to build up. In my experience, three years is about the minimum.

But the small and growing new venture cannot afford a top management team; it cannot sustain half a dozen people with big titles and corresponding salaries. In fact, in the small and growing business, a very small number of people do everything as it comes along. How, then, can one square this circle?

Again, this remedy is relatively simple. But it does require the will on the part of the founders to build a team rather than to keep on running everything themselves. If one or two people at the top believe that they, and they alone, must do everything, then a management crisis a few months, or at the latest, a few years down the road becomes inevitable.

Whenever the objective economic indicators of a new venture—market surveys, for instance, or demographic analysis—indicate that the business may double within three or five years, then it is the duty of the founder or founders to build the management team the new venture will very soon require. This is preventive medicine, so to speak.

First of all the founders, together with other key people in the firm, will have to think through the key activities of their business. What are the specific areas upon which the survival and success of this particular business depend? Most of the areas will be on everyone's list. But if there are divergencies and dissent—and there should be on a question as important as this—they should be taken seriously. Every activity which any member of the group thinks belongs there should go down on the list.

The key activities are not to be found in books. They emerge from analysis of the specific enterprise. Two enterprises that to an outsider appear to be in an identical line of business may well end up defining their key activities quite differently. One, for instance, may put production in the center; the other, customer service. Only two key activities are always present in any organization: there is always the management of people and there is always the management of money. The rest has to be determined by the people within looking at the enterprise and at their own jobs, values, and goals.

The next step is, then, for each member of the group, beginning with the founder, to ask: "What are the activities that *I* am doing well? And what are the activities that each of my key associates in this business is actually doing well?" Again, there is going to be agreement on most of the people and on most of their strengths. But, again, any disagreement should be taken seriously.

Next, one asks: "Which of the key activities should each of us, therefore, take on as his or her first and major responsibility because they fit the individual's strengths? Which individual fits which key activity?"

Then the work on building a team can begin. The founder starts to discipline himself or herself not to handle people and their problems, if this is not the key activity that fits him best. Perhaps this individual's key strength is new products and new technology. Perhaps this individual's key activity is operations, manufacturing, physical distribution, service. Or perhaps it is money and finance and someone else had better handle people. But all key activities need to be covered by someone who has proven ability in performance.

There is no rule that says "A chief executive has to be in charge of this or that." Of course, a chief executive is the court of last resort and has ultimate accountability. And the chief executive also has to make sure of getting the information necessary to discharge this ultimate accountability. The chief executive's own *work*, however, depends on what the enterprise requires and on who the individual is. As long as the CEO's work program consists of key activities, he or she does a CEO's job. But the CEO also is responsible for making sure that all the other key activities are adequately covered.

Finally, goals and objectives for each area need to be set. Everyone who takes on the primary responsibility for a key activity, whether product development or people or money, must be asked: "What can this enterprise expect of you? What should we hold you accountable for? What are you trying to accomplish and by what time?" But this is elementary management, of course.

It is prudent to establish the top management team informally at first. There is no need to give people titles in a new and growing venture, nor to make announcements, nor even to pay extra. All this can wait a year or so, until it is clear that the new setup works, and how. In the meantime, all the members of the team have much to learn: their job; how they work together; and what they have to do to enable the CEO and their colleagues to do their jobs. Two or three years later, when the growing venture needs a top management, it has one.

However, should it fail to provide for a top management before it actually needs one, it will lose the capacity to manage itself long before it actually needs a top management team. The founder will have become so overloaded that important tasks will not get done. At this point the company can go one of two ways. The first possibility is that the founder concentrates on the one or two areas that fit his or her abilities and interests. These are key areas indeed, but they are not the only crucial ones, and no one is then left to look after the others. Two years later, important areas have been slighted and the business is in dire straits. The other, worse, possibility is that the founder is conscientious. He knows that people and money are key activities and need to be taken care of. His own abilities and interests, which actually built the business, are in the design and development of new products. But being conscientious, the founder forces himself to take care of people and finance. Since he is not very gifted in either area, he does poorly in both. It also takes him forever to reach decisions or to do any work in these areas, so that he is forced, by lack of time, to neglect what he is really good at and what the company depends on him for, the development of new technology and new products. Three years later the company will have become an empty shell without the products it needs, but also without the management of people and the management of money it needs.

In the first example, it may be possible to save the company. After all, it has the products. But the founder will inevitably be removed by whoever comes in to salvage the company. In the second case, the company usually cannot be saved at all and has to be sold or liquidated.

Long before it has reached the point where it needs the balance of a top management team, the new venture has to create one. Long before the time has come at which management by one person no longer works and becomes mismanagement, that one person also has to start learning how to work with colleagues, has to learn to trust people, yet also how to hold them accountable. The founder has to learn to become the leader of a team rather than a "star" with "helpers."

—— "WHERE CAN I CONTRIBUTE?"

Building a top management team may be the single most important step toward entrepreneurial management in the new venture. It is only the first step, however, for the founders themselves, who then have to think through what their own future is to be.

As a new venture develops and grows, the roles and relationships of the original entrepreneurs inexorably change. If the founders refuse to accept this, they will stunt the business and may even destroy it.

Every founder-entrepreneur nods to this and says, "Amen." Everyone has horror stories of other founder-entrepreneurs who did not change as the venture changed, and who then destroyed both the business and themselves. But even among the founders who can accept that they themselves need to do something, few know how to tackle changing their own roles and relationships.

They tend to begin by asking: "What do I like to do?" Or at best, "Where do I fit in?" The right question to start with is: "What will the venture need *objectively* by way of management from here on out?" And in a growing new venture, the founder has to ask this question whenever the business (or the public-service institution) grows significantly or changes direction or character, that is, changes its products, services, markets, or the kind of people it needs.

The next question the founder must ask is: "What am I good at? What, of all these needs of the venture, could I supply, and supply with distinction?" Only after having thought through these two questions should a founder then ask: "What do I really want to do, and believe in doing? What am I willing to spend years on, if not the rest of my life? Is this something the venture really needs? Is it a major, essential, indispensable contribution?"

One example is that of the successful American post–World War II metropolitan university, Pace, in New York City. Dr. Edward Mortola built up the institution from nothing in 1947 into New York City's third-largest and fastest-growing university, with 25,000 students and well-regarded graduate schools. In the university's early years he was a radical innovator. But when Pace was still very small (around 1950), Mortola built a strong top management team. All members were given a major, clearly defined responsibility, for which they were expected to take full accountability and give leadership. A few years later, Mortola then decided what his own role was to be and converted himself into a traditional university president, while at the same time building a strong independent board of trustees to advise and support him.

But the questions of what a venture needs, what the strengths of the founder-entrepreneur are, and what he or she wants to do, might be answered quite differently.

Edwin Land, for instance, the man who invented Polaroid glass and the Polaroid camera, ran the company during the first twelve or eighteen years of its life, until the early 1950s. Then it began to grow fast. Land thereupon designed a top management team and put it in place. As for himself, he decided that he was not the right man for the top management job in the company; what he and he alone could contribute was scientific innovation. Accordingly, Land built himself a laboratory and established himself as the company's consulting director for basic research. The company itself, in its day-to-day operations, he left to others to run.

Ray Kroc, the man who conceived and built McDonald's, reached a similar conclusion. He remained president until he died well past age eighty. But he put a top management team in place to run the company and appointed himself the company's "marketing conscience." Until shortly before his death, he visited two or three McDonald's restaurants each week, checking their quality carefully, the level of cleanliness, and friendliness. Above all, he looked at the customers, talked to them and listened to them. This enabled the company to make the necessary changes to retain its leadership in the fast-food industry.

Similarly, in a much smaller new venture, a building supply company in the Pacific Northwest of the United States, the young man who built the company decided that his role was not to run the company but to develop its critical resource, the managers who are responsible for its two hundred branches in small towns and suburbs. These managers are in effect running their own local business. They are supported by strong services in headquarters; central buying, quality control, control of credit and receivables, and so on. But the selling is done by each manager, locally and with very little help—maybe one salesman and a couple of truck drivers.

The business depends on the motivation, drive, ability, and enthusiasm of these isolated, fairly unsophisticated individuals. None of them has a college degree, and few have even finished high school. So the founder of this company makes it his business to spend twelve to fifteen days each month in the field visiting branch managers, spending half a day with them, discussing their business, their plans, their aspirations. This may well be the only distinction the company has—otherwise, every other building materials wholesaler does the same things. But this performance of the one key activity by the chief executive has enabled the company to grow three to four times as fast as any competitor, even in recession times.

Yet another quite different answer to the same question was given by the three scientists who, together, founded what has become one of the largest and most successful companies in the semiconductor industry. When they asked themselves, "What are the needs of the business?" the answer was that there were three: "One for basic business strategy, one for scientific research and development, and one for the development of people—especially scientific and technical people." They decided which of the three was most suited for each of these assignments, and then divided them according to their strengths. The person who took the human relations and human development job had actually been a prolific scientific innovator and had high standing in scientific circles. But he decided, and his colleagues concurred, that he was superbly fitted for the managerial, the people task, so he took it. "It was not," he once said in a speech, "what I really wanted to do, but it was where I could make the greatest contribution."

These questions may not always lead to such happy endings. They may even lead to the decision to leave the company.

In one of the most successful new financial services ventures in the United States, this is what the founder concluded. He did establish a top management team. He asked what the company needed. He looked at himself and his strengths; and he found no match between the needs of the company and his own abilities, let alone between the needs of the company and the things he wanted to do. "I trained my own successor for about eighteen months, then turned the company over to him and resigned," he said. Since then he has started three new businesses, not one of them in finance, has developed them successfully to medium size, and then quit again. He wants to develop new businesses but does not enjoy running them. He accepts that both the businesses and he are better off divorced from one another.

Other entrepreneurs in this same situation might reach different conclusions. The founder of a well-known medical clinic, a leader in its particular field, faced a similar dilemma. The needs of the institution were for an administrator and money-raiser. His own inclinations were to be a researcher and a clinician. But he realized that he was good at raising money and capable of learning to be the chief executive officer of a fairly large health-care organization. "And so," he says, "I felt it my duty to the venture I had created, and to my associates in it, to suppress my own desires and to take on the job of chief administrator and money-raiser. But I would never have done so had I not known that I had the abilities to do the job, and if my advisors and my board had not all assured me that I had these abilities."

The question, "Where do I belong?" needs to be faced up to and thought through by the founder-entrepreneur as soon as the venture shows the first signs of success. But the question can be faced up to much earlier. Indeed, it might be best thought through before the new venture is even started.

This is what Soichiro Honda, the founder and builder of Honda Motor Company in Japan, did when he decided to open a small business in the darkest days after Japan's defeat in World War II. He did not start his venture until he had found the right man to be his partner and to run administration, finance, distribution, marketing, sales, and personnel. For Honda had decided from the outset that he belonged in engineering and production and would not run anything else. This decision made the Honda Motor Company.

There is an earlier and even more instructive example, that of Henry Ford. When Ford decided in 1903 to go into business for himself, he did exactly what Honda did forty years later: before starting, he found the right man to be his partner and to run the areas where Ford knew he did not belong—administration, finance, distribution, marketing, sales, and personnel. Like Honda, Henry Ford knew that he belonged in engineering and manufacturing and was going to confine himself to these two areas. The man he found, James Couzens, contributed as much as Ford to the success of the company.[1] Many of the best known policies and practices of the Ford Motor Company for which Henry Ford is often given credit—the famous $5-a-day wage of 1913, or the pioneering distribution and service policies, for example—were Couzens's ideas and at first resisted by Ford. So effective did Couzens become that Ford grew increasingly jealous of him and forced him out in 1917. The last straw was Couzens's insistence that the Model T was obsolescent and his proposal to use some of the huge profits of the company to start work on a successor.

The Ford Motor Company grew and prospered to the very day of Couzens's resignation. Within a few short months thereafter, as soon as Henry Ford had taken every single top management function into his own hands,

---

1. Couzens later became mayor of Detroit and senator from Michigan and might well have become president of the United States had he not been born in Canada.

forgetting that he had known earlier where he belonged, the Ford Motor Company began its long decline. Henry Ford clung to the Model T for a full ten years, until it had become literally unsalable. And the company's decline was not reversed for thirty years after Couzens's dismissal until, with his grand-father dying, a very young Henry Ford II took over the practically bankrupt business.

THE NEED FOR OUTSIDE ADVICE

These last cases point up an important factor for the entrepreneur in the new and growing venture, the need for independent, objective outside advice.

The growing new venture may not need a formal board of directors. Moreover, the typical board of directors very often does not provide the advice and counsel the founder needs. But the founder does need people with whom he can discuss basic decisions and to whom he listens. Such people are rarely to be found within the enterprise. Somebody has to challenge the founder's appraisal of the needs of the venture, and of his own personal strengths. Someone who is not a part of the problem has to ask questions, to review decisions and, above all, to push constantly to have the long-term survival needs of the new venture satisfied by building in the market focus, supplying financial foresight, and creating a functioning top management team. This is the final requirement of entrepreneurial management in the new venture.

The new venture that builds such entrepreneurial management into its policies and practices will become a flourishing large business.[2]

In so many new ventures, especially high-tech ventures, the techniques discussed in this reading are spurned and even despised. The argument is that they constitute "management" and "We are entrepreneurs." But this is not informality; it is irresponsibility. It confuses manners and substance. It is old wisdom that there is no freedom except under the law. Freedom without law is license, which soon degenerates into anarchy, and shortly thereafter into tyr-anny. It is precisely because the new venture has to maintain and strengthen the entrepreneurial spirit that it needs foresight and discipline. It needs to prepare itself for the demands that its own success will make of it. Above all, it needs responsibility—and this, in the last analysis, is what entrepreneurial management supplies to the new venture.

There is much more that could be said about managing the new venture, about financing, staffing, marketing its products, and so on. But these specifics are adequately covered in a number of publications. What this reading has tried to do is to identify and discuss the few fairly simple policies that are crucial to the survival and success of any new venture, whether a business or a public-

---

2. A fine description of this process is to be found in *High-Output Management* (New York: Random House, 1983), by Andrew S. Grove, co-founder and president of Intel, one of the largest manufacturers of semiconductors.

service institution, whether high-tech, low-tech, or no-tech, whether started by one man or woman or by a group, and whether intended to remain a small business or to become "another IBM."

——— DISCUSSION QUESTIONS

1. Compare the skills needed to launch a new venture with those needed to manage one. How can the experience of founding a company prepare the entrepreneur for the task of managing one? What qualities that are desirable in a founder may be undesirable in a manager?

2. Thomas Edison, we are told, "thought that 'managing' meant being the boss." How do the responsibilities of a boss differ from those of a manager of managers?

3. According to Drucker, the new venture must organize itself "to take advantage of the unexpected and unseen markets." Is it possible to plan systematically for the unknown? What policies and practices can equip companies to capitalize on surprises?

4. Conventional measures of success—booming sales, high profits, rapid growth—can dangerously mislead new venture managers. By what standards—financial and nonfinancial—would you judge the health of a venture that has just launched its product or service and is enjoying its first sales?

5. The small, growing venture cannot afford a highly paid top management team. Without such traditional incentives as high pay, prestigious titles, and extensive benefits, how can the chief executive motivate the management team to do its best work?

The Five Stages of Small Business Growth

21

NEIL C. CHURCHILL AND VIRGINIA L. LEWIS

Growing ventures inevitably differ in many ways—size, structure, managerial style, capacity for growth. After studying the histories of many small companies, however, the authors of this reading have concluded that organizations experience common problems and challenges at similar stages in their development. Their small business framework consists of five stages through which such companies pass: existence, survival, success, take-off, and resource maturity. They describe each stage, focusing on the key questions that arise in the course of the company's evolution. By assessing the stage at which their companies are operating, owners can better determine current requirements and priorities, make more informed choices, and prepare for future decisions.

Categorizing the problems and growth patterns of small businesses in a systematic way that is useful to entrepreneurs seems at first glance a hopeless task. Small businesses vary widely in size and capacity for growth. They are characterized by independence of action, differing organizational structures, and varied management styles.

Yet on closer scrutiny, it becomes apparent that they experience common problems arising at similar stages in their development. These points of similarity can be organized into a framework that increases our understanding of the nature, characteristics, and problems of businesses ranging from a corner dry cleaning establishment with two or three minimum-wage employees to a $20-million-a-year computer software company experiencing a 40% annual rate of growth.

For owners and managers of small businesses, such an understanding can aid in assessing current challenges; for example, the need to upgrade an existing computer system or to hire and train second-level managers to maintain planned growth.

It can help in anticipating the key requirements at various points—for example, the inordinate time commitment for owners during the start-up period and the need for delegation and changes in their managerial roles when companies become larger and more complex.

The framework also provides a basis for evaluating the impact of present and proposed governmental regulations and policies on one's business.

A case in point is the exclusion of dividends from double taxation, which could be of great help to a profitable, mature, and stable business like a funeral home but of no help at all to a new, rapidly growing, high-technology enterprise.

Finally, the framework aids accountants and consultants in diagnosing problems and matching solutions to smaller enterprises. The problems of a 6-month-old, 20-person business are rarely addressed by advice based on a 30-year-old, 100-person manufacturing company. For the former, cash flow planning is paramount; for the latter, strategic planning and budgeting to achieve coordination and operating control are most important.

─── DEVELOPING A SMALL BUSINESS FRAMEWORK

Various researchers over the years have developed models for examining businesses (see *Exhibit 1*). Each uses business size as one dimension and company maturity or the stage of growth as a second dimension. While useful in many respects, these frameworks are inappropriate for small businesses on at least three counts.

First, they assume that a company must grow and pass through all stages of development or die in the attempt. Second, the models fail to capture the important early stages in a company's origin and growth. Third, these frameworks characterize company size largely in terms of annual sales (although some mention number of employees) and ignore other factors such as value added, number of locations, complexity of product line, and rate of change in products or production technology.

EXHIBIT 1
Growth Phases

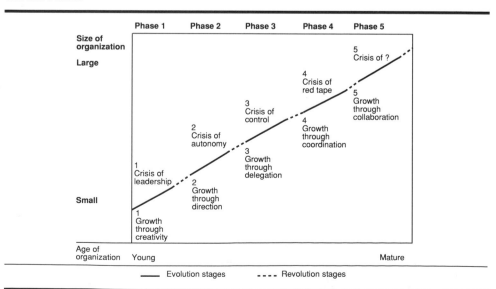

To develop a framework relevant to small and growing businesses, we used a combination of experience, a search of the literature, and empirical research. The framework that evolved from this effort delineates the five stages of development shown in *Exhibit 2*. Each stage is characterized by an index of size, diversity, and complexity and described by five management factors: managerial style, organizational structure, extent of formal systems, major strategic goals, and the owner's involvement in the business. We depict each stage schematically in *Exhibit 3*.

STAGE I: EXISTENCE

In this stage the main problems of the business are obtaining customers and delivering the product or service contracted for. Among the key questions are the following:

- Can we get enough customers, deliver our products, and provide services well enough to become a viable business?
- Can we expand from that one key customer or pilot-production process to a much broader sales base?
- Do we have enough money to cover the considerable cash demands of this start-up phase?

The organization is a simple one—the owner does everything and directly supervises subordinates, who should be of at least average competence. Systems and formal planning are minimal to nonexistent. The company's strategy is simply to remain alive. The owner *is* the business, performs all the

EXHIBIT 2
Growth Stages

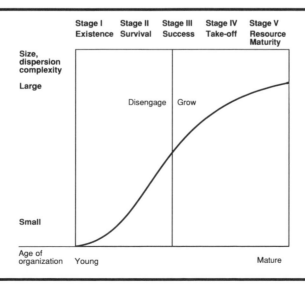

EXHIBIT 3
Characteristics of Small Businesses at Each Stage of Development

	Stage I Existence	Stage II Survival	Stage III-D Success- Disengagement	Stage III-G Success- Growth	Stage IV Take-off	Stage V Resource Maturity
Management style	Direct supervision	Supervised supervision	Functional	Functional	Divisional	Line and staff
Organization						
Extent of formal systems	Minimal to nonexistent	Minimal	Basic	Developing	Maturing	Extensive
Major strategy	Existence	Survival	Maintaining profitable status quo	Get resources for growth	Growth	Return on investment
Business and owner*						

*Smaller circle represents owner; larger circle represents business.

important tasks and is the major supplier of energy, direction, and, with relatives and friends, capital.

Companies in the Existence Stage range from newly started restaurants and retail stores to high-technology manufacturers that have yet to stabilize either production or product quality. Many such companies never gain sufficient customer acceptance or product capability to become viable. In these cases, the owners close the business when the start-up capital runs out and, if they're lucky, sell the business for its asset value (see endpoint 1 on *Exhibit 4*). In some cases, the owners cannot accept the demands the business places on their time, finances, and energy, and they quit. Those companies that remain in business become Stage II enterprises.

STAGE II: SURVIVAL

In reaching this stage, the business has demonstrated that it is a workable business entity. It has enough customers and satisfies them sufficiently with its products or services to keep them. The key problem thus shifts from mere existence to the relationship between revenues and expenses. The main issues are as follows:

- In the short run, can we generate enough cash to break even and to cover the repair or replacement of our capital assets as they wear out?

EXHIBIT 4
Evolution of Small Companies

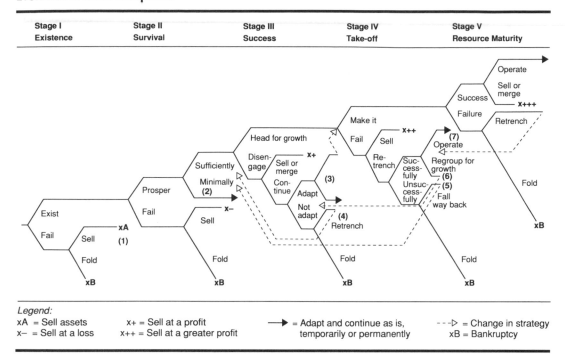

Stage I	Stage II	Stage III	Stage IV	Stage V
Existence	Survival	Success	Take-off	Resource Maturity

Legend:
xA = Sell assets   x+ = Sell at a profit   ──▶ = Adapt and continue as is,   ---▷ = Change in strategy
x− = Sell at a loss   x++ = Sell at a greater profit   temporarily or permanently   xB = Bankruptcy

- Can we, at a minimum, generate enough cash flow to stay in business and to finance growth to a size that is sufficiently large, given our industry and market niche, to earn an economic return on our assets and labor?

The organization is still simple. The company may have a limited number of employees supervised by a sales manager or a general foreman. Neither of them makes major decisions independently, but instead carries out the rather well-defined orders of the owner.

Systems development is minimal. Formal planning is, at best, cash forecasting. The major goal is still survival, and the owner is still synonymous with the business.

In the Survival Stage, the enterprise may grow in size and profitability and move on to Stage III. Or it may, as many companies do, remain at the Survival Stage for some time, earning marginal returns on invested time and capital (endpoint 2 on *Exhibit 4*), and eventually go out of business when the owner gives up or retires. The Mom-and-Pop stores are in this category, as are manufacturing businesses that cannot get their product or process sold as planned. Some of these marginal businesses have developed enough economic viability to ultimately be sold, usually at a slight loss. Or they may fail completely and drop from sight.

STAGE III: SUCCESS

The decision facing owners at this stage is whether to exploit the company's accomplishments and expand or keep the company stable and profitable, providing a base for alternative owner activities. Thus, a key issue is whether to use the company as a platform for growth—a substage III-G company—or as a means of support for the owners as they completely or partially disengage from the company—making it a substage III-D company. (See *Exhibit 3*.) Behind the disengagement might be a wish to start up new enterprises, run for political office, or simply to pursue hobbies and other outside interests while maintaining the business more or less in the status quo.

Substage III-D   In the Success-Disengagement substage, the company has attained true economic health, has sufficient size and product-market penetration to ensure economic success, and earns average or above-average profits. The company can stay at this stage indefinitely, provided environmental change does not destroy its market niche or ineffective management reduce its competitive abilities.

Organizationally, the company has grown large enough to, in many cases, require functional managers to take over certain duties performed by the owner. The managers should be competent but need not be of the highest caliber, since their upward potential is limited by the corporate goals. Cash is plentiful and the main concern is to avoid a cash drain in prosperous periods to the detriment of the company's ability to withstand the inevitable rough times.

In addition, the first professional staff members come on board, usually a controller in the office and perhaps a production scheduler in the plant. Basic financial, marketing, and production systems are in place. Planning in the form of operational budgets supports functional delegation. The owner and, to a lesser extent, the company's managers, should be monitoring a strategy to, essentially, maintain the status quo.

As the business matures, it and the owner increasingly move apart, to some extent because of the owner's activities elsewhere and to some extent because of the presence of other managers. Many companies continue for long periods in the Success-Disengagement substage. The product-market niche of some does not permit growth; this is the case for many service businesses in small or medium-sized, slowly growing communities and for franchise holders with limited territories.

Other owners actually choose this route; if the company can continue to adapt to environmental changes, it can continue as is, be sold or merged at a profit, or subsequently be stimulated into growth (endpoint 3 on *Exhibit 4*). For franchise holders, this last option would necessitate the purchase of other franchises.

If the company cannot adapt to changing circumstances, as was the case with many automobile dealers in the late 1970s and early 1980s, it will either fold or drop back to a marginally surviving company (endpoint 4 on *Exhibit 4*).

Substage III-G   In the Success-Growth substage, the owner consolidates the company and marshals resources for growth. The owner takes the cash and the established borrowing power of the company and risks it all in financing growth.

Among the important tasks are to make sure the basic business stays profitable so that it will not outrun its source of cash and to develop managers to meet the needs of the growing business. This second task requires hiring managers with an eye to the company's future rather than its current condition.

Systems should also be installed with attention to forthcoming needs. Operational planning is, as in substage III-D, in the form of budgets, but strategic planning is extensive and deeply involves the owner. The owner is thus far more active in all phases of the company's affairs than in the disengagement aspect of this phase.

If it is successful, the III-G company proceeds into Stage IV. Indeed, III-G is often the first attempt at growing before commitment to a growth strategy. If the III-G company is unsuccessful, the causes may be detected in time for the company to shift to III-D. If not, retrenchment to the Survival Stage may be possible prior to bankruptcy or a distress sale.

STAGE IV: TAKE-OFF

In this stage the key problems are how to grow rapidly and how to finance that growth. The most important questions, then, are in two areas.

Delegation   Can the owner delegate responsibility to others to improve the managerial effectiveness of a fast-growing and increasingly complex enterprise? Further, will the action be true delegation with controls on performance and a willingness to see mistakes made, or will it be abdication, as is so often the case?

Cash   Will there be enough to satisfy the great demands growth brings (often requiring a willingness on the owner's part to tolerate a high debt/equity ratio) and a cash flow that is not eroded by inadequate expense controls or ill-advised investments brought about by owner impatience?

The organization is decentralized and, at least in part, divisionalized—usually in either sales or production. The key managers must be very competent to handle a growing and complex business environment. The systems, strained by growth, are becoming more refined and extensive. Both operational and strategic planning are being done and involve specific managers. The owner and the business have become reasonably separate, yet the company is still dominated by both the owner's presence and stock control.

This is a pivotal period in a company's life. If the owner rises to the challenges of a growing company, both financially and managerially, it can become a big business. If not, it can usually be sold—at a profit—provided the owner recognizes his or her limitations soon enough. Too often, those who bring the business to the Success Stage are unsuccessful in Stage IV, either because they try to grow too fast and run out of cash (the owner falls victim to the omnipotence syndrome), or are unable to delegate effectively enough to make the company work (the omniscience syndrome).

It is, of course, possible for the company to traverse this high-growth stage without the original management. Often the entrepreneur who founded the company and brought it to the Success Stage is replaced either voluntarily or involuntarily by the company's investors or creditors.

If the company fails to make the big time, it may be able to retrench and continue as a successful and substantial company at a state of equilibrium (endpoint 7 on *Exhibit 4*). Or it may drop back to stage III (endpoint 6) or, if the problems are too extensive, it may drop all the way back to the Survival Stage (endpoint 5) or even fail.

STAGE V: RESOURCE MATURITY

The greatest concerns of a company entering this stage are, first, to consolidate and control the financial gains brought on by rapid growth and, second, to retain the advantages of small size, including flexibility of response and the entrepreneurial spirit. The corporation must expand the management force fast enough to eliminate the inefficiencies that growth can produce and professionalize the company by use of such tools as budgets, strategic planning, management by objectives, and standard cost systems—and do this without stifling its entrepreneurial qualities.

A company in Stage V has the staff and financial resources to engage in detailed operational and strategic planning. The management is decentralized, adequately staffed, and experienced. And systems are extensive and well developed. The owner and the business are quite separate, both financially and operationally.

The company has now arrived. It has the advantages of size, financial resources, and managerial talent. If it can preserve its entrepreneurial spirit, it will be a formidable force in the market. If not, it may enter a sixth stage of sorts: ossification.

Ossification is characterized by a lack of innovative decision making and the avoidance of risks. It seems most common in large corporations whose sizable market share, buying power, and financial resources keep them viable until there is a major change in the environment. Unfortunately for these businesses, it is usually their rapidly growing competitors that notice the environmental change first.

——— KEY MANAGEMENT FACTORS

Several factors, which change in importance as the business grows and develops, are prominent in determining ultimate success or failure. We identified eight factors in our research, of which four relate to the enterprise and four to the owner. The four that relate to the company are as follows:

1. Financial resources, including cash and borrowing power.
2. Personnel resources, relating to numbers, depth, and quality of people, particularly at the management and staff levels.
3. Systems resources, in terms of the degree of sophistication of both information and planning and control systems.
4. Business resources, including customer relations, market share, supplier relations, manufacturing and distribution processes, technology and reputation, all of which give the company a position in its industry and market.

The four factors that relate to the owner are as follows:

1. Owner's goals for himself or herself and for the business.
2. Owner's operational abilities in doing important jobs such as marketing, inventing, producing, and managing distribution.
3. Owner's managerial ability and willingness to delegate responsibility and to manage the activities of others.
4. Owner's strategic abilities for looking beyond the present and matching the strengths and weaknesses of the company with his or her goals.

As a business moves from one stage to another, the importance of the factors changes. We might view the factors as alternating among three levels of importance: first, key variables that are absolutely essential for success and must receive high priority; second, factors that are clearly necessary for the enterprise's success and must receive some attention; and third, factors of little immediate concern to top management. If we categorize each of the eight factors listed previously, based on its importance at each stage of the company's development, we get a clear picture of changing management demands. (See *Exhibit 5*.)

——— VARYING DEMANDS

The changing nature of managerial challenges becomes apparent when one examines *Exhibit 5*. In the early stages, the owner's ability to do the job gives life to the business. Small businesses are built on the owner's talents: the ability

EXHIBIT 5
Management Factors and the Stages

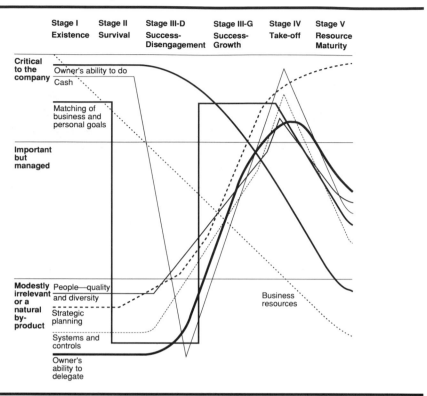

to sell, produce, invent, or whatever. This factor is thus of the highest importance. The owner's ability to delegate, however, is on the bottom of the scale, since there are few if any employees to delegate to.

As the company grows, other people enter sales, production, or engineering and they first support, and then even supplant, the owner's skills—thus reducing the importance of this factor. At the same time, the owner must spend less time doing and more time managing. He or she must increase the amount of work done through other people, which means delegating. The inability of many founders to let go of doing and to begin managing and delegating explains the demise of many businesses in substage III-G and Stage IV.

The owner contemplating a growth strategy must understand the change in personal activities such a decision entails and examine the managerial needs depicted in *Exhibit 5*. Similarly, an entrepreneur contemplating starting a business should recognize the need to do all the selling, manufacturing, or engineering from the beginning, along with managing cash and planning the business's course—requirements that take much energy and commitment.

The importance of cash changes as the business changes. It is an extremely important resource at the start, becomes easily manageable at the

Success Stage, and is a main concern again if the organization begins to grow. As growth slows at the end of Stage IV or in Stage V, cash becomes a manageable factor again. The companies in Stage III need to recognize the financial needs and risk entailed in a move to Stage IV.

The issues of people, planning, and systems gradually increase in importance as the company progresses from slow initial growth (substage III-G) to rapid growth (Stage IV). These resources must be acquired somewhat in advance of the growth stage so that they are in place when needed. Matching business and personal goals is crucial in the Existence Stage because the owner must recognize and be reconciled to the heavy financial and time-energy demands of the new business. Some find these demands more than they can handle. In the Survival Stage, however, the owner has achieved the necessary reconciliation, and survival is paramount; matching of goals is thus irrelevant in Stage II.

A second serious period for goal matching occurs in the Success Stage. Does the owner wish to commit his or her time and risk the accumulated equity of the business in order to grow or instead prefer to savor some of the benefits of success? All too often the owner wants both, but to expand the business rapidly while planning a new house on Maui for long vacations involves considerable risk. To make a realistic decision on which direction to take, the owner needs to consider the personal and business demands of different strategies and to evaluate his or her managerial ability to meet these challenges.

Finally, business resources are the stuff of which success is made; they involve building market share, customer relations, solid vendor sources, and a technological base, and are very important in the early stages. In later stages the loss of a major customer, supplier, or technical source is more easily compensated for. Thus, the relative importance of this factor is shown to be declining.

The changing role of the factors clearly illustrates the need for owner flexibility. An overwhelming preoccupation with cash is quite important at some stages and less important at others. Delaying tax payments at almost all costs is paramount in Stages I and II but may seriously distort accounting data and use up management time during periods of success and growth. "Doing" versus "delegating" also requires a flexible management. Holding onto old strategies and old ways ill serves a company that is entering the growth stages and can even be fatal.

AVOIDING FUTURE PROBLEMS

Even a casual look at *Exhibit 5* reveals the demands the Take-off Stage makes on the enterprise. Nearly every factor except the owner's "ability to do" is crucial. This is the stage of action and potentially large rewards. Looking at this exhibit, owners who want such growth must ask themselves:

- Do I have the quality and diversity of people needed to manage a growing company?
- Do I have now, or will I have shortly, the systems in place to handle the needs of a larger, more diversified company?
- Do I have the inclination and ability to delegate decision making to my managers?
- Do I have enough cash and borrowing power along with the inclination to risk everything to pursue rapid growth?

Similarly, the potential entrepreneur can see that starting a business requires an ability to do something very well (or a good marketable idea), high energy, and a favorable cash flow forecast (or a large sum of cash on hand). These are less important in Stage V, when well-developed people-management skills, good information systems, and budget controls take priority. Perhaps this is why some experienced people from large companies fail to make good as entrepreneurs or managers in small companies. They are used to delegating and are not good enough at doing.

——— APPLYING THE MODEL

This scheme can be used to evaluate all sorts of small-business situations, even those that at first glance appear to be exceptions. Take the case of franchises. These enterprises begin the Existence Stage with a number of differences from most start-up situations. They often have the following advantages:

- A marketing plan developed from extensive research.
- Sophisticated information and control systems in place.
- Operating procedures that are standardized and very well developed.
- Promotion and other start-up support such as brand identification.
- They also require relatively high start-up capital.

If the franchisor has done sound market analysis and has a solid, differentiated product, the new venture can move rapidly through the Existence and Survival Stages—where many new ventures founder—and into the early stages of Success. The costs to the franchisee for these beginning advantages are usually as follows:

- Limited growth due to territory restrictions.
- Heavy dependence on the franchisor for continued economic health.
- Potential for later failure as the entity enters Stage III without the maturing experiences of Stages I and II.

One way to grow with franchising is to acquire multiple units or territories. Managing several of these, of course, takes a different set of skills than managing one and it is here that the lack of survival experience can become damaging.

Another seeming exception is high-technology start-ups. These are highly visible companies—such as computer software businesses, genetic-engineering enterprises, or laser-development companies—that attract much interest from the investment community. Entrepreneurs and investors who start them often intend that they grow quite rapidly and then go public or be sold to other corporations. This strategy requires them to acquire a permanent source of outside capital almost from the beginning. The providers of this cash, usually venture capitalists, may bring planning and operating systems of a Stage III or a Stage IV company to the organization, along with an outside board of directors to oversee the investment.

The resources provided enable this entity to jump through Stage I, last out Stage II until the product comes to market, and attain Stage III. At this point, the planned strategy for growth is often beyond the managerial capabilities of the founding owner, and the outside capital interests may dictate a management change. In such cases, the company moves rapidly into Stage IV and, depending on the competence of the development, marketing, and production people, the company becomes a big success or an expensive failure. The problems that beset both franchises and high-technology companies stem from a mismatch of the founders' problem-solving skills and the demands that "forced evolution" brings to the company.

Besides the extreme examples of franchises and high-technology companies, we found that while a number of other companies appeared to be at a given stage of development, they were, on closer examination, actually at one stage with regard to a particular factor and at another stage with regard to the others. For example, one company had an abundance of cash from a period of controlled growth (substage III-G) and was ready to accelerate its expansion, while at the same time the owner was trying to supervise everybody (Stages I or II). In another, the owner was planning to run for mayor of a city (substage III-D) but was impatient with the company's slow growth (substage III-G).

Although rarely is a factor more than one stage ahead of or behind the company as a whole, an imbalance of factors can create serious problems for the entrepreneur. Indeed, one of the major challenges in a small company is the fact that both the problems faced and the skills necessary to deal with them change as the company grows. Thus, owners must anticipate and manage the factors as they become important to the company.

A company's development stage determines the managerial factors that must be dealt with. Its plans help determine which factors will eventually have to be faced. Knowing its development stage and future plans enables managers, consultants, and investors to make more informed choices and to prepare themselves and their companies for later challenges. While each enterprise is unique in many ways, all face similar problems and all are subject to great changes. That may well be why being an owner is so much fun and such a challenge.

—— DISCUSSION QUESTIONS

1. During the Survival Stage, the authors say, formal planning consists, at best, of cash planning. By the next stage, Success, "strategic planning is extensive." Once survival of your business was no longer in doubt, what business goals would be important to you? What issues would you have your strategic planners tackle?

2. According to *Exhibit 5*, matching of business and personal goals is critical at the Existence Stage and at the Success and Take-off Stages. If you were evaluating your personal goals at the Existence Stage, what questions would you ask yourself? How would your personal concerns change at the Success and Take-off Stages?

3. As the venture grows and becomes more complex, the entrepreneur faces the difficult task of delegating. Suppose your venture were entering the Success phase and "hiring managers with an eye to the company's future." What management positions would you create? What backgrounds would you look for? What questions would you ask of job candidates?

4. As *Exhibit 5* shows, the importance of cash fluctuates as the company progresses from one stage to the next. Suppose you are a financial planner for a new venture. What questions would you ask about the flow and deployment of cash at each of the five stages described in the reading?

5. Mature companies, the authors say, must preserve their entrepreneurial spirit or risk ossification. What elements of an entrepreneurial spirit are most important to preserve? Are there any that should be discarded? What actions can companies take to keep the entrepreneurial spirit alive?

Compensation Planning for Entrepreneurs

22

HOWARD H. STEVENSON AND JAMES Z. TURNER

Designing the appropriate compensation package is a challenge for all companies. Because start-up companies lack the resources and financial stability of the large corporation, they must be especially creative and flexible in producing packages that will attract and motivate first-rate managers. At the same time, it is essential that executives of start-ups recognize the complex legal issues that arise in planning compensation packages.

This reading describes the building blocks of a basic compensation program. Equally important, it illustrates the impact of the tax code as of 1985 on compensation planning. Of course, tax laws change on a regular basis and the reading is not a guide to the laws as they currently exist; what matters is that the importance of these laws to compensation planning remains constant. As the reading shows, an understanding of the legal implications of different compensation options must be an intrinsic part of the planning process. And because tax laws are complex and changing, it is vital that entrepreneurs designing compensation packages employ the counsel of well-qualified, specialized advisers. The reading points out, moreover, that as a company matures, different compensation programs become appropriate; entrepreneurs must therefore think strategically, addressing the immediate needs of their businesses and envisioning the impact on compensation of such future events as harvesting and the termination of key shareholders.

A major reason for the use of equity-based compensation in new companies is that most start-ups simply do not have sufficient cash to pay executives handsome salaries. Options for sharing ownership also seem consistent with the entrepreneurial style and risk profile of business founders. Nonetheless, employees' needs for adequate salary and fringe benefits cannot be ignored: cash, not stock options, pays the mortgage and buys the groceries. An equitable salary structure and protection from financial catastrophe, in the form of group insurance providing life, medical, and disability benefits, must be basic components of any new venture's compensation program. Even if a start-up firm's benefits package is modest compared with that of an established corporation—for example, it may not, initially, include a qualified retirement plan—a well-designed program will send an important psychological message to all levels of management.

The attitudes of the entrepreneur will also be reflected in the design of perks (e.g., use of company cars) that are attractive to the recipient, yet establish a principle of respect for the company. In a small corporate environment, junior employees will quickly confuse corporate and personal purpose if they see their bosses doing so.

———— RECEIVING OWNERSHIP

FOUNDERS' STOCK

The first building block of any start-up corporation's compensation program is "founders' stock," stock issued to the initial shareholders or assigned to early key executives on approximately the same basis. This cheap stock can make paper millionaires of the founders when the corporation goes public. Immediately, however, it presents several tax questions.

First, it is not unusual for some of the founders to receive this stock in exchange for past or future performance of services. If so, according to Internal Revenue Code Section 83 (IRC §83), the value of the stock counts as compensation income and is, therefore, taxable. Under this rule, the employer is entitled to claim a corresponding deduction for compensation expense, although the value of the deduction is minimal to a corporation in the start-up phase because of its lack of taxable income.

Second, and more important, is the tax time bomb that can be disastrous if the hoped-for appreciation in the value of the founders' stock occurs. Section 83(a) of the IRC provides that if a person receives property (e.g., founders' stock) in return for services, that person must declare as income the amount of the gain in value in the first taxable year in which his or her rights in such property are "transferable and not subject to a substantial risk of forfeiture." Since founders' stock is generally subject to restrictions that make it nontransferable and subject to a substantial risk of forfeiture, taxation is generally delayed until such restrictions lapse. However, to avoid a whopping tax bill at that time, IRC Section 83(b) enables a taxpayer to elect to include in income in the year of such transfer the excess of the fair market value of the restricted property over the amount paid for it. The election must be filed by the taxpayer within 30 days after the transfer of restricted property; it ensures that all future appreciation will be treated as a capital gain.

For example, suppose you receive founders' stock in 1981 with a value of $1,000 (or stock worth $2,000 where you pay $1,000). The stock is not transferable and is subject to forfeiture. In 1983, the restrictions lapse and the value of the shares is $1,000,000. The IRS would send a tax bill based on taxable income of $999,000. The recognition of the gain can be deferred by filing an 83(b) election within 30 days of receipt of the stock and by treating as income in the year received the difference between its fair market value and its cost ($1,000 in this case). The gain would not be recognized until the stock was sold and any gain realized would be considered a capital gain rather than ordinary income.

Sometimes outside investors have a substantial effect on the amount of compensation income recognized by founders under IRC §83. If the corporation attracts seed money and additional rounds of working capital through private equity placements, it sometimes becomes obvious that the founders acquired their stock at a bargain price—the bargain element of which will be taxable as compensation income. Thus, it is not that the outside financing creates compensation for the founders; rather that the outside financing provides a measure of the founders' compensation.

A clever solution to this measurement problem is to issue convertible preferred stock to the outside investors and reserve the common stock for founders and new key employees. The convertible preferred stock should carry a liquidation preference designed to be large enough, upon liquidation, to eliminate the book value of the corporation, thereby leaving nothing for the common stock. In subsequent rounds of outside financing, the liquidation preference of each class or series of preferred stock should be increased to cover current book value. In addition, the convertible preferred stock should have senior dividend, preemptive, and redemption rights, as well as registration rights and the rights of co-sale by contract. Holders of the common stock own only the shareholders' equity remaining after satisfying the preferences accorded the convertible preferred stock. Accordingly, the superior rights attached to the convertible preferred stock, when coupled with the likelihood in most cases of negative earnings, should substantially depress the fair market value of the common stock taxable under IRC §83. This enables the founders and new key employees to receive common stock at prices and at tax liabilities significantly lower than those paid by outside investors.

INCENTIVE STOCK OPTIONS

An incentive stock option plan (ISO) allows employees to acquire stock and receive favorable tax treatment provided certain conditions are met. To be an ISO, or a qualified stock option, an option must satisfy numerous conditions.

- The plan must be approved by stockholders within 12 months before or after its adoption. It should state the aggregate number of shares subject to option and the employees who can receive them.
- The option must be granted within 10 years from the date the plan is adopted or approved by the stockholders, whichever is earlier.
- The term of the option must not be longer than 10 years.
- The option price must not be less than the stock's fair market value at the time the option is granted.
- The option, by its terms, must not be transferable except in the event of death.

- The optionee, at the time the option is granted, may not already own more than 10% of the company's combined voting power. This condition is waived if the option price is at least equal to 110% of the stock's fair market value at the time the option is granted and if the option term does not exceed five years.
- The option, by its terms, must not be exercisable while there is a previously granted ISO outstanding (i.e., options must be sequentially exercised).
- The plan must limit the fair market value of stock for which an optionee is granted options in any one year to $100,000 plus any unused-limit carryover to such year. This unused-limit carryover equals one-half of the excess of $100,000 over the fair market value of the stock for which the optionee was granted ISOs in any calendar year since 1980, and it may be carried over for three succeeding calendar years.
- At all times from the date of the grant of the option to the date three months before the exercise of the option, the optionee must be employed by the corporation granting the option or by an affiliated corporation.

If the stock option meets all of the conditions noted above, several tax consequences flow to the employer and employee. First, the employee need not count the value of the shares as income on either the granting or the exercise of an ISO. However, the excess of the fair market value of the shares on the date of their transfer pursuant to the exercise of an ISO over the option price is an item of tax preference and may be subject to the 20% alternative minimum tax. Second, provided the stock acquired on the exercise of an ISO is held for at least two years from the date of grant *and* at least one year from the date of exercise, all gain on the sale of the stock will be taxed as long-term capital gains.[1]

Finally, if the employee disposes of stock acquired on the exercise of an ISO within either the two-year or one-year holding period referred to above (a "disqualifying disposition"), the employee must include as ordinary income in the year of disposition the lesser of (a) the excess of the fair market value of the stock on the date the option is exercised over the exercise price, or (b) the excess of the amount realized on the sale or exchange over the exercise price. Any additional gain will be treated as a long-term or short-term capital gain in the year of disposition, depending on how long the stock is held.

In spite of the rules for ISOs outlined above, numerous traps lie in wait for the unwary. The principal ones are discussed below.

---

1. Insiders (officers, directors, or 10% stockholders) must hold exercised options for six months before selling [IRC §16(b)]. This holding period prevents them from simultaneously exercising and selling their options; it also prevents them from capturing any short-swing profits in the same time period through other securities the SEC treats as equity securities (i.e., call or put options, warrants, subscription rights, etc.). Insiders who breach this provision may be sued and all profits from the sale will be paid back to the company.

Alternative Minimum Tax   The employee's exposure to the alternative minimum tax on the exercise of an ISO can create serious problems. The alternative minimum tax is the excess, if any, of (a) 20% of the amount by which a taxpayer's adjusted gross income exceeds an exemption amount of $30,000 ($40,000 if a joint return is filed) over (b) the regular income tax paid. Consider the following nightmare: Company X grants an ISO to a key employee to purchase 100,000 shares of its stock at $.60 a share, its current fair market value (total exercise price: $60,000). Four years later, after several rounds of venture capital financing and the introduction of a spectacular new product, the company goes public at $10 a share. The employee exercises his or her option and acquires 100,000 shares of stock for $60,000. The amount of tax preference potentially subject to alternative minimum tax is $940,000 ($1 million − $60,000); thus the employee could face a staggering tax bill without having sufficient funds to pay the tax.

In the above example, a taxpayer with no other income would incur an alternative minimum tax of $188,000 (20% of $940,000). However, since the employee probably has other taxable income, and since the alternative minimum tax is 20% of the excess over the regular income tax paid, minus an exemption, a taxpayer in the 50% tax bracket would only need about $450,000 in other income to negate the alternative minimum tax. The reality is that with proper financial planning the effect of the alternative minimum tax can often be nullified.

Sequential-Exercise Rule   The sequential-exercise rule prevents an employee from exercising an ISO while a previously granted ISO is outstanding. For example, if an ISO was granted at $25 a share in year 1 and at $20 a share in year 2, the employee is required to exercise the higher priced year-1 option before exercising the more favorable year-2 option. This problem is particularly acute in installment-exercise options (e.g., an option exercisable in 20% increments over five years) because all installments of the year-1 option need to be exercised before the exercise of any year-2 options. One solution to this problem is to grant immediately exercisable options that are subject to a right of repurchase in favor of the employer at the option price. This repurchase right could lapse at intervals corresponding to the intervals at which an installment option is exercisable.

Effect of Modification on Sequential-Exercise Rule   If an ISO is modified so that it is considered the granting of a new option, the original option is deemed to continue for purposes of the sequential-exercise rule and may, therefore, prevent the exercise of the "new" ISO until the "old" ISO has, in accordance with its original terms, expired.

Loans   Serious problems may arise if the employer lends the employee the cash needed to exercise the ISO or simply allows him or her to exercise the

ISO by giving a note as payment. In the latter case, the note must constitute full recourse for purposes of commencing the one-year holding period; and if the term of the note extends beyond 12 months, it must bear an annual rate of interest at least equal to the current federal rate. In addition, the terms of the ISO must specifically permit the use of notes as payment to avoid the risk of having the ISO deemed a modification.

Holding-Period Requirements   For purposes of the two-year and one-year holding requirements referred to above, a "disposition" generally includes a sale, exchange, gift, or any transfer of legal title. For example, the IRS has held that the transfer of option stock into a blind trust by a taxpayer before entering public service constitutes a disposition for this purpose. The implications for tax planning are obvious. Holders of an ISO or founders, in general, should always maintain a prudent awareness of the tax regulations to avoid unnecessary and undesirable tax consequences. For instance, a founder might consider initially registering some founder's stock in a child's name to avoid the double taxation that would result from a later transfer.

Conditions on Exercise of an ISO   It is not uncommon for an employer to place conditions on an ISO that must be met before the ISO can be exercised. However, care must be taken to ensure that such conditions are not deemed conditions on the granting of the ISO or the two-year holding period will not commence until the condition is met.

Stock-for-Stock Exchange   Optionees may exercise their ISO options by transferring previously acquired stock to the employer. This is a popular ISO term because the surrender of the stock is generally a nontaxable event. However, if the surrendered stock is also ISO stock, the dual holding-period requirements must have been met at the time of transfer to qualify for the tax protection afforded by an ISO. This limitation prevents abuse of ISOs.

Fair Market Valuation   Determining the fair market value of stock purchasable by exercise of an ISO is necessary at the time of granting the ISO because of the requirement that the option price not be lower than the then-current fair market value. The officers of a closely held corporation must, for this reason, institute procedures enabling them to determine fair market value at frequent intervals. Outside appraisals by completely independent and well-qualified experts provide the best means of demonstrating an employer's good faith attempt to evaluate a stock's market value.

However, since such outside appraisals may be prohibitively expensive, smaller or newer corporations desiring to grant options over an extended period may choose to do an in-house valuation. The IRS permits the use of any reasonable valuation method, including specifically the methods used for estate-tax purposes.[2]

The architect of an ISO plan should be closely acquainted with the factors the IRS considers fundamental to any fair market stock price valuation. If such a valuation results in a substantial understatement of tax liability (as determined by the IRS), penalties can be severe. The IRS, in addition to collecting the tax owed and the corresponding fines, will suspend the statute of limitations provision. No start-up company flourishes under constant IRS scrutiny.

One last factor to consider when establishing a stock's fair market value is the extent to which a company may legitimately discount the value of its stock. This is done to reflect factors such as lack of a market for the stock, lack of control, potential loss of key management, and restrictions on the sale of stock. The last of these factors is the most significant since the sale of unregistered securities is generally prohibited by SEC Rule 144 for two years after their acquisition. A 1982 tax court ruling allowed the taxpayer to discount the value of restricted stock acquired by exercise of a qualified stock option by 33 1/3% in determining the fair market value for purposes of calculating the alternative minimum tax on tax preference items. Presumably (and here counsel is advised), this ruling also permits an employer to discount a stock's value for purposes of determining the option price on the date of the grant.

NONQUALIFIED OPTIONS

In spite of the advantageous tax rules for ISOs, nonqualified stock options continue to play an important role in compensation planning for a number of reasons. These include:

- The $100,000 limit on the value of stock for which ISOs may be granted in any one year. Nonqualified options are used to attract new key employees and to reward continuing key employees for unusual successes.
- Situations in which the option price of outstanding ISOs is significantly higher than the current fair market value of the stock. Because the sequential-exercise rule prevents the exercise of a new ISO at current option prices, the only way to give an option to an employee at the lower, current value is a nonqualified option.
- The unattractiveness of ISOs for employees with on-going alternative minimum tax because of large tax preference items. Such employees may prefer to have some of their compensation in the form of nonqualified options.

---

2. The 1985 IRC §2031(b) states that "the value [of unlisted stock and securities] shall be determined by taking into consideration, in addition to all other factors, the value of stock or securities of corporations engaged in the same or a similar line of business which are listed on an exchange."

- Cases in which a company wants to grant an option to an outside director, consultant, scientific adviser, or service provider. ISOs may be granted only to employees.

Nonqualified stock options are governed by the same tax rules as ISOs (IRC §83), but the consequences are stiffer. The main difference is that the IRC §83(b) provision (the election) is not available at the time the option is granted unless it has a readily ascertainable fair market value. If the option does not have such a value when it is granted, the rules of IRC §83(a) and the election described in §83(b) apply to the option at the time it is exercised and the stock is acquired. In either case, the employee includes the value of the option in ordinary income in accordance with the above rules, and his or her basis is adjusted by that amount. Any additional gain upon disposition of the stock is treated as long-term or short-term gain, depending on how long it has been held.

The key words for allowing an employee to seek the protection of a Section 83(b) election at the time of the option's grant are "readily ascertainable fair market value." If an option is not actively traded on an established market, it does not have such an ascertainable value unless the taxpayer can show that all four of the following conditions exist:

1. The option is transferable by the optionee;
2. The option is exercisable immediately in full by the optionee;
3. The option is not subject to any restriction or condition that has a significant effect on the fair market value of the option; and
4. That in determining the fair market value of the option it is necessary to consider the value of the property subject to the option, the probability of the ascertainable value of the property increasing or decreasing, and the duration of the period in which the option can be exercised.

Nonqualified options are not statutory options and, as such, are free from some of the limitations and regulations of the IRC. Even so, there are a number of important issues to consider when designing a compensation program that includes nonqualified stock options.

Inadvertent ISO   An IRS regulation states that a stock option granted after April 9, 1984, that meets all of the requirements of an ISO will be treated for tax purposes as an ISO, even if it is labeled a nonqualified option. Given the desirability of granting nonqualified options rather than ISOs, in some cases avoiding this requirement can become critical. This can be done by extending the option beyond that permitted for ISOs (e.g., 11 years rather than 10) or by making it exercisable four months after termination of employment rather than only three.

Withholding   To ensure that a company receives the deduction for an employee's exercise of a nonqualified option, it must institute procedures to withhold the appropriate amount from the employee's compensation income (generally 20% of the compensation income recognized by the employee). This may be done a variety of ways (e.g., through direct withholding against other compensation payable to the employee or by having the employee make cash payments as needed to the employer). In any event, the terms of the option should give the employer broad enough powers to enable it to meet this requirement.

Grants by Shareholders   The rules of IRC §83 cannot be avoided by having another shareholder, rather than the employer, grant a nonqualified option. If this occurs, when the option is exercised the shareholder will be deemed to have made a capital contribution to the employer, and the actual transfer of stock will then be deemed to have been made by the employer to the employee. In this case, however, the withholding obligation will fall to the shareholder, although it can be satisfied within the employer's withholding system.

Loans   As in the case of ISOs, loans for nonqualified options may create a number of problems. First, although a no-interest or low-interest loan cannot "disqualify" a nonqualified option, it can cause an employee to incur additional compensation income because of imputed interest rules. For example, if an employee exercises a nonqualified option with an option price of $50,000 by giving a no-interest note for that amount payable in five years, the IRS will treat a portion of the amount paid as interest imputed at the federal rate. At a 10% rate, it would reduce the principal amount of the note to about $30,000. If the fair market value of the stock on the date of exercise is $100,000, the employee will have to recognize compensation income of $70,000 (i.e., $100,000 – $30,000) rather than $50,000. Although arguably entitled to an offsetting deduction, the employee may not be entitled to it until the loan is paid off. The second problem then becomes the IRS limitation on deductions for investment purposes as IRC §103 limits the deduction in any one year to $10,000 plus net investment income for the year. The third problem is that the loan must constitute full recourse. If it does not, the stock will be deemed transferred only when the note is paid off and the employee risks having further appreciation taxed as ordinary income.

Valuation   The same valuation concerns apply to nonqualified options as to ISOs. Although a failure to determine the fair market value of stock acquired upon exercise of a nonqualified option will not disqualify the option (as it would in the case of an ISO), it is nevertheless important for the employer to implement procedures enabling fair market value determinations of the stock to be readily made. Valuation at the time of exercise is also important from an employer's viewpoint, because it determines the amount of the compensation deduction.

Comparison of ISOs and Nonqualified Options   Considering the merits and problems of both ISOs and nonqualified options, it is natural to ask which form of compensation is more attractive. The main difference between them is that in ISOs the 20% alternative minimum tax applies not only at the time of exercise but also at the time of disposition, to the extent of the long-term capital gain deduction. In other words, appreciation in the value of the stock is subject to the alternative minimum tax both at exercise and again at disposition. The following *Exhibit* compares the tax consequences of the two types of options and assumes that the employee has used up his or her minimum tax exemption by a substantial margin.

Mathematically, the maximum possible difference can be quantified by considering the tax treatment of pre-exercise appreciation only. Under the ISO, the maximum alternative minimum tax is 32% (20% at exercise and 12% upon disposition), and the maximum long-term capital gain is 20%. Therefore, the maximum total tax on the ISO stock is 52%. In the case of a nonqualified option, there is only one tax, at the time of exercise, at the rate of 50% of the pre-exercise appreciation. With respect to post-exercise appreciation, the ISO and nonqualified option are treated identically.

Therefore, in some cases a nonqualified option is slightly more advantageous to the employee than an ISO. However, two factors swing the pendulum back in favor of the ISO. First, as can be seen from the *Exhibit*, a nonqualified option has a higher tax at exercise, and the time value of money therefore favors the ISO. Second, and more important, the imposition of the alternative minimum tax upon the sale of the ISO occurs only if the taxpayer has substantial tax preference items other than the 60% long-term capital gain deduction applicable to the sale of the stock. If the only tax preference item is this 60% deduction there is no alternative minimum tax since the taxpayer would already have paid a long-term capital gain tax at the rate of 20%. Also, a reduction in the marginal tax rate (due to tax shelters) favors ISOs because the capital gain at disposition for an ISO is the difference between the selling price and the option price, whereas for a nonqualified option it is the difference between the selling price and the exercise price.

EXHIBIT

	INCENTIVE STOCK OPTION		NONQUALIFIED OPTION	
When Taxed	*Type of Tax*	*Rate of Tax*	*Type of Tax*	*Rate of Tax*
At exercise	Alt. min. tax	20% (EP–OP)[a]	Ord. inc.	50% (EP–OP)
At disposition	L–t cap. gain	50%x40%(SP–OP)[a]	L–t cap. gain	50%x40%(SP–EP)
	Alt. min. tax[b]	20%x60%(SP–OP)	Alt. min. tax[b]	20%x60%(SP–EP)

a. The option price (OP) is less than the exercise price (EP), which is less than the selling price (SP).

b. The 60% represents the long-term capital gains deduction.

JUNIOR COMMON STOCK

Another form of compensation for aggressive start-up firms is junior common stock. The objective of these stock plans is to allow key employees to acquire a junior class of common stock at a fraction of the value of the regular class of common stock and to extend the possibility that it might some day be converted into regular common stock. Unlike founders' stock, where the payoff comes from going public or being acquired by another company, the rewards of junior common stock come from substantial improvements in the employer's sales and/or earnings.

Typically this separate class of common stock conveys rights inferior to those of the regular common stock. For example, it may have only 1/10th the voting and dividend rights of the regular stock, as well as inferior liquidation rights. If the corporation achieves certain specified goals (e.g., $250 million in sales and $25 million in net income for four consecutive quarters), the junior shares automatically convert to regular shares on a one-for-one basis. In addition, junior stock plans usually include transfer limitations, repurchase provisions, and/or rights of first refusal in order to restrict ownership of shares to continuing employees of the corporation. Such stock may be purchased outright by the employee or offered through ISOs or nonqualified stock options.

If an employee purchases the junior common stock outright and makes a Section 83(b) election at the time of purchase, the purchase is tax free under IRC §83 at both the time of purchase and upon lapse of any restrictions. Conversion of the junior shares is a tax-free exchange of common stock for common stock. The employee's basis in the junior shares carries over to the regular shares, as does credit for the period the employee has held the junior shares for purposes of meeting the holding-period requirements for long-term capital gain treatment upon disposition. If junior common stock is offered under an ISO or nonqualified stock option, the risks for each option outlined earlier apply.

The IRS has not yet taken a public position with respect to the tax treatment of junior stock. There are several reasons why the IRS may challenge the application of desired tax consequences to this stock.

- *Valuation.* Given the peculiarities of junior stock, valuation is the critical issue; in the case of a private company it is especially speculative.
- *Lapsable Restrictions.* The IRS might argue that the acquisition of junior stock is nothing more than the acquisition of regular stock subject to lapsable restrictions and that, therefore, taxation should be deferred until the conversion event.
- *Conversion.* The IRS might take the position that conversion does not represent a tax-free exchange by arguing that one or the other class of common stock was in reality preferred stock.

In addition, accounting issues in regard to junior common stock remain clouded. In December 1984, the Financial Accounting Standards Board (FASB) proposed that when conversion of the junior stock to regular stock becomes "probable," the difference between the price paid for the junior stock and the current fair market value of the regular stock be treated as a compensation charge against the corporation's earnings. This was indeed a major change and was to apply regardless of whether the stock was acquired under a purchase plan or an option plan. On March 14, 1984, FASB issued a substantially equivalent "Interpretation," and that date became the proposed grandfather date. The issue is still being debated.

It is useful to compare the purposes of junior stock with the clever use of convertible preferred stock discussed in the section on founders' stock. While convertible preferred stock and junior common stock seem to possess many of the same features, the goals of the two techniques are exactly the opposite. In the case of convertible preferred, the goal is to depress the value of the regular class of stock into which the secondary class will be converted; in the case of junior common, the goal is to depress the value of the secondary class that will be converted into the regular class.

─── HARVESTING OWNERSHIP: RULE 144 TRANSACTIONS

Founders' stock, also known as "144 stock," has substantial restrictions on both its transferability and liquidity. Entrepreneurs should clearly understand Rule 144 transactions so as to avoid the pitfalls of noncompliance with the Securities and Exchange Commission (SEC) in designing a compensation package. In this section, therefore, we briefly explain the terminology of Rule 144, highlight some of its technical aspects, and discuss its basic operating procedures.

Rule 144 provides a uniform set of standards and procedures by which restricted and control stock may be sold. The SEC adopted Rule 144 in 1972 and amended it in 1978, 1979, and 1981. The rule specifies when, how, and how much restricted stock and control stock may be sold in the public marketplace by owners. Failure to comply with Rule 144 may result in a violation of Section 5 of the Securities Act of 1933, which makes public sale of stock not registered with the SEC unlawful.

TERMINOLOGY

The terminology of Rule 144 is replete with SEC legalese, but three terms deserve special mention.

144 Stock   So-called 144 stock refers to restricted stock, which is a generic term covering two categories of securities that have limitations on their salability: restricted stock and control stock.

Restricted Stock   Restricted stock is stock that is acquired from the issuing corporation and has not been registered with the SEC. Usually, restricted stock is obtained through a private placement; that is, the stock is acquired directly from the issuing corporation by the buyer in some type of negotiated transaction. Restricted stock transferred to a second party retains its restricted nature. Basically, all nonregistered stock acquired from the issuing corporation is restricted stock; this includes nonregistered stock issued upon the exercise of stock options or pursuant to a stock option plan.

Control Stock   Control stock is stock owned by people who control the business affairs of the issuing company, i.e., officers, directors, 10% stockholders of the company, or any other persons who can influence management decisions. Such people are called affiliates of the company; a nonaffiliate is someone who is not an officer, director, or 10% stockholder. This distinction is only material when either is selling restricted stock, but the rules for nonaffiliates are less stringent.[3]

TECHNICAL ASPECTS OF RULE 144

Rule 144 attempts to clarify the procedures for selling restricted and control stock. The rule is highly technical and must be complied with fully to obtain the protection it affords. Its general guidelines are:

1. There must be current information available to the public about the company.
2. In some instances only a limited quantity of the stock can be sold in any period.
3. The securities must be sold in a broker's transaction or directly to a market maker.
4. In some instances a notice of intention to sell the stock must be transmitted to the SEC and the stock exchange on which the stock is listed.
5. In the case of restricted stock, the stock must have been owned and fully paid for for a specified period of time before the sale.

The distinction between an affiliate and a nonaffiliate in the sale of restricted stock is important. A nonaffiliate need not comply with the provisions of Rule 144 if: (a) there is current information available to the public about the

---

3. Note that in the hands of an affiliate, control stock may also be restricted stock. It is restricted stock if it was acquired directly from the company and was not registered with the SEC, or if it was acquired from a person who acquired it from the company. All of the provisions of Rule 144 apply to restricted stock held by an affiliate. If it is only control stock, however, there is no requirement that the stock be held for a required period of time (point 5 above); all the other Rule 144 guidelines, however, do apply.

company; and (b) the seller has owned and fully paid for the stock for three years. A nonaffiliate who has held restricted stock for two, but not three years, must sell restricted stock in accordance with the provisions of Rule 144.

The salient features of the general guidelines refer to a detailed set of procedures and requirements in five areas.

Public Information   This guideline pertains to the issuer's compliance with SEC reporting requirements: that is, that all current 10-K and 10-Q reports have been filed on time; if they have not, the sale must be deferred. A company that has fewer than 500 shareholders is a nonreporting public company and does not need to file 10-Qs or 10-Ks. This kind of company is best described as semi-public, since it falls in between the private and public ends of the spectrum. Rule 144 also provides other means for nonreporting companies to satisfy the current public information requirement.

Volume Limitations   The volume limitations for sales of control stock by an affiliate or for sales of restricted stock by a nonaffiliate (provided the special nonaffiliate case noted above does not apply) are the same: the combined sales of all stock of the same class by a person within the preceding three months may not exceed the greater of (a) 1% of the shares or other units of the class outstanding (as shown by the most recent report or statement published by the issuer) or (b) the average weekly reported volume of trade in the stock either on all securities exchanges or as reported through the automated quotation system during the four calendar weeks preceding receipt of the sell order. Note the word *person* includes any relative or spouse of the seller, or any relative of a spouse who resides with the seller. It also includes certain trusts, estates, or corporations that collectively own 10% or more of any class of the company's equity securities. Also, the seller should be aware that certain sales (e.g., for the account of a pledgee or purchaser, or for a donee or trust) must be aggregated into the total sales figure. (Expert financial advice is highly recommended.)

Manner of Sale   This very technical point forbids the seller or the broker to solicit or arrange for the solicitation of orders to buy the stock in anticipation of or in connection with a Rule 144 sale. Certain additional payment and commission restrictions are imposed on both seller and broker. A seller, however, retains the alternative of executing a sale directly with a market maker.[4]

---

4. A *market maker* as defined in Section 3(a) of the Securities Exchange Act of 1934 means any specialist permitted to act as a dealer, any dealer acting in the capacity of block positioner, and any dealer who, with respect to a security, holds himself out (by entering quotations in an interdealer communications system or otherwise) as being willing to buy and sell a security for his own account on a regular or continuous basis.

Notice of Intent to Sell   Prior to or concurrent with the placing of the sell order with the broker, three copies of a "Notice of Proposed Sale" (Form 144) must be deposited with the SEC. If the stock is listed, a copy of the notice must be concurrently sent to the principal exchange on which the stock is trading. The seller must have a bona fide intention to sell the stock within 90 days after filing the notice. If more than 90 days elapse, a new notice must be filed. The above rules do not apply if the amount of stock to be sold during any three-month period does not exceed 500 shares or other units and the aggregate sale price thereof does not exceed $10,000.

Holding Period   The holding-period requirements apply only to sales of restricted stock and require that the seller has owned the stock for at least two years prior to the sale (note the exception cited previously for nonaffiliate sales of restricted stock). In the case of successive private placements of the same stock, the purchaser is not permitted to include the holding period(s) of prior owners; each purchaser starts the two-year holding period anew. In order to meet the holding requirement, the SEC has fleshed out this requirement with numerous subclauses, including:

- "Tacking" of holding periods is permitted in certain relationships (i.e., decedent-estate-beneficiary).
- Stock acquired in recapitalizations is deemed to have been acquired when the stock to which it relates was acquired.
- The holding period is suspended during any period in which the holder has a short position in equity securities of the same class.
- The holding period does not begin to run until the full purchase price or other consideration has been paid. Although collateral having a fair market value at least equal to the purchase price of the stock purchased is acceptable, the stock must be fully paid for prior to sale.

OPERATING PROCEDURES

It should be obvious that full compliance with Rule 144 is a very technical, time-consuming matter for both the seller, who has to follow complex regulations, and the broker, whose actions are restricted by the solicitation rule. To avoid a conflict of interest, the broker should also discontinue making recommendations with respect to the stock pending completion of the sale. Consequently, not all brokers will be willing to participate in a Rule 144 sale.

Responsible brokers should, however, be well able to execute a Rule 144 stock sale. Such a sale entails accepting the order, executing Form 144, obtaining a seller's Rule 144 letter, confirming the issuer's SEC reporting requirements, determining the volume and holding-period requirements, making additional inquiries (e.g., making sure the seller is not an underwriter), placing the stock on the firm's unsolicited list, entering the order ticket, notifying the SEC and the appropriate stock exchange, and executing the sale.

The purpose of Rule 144 is to create conditions for the orderly transfer of restricted and control stock, an issue of particular importance to entrepreneurs as it directly affects their ability to harvest value they have created. The amendments to Rule 144 have both liberalized the regulations and strengthened the Rule's power. Rule 144 is not, however, the sole means of selling restricted stock: the seller can also apply to the SEC for permission to sell restricted stock that does not meet Rule 144 guidelines on the basis of a change of circumstances. A sale under this doctrine, however, requires the seller's counsel to confirm such a change and is, therefore, expensive and time consuming for the seller.

As the above discussion illustrates, the restrictions placed on founders' or Rule 144 stock are substantial and should be carefully considered when designing a compensation package. More important, the recipient should seek expert counsel prior to accepting Rule 144 stock or before attempting to dispose of such stock. This area of the law is rapidly changing and, as mentioned at the beginning of this section, the penalties for noncompliance with the SEC regulations are severe. The purpose of this discussion, however, is not to discourage the use of founders' or Rule 144 stock but to highlight some of the issues involved in exiting from such holdings.

──── RETURNING OWNERSHIP

TERMINATIONS

Every company needs to be protected when founders or large initial shareholders leave the company or are fired; in addition, there is a large gray area surrounding issues like disabling illnesses and death. Corporate buy/sell agreements are the traditional vehicle for addressing these issues; they provide the start-up company with the ability to recapture the economics of the stock and ownership of the firm.

There are several kinds of buy/sell agreements, which can apply equally well to a deceased or departing employee.[5] In one type the corporation (or, if it cannot, the surviving shareholders) agrees to buy and the estate or individual agrees to sell the holdings. In another, first the corporation, then the surviving shareholders, have an option to buy the stock; if the option is exercised, the estate or individual is obligated to sell. Yet another agreement may specify that the estate or stockholder has the right to offer the stock to the survivors or to the corporation and that, if it does so, either survivors or the corporation is

---

5. This section is based extensively on the chapter "Corporate Buy/Sell Agreements" in *The Lawyer's Desk Book*, 6th ed., 1980.

obligated to buy. In other cases there may be no specified obligation either to buy or to sell, but if a stockholder or an estate wants to sell, the stock must first be offered to the other stockholders or the corporation before it can be sold to an outside party.

The next question, of course, is how to set the price in a buy/sell agreement. Any reasonable valuation method may be used (such as fixed price per share, appraisal, or book value); the important factor is prior agreement on the method to be used. A method of payment should also be devised and, in case of death or disability, an insurance policy to fund the buy/sell agreement. The types of policies available range from a standard disability income contract to a lump-sum contract.

Although buy/sell agreements are the most obvious form of protection for a start-up venture, they are difficult to structure, especially in the euphoria surrounding the launching of a new company. If they are not in place, however, the entrepreneur may be forced to accept a return on his or her efforts that is well short of the maximum possible. Of course, more subtle forms of protection are available through vesting programs for stock options (which ensure a gradual transfer of ownership to the employee) or profit-sharing plans. As the company matures these kinds of vesting plans can sometimes secure employee loyalty by acting as "golden handcuffs."

——— SUMMARY

One of the underlying themes of this reading is that a firm's choice of a particular compensation program should reflect not only its ability to reward employees, but also the company's stage of growth. Techniques such as founders' stock, ISOs, or nonqualified option plans are best suited for the early period, whereas a junior common stock plan is perhaps more appropriate for companies that have recently gone public. The main point is that as a company matures different and additional compensation techniques become available and should be employed. As a start-up firm grows and begins to contemplate going public, it should consider such compensation techniques as stock appreciation rights, performance awards, employee stock-purchase plans, qualified retirement plans, convertible-debenture plans, venture capital partnerships, and financial planning for its executives. In addition, it is wise to grapple early on with the issues of harvesting and terminations.

The issues involved in planning an effective and appropriate compensation package are extensive and complex. The laws governing their design and implementation change constantly. Thinking ahead, learning the right questions to ask, and seeking the guidance of knowledgeable, experienced advisers are crucial—to save the entrepreneur future anguish and to create a plan that will best serve the interests of the new venture and its managers.

─── **DISCUSSION QUESTIONS**

1. What are the minimum benefits you would provide at the outset of your venture's life? What benefits would you postpone until your company was on a stronger financial footing? What perks would you use to supplement a no-frills benefits package?
2. Compare the rewards and time horizons of the compensation packages described in the reading. What performance incentives do the different packages provide?
3. The authors compare the merits of incentive stock options and nonqualified options. Given the pros and cons of each, under what scenarios would you include one or the other or both in a compensation package?
4. The authors advise entrepreneurs to consult outside professionals when designing a compensation package. After familiarizing yourself with the basics as outlined in this reading, what questions would you ask a professional if you were first attempting to design a compensation program?

How Small Companies Should Handle Advisers

23

HOWARD H. STEVENSON AND WILLIAM A. SAHLMAN

There was a time when a small business owner could rely on one all-knowing accountant or one all-knowing banker over the lifetime of a business. Now, the advising world is in a whirlwind of change as mergers and reorganizations have reshaped service organizations and laws and regulations have multiplied. At the same time, operating a small business is more complex than it was even a decade ago, in areas ranging from toxic waste disposal to choosing the right computer system.

Getting good advice—always difficult for a company with limited resources— is more important than ever. In this reading Stevenson and Sahlman recommend that the small business owner build a new kind of relationship with advisers: he or she must manage them, not the other way around. Being an activist manager means doing two seemingly contradictory things: seeking out the best advisers—specialists if necessary—and involving them more thoroughly and earlier than might have been done before. At the same time, the manager must be more skeptical of their credentials and advice. The authors suggest approaches for building these new relationships, pointing out that the manager's own knowledge and attitude are the best tools for ensuring that he or she gets the best advice possible.

Managing your outside advisers and service providers—the accountants, lawyers, bankers, ad agencies, and others who help you compete—has become a new ball game.

Once upon a time, Japan, South Korea, Taiwan, and Hong Kong were still exporting junk; the Clean Air Act, ERISA, 401(k) plans, and OSHA did not exist yet; and computers were just for the biggest of companies. The stuff the accountants, bankers, and lawyers worried about did not affect the bottom line much. So you'd call a CPA when you needed the taxes done, but not before. And when you wanted the legal effect of a contract explained (maybe even after it was signed), you'd get your lawyer. Back then, the pace of change in products and the financial markets was slow enough that even the most lackadaisical professional could keep up with it.

All of that is no longer true. The environment for small business is more competitive and confusing than it was even a decade ago. The chance of error is higher while the results of error are more damaging. That piece of real estate you bought for a new distribution center could trap you in a $50 million lawsuit if your lawyer did not warn you beforehand to have it tested for toxic waste. A consultant's bad advice on a computer system could throw your entire business into turmoil and threaten your ability to compete.

The problem is that as your world is changing, so is the world of the adviser and service provider, and getting timely, accurate advice—always tough for the small company with limited resources—is more difficult than it used to be.

Competition has led once-staid professions like accounting and law into waves of mergers and reorganizations in a search for efficiency and resources; higher operating costs have enticed firms into pursuing more profitable, short-term consulting roles, which are sometimes in conflict with long-term relationships; complex laws and regulations (as well as a myriad of new marketplace niches) have made it impossible for any adviser to know deeply the broad range of concerns that a business faces today.

In that environment, the notion that a company can have one all-knowing accountant or one all-knowing banker over the life of a business seems about as quaint as a Norman Rockwell painting. Experience has taught us that these days, the all-knowing adviser does not know enough to really help you and has probably been asked too late anyway to keep your company from bearing unnecessary risk.

We recommend creating a new relationship with your outside advisers. Become an activist manager of the advice-giving process by doing two seemingly contradictory things: seek out the best advisers—specialists if you have to—and involve them more thoroughly, and at an earlier stage, than you have in the past. At the same time, be more skeptical of their credentials and their advice. The link in the process is your knowledge and attitude, as well as the resources you are willing to use. You will have to work harder and probably spend more money, but you will save time and money at the other end.

—— A NETWORK OF SPECIALISTS

Operating a business always means managing risk. Successful entrepreneurs endlessly educate themselves about opportunities and dangers to help narrow the odds in a changing environment.

It goes without saying that you should read voraciously and have a wide network of friends inside and outside your industry whom you can call and ask how they handled particular problems, what experts they used, and what their successes and failures were. By doing so, you broaden your base of experience before the fact—and you can weed out many a bad service provider.

Getting the best advice today, however, means more than networking with friends and associates or relying on your old standby adviser. It also means specialists. In medicine you would go to your general practitioner for a cold, but if you have a kidney problem you go to a urologist and to a neurosurgeon if you have a brain tumor.

The same principle applies to the business adviser. You no longer can rely on the GP to give you the sophisticated advice you may need on handling taxes or financing—not to mention toxic waste. Sometimes you may need a securities lawyer, at other times a tort lawyer, a contracts lawyer, or an intellectual property lawyer. You may not need an accounting firm but a consulting firm specializing in high-tech start-ups, which has contacts and intimate knowledge of the problems facing new businesses.

In the new world, you need multiple relationships to diversify your sources (just as you do for capital and other resources) to get the best advice. You will also need that diversity in case something happens, as when your accountant fails to keep up with a changing world, or her firm is acquired and she is transferred.

The general practitioner has not lost importance. Far from it. The GP remains the most important link in the information chain, usually being more familiar with the business over a longer period of time. But you have to find one whose ego is not threatened by an occasional request to see a specialist.

In some cases, hooking up with the vast resources of a large law firm or Big Eight accounting firm may be the best course, but we do not necessarily advise that strategy. You can usually get reasonable tax or estate-planning advice from a big law firm merely by picking up a telephone. The trade-off is that, if you are a small company and they have a dozen General Electrics as clients, you may get short shrift. One- or two-person firms can have an excellent network of specialists to refer to for problems outside their bailiwick. The point is, you'd better use the specialists when you have to.

MANAGING ADVICE SUPPLIERS

Big companies can afford to have many of their experts on the inside. Little companies cannot do that. And specialists are temporary help; they are called on in limited circumstances, and it's difficult to make them part of a permanent team. But you can manage your outside experts as you do the other parts of your business. You are simply managing people you do not control hierarchically.

You have parts suppliers, inventory suppliers, and money suppliers. Consider your outside advisers as advice suppliers, and deal with them accordingly. You would not order a part without knowing its cost, whether it will meet your requirements, or whether the supplier can produce it. The same rules apply to your advice suppliers. That implies a more tough-minded attitude than many people bring to their relationships with professionals.

So it's important to be up front with an accountant or lawyer and ask directly about fees and other essential matters: "How much is this going to cost me? Who is actually going to perform the work? What are the person's credentials? What if I don't like her?" Demand interim, itemized bills that will show who performed what task.

But this line of questioning is just a small part of the new relationship. The product of advice suppliers is not worth much if it is set in stone by the time you see it. Managing the advice suppliers means you work with the experts as they develop their recommendations. To do this you have to find out the skills and weaknesses of the people making the product. What are their incentives? How do they make money? What helps them with their employer, and what gets them into trouble? Does the loan officer at your bank get rewarded when a loan is placed—if you default does it count against him?

Ask yourself, does the professional see you as a hockey ticket—a one-shot event—or a meal ticket, an important repeat client? The system of compensation sets up a tug on the service provider as it does on anyone else (when you grab advisers by the wallet, their hearts and minds will follow). Knowing the direction of the pushes and pulls, you'll be in a better position to judge the value or reliability of the advice or service and act accordingly. If your bank has just lost a bundle in your industry, the lending officer may be overly negative in assessing your company's financial needs. Perhaps you should switch to a firm that has not been burned, at least not recently.

You may prefer to seek a big hunk of your financing from a local bank—it will be more likely to see you as a meal ticket rather than as a hockey ticket. Storage Technology Corporation, a Colorado computer equipment supplier, borrowed hundreds of millions of dollars, all from New York bankers. When Storage ran into financial problems, the New York banks, rather than work to solve the problems, pulled the plug and forced the company into Chapter 11 and a costly, complex reorganization.

A large West Coast bank pulled a similar strategic reversal only a few months after advertising heavily that it was a bank that welcomed long-term relationships with high-tech start-ups on the East Coast. It abandoned all non-California, small and medium-sized high-technology companies in its new $150 million loan portfolio, even those at a fragile stage of growth. The companies summarily were told to find a new bank. You may want help from a heavyweight financial institution, but a local bank has a strong incentive not to harm the local economy, its reputation, and its own balance sheet, and will think twice about the impact before it pulls the plug.

QUESTION THE LOGIC

With expert advisers, you must be skeptical in other ways. Question their advice; find out the reasons behind it, the logic they relied on to reach it. Do not be afraid to sound dumb. If you fail to understand, take it as a sign of your adviser's incompetence, not your own. Even when you have found a so-called expert, be careful. Specialists themselves quickly become obsolete if they do not spend hours assimilating the latest developments in their field. You are entitled to find out what they know.

Be like the vice president who thought his small company's annual payment to the union pension fund was much too high. He kept questioning the charge, but the insurance company funding the plan kept saying he was wrong. He even spoke to a pension consultant who said the calculation was made according to the "best methods."

The VP finally called on the insurance company's chief actuary, who said the insurer used the particular methodology because it was traditional for such companies. But the VP also learned that the methodology incorporated incorrect assumptions based on another industry—for example, that employees remained many years on the job and as a group were older. The VP's company actually had a high turnover, and the workers' average age was 26. Eventually the actuary changed the assumption and the methodology. The company recaptured 80% of its pension fund contributions for the previous nine years.

That vice president (who incidentally was not an accountant) showed the necessary attributes in today's climate: skepticism and persistence. Belief in experts' infallibility is one of the least likely-to-succeed strategies in the new world of business. You have to test continually to be sure the expert is providing you adequate service or advice. Don't assume anything.

Here is an example of a service buyer who did not ask the right questions up front. He allowed himself to be snowed by a sophisticated selling job. As the owner of a small company who wanted to sell out, he hired a big investment bank after one glitzy presentation at which top executives displayed reams of charts and statistics to prove the investment bank's competence. After the contract was signed, the owner discovered that the team leader assigned to the project was four years out of business school and the other team members were either one year out of business school or one year out of college. As low-level as the team was, moreover, it was quite busy and devoted little time to the deal. The investment bankers seemed to think they had spent enough time and money just getting the contract—which was too small to justify further effort.

The owner should have insisted that the contract call for the assignment of a partner to the sale, to the extent of a minimum percentage of the time required. If the bank had balked, the owner would have learned its level of commitment before signing. He learned, however, that in investment banking circles, what is done cannot be easily undone. He was told by other bankers that he had better stick with his choice of investment banker or he would look like a "flake" to potential investors. Maybe that advice was sound. But we think it's axiomatic to dump a bad adviser if the potential damage from bad advice or inattention will be higher than the added cost of getting someone else.

GET THEM IN EARLY

Your goal is to get the best advice or service early enough to do you some good. You cannot do that by telling the experts, "I know where you fit, and you should stay in your little box." You cannot treat them like fire fighters whom you call in only to put out your little conflagrations or (more to the point) like janitors to clean up your messes. By then, it is too late. You have lost your most valuable commodities: time and the control of your own destiny.

So another important part of managing the experts is to anticipate the events—positive and negative—that may affect your organization. This is not new advice. The good business manager has always been someone who increases the odds in his or her favor. Today, however, planning and anticipating are absolutely mandatory if you want to control your adviser instead of your adviser controlling you.

You have to ask what can go right and what can go wrong in a given situation—not all the things in the world that can go wrong or right, but which are likely to do so. What are the consequences across your business if you switch to foreign parts suppliers? What if your product has a defect—what kinds of liabilities do you face, and can you prepare for them now? What if your earnings take off—what steps do you take now to minimize taxes later? If your business might generate a healthy cash flow, should you set up a Subchapter-S corporation so you can funnel money through without paying double taxes? If you hope to expand your business into other states someday, do you want to register your business name and logo there now?

If you sat down and took half an hour each day to think about them, you might think of hundreds of questions about your business. Many you will be able to answer yourself with more thought or through reading or by asking your network of friends; but some questions take experts to answer. You should seek their help especially in ascertaining the consequences of a given strategy. To provide such advice, they must first understand the business aspects of a decision, not just the legal or accounting aspects. They need to see the whole picture and the context in which the activity is taking place.

You want your important suppliers to think of themselves not as mere sellers of a product but as an integral part of your business. That way they will recognize that it is in their interests to keep product quality high, costs down, and delivery on time. So too for the professional adviser. Using the adviser to help anticipate not only keeps you in the driver's seat, it helps you forge the bond needed to generate sound, timely advice under the right constraints. The head designer at an ad agency producing your catalog might not worry about the indirect costs of any design decision unless warned that cost is important. The lawyer negotiating an agreement might be so zealous in protecting your interests as to lose the deal, unless you spell out how important the deal is and how far you are willing to go to make it.

Unless they understand your path of evolution, the experts may build in their own constraints. You have expansion plans, say, and you are dealing with architects. It makes sense to let them know your long-term needs. By letting the architects understand where you may be in five years, they can build in the essentials that allow you to connect to the next phase—like raceways for new cables, or knockout doors. You may spend a little more money now, but you save a lot in terms of flexibility of the building.

That is true of advice in general. Going to a variety of experts in the beginning will probably cost you more money up front. Getting the right advice is rarely cheap. But staying out of trouble is vastly more cost efficient than trying to get back out once you have stepped in. The negative side of excluding the adviser is needless risk.

You may think you are saving money by not consulting a lawyer before expanding the sales of your chemical product to the West Coast. But how much have you saved if you are ordered to pay an injured California worker $500,000 in damages because you failed to supply warning labels in Spanish as required by California law? If you have set up a Sub-S corporation to get favorable tax status, you may jeopardize that status by making what seem like trivial changes—moving from 75% to 80% ownership of a subsidiary, for example, or having 36 shareholders instead of 35.

So you should be up front with your accountant and lawyer, saying that next year you are going to be 20% larger, or you are going to have 20 more employees, or be selling in 15 states. Or you are changing your production process and using new materials. And you ask whether there are any things you should know or be thinking about—like agencies to notify, tests to run, documents to distribute. In other words, you must communicate the nature of the future you are planning.

THE HUMAN TOUCH

We're saying the obvious: your advisers are, after all, people. People you do not control hierarchically you must manage in other ways.

In dealing with service providers, you want every advantage you can get. So take those little steps that will bring added dimensions to their services. Closer involvement with your company gives advisers practical rather than abstract knowledge of your needs.

Sincere flattery is another way to make your relationship more human and helpful. Obviously you do not want to puff the firm, but if it does a good job, recommend other clients. Tell the senior partner how well the junior associate has handled your problem—it ratifies the senior partner's choice of the associate and the associate will think of you as a friend. It is simple psychology. They'll think better of you and you will have better access to them on the next go-round.

There is another psychological benefit from greater involvement: an implication of future interaction that may motivate the experts to do a particularly good job on this assignment. You are saying that if they help you on this one, the future is bright for them as well as for you, that you will work with them as long as you work well together.

In today's world, you have to manage your advisers—lead your guides. But first you must manage yourself, and that implies a much larger set of analytical responses to the environment than you have probably been making. You must know what path you are on and anticipate its twists and turns. You have to know a lot simply to ask the right questions. Feel free to ask enough questions to understand your advisers' motives. Find out what is in it for them. Be more cautious, more inquisitive, more persistent, more independent. Be willing to switch horses in midstream—better that than drown halfway across.

At the same time, involve the expert more directly at an early stage. Explain up front your expectations and requirements. Be at once distant and reliant. In a sense you must become an expert on using experts. That's a tall order, but your company can only benefit if you do.

———————————

Copyright © 1988; revised 1991.

——— DISCUSSION QUESTIONS

1. No adviser is infallible. Few will devote themselves wholeheartedly to the well-being of any single client. Working with advisers can consume large amounts of an entrepreneur's time, money, and energy. Why, then, is it crucial for entrepreneurs to seek out the counsel of advisers? What can advisers provide that entrepreneurs cannot provide for themselves?

2. According to the reading, entrepreneurs must seek the best advice they can get—and treat it with a healthy skepticism. What kinds of knowledge must entrepreneurs cultivate, without spending years becoming legal or accounting experts themselves, in order to challenge the wisdom of the experts?

3. Specialists bring to the new venture the benefits of experience, knowledge, and sophistication. What limitations inherent in the specialist's perspective should the entrepreneur be alert for? How can the entrepreneur test the quality of the advice he or she is receiving from a specialist?

4. What are some similarities and differences between managing relationships with employees and managing relationships with suppliers of advice?

5. Imagine yourself interviewing prospective legal or accounting advisers for your new venture. Given the nature of your venture, what abilities and attributes in an adviser are most important to you? What questions would you ask to ascertain whether the candidates will meet your standards?

Confessions of a So-So Controller   24

DEREK F. DU TOIT

After the excitement of launching their ventures and seeing the first signs of growth, few entrepreneurs can easily step back and assume the more special- ized and distant executive role. As operations expand, however, owners need to concentrate their efforts on the tasks they do well and delegate other functions to managers better suited to them by temperament and training. In this reading, the founder of a cookware manufacturing and sales company recalls the control problems that plagued his organization and jeopardized its prosperity. He attributes these problems to his own failure to assess his strengths and weaknesses and to build expertise and commitment throughout the organization. From his experiences, he draws some hard-won lessons about the importance of hiring first-rate managers, delegating authority and responsibility, and maintaining close communications.

From 1969 through 1981, the South African cookware sales company I helped found had a 96% average annual revenue growth. But steep as the growth curve was, my learning curve for the control function of the business was even steeper—at times it seemed almost vertical.

My problem was that, like many entrepreneurs, I was not an adept administrator. Good administrators strive for detailed policy execution and orderly business operations. They are happiest when circumstances are con- trolled and actions are predictable.

The person who starts a business has a much different mindset. This individual often comes from a manufacturing or sales background, where the accent is on getting the job done as quickly as possible, even if this means disregarding the rules laid down by methodical administrators. The entrepre- neur paints with a broad brush and prefers planning new projects to learning from experience how to run the business effectively.

Successful entrepreneurs thus face a dilemma: they succeed in building sales, installing plants and machinery, and organizing production runs, but they often fail to concentrate sufficiently on administration and control so that their increasing sales and large production runs will be converted into commensurate profits.

I suspect that many entrepreneurs start off—as I did—believing that if the business grows, everyone working in it will be as enthusiastic as the founders and will support the organization's aims and objectives. They envision that profits will flow and success will breed success. The average entrepreneur can easily be lulled into thinking that if things seem to be going well, all *is* going well. Unfortunately, this is not always so.

—— GROWTH AND FRONTING

The first control problem I encountered concerned inventory. I knew that if our business—selling imported stainless steel cookware—were to grow, we would have to open offices and warehouses in South Africa's major cities. Recognizing that control problems would be aggravated by distance, I decided to test a system of management from afar by setting up a branch office in Paarl, 30 minutes from Cape Town, and forbidding anyone, myself included, from visiting or even telephoning the new office. I limited my communication to the mails and had merchandise sent by train.

To carry the plan forward, I recruited our most promising salesman with an offer to become our future Johannesburg branch manager; first though, he would manage the Paarl branch for three or four months to set up the systems and implement the branch manual I had written.

The new manager, who was paid entirely on a commission basis, reported slow sales at first; but they increased satisfactorily near the end of the trial period, with inventory drawn from the Paarl stockroom. Two days after he left for Johannesburg, I got a call from the Paarl office administrator, who said she wanted to see me immediately. A sorry tale unfolded!

The sales manager had worked hard but had not achieved hoped-for sales. So he resorted to "fronting." He made down payments on goods sold fictitiously, reimbursed himself with a commission, and took the merchandise to a secret warehouse. His intention, he later told us, was to ship the goods to Johannesburg and sell them legitimately, thus covering his fronting operation. Shortly thereafter I hired an accountant who had more practical experience than I in writing systems, implementing accounting controls and procedures, and overseeing the administrative process.

—— GROWTH AND ROLLING CASH

Most people working in a fast-track growth company find the experience to be intensely emotional. Salespeople join such a business because it offers an opportunity to quickly boost their earnings. The public praise and congratulation they receive in a direct sales company is often a new experience for them and typically fuels their ambition to earn more. They earn additional income by recruiting friends and neighbors. Before long, many are handling sums of money that are enormous by their previous standards. They and other employees handling cash can also quickly notice and take advantage of any weaknesses in the control system.

My next major control problem developed in this way. The company had grown to six offices spread across the country; in each, the cashier received large sums of cash from customers' monthly installment payments. Our accountant put off visiting the outlying offices on a regular basis because more urgent home-office matters always seemed to occupy his time.

One day, the husband of one of our most trusted cashiers came to my office to confess that his wife had stolen $25,000 by rolling-cash installments. This is a process whereby a cashier receiving large sums of money delays depositing the cash; without supervision, deposits can be "rolled" for two or three weeks, until one has a cash float equal to the total cash inflow for the period.

When the cashiers also control all primary bookkeeping entries, they have even more latitude, since they can simply wait until customers complain that their payments have not been acknowledged on their statements and then write out journal vouchers. The cashiers can also print secret supplies of cash receipts or prepare receipts without carbon copies. The copies are filled in after the customer leaves with a figure much lower than that shown on the customer's receipt.

The one constant in a rolling-cash situation is that the cashier invariably says that the money was only borrowed and will be repaid. In this case, the offending cashier determined that our controls had failed to detect a "temporary loan," so she "borrowed" increasing sums to finance her husband's growing business.

——— GROWTH AND INVENTORY

As the business continued growing, we had moved from importing inventory to producing it in our own factory. It was an exciting time as we strove to implement various imported processes, train unskilled labor, and still meet production targets that rose every month. I naively assumed that there was little in the factory for employees to steal early in the production process; once the product was finished, I further reasoned, the cookware would be too large for the staff to carry out the door unnoticed.

But our monthly accounts had for some time been showing an ever-increasing percentage of unexplained losses. More aware than ever that control weaknesses attract losses, I tried an experiment in our factory. At one minute before closing one evening, a number of previously briefed senior administrative officers locked all doors and allowed the people to leave only after methodically searching them and their parcels. The process took some time to complete and, as you might imagine, many employees were quite upset.

Our search yielded nothing out of the ordinary, and as we returned to our offices to figure out what to do next, we were amazed to find cookware, raw materials, and small tools in every nook and cranny of the factory. These items looked as though they had been tossed aside in a hurry; once news of the holdup at the front door had spread among the employees, they apparently disposed of the incriminating evidence on the spot.

I was by this time somewhat cynical about the ability of some people to resist the temptations posed by our less-than-perfect control systems. I encouraged our accountant to install a tighter and more effective system so that people with direct access to goods and cash would steal less from us.

Although we worked hard to implement effective controls, we still suffered theft of all kinds. I finally realized the situation was my fault. I had not conducted sufficiently rigorous recruitment interviews, and I had not hired an accountant who was up to the job. Perhaps we were unable to attract the right talent because we were so small and puny when we hired the accountant.

Whatever the reason, I then asked our auditing firm to help me in the employee-selection process by asking all candidates the right questions about control, accounting, and administration. (I had only recently hired this firm because the previous one seemed to lack the skills and experience necessary to offer us the kind of advice we needed.) The new firm not only aided us in the recruitment process but also gave us solid and useful advice on weaknesses and loopholes in our control systems.

——— ELEMENTARY CONTROLS

The three incidents I have described are not unusual; they reveal what happens when, during periods of growth, ambitious entrepreneurs do not concern themselves with the mundane tasks of control.

In hindsight, I can determine how I might have prevented these incidents from occurring. First, our top salesman would have been unable to front his sales if my systems manual had enforced even perfunctory checks on the creditworthiness of the alleged purchasers. These checks would have quickly revealed fictitious names and addresses. An additional safeguard would have been to pay only a percentage of the commission for credit sales at the time of delivery.

Second, I should never have allowed our cashiers to do all the primary bookkeeping entries relating to cash payments without having continual audit checks. The way I had set up the system practically ensured there would be temporary borrowings and eventual theft.

And finally, because I had assumed it would be difficult to take finished cookware out of the factory, I believed no one would. Thus stolen items left the premises in delivery vehicles, in scrap and waste containers, and through staff toilet windows that abutted an empty site. Other items were brazenly taken out through the front door. All this came to light after we hired a security firm to advise us on physical control of all movables in the factory.

Such problems are elementary to experienced administrators. Most entrepreneurs, however, have no experience or formal training in these areas, nor are they temperamentally inclined toward administrative functions. In envisioning the big picture, they tend to ignore the many details of administration, to the detriment of their businesses.

UNDERSTANDING THE PROBLEMS

By now I had realized that I did not have the mindset of even an average controller. I knew that if I wanted to reap the benefits of our excellent growth, I would have to solve the control problem and instill law and order before our success was destroyed by the company wobbling out of control. By the time our auditors recommended we hire a financial director—the business had grown to $10 million volume per year and required more than the services of an accountant—any number of entrepreneurial management problems were coming to light. We had an ever-growing backlog of orders; customers were complaining about incorrect statements; we had difficulty in collecting customers' accounts; we were making more mistakes in every segment of the business; and our salespeople were saying that we had a great product but everything else was terrible. This tale of woe resulted from four factors:

1. The business had grown so large that my managerial style—hands on, with all decisions resting with me—had become inadequate. I could not attend to everything.
2. We lacked good administration and control, largely because they were low on my list of priorities. I had not insisted that they be installed.
3. Our management team was not up to the task of controlling a large and growing company. We, myself included, were good at running a small company, but the strains of growth imposed the need for problem solving of a kind for which we were not temperamentally suited.
4. My desire for complete control had led me to buy out my coshareholders in a way that placed financial and other burdens on the company.

FINDING SOLUTIONS

Ironically, many entrepreneurs do set store by control of the venture; yet they often fail to install effective financial and administrative discipline. The important lesson I learned from my experiences was that although I would have to ensure that proper administrative controls were set up, I was not the person to do it. I resolved our difficulties in a number of ways.

First, I hired the best management team I could find and tried to make sure it was strong and aggressive enough to withstand my domineering behavior.

Second, I set up a participatory form of decision making whereby five of us thrashed out the company's problems for two days every month for the first year. We allowed no interruptions of these meetings. They got pretty combative at times, but we had all taken a management course that made us aware that it was better to beat problems to death in the open than to sweep them under the carpet.

Third, in addition, I pushed decision making down the line by giving managers responsibility *and* authority. This was not easy for me, and many times I had to stand by biting my tongue while subordinates made errors. My consolation was that we learn from our mistakes.

Fourth, I consulted with my top people often on an informal and sometimes a formal basis. Previously, I had tended to leave them alone and had not bothered to review their performance in any detail because I was too busy being an entrepreneur. Now, through my daily contact with them, I became more aware of executive performance, and I realized at last that my most important task was to provide the right environment for my senior executives. I made their remuneration package as creative as possible.

Fifth, even as I understood the need for control, I knew I was incapable of implementing it. I gave that responsibility and authority to our new financial director, a strong and talented executive. Although we buckled under the strain of his rules and regulations, we were ultimately better able to cope with another period of fast-track growth.

——— THE EMOTIONAL BARRIER

Those entrepreneurs who, like me, discover that they are mishandling the control function will almost certainly need to do some soul searching before they can recognize intellectually and emotionally that they must act. Essentially, they must temper their need for control with the need to vest responsibility for control in someone who has the right personal and professional qualifications.

Because entrepreneurs are not inclined to accept advice from others, I do not expect readers to change their approaches to this subject overnight. I certainly didn't change that quickly. The episode that finally tipped me toward accepting the necessity of changing my ways occurred during the management course I referred to previously. During an evening discussion, one participant said he was unconcerned about the detailed evaluations each participant wrote of the others' performance in the program. Because most of us had never before been exposed to uninhibited comment about our behavior, nearly everyone else was apprehensive.

I could not believe that this individual had no qualms whatsoever—in fact, I suspected that this was his way of whistling in the dark. To confirm my suspicion, I engaged him in a Socratic dialogue that had him admitting after 15 minutes that, yes indeed, he was concerned. Because I had always loved an energetic argument and in fact arrived at most of my decisions this way, I was unprepared for his reaction to my triumphant cry of, "Aha! So you really were concerned about it and were just saying you weren't to relieve your anxiety. Was this the best way to do it?" His reaction to having his weakness exposed to the fascinated group observing this interplay was such that we had to be forcibly separated.

This incident made a deep impression on me. I realized that not everyone enjoys arguing in such a logical, bare-knuckled way. As I became more and more aware of my entrepreneurial orientation toward the task at hand rather than toward the finer feelings of the people I worked with, I concluded that I would have to reduce my intensity that everyone but I saw in my approach to getting the job completed.

Entrepreneurs who have headed their organizations for any length of time are generally spared these chastening experiences, since subordinates are unlikely to press their point with such vehemence. The only situation in which such open confrontation could be expected is in an environment separated from the work environment, where the participants are mostly strangers, equals in status, and unlikely to meet again.

This valuable experience enabled me to accept emotionally something I had come to realize intellectually—that I would have to change my ways of managing the company's affairs. Changing turned out to be one of the most difficult things I have ever attempted. The key to success was step 3. Transferring responsibility and authority means having to watch your managers make mistakes you could have avoided had you done the job yourself. The object of the strategy, however, is to develop your subordinates' skills and reduce your workload, so be careful and gentle when you review their performances with them. Step 4 allows you frequent reviews so that you can step in to prevent a brush fire from developing into the forest inferno.

Many entrepreneurs will instinctively balk at my suggestions because they will have to give up much of their authority and responsibility, something no entrepreneur does easily. If, however, you want to avoid spending most of your time on crisis management and you want your business to grow significantly, you will have to recognize that there are some things that you do well and others that you are unsuited for by temperament.

I think that the most profitable area for an entrepreneur to delegate is the control aspect of the business. This enables the entrepreneur to build a stable foundation and concentrate efforts on growth. Ignoring the control and administrative requirements of a business will lead to problems more fundamental than a few lost sales or a slow production line.

——— DISCUSSION QUESTIONS

1. Suppose the author had hired you as a management consultant. Do you agree with his assessment of the company's failings? How would you diagnose the company's problems, and what steps would you take to solve them?

2. At a minimum, a controller must be precise, methodical, detail-oriented. What other qualities would you look for when hiring a controller?

3. The key to success, the author says, was giving his managers responsibility and authority. How do you define these terms? In what tangible ways can an executive transfer responsibility and authority to managers? How can the executive accomplish this transfer without abdicating his or her own responsibility?

4. What actions can an executive take to win the commitment, trust, and loyalty of a venture's support staff?

5. Given your own strengths, weaknesses, and interests, what areas of your business would you delegate to managers? How much contact, formal and informal, would you want to have with your management team? What reporting mechanisms would you establish?

The Family Venture   25

WENDY C. HANDLER

Of the more than 18 million businesses in the United States, points out Wendy C. Handler, nine out of ten are family-dominated; family firms produce half the gross national product. People are attracted to family ventures for many reasons: compared with life in a corporation, they may afford more flexibility, control, compatibility, trust, and opportunity. Naturally, great potential for conflict and misunderstanding also exists when work and personal relationships converge. In this reading, Handler surveys the family business from three perspectives: (1) joining a start-up or buyout as a partner or member of the entrepreneurial team, (2) joining a recently launched family venture, and (3) joining a family business as a second- or third-generation member. She explores the benefits and potential conflicts present in each of these situations, pointing out key issues and questions that family members must recognize and resolve if they are to achieve balance and success in both their work and personal lives.

Family businesses are very popular today: "All over the country, the bright young types who formerly opted for management consulting or the fast track at blue-chip corporations are eagerly joining family businesses . . . Changed attitudes and a changing economy account for this turnaround." (*Business Week,* July 1, 1985). People are tired of bureaucracy, and have turned to family ventures in hopes of success, security, and humanistic work values. However, many are finding that the complexities of putting together a venture team are compounded when family members and other relatives become involved in the business.

Historically, the family's involvement in business has been the least-understood aspect of new-venture creation. Yet, of the more than 18 million businesses in the U.S., nine out of ten are family-dominated. Family firms range in size from small local stores to large multinational corporations, and produce half the gross national product.

Family members may become involved in a venture at one of three stages:

1. At start-up (or buyout) as a partner or member of the entrepreneurial team.
2. Joining a recently launched family venture early in its operation.

3. Joining a family business anytime during the life of the organization as a second- or third-generation member.

─── LAUNCHING A VENTURE WITH A FAMILY MEMBER

Everything that has been said about choosing entrepreneurial teams and practicing teamwork applies to new family ventures. There are also special advantages: Initial costs and early losses may be more easily shared, and later success benefits the family as a whole. It also enables the family to be together, one of the major reasons couples choose to go into business with one another. One form of partnership that has gained popularity is the enterprise owned and run by a married couple.

Cheryl and Jeffrey Katz of Boston insist that they would rather work with each other than anyone else. Their design studio allows them to fulfill a mutual interest together. Bridget and Greg Martin, owners of an ice cream shop, believe that their business is so all-consuming that it would be difficult for them if they did not both work there. They both have enthusiasm about the business, so neither minds if the other wants to talk about work.

Couples may have certain benefits that are atypical of nonfamily partnerships, because they share the same family needs. If a child is sick and must stay home from school, the couple makes the necessary business adjustments so that one parent can be at home. Many couples deal with the equity issue by agreeing that there is no single "boss." Major decisions, especially financial, are made together, while smaller ones depend on who is available.[1]

Family members may also trust one another more than they do people outside the family. The issue of trust is paramount in the wholesale diamond business, as one member of a family firm in that industry explained it: "Dealing with diamonds is basically a family business, because you're dealing with these small things that are very expensive, and you must have a lot of trust in whoever you work with. So you don't hire [nonfamily] salesmen."

A family partnership can work well when the partners have abilities and responsibilities that complement each other, like brothers Ernest and Julio of Gallo Vineyards.

Ernest, 77, is chairman and in charge of marketing, sales and distribution. Julio, 76, is president and oversees production. Julio describes himself as a farmer at heart, who likes to "walk in the fields with the old-timers." Ernest's office, on the other hand, is cluttered with mementos from selling. The brothers mesh well: Julio's goal is to make

---

1. R. O'Gorman Flynn, "For Love and Money," *Boston Woman*, June 1987.

more wine than Ernest can sell. Ernest's goal is to sell more wine than Julio can make.[2]

But partnerships can turn sour when a business partner or boss is also a relative. This may also have serious implications for family relationships. Problems of control, fairness, and equity are common. Conflicts over control result when each partner has a different idea of how to run the business, and both are unwilling to compromise. Issues of fairness and equity arise over division of work and how much each partner is contributing to profit. And, in a business run by a couple, difficulties in the personal relationship may undermine the business.

> Esprit, the billion-dollar international clothing company, has experienced plummeting sales, largely blamed on founder-owners Doug and Susie Tompkins being "at each other's throat," according to *Newsweek* magazine (May 23, 1988). They moved into separate buildings on their estate overlooking San Francisco Bay.
>
> They disagree as well about the future direction of the company. She wants to produce more mature clothes for the aging baby boomers, while he insists on sticking with the youth market. In May of 1988, to placate concerned stockholders, the couple agreed to reorganize the company, and have given up some of their personal control of it.

If you are thinking about going into business with one or more members of your family, it is important to understand that you are entering a business relationship. Make adequate plans for managing its future. It is fatal to the life of a venture to assume that these issues are "understood" because "it's all in the family."

Of special urgency is the need to have a clear understanding about the following issues:

- Who (if anyone) is the lead entrepreneur?
- What are the specific strengths and weaknesses of each member of the team?
- What are the backgrounds of each in other areas of business?
- What are the specific responsibilities of each?
- How much money will each put up, and how will equity be divided?

Often family members in business together have trouble communicating honestly and willingly with one another. It is important that differences of opinion about the business be discussed in a professional manner. Regular meetings to take up day-to-day matters and longer range plans are a good idea.

Finally, the family must decide under what circumstances, and on what terms, nonfamily will be brought into the venture. While keeping a venture strictly in the family ensures complete control, this approach may also limit

---

2. J. Fierman, "How Gallo Crushes the Competition," *Fortune*, Sept. 1, 1986.

growth by discouraging able and potential partners from joining, if the inner circle is closed to them. It may also discourage potential investors who may question the growth potential of a tightly held operation.

JOINING A NEW FAMILY VENTURE EARLY IN ITS OPERATION

A typical scenario for joining a new family venture early might be an entrepreneur who starts small, with the understanding that a sibling (employed elsewhere or still in school) or a parent will join the venture as it grows. In this instance the lead entrepreneur has already declared himself or herself, and presumably has identified the areas in which the venture needs the help of potential family partners, employees, and backers.

There are various advantages to having family members join a new venture. They can help during the development period. They may welcome the opportunity to help the business because it benefits the family. Flexible hours and days (and pay) may be attractive to family members struggling to get the business going while using minimum resources. Working together also enables the family to be together.

> One member of a family that owns a successful restaurant chain in Boston talked about his father's desire to have the family together in business: "He wanted to have his family around—I think that was one of his greatest priorities. We went to school in different places and we did different kinds of things. Each one of us moved away for a little while. But his goal always was, as well as my mother's goal always was, to have the family close by . . . because he looks at a lot of people he knows and the kids are all over the country, all over the world, and maybe they're successful, but the parents never see them."

Many family members join a family business because they are uncomfortable with close supervision, or with working in a bureaucratic atmosphere—and are welcomed because family members are typically more trustworthy and responsible (or seen as so) than outsiders.

> A woman's specialty clothing shop in Boston is run by two sisters, ten years apart in age. The younger sister started working for the older sister because it gave her autonomy without working alone. The older sister is happy because she thinks family is more reliable and cares more about the business.

The problems of a family business early in its operation are largely interpersonal. An entrepreneur employing a parent may experience role reversal, which can be awkward, given the history of relating as a son or daughter. The parent may be resentful, if the work is unrewarding, tedious, or difficult.

In the case of siblings, issues of power, rivalry, and jealousy may crop up if the relationship is not carefully managed—especially if they are close in age and of the same gender. It is important to delineate areas of responsibility clearly, and they should be based on personal interest, skills, and training.

For the case of family members joining a venture early in its operation, therefore, many issues must be worked out:

- What, exactly, is the area of responsibility of each family member, and to whom is he or she responsible?
- What is the compensation: salary, bonus, equity shares, or some mixture?
- What will be done in the event of a disagreement, or if one family member is not pulling his or her weight?
- What is the ante—can it be redeemed if the joining family member changes his or her mind?

Discussion of questions like these are best done in periodic family meetings, so that the experience of working in the family business is beneficial and productive.

——— JOINING A FAMILY COMPANY AS A LATER-GENERATION MEMBER

Joining a family company as a later-generation member is probably the most common path—and is filled with stories of success and failure. Thomas Watson Jr., for example, "got his job from his father, but built IBM into a colossus big enough to satisfy even the wildest of the old man's dreams."[3] In contrast are the Bingham heirs of Louisville, Kentucky, whose squabbling led to the downfall and sale of a $400 million media empire.

There are three broad categories of next-generation members of a family firm, described below. Which category an individual fits depends on personal qualities, interests, and needs. Furthermore, the decision to join a family venture is subtle and dynamic, and can take many years and several periods in and out of the business to solidify.

> A woman actively involved in her family's printing business talked about her tenuous existence during the early years: "There was a lot of aggravation. I quit twenty times. [My father] fired me twenty times. I fired him twenty times. We fired each other—we both walked out. We were gonna close the whole place."

THE HELPER OR FAITHFUL APPRENTICE

The helper is the individual who joins to help out in the organization and is often unsure how long his or her tenure will be. Often the helper joins at

---

3. "The Greatest Capitalist in History," *Fortune*, August 31, 1987.

the early stages of development, when the entrepreneur may rely heavily on family members for flexible work hours and pay.

Sometimes the helper stays on as the dutiful apprentice to learn the business "from the bottom up." The helper or apprentice may not have a regular title or position, but is expected to be a factotum—someone who does all kinds of work.

Perhaps the best example of the dutiful apprentice is Edsel Ford, only son of the original Henry Ford and father of Henry II, who, even as president of Ford Motor Company, found himself overshadowed by his father, the real power in the company. . . .

Nevertheless, one of the benefits of being the helper or faithful apprentice is that you are helping the family. The son of the founder of an industrial development firm said this was what he liked about working for his father:

> You're contributing to the family, you're helping reach a goal, you're getting something done that needs to be done, you can see progress on the work that you're doing, which is always nice when you're doing work. But I think that the underlying thing is that it's our business. This is what we do, this something that my father does. That kind of attitude or thought process is the main thing that made me want to work for him more and work hard.

There is also the added incentive to help out when there are direct benefits as a member of the family. The young man above noted that his college expenses were affordable because of the family business.

THE STEPPING STONE

Some individuals use the family firm as a stepping stone on a career path. They are interested in it as a convenient career opportunity, a launching pad to other job choices.

> Two sons of restauranteur Anthony Athanas, owner of Anthony's Pier 4 in Boston, set up a seafood supply company in Maine, with the intent of having their father be one of their most loyal customers.
>
> Ira Riklis, son of conglomerateur Meshulam Riklis, of Rapid-American Corporation, worked for his father for one year, developing an ulcer and the conviction that the role was not for him. However, the contacts he made enabled him to start a successful company of his own.

There are several benefits to using the family business as a stepping stone. It resolves the Catch-22 confronting beginners—the need to possess work experience to get the job that gives it. It fulfills the feeling of personal obligation members of the next generation are likely to feel toward the family business. Finally, it allows for personal growth and development of the business skills needed to move into a desirable job or to begin a business.

THE SOCIALIZED SUCCESSOR

This individual joins and becomes socialized into the family business, with the strong likelihood of becoming the next-generation president.

> One notable example is the Bechtel Corporation, begun by Warren Bechtel to build railroads. His son Steve Sr. directed the firm into construction of pipelines and nuclear power plants. Today, Steve Jr. heads the $3 billion company, which has further diversified.

The benefits of being socialized into the family business are similar to the benefits of starting a business: the opportunity to be creative, innovative, and goal-oriented. Entrepreneurial success within the family business depends to a great extent on company growth. Is there room for the next generation to expand? Is the company growing fast enough to accommodate new ideas, new divisions? Does the management style permit the type of latitude the next generation seeks?

—— IMPORTANT ISSUES THAT CONFRONT THE NEXT GENERATION

Three major issues confront the next-generation member of a family firm. First is the classic problem of the owner who can't let go. To many founders, the company is child and lover. The founder cannot stand to relinquish any part of it, and will often deny the successor the training necessary to qualify to take it over.

In addition, parents do not like to take orders from their children; the generation gap is magnified in the setting of the family business. Often the second-generation entrepreneur becomes a permanent person-in-waiting. A survivor of this syndrome describes his good fortune as follows, "Fortunately, my father died one year after I joined the firm."

A seasoned observer summarizes the dilemma: "Dad's successor is an entrepreneur in training. He's expected to be the trail blazer when Dad passes on his machete. He's expected to be independent, yet he is forced to work for one of the most domineering bosses in existence, a successful business owner. To make it worse, the boss is also the successor's father."[4]

A well-known family business consultant explained that the practice of choosing your own successor is "an organizationally hazardous activity that might better be abolished."[5] Unconsciously, owner-founders may want to prove no one can fill their shoes. Several successors I have spoken to were aware of this dynamic; one in particular was still trying to come to grips with his father's

---

4. L. Danco, *Inside the Family Business* (Center for Family Business, 1980), 131.
5. H. Levinson, "Don't Choose Your Own Successor," *Harvard Business Review* (March–April 1971).

words: "If anything happens to me, don't think for one minute that you could ever run this business without me."

A second, related issue is establishing credibility. Founding parents have difficulty believing that their children ever grow up. They push their children to enter the business, but then fail to give them responsibility or encouragement. Few next-generation family members appear to be given direct positive feedback about their performance. Typically, they find out from others if the parent thinks they are doing a good job.

Gaining credibility is a slow, gradual dance between parent and child. The parent (particularly the founder) has worked hard and expects the child to do the same. Family often have higher expectations of family members in the firm, with one implication being that *because* they are family, they do not have to praise their work.

A third complication of entering a family business is family dynamics and conflicts. Boundaries should be set between family life and the business, so that tensions from one do not spill over into the other—although this is very difficult, and often impossible, to do.

While family closeness can be a positive feature, certain family patterns can be counterproductive.

> One man spoke to me of coming from an "alcoholic family." The family auto dealership had been very successful, but the alcoholic father had never given him the recognition he deserved because he sought attention for himself as he battled his alcoholism. The son is now in charge, but doubts his abilities because his father had given him so many bad messages. His father also will not give up control or the presidency, even though he no longer has any real responsibilities in the company.[6]

Even more extreme are cases where the family business has been nearly destroyed by family feuds.

> Cesare Mondavi, founder of Mondavi Vineyards, before he died, mediated disputes between his two sons over running the family's Charles Krug Winery. The sons, Robert and Peter, had been known for fist fights at their grape-shipping plant. By 1972, Robert was suing Peter for his investment in Krug, and being countersued for trying to monopolize the Napa Valley wine industry. In 1978, a California Superior Court judge ordered that Krug be sold. One month before the sale, Peter bought out Robert's share and saved the business from the auction block.

There is little a next-generation family member can do about the owner who can't let go, but there are direct ways of coping with the issues of credibility and family conflict.

---

6. E. Topolnicki, "Family Firms Can Leave the Feuds Behind," *Money*, July 1983.

CREDIBILITY

There are four strategies for dealing with the credibility issue. First, if you are a next-generation family member, express interest in the family business. Do not assume that your parents know that you are interested. It is important to communicate your interest, and discuss goals with your parents. Be direct and forthright about the responsibility you want and what you are capable of. My research clearly indicates that next-generation family members are more likely to achieve for themselves and the business when they are clear about their needs, and communicate them directly to the owner in charge.

Second, take responsibility for your own development. Decide what your personal goals are and how—or if—they are to be met by the family business. Ask yourself:

- What are my strengths and what do I need to work on?
- What other aspects of the business do I need to learn?
- Do I have the qualities to be a leader?
- Am I happy working in the business?
- Is there anything else I should do to meet my goals?

If you hope to become head of the business, you should learn as much about the business as you can. A leading family business expert suggests an initial learning stage to understand the business better, followed by a specialization stage to acquire a specific skill. Then become a generalist and learn to manage.[7] How appropriate these steps are, however, depends on the nature, complexity, and size of the business.

Third, develop a relationship with a mentor, or with several people who can act as coach, protector, role model, counselor, or even friend. It may not be wise to look only to a parent for mentoring because of possible inherent conflict of interest. Parents play many roles with children; they may not want them to grow up, and may have subconscious difficulty accepting this reality. Look to respected individuals outside the family for counseling and long-term developmental support.

Fourth, and most important, acquire practical business experience outside the family business. This helps increase knowledge, experience, and confidence. It is also likely to enhance credibility with employees in a family business, who may be skeptical about the qualifications of family members.

A son of the founder of a software marketing and consulting company in New York was adamant about gaining experience elsewhere: "I think it gives you a very narrow perspective on life to go at age 21 into your family business and be there for the rest of your life. I think it limits your exposure; I don't think you can become as broad and as developed an individual if you're involved in one thing for your entire life . . ."

---

7. S. Nelton, "Making Sure the Business Outlasts You," *Nations Business*, January 1986.

FAMILY CONFLICT

There are three ways to minimize the likelihood of family conflict. One is to define different responsibilities clearly and with minimum overlap, and assign them according to personal capabilities and interests. In every well-managed family business I have observed, this approach has been used. On the other hand, in family businesses plagued with conflict, siblings typically perform similar jobs, competing with each other and vying for attention from parents and other family members.

Second, fight issues, not emotions. A woman, whose husband entered then quit her father's business, explained:

> Two years ago, my husband was determined to make my father see the importance of expanding. After plotting and pushing, he got the ok. But this was the beginning of almost daily confrontations. He and my father began to fight over people hired and money being spent. If they had discussed plans for company expansion rationally, before my husband began working for my father, much of this could have been resolved.[8]

Finally, establish a family council, composed of all family members key to the future of the business: the founder, spouse, and children, as well as other relatives who have a significant interest in the business.[9] Having regular family meetings allows the airing of problems or differences that might otherwise be ignored—but that won't go away. A family council helps establish open communication, understanding, and trust. It also serves as a forum for planning the future of the family and the business.

——— FINAL NOTE

One last suggestion is in order. Becoming involved in a peer network is highly recommended. There are a variety of national and regional organizations for individuals involved in family ventures. Through the Family Firm Institute (Johnstown, New York), you can become affiliated with local professionals and personal support groups. The Young President's Association is geared to presidents of entrepreneurial and family businesses. Other organizations with a family-business focus include the National Family Business Council and the Small Business Association of New England.

Whatever issues you and a parent or other family business member might be struggling with, it is likely that others have confronted it, or know

---

8. M. Crane, "How to Keep Families from Feuding," *INC.*, February 1982.
9. I. Lansberg, "The Succession Conspiracy," *Family Business Review*, Summer 1988.

someone who has. Sharing experiences can be useful and therapeutic for people involved in family ventures.

——— DISCUSSION QUESTIONS

1. "People . . . have turned to family ventures in hopes of success, security, and humanistic values." From what you have read here and from what your experience may tell you, do you think these hopes are realistic? What are some of the attractions and pitfalls of joining a family business?

2. According to the reading, many couples in business agree that there will be no single "boss." What are the advantages and disadvantages of traditional hierarchical relationships in a workplace? How can couples resolve disagreements over goals, strategy, and tactics when each individual is an equal partner?

3. The author proposes regular meetings in which family members have the opportunity to communicate honestly with one another about day-to-day matters as well as long-range plans. If you were in charge of these meetings, what ground rules would you establish?

4. Family dynamics will inevitably shape and possibly damage business operations. Is it possible, as the author suggests, to set boundaries so that family tensions do not spill over into the business? What can family members do to minimize tensions during working hours?

5. What are the advantages and disadvantages of bringing nonfamily into the business? What can family members do to ensure that nonfamily employees feel welcome, involved, and committed to the business?

FINANCIAL STRATEGY FOR THE GROWING VENTURE

The Financial Perspective: What Should Entrepreneurs Know?

WILLIAM A. SAHLMAN

Are concepts and tools from finance useful to entrepreneurial managers? Describing finance as a way to think about cash, risk, and value, this reading says that the answer is an unequivocal yes. Entrepreneurs start out with few resources; to survive and to create value, they must consider the financial perspective as well as other perspectives when making decisions. The reading explores some fundamental concepts from finance that are particularly useful to entrepreneurs and points out their relationship to managerial decision making. It concludes with several observations on the benefits and limitations of the financial perspective.

Finance is the study of the allocation of scarce resources within the firm. It helps managers in companies of all sizes to ask the right questions: How should they make investment decisions, that is, decisions entailing current sacrifice for future gain? How should they arrange for the financing of investment decisions? What effect do the decisions managers make have on value for shareholders and other constituencies—management, labor, suppliers, customers, government, society?

This definition of finance relies on two important premises. First, finance is the study of how decisions *should* be made. Second, finance is not just the domain of the financial manager; properly considered, it is also a task for general managers.

Like any management tool, finance cannot stand alone. Managers who view decisions only from the finance perspective are not doing their jobs. They must remember that the numbers they manipulate are generated by real people selling real products in a competitive market. To ignore the human or the production perspective would be just as fatal as ignoring the finance perspective.

If finance is useful to general managers of large firms, it is especially useful to entrepreneurs, for they are the ultimate general managers, responsible for making many, if not most, of the decisions in their enterprises. Entrepreneurs are value creators, investing today in hopes of generating cash flows tomorrow. They must understand what cash flow will do; they must understand and manage risk; they must understand how value is determined. Indeed, the importance of thinking through problems from the finance perspective is probably even more important for entrepreneurial firms than it is for larger companies. A key goal of the entrepreneur must be to keep playing the game; ignoring finance risks being forced to stop playing.

In the following paragraphs, I identify certain concepts and tools of finance that are useful to general managers and critical to entrepreneurs. The list is divided into three sections—cash, risk, and value.

—— CASH

The first principle of all financial thinking is that cash is what is important. Because cash can be consumed—traded for other assets in the economy that have utility—all analysis of investment or financing decisions must focus on cash.

ACCOUNTING INCOME VERSUS FREE CASH FLOW

Cash income is not, however, the same as accounting income. Finance relates to financial accounting only in that the financial analyst must be able to infer from reported financial statements what cash is doing. Whereas the accountant tries to match revenues with expenses, the manager focuses on the difference between cash inflow and cash outflow. Accountants distinguish between *expenditures* and *expenses;* they define *net income* as the difference between revenues and expenses. Managers define economic income as the difference between cash income and the sum of all cash outlays required to produce the cash income, whether called expenses or expenditures. That difference, called *free cash flow,* is the amount of cash income that can be consumed in any period (or invested in new projects) without hurting the cash flow stream. Free cash flow is defined as net income plus depreciation, minus required investments in working capital, plant, and equipment. It takes into account both the benefits and the costs of investing.[1]

---

1. A more complete definition of free cash flow is as follows:
   Earnings Before Interest and Taxes (EBIT)
   Less Tax Rate x EBIT
   Plus Depreciation
   Less Change in Required Working Capital
   Less Change in Required Gross Fixed Assets
   Equals Free Cash Flow
   This definition does not reflect how the free cash flow stream has been financed. That is, interest expense, loan amortization requirements, and common stock dividends have not been taken into account. Free cash flow is a measure of the net cash generated by a decision, before considering how it should be financed.

MEASURING PROFITABILITY

The manager's measure of profitability differs from the accountant's. Managers measure profitability on the basis of *net present value:* the difference between the present value of the future free cash flows and the initial investment, given the assessed riskiness of the flows. The accountant's measure of profitability (e.g., book return on equity) is probably unrelated to the manager's measure. Book return reflects the concept of matching income and expenses and ignores the expenditures necessary to produce the income. Moreover, book value is not the same as market value.

PERFORMANCE EVALUATION AND INCENTIVE COMPENSATION

A basic tenet of finance is that individuals act to maximize their own wealth. A company's incentive compensation system will therefore have a strong effect on the actions of its managers. If the firm's objective is to maximize *value,* and value depends on *cash* and *risk,* then the incentive compensation system must focus on all three factors. If, instead, it focuses on the accountant's measure of performance, the results are likely to be counterproductive; acting in their own self-interest, managers will make decisions that maximize accounting income rather than value. When performance evaluation systems focus on accounting systems, managers usually consider sunk costs when making decisions and often refuse to make a decision that would ultimately enhance value because the result would be to lower accounting income.

TAXES AND CASH

An important determinant of cash flow is taxation. Four kinds of decisions affect taxes: legal (e.g., incorporation), investment, financing, and accounting. Managers must try to minimize the resources (corporate and personal) siphoned off to the government within the constraints of the law. To do otherwise would be to ignore one of the key responsibilities of management: to minimize costs in order to compete effectively. If one firm pays more taxes than an essentially identical competitor, the first firm will fail. The ultimate losers will be the firm's constituencies: management, shareholders, labor, consumers, and so on.

CASH AND GROWTH

Another important determinant of cash flow is the rate of sales growth. Growth in sales must be supported by growth in assets (working capital and fixed assets). In turn, growth in assets must be supported by increases in stockholders' equity through retained earnings, stock sales, or increases in external liabilities. High growth rates may require successful firms to rely heavily on external funding.

It is essential that managers distinguish between real growth and growth in prices—that is, inflation. High inflation rates can have a much more damaging effect on a company's long-term financial health than high rates of real growth, especially in view of the historical cost basis for tax accounting used in the United States.

PATTERN RECOGNITION

A critical skill for managers is the ability to recognize and respond to patterns. Many patterns affect cash: cyclical, seasonal, competitive, technological, regulatory, and tax. A hallmark of good managers is their ability to recognize an opportunity to create value *and* to act on it. Becoming proficient at pattern recognition enables them to commit resources quickly to a perceived opportunity. By recognizing and responding to patterns of cash flow behavior, and by using past and current information, successful managers seek to predict the future and to take action.

Pattern recognition helps managers make both defensive and offensive decisions. Consider the effects of a recession. Battening down the hatches when the recession has been recognized is an example of a defensive action. Deciding to accelerate an investment in capacity during a recession precisely because the competition is battening down the hatches is an example of an offensive decision. Recognizing the event—a recession—and anticipating how the competition will react to it drives the company's decisions.

Of course, managers cannot always identify the patterns that are affecting cash flows at a particular time. They may not know, for example, when a recession begins or even ends; their reactions will therefore be delayed. If, however, they have studied the issues before they arise and have come up with a plan of action, they will do a better job than if they had not thought about the problem in the first place.

SCENARIO PLANNING

Scenario planning can be a useful way to analyze cash flows. A scenario is a numerical depiction of a logically consistent set of events that are likely to occur in the future. The scenario reflects past and potential management decisions. It also considers the probable moves of competitors. It is a way to manage in an uncertain environment.

Scenario planning is not the same as worst-case, expected values, and best-case forecasting. These simplistic depictions of future events are not particularly useful. The reason is simple. Consider the worst-case scenario. Rarely will all the elements of a worst-case scenario occur simultaneously. Moreover, these scenarios often fail to account for an explicit change in management decisions. They assume that management will keep making the same decisions it would have made had the expected outcomes occurred; in reality, managers may go so far as to abandon a project altogether. Best-case scenarios have the same pitfalls.

Nor is scenario planning the same thing as linear extrapolation. Few trends persist without interruption. Many planning errors are made because the planners extrapolate from past data. During the 1970s, many banks lent to energy companies based on values that reflected a continuation of rapidly escalating oil and gas prices—at rates above the expected rise in general prices. When oil and gas prices fell, both in absolute terms and relative to other prices in the economy, the values on which loans had been made vanished. This example, which admittedly relies on hindsight, is nonetheless useful because the pattern has been and will be repeated time and time again.

An unwritten rule states that every forecast a manager makes will turn out with hindsight to be wrong. But by making internally consistent forecasts that reflect reasoned management decisions and that are economically significant (i.e., not so unlikely as to be irrelevant), managers can manage in an uncertain world.

One final note: there is a crucial distinction between evaluating the effects of a particular event occurring and being able to predict the occurrence of the event with certainty. A good example is interest rates. No evidence indicates that any individual or group of individuals can predict interest rates with any precision. Nevertheless managers must evaluate the consequences of interest rate changes.

CONSIDER ALL THE CASH FLOWS

Suppose I am considering an investment strategy that involves acquiring at least three companies in the hand tool business over the next few years.[2] I already own a hand tool division that sells a narrow product line, and I have chosen this acquisition strategy because adding the three companies will produce significant economies (cost savings) in distribution.

However, my financial vice president has come up with financial projections for the first acquisition candidate that do not justify making the investment. What should I do?

The first question to consider is: Does the analysis take into account all the cash flow effects of the investment? Does it include the potential savings to

---

2. This example is drawn from "Cooper Industries, Inc.," Harvard Business School Case No. 9-274-116.

be realized by adding the new business to my existing business? Do the figures reflect any synergies (increased revenues) that might result from being able to offer the market a broader line of products? Finally, do they allow for the fact that the next acquisition will look even better because the division will already have two hand tool companies rather than one?

As this example suggests, any prediction of cash flows must take into account all the cash flow effects of the decision. The relevant question to ask is simple: If I make this investment, what cash flows will I get? If I don't make this investment, what cash flows will I get? Will I create opportunities to invest profitably in other new projects because I invest in the project under consideration? Considered in this light the acquisition strategy appears to be eminently sensible, and carrying it out will add measurably to the value of the company. Viewed individually, however, the investments do not look attractive. Focusing on the trees rather than the forest would be a serious error.

One element of successful pattern recognition is the ability to recognize how current investment or financing decisions affect cash flows from the firm's existing assets or from future investment and financing decisions. Attributing these effects (whether positive or negative) to the decision under consideration is an important element of financial thinking.

DON'T RUN OUT OF CASH

This is a fundamental rule of finance (and of business generally). Just as blood sustains living organisms, cash sustains a business. Most competitive moves can be thought of as investments; even the decision to cut prices temporarily is an investment decision. In a competitive economy, the inevitable result of being unable to invest due to a cash constraint is atrophy and death. Not only is the company unable to seize profitable investment opportunities, but financial weakness might encourage the competition to attack. By forecasting and planning for future cash flow patterns, managers can avoid jeopardizing their firms' survival.

Note that the definition of cash I use is very broad. What I really have in mind is the potential to raise cash from inside and outside the firm. To obtain cash from external sources, however, there must be value within the firm that can be sold off.

──── RISK

The riskiness of a particular cash flow stream determines its value. How is risk measured? How do managers deal with uncertainty?

HOW IS RISK MEASURED?

There are really two answers to this question. One way to define risk is as the total amount of uncertainty about future cash flows. A manager will never be able to predict future events with certainty. The managers of a rocket-launching company may have a good idea what cash flows will be if the rocket is successfully launched or if it dies on the launching pad; they cannot predict exactly which of these two events will occur. This first notion of risk focuses on that total uncertainty about future events.

Another notion of risk deals with only a portion of total risk: the portion of the total risk that cannot be diversified away. Suppose, for example, that an investor had the following choices: invest in a suntan lotion manufacturer on a small tropical island; invest in an umbrella manufacturer on the same island; or invest in both. The expected return from investing in either company is 10%. The actual return depends on whether the island has a sunny year, a normal year, or a rainy year. In the first case, the suntan lotion producer will do well and the return on investment will be 30%. The umbrella manufacturer, on the other hand, will do poorly in the sunny year and will report a negative 10% return. The opposite pattern will occur in a rainy year. During a normal year, the investor will earn a 10% return on an investment in either company. Unfortunately, no one on the island had developed a foolproof way to predict the weather for the forthcoming year. What should the investor do? [3]

The answer is obvious when you think about it. Investing in both companies rather than in just one eliminates the uncertainty about the investor's return. The investor is certain to get a 10% return on his or her money *regardless* of the weather during the next year. By combining the two companies, the investor gets the expected level of return while removing all risk.

A fundamental principle of finance is that investors will seek to maximize return for a given level of risk and minimize risk for a given level of expected return. In the preceding example, the only rational decision for an investor unable to forecast the weather is to invest in both the umbrella manufacturer and the suntan manufacturer. Investing in only one of the two would expose the investor to unnecessary risk. Investors will not be compensated for bearing any risk they can get rid of without cost; that is, they cannot expect higher returns for bearing diversifiable risk.

This example demonstrates a powerful principle: don't put all your eggs in one basket. Successful professional investors obey this rule. To the extent that they do the price of risk in the capital markets depends on that part of total risk that cannot be diversified away, not on total risk. Phrased another way, the discount rate that will be applied to future cash flows to convert them to current dollars (present value) will depend principally on the systematic riskiness of

---

3. This example is drawn from David W. Mullins, "Does the Capital Asset Pricing Model Work?" *Harvard Business Review* (January–February 1982): 105–14.

the cash flows. *Systematic risk* is defined as the covariability of the return on the particular asset with the return on a portfolio comprised of all risky assets in the economy (the ultimate diversified portfolio).

Outside the world of academic finance, this is a controversial assertion. It shouldn't be. Still, the principle should not be carried to an illogical extreme. The statement that the price of risk depends solely on the undiversifiable (i.e., systematic) risk applies only to investors with diversified portfolios.

Many rational investors have undiversified portfolios. It is important, then, to distinguish between active and passive investors. Active investors have significant control over the returns they will receive on their investments. An example would be an owner-manager of a company. The owner-manager generally has an undiversified portfolio and must therefore be concerned with total risk, not just systematic risk. Passive investors exercise essentially no control over their investments. It would be irrational for these investors not to diversify their investments, and they will, therefore, measure risk as the systematic component.

For managers acting in the best interests of their diversified shareholders, the cash flows from investing should be discounted at a rate that reflects only the systematic riskiness of the project, not the total risk. This rule applies even to managers who are personally undiversified but are making decisions on behalf of diversified investors.[4] An important corollary is that diversified investors will pay no premium for diversification by companies because they can achieve such diversification on their own at no cost.

RISK, DISCOUNT RATES, AND BENCHMARKS

Modern finance textbooks put great emphasis on determining the "right" discount rate or the "correct" cost of capital and often provide complicated formulas for calculating the discount rate. This preoccupation is misguided. The current state of finance theory and experience suggests that the search for exactitude will not be successful. We simply cannot be precise in our calculations.

The inability to be precise does not alleviate managers' responsibility for estimating the opportunity cost of investing. When making decisions based on value, managers must estimate discount rate, just as they estimate future cash flows.

What, then, is a reasonable discount rate? While a complete discussion of this issue is beyond the scope of this reading, some elementary principles can

---

4. This statement is intended to be normative rather than descriptive. Inevitably, managers will take their own personal risk exposure into account in evaluating any decision. The point here is that the performance evaluation and incentive compensation systems should be set up to encourage managers to take risks, per se, and to make decisions using as a metric the effect of the decisions on the wealth of the shareholders.

be outlined. First, it is most useful to think of the determinants of the discount rate as follows:

$$\text{discount rate} = \text{risk-free} + \text{business-risk} + \text{financial-risk}$$
$$\qquad\qquad\quad \text{rate} \qquad\quad \text{premium} \qquad\quad \text{premium}$$

As this equation shows, the discount rate has three elements. The base level is the rate of return required on investments that have no business or financial risk. An example would be a government bond. A premium must be added to reflect business risk. The preceding discussion about what constitutes risk then becomes relevant: for diversified investors and for managers of companies acting on behalf of diversified investors, business risk is measured relative to all risky investments; for undiversified investors, total risk is what matters. Next, a premium for financial risk must be added. When a company or project is financed by using debt, the returns accruing to the equity owner are riskier. The interest must be paid before the shareholder gets any return. Therefore, equity investors will require higher returns (holding all other things constant) from debt-financed investments than they will from equity-financed projects.

This simple description of the determinants of the discount rate does not imply an equally simple way to estimate discount rates in the real world. However, there are some guiding principles. The first source of data must be the capital market's current risk-free interest rate. This is the fundamental benchmark. Then, the appropriate premiums must be added, depending on the assessed degree of basic business risk and the financial strategy employed by the company. Once again, a useful, but not infallible, source of data on the riskiness of relevant cash flows and on the required premiums is the capital market.[5]

In estimating discount rates for most complex projects, the best managers can hope to do is decide whether a project is low, middle, or high risk. To expect an analysis to yield more exact estimates would be inappropriate and even dangerous.

RISK MANAGEMENT

The preceding discussion focused on how the capital markets charge for risk. An issue of greater importance is managing total risk. The basic tools have already been described: pattern recognition and scenario planning. What are the events that will affect the company? How likely are they to occur? How

---

5. One measure of risk from the capital markets is known as *beta*. Beta is a measure of how sensitive the returns on a given stock are relative to returns on the market. The process of estimating risk and an associated discount rate from capital markets data is fraught with pitfalls. But, these data, when combined with common sense, often offer reasonable guides to the appropriate discount rate. Moreover, there is usually a very close correspondence between virtually all measures of risk, including systematic and unsystematic.

will we respond when and if they occur? What are the likely consequences of the event and the reaction to the event in terms of cash, risk, and value?

Another principle of risk management has already been discussed. Managers should try to get rid of risks if they can do so at relatively low cost. (For passive investors, getting rid of exposure to certain kinds of risk turns out to be simple and cost free: hold a diversified portfolio.) Managers should transfer risk to those most able and willing to bear it. Certain kinds of risks can be transferred to others at low cost. If a major risk confronting a company is the possible death of a top executive, then the company can purchase life insurance on that executive's life. This is an example of an event outside the control of management that can and should be guarded against. The insurance company charges a low premium for the policy, implying a favorable benefit-to-cost ratio. The policy premium is low because the contribution to the risk of the insurance company of adding one more insurance policy to its portfolio is negligible.

Another example of transferable risk is the technological risk inherent in buying a computer. Certain leasing firms specialize in bearing this risk. The larger leasing companies often hold widely diversified portfolios of assets, including many different kinds of computers. By virtue of their diversification and their expertise in managing technological risk, these firms are better able and more willing to bear the risks associated with purchasing a computer. A firm that only needs the services of the computer might be well advised to lease rather than buy one.

The underlying principle of risk management is that company officers should choose with deliberation the risks they are willing to bear.

RISK, TIME, AND INVESTMENTS IN RISK REDUCTION

Risk is not constant over time; with the passage of time uncertainty is usually resolved. A large R&D project may look quite risky at first, but preliminary results, whether good or bad, will gradually reduce the uncertainty.

A useful way to take likely changes in risk into account is to break down the elements of a project into modules, or stages. While the potential returns from such a strategy may be lower than if the project is undertaken all at once, the reduced risk may more than compensate for the lower return.

RISK, PERFORMANCE EVALUATION, AND INCENTIVE COMPENSATION

An important issue for top management is how to evaluate and reward managers operating in uncertain environments. Here are three useful guidelines:

- Measure performance in a relative rather than an absolute sense;
- Assess performance on the basis of value rather than single-period accounting data;
  Compensate managers accordingly.

For example, the absolute performance of a manager's business unit may be poor; but this may not mean the manager has done a poor job if the reasons for the poor performance were beyond his or her control—say an economic recession or an unexpected change in the regulatory environment. To keep managers from avoiding all risky decisions, even those with positive net present values, it is essential to compensate them on the basis of how well they respond to actual opportunities. Identifying scenarios for future cash flows and managerial decisions will help top management assess and reward performance.

In assessing performance, top management must also focus on how decisions contribute to long-term value rather than short-term operating results.[6] Managers supervising major strategic investments can have poor current results—low profits or even losses—while doing an outstanding job of creating long-term value. Penalizing these managers could lead to missed investment opportunities and long-term competitive decline. An incentive compensation system that focuses on short-term accounting performance will discourage long-term value building.

RISK AND THE RULES OF THE GAME

Certain rules and regulations—for example, tax policies, antitrust regulations, health and safety regulations—govern every business decision. Naturally, these rules change over time, and the effects of change can be devastating. Planning for alterations in the rules of the game is an essential part of management thinking.

Suppose, for example, that the level of allowable depreciation changes. Depreciation is a noncash charge to pretax income. Increases in allowable depreciation expense would lead to increased cash flow from any given investment project. A company that has made a high capital expenditure under the prior rules will be at a cash flow disadvantage compared with a competitor that has delayed investing until the new rules were passed.

The point here is simple: ignoring the ways in which changes in the rules of the game can affect the absolute and relative position of the company is a serious mistake.

---

6. A consistent theme of this reading has been that value is a useful metric for evaluating the consequences of decisions. This does not mean that managers of publicly traded companies should build corporate strategies based on current stock price. Rather, managers should focus on the long-term fundamental valuation implications of their decisions; in doing so they should not ignore current information from the capital market.

——— VALUE

Value is determined by the interaction of cash and risk and is affected by investment decisions that create future cash flows and by financing decisions that market the existing and future cash flow streams to shareholders and bondholders.

GETTING YOUR MONEY OUT

A simple rule of finance is that the present value of nothing is nothing. Professional managers and investors must ask a fundamental question before committing resources to any investment: How will I get my money out?

POSITIVE NET PRESENT VALUE DECISIONS

A decision has a positive net present value if the discounted present value of the expected cash flow exceeds the purchase price. If you buy a project and the expected rate of return exceeds the opportunity cost of capital for a project with the same level of risk, then the project has a positive net present value.

Managers who find a project that seems to have a very high expected return and a high net present value must ask and answer one simple question: How will the return be achieved? If this question cannot be answered, the project probably does not have a positive net present value. Investments only have positive net present values when there exists, or is likely to exist, a specific advantage for the company making the investment. These advantages may include superior management, controlled access to scarce resources, product differentiation, economies of scale, or other cost advantages unavailable to the competition.

Once again, a key component of successful pattern recognition is the ability to identify potential positive net present value decisions and to respond to them before the competitive advantage disappears.

SENSITIVITY ANALYSIS

All financial analysis seeks to identify critical assumptions and key managerial concerns. Sensitivity analysis accomplishes this goal through asking a series of simple questions, the answers to which are important because they affect both the initial decision and the way in which subsequent decisions are made.

The objective in sensitivity analysis is identification of the major determinants of value by creating an economic model of a decision. The first step is to break down an aggregate estimate of the cash flow effects of a given decision into major components. The value of each of the component streams can then be calculated, given the magnitude, timing, and estimated riskiness of the relevant cash flows. The values of the component cash flow streams add up to the value of the entire project.

The next step is identifying the key determinants of the project's ultimate value. Almost invariably, the value of the project is highly sensitive to changes in the major assumptions. In measuring the sensitivity of value to these changes, managers must consider not only changes in the level of certain variables but also changes in the timing of certain events.

Consider a typical investment project. Among the questions one might ask would be the following:

- What will happen to value if target market share is never attained?
- What will happen if the target share is attained one year later than projected?
- What will happen if there is a major cost overrun in construction?
- What will happen if inflation differs from the projected level?
- What will happen if interest rates differ from the projected level? (If inflation is different, interest rates are also likely to change.)
- What will be the effects of a typical economic recession? Of a typical economic boom?
- What will happen if unit variable costs are different?
- What will happen if fixed costs vary from those projected?
- What will happen if the competition responds to our moves by lowering price 10% below projections for a period of one year?
- What will happen if the competition's unit costs are lower than ours?
- How low could estimated terminal value fall before the net present value of the decision is zero?
- How high could the estimated discount rate rise before the net present value of the project falls to zero?
- Does making this investment create opportunities to invest later that would not otherwise exist? If so, how valuable are these growth options?

The particular set of questions to be addressed in sensitivity analysis depends on the nature and importance of the decision being analyzed. The skill described earlier as pattern recognition will guide the questioning process; past events that have had a strong impact on the success or failure of projects will be the focus of attention in evaluating future projects. The objective of sensitivity analysis is clear: to locate the crucial determinants of the success or failure of the current decision, taking uncertainty into account.

Like scenario planning, sensitivity analysis focuses on the effects of possible events that are economically important. The difference is that sensitivity analysis seeks to identify the critical assumptions by measuring the degree to which a change in each assumption affects value.

GENERAL EQUILIBRIUM VERSUS PARTIAL EQUILIBRIUM

Economists distinguish between two modes of analysis: partial and general equilibrium. In *partial analysis,* the objective is to determine the implications of changing an assumption, holding all other related values constant. In *general equilibrium analysis,* the objective is to determine the effects of changing an assumption, while simultaneously allowing all other related variables to change.

For scenario planning or sensitivity analysis to have meaning, managers must have an understanding of the fundamental economic relationships among certain variables. Consider, for example, the relationship between the level of interest rates and the level of anticipated inflation. Loosely put, the nominal interest rate is equal to the sum of the real interest rate and the expected inflation rate. If a manager wishes to understand the effect of changing the assumed level of anticipated inflation on the value of a specific project, he or she must also consider the effects of changes in the level of interest rates: these two economic quantities are interdependent. Furthermore, the level of economic activity is almost always affected by the level of interest rates and inflation. In turn, the level of revenues (for a cyclical product) are likely to be affected by changes in the assumed level of inflation or interest rates.

The economic conditions in an industry are greatly affected by decisions made by the major participants. If management is studying a decision to cut prices, it must simultaneously consider the response of each of the actual and potential competitors, including indirect competitors that supply substitutable products. Management cannot make a reasonable decision by focusing solely on a partial equilibrium analysis of its own particular situation.

A requisite skill for successful pattern recognition is the ability to see the way in which certain economic variables are related. Some patterns occur time and time again. Analyzing decisions by making assumptions that ignore these fundamental economic relationships is a serious mistake.

VALUE CREATION POTENTIAL FROM FINANCING DECISIONS

Financing a company is the process of marketing claims about the company's current and future economic cash flows. That is, financial decisions entail selling the rights to the free cash flows the company generates. The way in which a company is financed can affect its value in three different ways.

1. By substituting debt for equity in the capital structure, a company can increase the amount of income that can be distributed to and retained by shareholders and bondholders, because interest is a tax-deductible expense. There are, of course, limits to the degree that debt can be added, for increasing debt raises the probability that the company will get into financial difficulty or go bankrupt.

2. At certain times, financial decisions result in value transfers among
   the various owners of the firm.
3. The method of financing can affect the incentives of the various
   players, especially management.

Even though employing debt capital to finance a business increases the
risk to shareholders, most companies do use debt. The key reasons for concern
in these decisions are usually taxes, financial distress, and bankruptcy. First,
U.S. tax laws are biased toward debt financing. Interest is a tax-deductible cost;
dividends are not. Offsetting this tax advantage is the fact that for the recipient
interest income is generally taxed at higher rates than returns from owning
common stocks (i.e., dividends and capital gains). On balance, a bias toward
debt persists because the total amount of cash flow that can be paid out to and
retained by owners (stockholders and bondholders) increases as debt is introduced to the capital structure.[7]

The second factor is financial distress. Companies that have debt outstanding are more likely to find themselves in a position in which they are
financially weak and therefore vulnerable. Consider events at Chrysler Corporation in 1980. Many potential car buyers probably avoided buying Chrysler
products because they thought the company would go bankrupt and be unable
to fulfill warranty obligations. Some suppliers undoubtedly balked at giving
credit to Chrysler for the same reason. General Motors, Ford, Toyota, and the
other car manufacturers had an incentive to force Chrysler into bankruptcy.
Because of its precarious financial position Chrysler would be unable to respond
or even threaten to respond to competitors' actions.

Debt in the capital structure did not cause Chrysler's problems; the
existence of debt in the capital structure detracted significantly from the basic
value of the company; it caused free cash flow and value to be lower than it
would have been had the company been all equity financed.

The final factor in the capital structure decision is the risk and cost of
bankruptcy. Filing for bankruptcy entails significant losses: management must
spend most of its time negotiating with creditors; legal and administrative costs
are high; bankrupt companies have great difficulty persuading suppliers and
customers to continue to do business with them; companies in bankruptcy often
lose the value of options to invest in profitable projects in the future, options
that have been created and nurtured in the past. These potential costs of
bankruptcy deter the use of debt capital.

In summary, substituting debt for equity in the capital structure increases the risk to which the shareholders are exposed while increasing the
expected return. Because the U.S. tax code has a bias toward debt financing, the
increase in expected return more than compensates for the increased risk. There

---

7. For a more complete discussion of the capital structure decision, see Thomas R. Piper
and Wolf A. Weinhold, "How Much Debt Is Right for Your Company?" *Harvard Business Review*
(July–August 1982): 106–14.

are limits, however, to the amount of debt capital that can be employed. These limits result from possible adverse cash effects when a company faces financial difficulty and bankruptcy.

The process of debt financing I have described is one in which the total cash flows that a company can distribute, and hence its total market value, is affected by the capital structure decision. Another way in which financial decisions can affect value has more to do with value transfers than with value creation. The total size of the (value) pie is not changed by these decisions, but the size of the different slices is.

For example, some financial decisions entail selling or buying securities that are incorrectly priced. An example would be the decision to issue stock when the manager believes the stock is overvalued. If the stock is too high, given the firm's prospects, this decision results in a value transfer from new shareholders (they paid too high a price) to old shareholders and management, who benefit to the extent of the overvaluation.

Another example of value transfer is when a management decision changes the character of the cash flow stream in a way unanticipated by former capital suppliers. If management changes from a conservative to a risky company strategy, the suppliers of debt will suffer a capital loss, and their loss will accrue to the owners of the equity. An essential element of both these examples of value transfers is the ability of management to fool some group of suppliers of capital.

Finally, the way in which a company is financed can affect its value by changing managers' incentives in positive or negative ways. I will return to this point in the next section.

It is important to keep in mind the degree to which making financial decisions can add value to a company. The ability to create value by purely financial machinations pales in comparison to the potential to create value by making investment decisions. That is, opportunities to create value are more likely to reside on the lefthand than on the righthand side of the balance sheet.[8]

VALUE, CONTRACTS, AND INCENTIVES

As we noted in the section on cash, a company's performance evaluation and incentive compensation systems can affect managerial behavior. Similarly, the nature of the contracts between the managers of the firm and the suppliers of capital will affect managerial behavior. The goal of the manager (and of the investor) should be to negotiate individual contracts that make sense in terms

---

8. One way in which financial decisions might affect value has been omitted from this list. In some cases, potential buyers of streams of free cash flows will disagree over value, even if they have exactly the same information. Reasons for disagreement might include different assessments of risk or different cash flow expectations. To the extent managers can identify the groups willing to pay the highest price for an equity or debt stake, value can be enhanced.

of cash, risk, and value, and to select a mix of contracts (e.g., debt and equity) that create rather than detract from value. Two problems may appear in connection with contracts. First, contract provisions may be counterproductive to increasing value. Consider bank loan covenants that often prescribe minimum levels of working capital or coverage ratios. Such covenants may be drafted in such a way as to cause managers seeking to avoid technical default to make decisions that lower value—either by increasing risk or decreasing cash potential. In such cases, the banker who wrote the covenant ends up detracting from what is, after all, the only possible source of repayment: the value of the company.

Second, the *mix* of contracts might affect behavior. Consider, for example, the existence of debt in the capital structure. A management acting in the best interests of shareholders may decide to forgo investing in a project that would increase net present value because all the gains would accrue to the owners of the debt and not to the shareholders. In this case, the existence of debt has caused management to make a decision that detracts from value. However, in situations in which a firm is near bankruptcy, there may be an incentive for management to invest in a very risky project, even if it has a negative net present value. The reason is simple: the shareholders have a worthless claim unless the firm strikes it rich.

On the other hand, having debt outstanding might have a positive effect on managerial decision making. Evidence suggests, for example, that managers perform better after leveraged buyouts than before; these managers often end up with a larger share of equity after the buyout than they had before and thus have strong incentives to perform well. In contrast to the destructive incentive effects described above, the effect in the case of issuing large amounts of debt in leveraged buyouts seems to be positive.

The nature of the contract between the managers and the suppliers of capital can also act as a mechanism for separating highly capable from less capable managers. Consider, for example, two possible contracts governing an infusion of capital into a venture. In the first, the entrepreneur demands 51% of the business. In the second, the entrepreneur expresses a goal of 51% ownership but is willing at the beginning to give 100% of the equity to the supplier of capital while earning the 51% on the basis of actual performance set forth in a plan. Such an entrepreneur is making a strong statement of faith in his or her own abilities to perform; willingness to accept capital on these terms signals commitment and may result in superior performance in the long run.

THE CONCEPT OF MARKET EFFICIENCY

One of the most pervasive notions in financial economics is that the capital markets are efficient. An efficient capital market is one in which prices accurately reflect all relevant information at each point in time. If prices reflect information in this way, then prices are said to be fair: investors cannot expect to achieve returns on their investments that exceed the opportunity cost of investing in the asset. Therefore, according to economists, there are no positive net present value investment opportunities in efficient capital markets: all decisions have a zero net present value. Capital markets are efficient simply because they are extremely competitive. There are lots of well-informed, rational, intelligent players trying to gain an advantage.

Many professional managers and investors, however, do not believe the capital market is efficient. They cite numerous examples of incorrect pricing or irrationality. It is not essential that managers accept the economist's view of capital market efficiency without question. The important point is that managers should, in fact, be skeptical. Assuming that every price observed in the capital markets is always wrong is more dangerous than assuming the opposite. The road to bankruptcy is littered with companies whose executives acted on the belief that prices were wrong. Such dangerous beliefs may be reflected in statements that:

- We should defer raising the money needed for capital expenditures because interest rates are going to fall.
- We should borrow short term because short-term rates are a lot lower than long-term interest rates.
- We should issue debt rather than equity because our stock price is grossly undervalued.

Clearly, the level of interest rates or stock prices is of great importance to managers, and some projects do not make sense when the cost of capital is too high in an absolute sense. The question posed here, however, is whether managers are capable of identifying incorrect rates or prices. Basing strategic decisions on faith in such skills appears to be ill advised.

Managers should also be wary of basing decisions on the perception that certain kinds of financial decisions affect capital market valuations. For example, some analysts recommend that companies not enter into mergers when the effect of the merger would be to dilute earnings per share. Managers' assumption should be that the capital market cannot see through the short-term accounting effects of the merger to the real, long-term economic effects. Moreover, if some managers or investors can see the true economic effects of the merger, then they can profit at the expense of those who do not understand. It is exactly this phenomenon—the reaction of smart investors to profit potential from economic analysis—that suggests that markets do react to real effects, not solely to financial or accounting effects. Although many strictly financial decisions are benign (e.g., stock splits or stock dividends), others—such as a decision not to make an acquisition that would create true economic value because of earnings-per-share dilution—are not defensible in a reasonably competitive and efficient capital market.

In summary, when managers believe they have identified potential market inefficiency, they should be prepared to say why it exists and why they alone have been smart enough to identify the inefficiency. Generally, prolonged inefficiencies will only exist in situations in which there are few competitors or in which information necessary to value a security is not freely available.

OPTIONS AND VALUE

An option is defined as the right to do something at some future date under a predetermined set of conditions. In securities markets, for example, the owner of a call option has the right to purchase a common stock at a set price (the exercise price) at any point over a specified period of time (time to maturity). A put option gives someone the right to sell a stock at a fixed price during the relevant period.

For the entrepreneur and general manager, it is important to understand the characteristics of options and their valuation. It is not easy to value options correctly using traditional discounted cash flow techniques. But understanding the determinants of the value of options is essential because many of the decisions managers make are similar to the decision to exercise an option or have the effect of creating new options that can be exercised later. The optional element in various decisions is described below.

- A decision to enter a new product market on a small scale may create options to invest more at a future date. Viewed in isolation, the entry decision may not make sense (i.e., has a negative net present value). But if the initial foray into the market enables the company to invest heavily and profitably once a position has been established, it should not be rejected without taking into account the value creation potential from subsequent decisions.

- Expenditures on research and development create options to invest in subsequent product development. That is, R&D spending creates value indirectly by providing a company with the ability to pursue (or abandon) commercial introduction of ideas that result from it.

- When considering any investment decision, managers should assess the option to abandon the project at an intermediate stage. In some cases, it will make sense to scrap the project (i.e., exercise the option) rather than to continue. The value associated with the option to abandon may make a marginal project economically attractive.

- Venture capitalists often insist on investing money in stages. This reflects their perception of the value of the option to abandon the venture at different points in time. Similarly, the demand of many venture capital investors for a right of first refusal constitutes an option to put in more money where warranted.

- Financial securities often involve options. For example, a convertible bond is a regular bond with an option that gives the holder the right to buy common stock at a fixed price over some specified period of time. A callable bond is one that grants the issuer the option to buy the bond back at a fixed price at some point in the future.

- A line of credit is equivalent to an option granted to a company to borrow at some point in the future under predetermined conditions.
- Incentive compensation schemes sometime involve options. Managers are often given options to purchase stock at a fixed price for some specified time period.
- A company pension plan has two separate option elements. First, beneficiaries of the plan have a call on the assets of the firm equal to the value of the liability. This liability is offset by the value of the existing assets invested in the pension fund. In addition, the company has the option to put the liability to the Pension Benefit Guarantee Corporation in the event of bankruptcy.
- At a more general level, owning stock in a company with debt outstanding is like having the option to buy the whole company at a fixed price—the value of the outstanding bonds. In some sense, the bondholders own the company but have issued the stockholders the right to buy the company back by paying off the bonds.
- Limited liability can be thought of as an option granted to the stockholders of a company to transfer ownership of the company to the bondholders by defaulting when the total value of the firm is less than the face value of the debt.
- A warrant contract provides the consumer with the option to put the equipment back to the producer to be fixed or replaced. This option is valuable to the consumer and therefore represents a liability to the company issuing the warranty.
- A loan guarantee is an option to transfer a liability to the guaranteeing party.

Options have value. Determining the value of particular options can be tricky, but there are some fundamental principles. In assessing the value of a simple call option on a publicly traded common stock, four factors are important.

1. *Time to Maturity.* The longer the option exists, the more valuable it is.
2. *Level of Uncertainty.* The greater the uncertainty (as measured by the standard deviation of expected returns) about the value of the common stock, the more valuable the option.
3. *Level of Interest Rates.* The higher the interest rates, the higher the value of the option.
4. *Level of the Exercise Price.* The higher the exercise price relative to the value of the stock, the lower the value of the option.

An intuitive explanation can be provided for each of these factors. The first is obvious: having a longer period of time in which to decide whether or not to exercise an option increases the likelihood that the stock price will exceed the exercise price.

With respect to uncertainty, consider the case in which the exercise price exceeds the current price of the stock. If there were no uncertainty about the future price of the stock (i.e., the price remains constant), the option would be worthless. However, if the future price is unknown and might exceed the exercise price, then the option has value. The higher the degree of uncertainty about the future price, the more one should be willing to pay for the option.

The fact that a high degree of uncertainty is associated with a high value for an option seems counterintuitive. Normally, one would expect a lower value because of the high risk. In this case, however, because the value of an option cannot be less than zero, increased uncertainty is associated only with an increased probability that the value of the stock will be high relative to the exercise price.

The level of interest rates affects the value of options because buying an option to purchase a stock in the future at a fixed price is like getting a free loan. The amount of the loan is the exercise price. The higher the level of interest rates, the more valuable the loan.

Finally, if the exercise price is high relative to the current stock price, the value of the option to buy the stock is not high, because it is unlikely that the stock price will ever exceed the exercise price.

One element missing from the above list is the expected return on the common stock. Investors can create a perfect hedge by buying a stock and selling call options on the stock. A perfect hedge is one for which the expected return is risk-free: there is no uncertainty about the income that will result from the strategy. The return is the same whether the stock price increases or decreases. The value of an option is determined in relation to the stock price, given the expected volatility, interest rates, exercise price, and time to maturity. Whether the stock price is expected to increase or decrease does not change the value of the option.

However, expected return is absent from the list of determinants of an option's value only when a hedged position can be created. For many option-like decisions confronting managers, it is simply not feasible to find the publicly traded options necessary to create hedges. In these cases, the value of the underlying option will depend in part on the expected return or price of the underlying asset, as well as on the level of uncertainty about the expected return. The other factors in the list will also be important. The fact that both expected return and uncertainty enter the valuation equation suggests that a fundamental role of management is to manage the risk/reward trade-off. And even though high uncertainty is associated with high option values, managers must still manage risk in order to maximize return for a given level of risk.

The manager confronts many investment and financing decisions that have option-like characteristics. Understanding how to value the options is essential to making reasoned decisions. For entrepreneurial ventures in particular, a great deal of the firm's value lies in options to invest rather than in assets already in place. Knowing what constitutes a valuable option, knowing when to exercise the option, and understanding the factors that influence the valuation of the option are all skills required to be successful in new ventures.

THE VALUE OF FINANCIAL FLEXIBILITY

Opportunities to invest can arrive without warning. To survive in a competitive product market, firms must be able to invest when the time is right. Financial flexibility is defined as the ability to invest or threaten credibly to invest when needed. Maintaining financial flexibility is like owning an option to exercise the option to invest.

Financial flexibility has value. Maintaining financial flexibility, however, entails incurring costs. For example, a firm may decide to keep cash balances on hand that exceed the level required to meet transaction balances. The interest income on these balances may be taxed at the corporate level and at the individual level if the income is paid out in the form of dividends. Shareholders of companies with large cash balances would in some sense be better off if the cash were distributed to them and they invested in marketable securities on their own account. Then the income would be taxed only once at the individual level. Corporations are simply not tax-efficient banks.

Does this mean that companies should never hold excess cash balances? No, because having excess cash gives a company the ability to exercise valuable investment opportunities as need arises. And since the competition knows that the company can afford to respond to competitive thrusts by retaliatory investing, the competition may decide not to attack the firm's position in the product market in the first place.

Maintaining financial flexibility clearly has some obvious benefits. However, because it is costly to keep financial reserves on hand, whether in the form of excess cash, unused debt capacity, or lines of credit, firms do not maintain unlimited flexibility.

Financial flexibility, per se, does not necessarily mean that a company can invest or threaten credibly to invest when the need arises. The organization must also be able to respond to changes in the economic environment. If, for example, a company has a rigid capital budgeting system, it may be difficult to exercise valuable investment options that arise outside the normal budgeting cycle. Some investment options decline precipitously in value if they are not acted upon quickly.

Finance is a way of thinking about cash, risk, and value. Managers must be able to view problems from the financial perspective as well as from other perspectives. But finance does not answer questions; it does not make decisions. Finance can help identify the right questions to ask and narrow down the options. When viewed from the finance perspective, some decisions will turn out to be illogical or unfeasible. Deciding what should not or cannot be done is a valuable aid to general managers.

Finance also teaches skepticism. The number of profitable investment opportunities people think exists far exceeds the actual number. Figuring out how a particular decision will create value is a key responsibility of management and does not require elaborate systems. Financial analysis can be carried out in the mind as well as on paper. Finance is thinking hard about the future course of events and trying to chart a sensible path.

Finally, financial thinking is useful only to the extent it helps managers make better decisions. The emphasis must be on action. A recurrent danger in employing the financial perspective is that it can easily become an excuse for inaction.

—— DISCUSSION QUESTIONS

1. As this reading suggests, a finance perspective is both vital and risky. In what ways can a preoccupation with financial analysis jeopardize a firm's well-being? How can the finance perspective help the general manager make sound decisions in other functional areas—personnel, marketing, and production, for example?

2. How do the responsibilities and objectives of the accountant differ from those of the general manager employing a financial perspective?

3. Choose a type of business that interests you—in retail, high technology, or service, for example. Identify important patterns that would affect cash flow.

4. Suppose you are an executive sketching scenarios in the business you chose in question 3. What kinds of decisions could you or your managers make if your goal was to maximize accounting income? What kinds of decisions could help build long-term value? What risks do the latter decisions entail?

5. "If the firm's objective is to maximize value, and value depends on cash and risk, then the incentive compensation system must focus on all these factors." What kinds of compensation policies and practices in an organization will encourage managers to focus on opportunities to maximize value?

27   Small Company Budgets: Targets Are Key

JERRY A. VISCIONE

As companies graduate from merely surviving to growing and prospering, budgeting often becomes just another way of formalizing operations. Entrepreneurs begin to see it as a reaction to events rather than as an important factor in determining events. Using a case model, Viscione argues that managers of smaller companies should adopt a budgeting procedure almost immediately after they start up in business. Deviations from what has been budgeted, he reasons, enable managers to anticipate potentially serious financial problems early enough to take corrective action. He advocates establishing a budget system whereby the chief executive oversees subordinates in setting realistic spending and income targets. The targets represent managers' commitments and can thus be changed only to adjust to business trends and developments.

Every business needs a control system or a budget to achieve an acceptable profit level. Unfortunately, many managers operate without satisfactory budget systems. In this reading I consider the most important issues and problems smaller businesses encounter in setting up and managing budget systems and suggest ways of making them effective. I hope to demonstrate that the obstacles to effective budgeting are not as great as frequently imagined.

The major objectives of a budget system are to:

1. Set acceptable targets for revenues and expenses.
2. Increase the likelihood that targets will be reached.
3. Provide time and opportunity to formulate and evaluate options should obstacles arise.

The targets are confined to the short term—to the next year—but raise issues like strategic planning that pertain to the long term as well.

To consider the issues that usually arise in managing a budget system, I shall rely primarily on a company I have studied, which for the purposes of this reading I shall call the J Company. I picked the J Company for four reasons. First, it has had a budget system for about ten years. Second, its system has been effective, for the company has attained its profit target. Third, despite its profit success, the company still faces problems in execution that are typical of many small businesses. Finally, and most important, the company's president and majority stockholder is firmly committed to the system.

The procedures that are appropriate for adopting and executing a budget depend on the company and are influenced by factors such as its industry, business, size, and the background and temperament of its key people. Any effective budget system, though, requires certain common ingredients.

The J Company distributes industrial supplies. It has 18 full-time employees, including a controller, and a number of part-time employees. *Exhibit 1* presents its target budget for 1991. It looks like an income statement but is really a summary of goals for revenues and expenses for the year. It is what management has decided to achieve in each category. The bottom-line figure has been its primary commitment.

Some managers confuse a target with an estimate or a forecast. An estimate is something we expect will happen. A target is something we make happen. One must do some forecasting, of course, to develop targets.

EXHIBIT 1
J Company's Operating Budget for Year Ended December 31, 1991 (in thousands of dollars)

Net sales	$2,471.6
Cost of goods sold	1,779.6
Gross profit	$ 692.0
Operating expenses	
Salaries and fringe benefits	$ 390.5
Heat, light, and power	8.9
Automobile expenses	27.1
Telephone	11.3
Advertising and selling	7.3
Legal and auditing fees	15.4
Insurance	13.9
Warehouse	17.8
Rent	18.9
Interest	9.5
Office supplies and postage	13.0
Miscellaneous	3.1
Contingency fund	10.5
Small operating expenses[a]	21.2
Total operating expenses	$ 568.4
Profit before taxes	$ 123.6

a. The company does not have this category. It is shown here only to simplify the table. The category represents ten types of operating expense.

Some operating expenses are harder to control than others. Various authorities suggest following the large-company practice of dividing operating expenses into two categories—controllable and uncontrollable. Uncontrollable expenses are the expenditures over which a manager has virtually no control, no authority, and no influence. The logic is that since the manager has no authority, he or she should not be held accountable. While this rationale seems sensible, I do not recommend it for small businesses. In a large company, someone is held responsible for the uncontrollable operating expenses of a unit. In a small organization, however, unless responsibility is assigned, no one is likely to take on this responsibility.

The J Company makes a target budget each year. Like most small businesses in which sales are not seasonal, the J Company does not divide its annual operating expense target because management believes that doing so would involve considerably more time than it is worth. My view is that taking the time to set targets by month or by quarter is generally worthwhile.

——— TIMING AND FORMAT

A budget system evolves through a process that includes the following elements: allocating time for the development of targets, summarizing the targets in writing, monitoring progress each month or quarter, and taking corrective action. So important is a budget system that a small business should establish one in its first year of operation. Many small businesses mistakenly avoid budgeting early on because their managers see no need for it. The J Company did not have a budget system for several years because the company was so small that the owner believed he could easily control all aspects of the operation without a formal system. Only when he encountered a profit sag did he realize that he needed one.

After drawing up a budget, he found that it took two or three years to make the system effective. He was fortunate that the J Company's profit problem was not very serious. The system provided enough short-term relief to give the company a chance to recover. Many small businesses are not so fortunate and, as a consequence, do not survive long enough for budget systems to help.

Not long ago, an investor in a small business asked me to investigate what he described as a minor problem. The business had an excellent product line with considerable market potential but no mechanism for controlling costs. By the time the investor became convinced that the company needed a budget system, the business was headed for insolvency. He certainly learned a lesson; it's too bad his education was so expensive.

Some managers of smaller companies shy away from budgeting because they believe it detracts from creativity. They argue that one cannot have a successful business if everyone thinks like a controller. They are probably right. In putting together a budget, keep this worry in mind. Situations in which everyone thinks like a controller do not mean that budget systems are inherently bad. Such situations suggest that the budget systems are poorly designed or managed. For instance, companies that do no strategic planning usually have poor budget systems that inhibit creativity and lead to other problems.

Does my strong backing of budgeting suggest that it can ward off poor years and somehow make a company immune to poor economic conditions? Of course not, but during uncertain times it warns a company of trouble, permits managerial control, and prevents crises. In a recent year, for example, the J Company was expecting a small sales growth because of the state of the economy while inflation was increasing its expenses. Some tough operating decisions had to be made. The company had a fix on its prospects in advance and the time to think through its problems. As it turned out, the first half of the year was worse than expected and the company had to make more hard decisions. If the J Company had had no budget system, its situation would have been even worse.

The company survived, and its budget system was successful because it was based on top management involvement, the clear designation of responsibility and authority, and the development and monitoring of targets.

TOP MANAGEMENT INVOLVEMENT

For a budget system to work in a large company, top management must be committed to the system and must communicate this commitment to its subordinates. In a small company the president or whoever has the major operating responsibility must do all this him- or herself and must play an active role in implementing the system as well. Obviously, the person responsible for the accounting-finance function is a key player, but very often in a small business that person has only a minor role and lacks the clout and personality to provide the needed leadership. Top management involvement is especially important for the first few years. Without it and the sense of commitment it fosters, you may as well not bother to install a budget system. Later on, the president can usually take a less active role.

The J Company's president did become committed to a budget system because he eventually saw that it would help the company achieve its profit objectives. At the outset he spent considerable time on the design and implementation of the system, and he still works at carrying it out. While the J Company has run into further problems, its budget system has been effective overall, primarily because its president has supported it.

DELEGATION OF RESPONSIBILITY

Every item on a target budget must be allocated to either an individual or a group. Most small businesses are best off assigning each category to one person.

The first three categories on the J Company's target budget—sales, cost of goods sold, and gross profit—are responsibilities of the sales manager. (Responsibility in this context means making an effort to deliver the agreed-on numbers.) All products at the J Company are purchased ready for sale and markup, and their prices are under the control of the sales manager. In any business that manufactures its own products, the person responsible for production should have a major role in setting and reaching the cost-of-goods-sold target.

The responsibility for salaries and fringe benefits at the J Company is split among the managers responsible for personnel. For example, a full-time bookkeeper and a part-time billing clerk assist the controller, who is thus held accountable for this portion of the salary budget. Each of the remaining operating expenses has one person assigned to it, but no one has complete control or authority over any of them. Everyone in the company uses office supplies and postage, for example. They could, of course, be divided by function in the company, but such sophisticated bookkeeping is beyond the scope of the J Company and many other small businesses.

The advent of the small computer and the requisite software, however, has made more sophisticated reporting systems increasingly feasible for small businesses and small not-for-profit organizations. The J Company assigns each of these expenses to the person who, in the judgment of the president, has the most control over it.

The person responsible for each target must believe it is reasonable to attain and must have the authority to control the expenditures it entails. The J Company adheres fairly well to this basic principle, but many companies have ineffective budget systems because they fail to do so.

In some organizations, the presidents review budget submissions, decide the bottom line is unacceptable, and order across-the-board cuts in expenses. I disapprove of this approach for two reasons. First, across-the-board cuts are seldom fair, for they penalize the managers who conscientiously request the minimum necessary and they reward the managers who pad their budgets; conscientious managers quickly learn how the game is played.

Second, the budget becomes the chief executive's budget and companies lose the commitment necessary to attain their targets.

In other organizations managers submit targets and, after reviewing them, the presidents talk their managers into different figures. A target must be bought; a target cannot be sold. Often, initial submissions need revision and presidents must help rewrite them. This is one of the more difficult tasks for presidents because they must persuade without selling and direct without commanding.

Budget items, like overhead expenses (often labeled general and administrative expenses), are difficult to assign. The J Company used to believe that one person should not take responsibility for them and thus that management as a group should be responsible. When this approach did not work, the

J Company began assigning each category on the budget. The result? Considerable improvement in most areas.

One tactic that helped the J Company was to subdivide its existing categories. Legal, audit, and insurance had been one item; now they are separate categories. The person who actually purchases the insurance is not the person who works with lawyers and auditors. While breaking down expenses will help considerably, it has limited benefits. Having too many items on the budget results in information overload.

The team approach to targeting can work. Indeed, it can be more effective than having one person in charge. Since it requires a team leader for each item, though, the team approach takes up more of management's time.

What is most important to keep in mind is that managers must be committed to controlling as many expenses as possible. The J Company's managers believe that expenses like heat, light, and power depend primarily on factors such as the weather and the price of oil and thus are virtually impossible for them to control. Whether they are correct is irrelevant. The point is that as long as managers believe an expense can't be controlled, it won't be.

The J Company assigns items like this to the controller, but I think that most operating expenses should be assigned to operating people. While the J Company has not encountered problems in controlling such expenses, other companies have. In one company, for instance, the president thought the amount for cleaning and maintenance was outrageously high, but the production people insisted that it could not be controlled. This expense was assigned to the controller. The result? A lower target for cleaning and maintenance expense and a facility that quickly became a mess.

─── SETTING REALISTIC TARGETS

The first step in implementing a budget system is to prepare a schedule specifying when each target is to be submitted. The president must insist that everyone stick to the timetable. The loss of a few weeks may not seem important at first, especially in the light of other short-term pressures, but it will cause problems later on.

When managers rush to complete their budgets, they may set unrealistic targets because they just do not have enough time to analyze the situation. Such environments cause new problems. One company's president made the mistake of setting the budget for a manager who was preoccupied with completing a major sale.

The J Company used to encounter such problems because it often let its schedule slip to accommodate other pressing matters. The key people did not involve themselves in setting targets. The result? Lack of commitment to the targets. On several occasions, changing economic conditions made attaining targets difficult, and the president could not generate the necessary enthusiasm and drive. Several such experiences inspired respect in the J Company's president for the importance of having a budget schedule.

For the next year, the budgeting process begins formally in early October with a memorandum from the controller; but prior to that time top managers hold several informal meetings—one at a local motel to avoid telephone interruptions—to discuss sales and gross profit margins as well as new employee positions and capital expenditures for future years. The big items on the budget thus receive attention before the budgeting process starts. Finally, in late September, the president and the controller decide on the schedule.

They send a memorandum about the schedule to the people responsible for the targets. It explains that submissions are due by a certain date and that each person will receive a rough sales target two weeks before the submission date. (The sales manager is responsible for submitting the sales target in time for distribution.) The memo also includes the president's thoughts about cost-of-living salary increases and merit raises. Finally, it gives a history of data for each manager's targets. The sales manager, for example, receives monthly sales figures for the previous five years as well as breakdowns by salesperson.

Of course, the sales manager and other executives already have these data somewhere in their files. Sending the data at this stage makes it easy for them to start work without the inevitable procrastination caused by a search through various files.

From the time they receive the memorandum to the time they submit their targets, the managers can ask the controller for more data and advice about costs and can discuss their ideas with the president—not only because they need feedback but also because they realize that it is unwise to have the president see something new for the first time in a budget submission. In one instance, the person responsible for the warehouse wanted to add an employee. This person justified the request by supplying data on the increase in the number of orders expected. In another instance, the sales manager requested funds for a new advertising program. The president asked the sales manager why such a campaign would be effective. After further discussion, they agreed it would not be a productive expenditure, given other priorities.

After each manager has submitted a target, the controller prepares a tentative consolidated budget so that the president can see an aggregate before he looks at each submission. When the president has reviewed the aggregate as well as each request, he discusses his concerns with the controller, talks with each manager further, and helps prepare a second target budget that incorporates the revisions made during the review process.

The managers complete the second tentative budget by early December. One year, because the profit projected was lower than the amount expected for the current year, the president and the controller recommended certain changes. For example, they suggested eliminating the two requests mentioned previously—the new warehouse employee and the advertising campaign. Following a lengthy meeting in mid-December, the revisions were accepted.

Everyone at the meeting agreed that the new person in the warehouse was needed and decided that if sales and gross profit were over budget for the first six months of the year, the new employee would be added. They also discussed what actions to take if sales and profits fell below budget, and they set a time for a review of the figures.

The J Company's budget for that year had a contingency item of $10,800 to protect its profit figure. If the company does not attain its gross profit figure or if one of its expenses is over budget, the funds come from this source. The president is responsible for allocating these funds and is stringent about it.

I urge you to resist the temptation to reduce the contingency item to produce an acceptable profit target. If you succumb, you will likely find that managers will look to it as a cushion. A simple policy that may help is not to allow the target for the contingency item to be set lower than the previous year's target.

MONITORING PROGRESS

In all successful efforts to formulate budget systems that I have observed, the chief executive has been firmly committed and has led by setting an example. He has made time to work on the budget. The top person usually spends considerable time persuading key people that a budget system is vital. In companies with ineffective budget systems, the chief executive either does not fully appreciate the importance of a system or believes that leadership of the budget can be delegated.

In addition, the J Company uses a bonus plan to motivate everyone to stick to the budget. The bottom line dominates the bonus plan. The J Company allocates a very healthy portion of its profits above a certain level to a pool divided among the managers. The president decides on the distributions.

To watch its progress toward its targets, the J Company issues a statement by the fifteenth of each month. This report covers each previous month. *Exhibit 2* shows the column headings used on one page of the statement.

Earlier I recommended a month-by-month breakdown of the target budget, even though the J Company does not make one. For most businesses, computing a year-to-date target budget by multiplying by the percentage of the year expired can produce misleading figures. For example, doing that for J Company's salary and fringe expenses for the end of March—one quarter

EXHIBIT 2
Monthly Statement

FOR MONTH	YEAR TO DATE	FOR YEAR	YEAR TO DATE	VARIANCE
Income statement	Income statement	Target budget	Target budget	

through the year—ignores the target's inclusion of overtime, most of which is incurred late in the year, and the fact that raises are usually granted in the second half of the year. To offset this weakness, the J Company's controller notes such facts in comments on the monthly statement.

I advocate a monthly breakdown of targets because I do not believe that the procedure at J Company is ideal for managing a small business. Managers love numbers presented in neat packages, and when they see a positive variance, they make an optimistic interpretation, regardless of caveats. Nevertheless, if you are convinced it is not possible, practical, or desirable to have a monthly breakdown, I suggest the J Company's method of adding comments.

A second page of the monthly statement prepared for management by the controller includes projections. One set shows actual results plus the budget for the remainder of the year. For example, the April statement will give a projection derived by adding the actual income statement for the first three months plus three quarters of the budget.

The two-page statement is sent to the key operating people, who analyze the data. If anyone is seriously concerned about progress, he or she requests a meeting of all top people. Regardless of special meetings, the J Company holds a regular meeting each quarter to discuss the budget even if progress is fine.

If in the monthly analysis an expense item is heading over budget for the year, the controller notes this point on the statement after she discusses the matter with the person responsible. This person would then have three options.

1. To take action to keep the expense on target.
2. To request an allocation from the contingency fund.
3. To request a revision of the target budget.

Given such a policy, total annual operating expenses have almost always been within budget and overages have been minor (2% to 3%). The president appreciates this record. His banker appreciates it even more. The system works not because the president is a tough guy when it comes to revisions but because he sees to it that the job of setting the budget and gaining the commitment of all those responsible for the initial budget is done.

These procedures do not mean that the J Company is inflexible once the budget is set. As noted earlier, if an unexpected opportunity arises during the year to introduce a new product line or to sell much more of existing products than anticipated, the company increases its operating expenses and need not go through red tape to effect a change.

Sometimes it becomes clear after the start of the year that an operating-expense target should be lower than anticipated even if the sales target is being reached or surpassed. When this is the case, the controller can note this fact and assume that the total should not be spent. Sometimes, with the approval of the president and the person responsible, the controller may lower the target.

The controller at the J Company believes strongly that revisions should be made in the budget and that the company should not incur unnecessary expense. Many managers share this view, but I believe that spending should be left to the discretion of the operating managers. Once an item is approved, the operating manager is the best judge of actual spending. This person may make errors at first, but the added costs are worthwhile investments when you think of the benefit the manager will get from the experience. Of course, if sales and/or gross profit targets are not met, revisions are in order.

What if the J Company is not attaining its sales or gross profit target? Usually, it postpones its planned expenditures. For example, it might put off the planned purchase of a new car. If the shortfall in gross profits cannot be offset by that kind of action, then management may eliminate a salary or accept reduced earnings.

What if the company is surpassing its sales and gross profit targets? It will most likely revise the targets, perhaps with appropriate adjustments to operating expenses. If sales and gross profit for the first six months of a year are over target, for example, the actual plus the target for the next six months will become the new target. The logic is that if the company sticks to its original sales and gross profit targets, it will face no challenge for the remainder of the year. Of course, there may be changes in operating expenses to support the higher sales or to replace a worthwhile expense that was removed during the budget preparation process.

———— GETTING STARTED

How do you begin? Sit down with your finance person (this may be the outside CPA). Review the model of the J Company and discuss how it can be adapted to your business. Then meet with your key people to discuss the system or the model you are planning.

The next step is to prepare a document outlining the procedures (the schedule, etc.). Remember that you will have to make numerous revisions as you go along. Also, make sure everyone realizes that implementing an effective budget system will take two to three years. Don't let that be an excuse for anyone to become sloppy or careless. After all, the budget system can begin to improve results much sooner, but only if you and your key people are committed to it.

———— DISCUSSION QUESTIONS

1. Do you think a formal budgeting process diminishes creativity in a small business? Why or why not? What can managers do to overcome this possibility?
2. If you were president of a small company, how would you persuade a group of skeptical operating managers that a new budgeting system is necessary?

3. Compare the advantages and disadvantages of individual and team responsibility for budget targets. For which budget items would each approach be suitable?

4. An important objective of a budget system is to "increase the likelihood that targets will be reached." By itself, setting targets is probably not sufficient. How would you ensure commitment to targets over the course of the fiscal year?

5. In your view, who should authorize expenditures, controllers or operating managers? Explain your reasoning. What is the proper role of the controller?

Budget Choice: Planning versus Control   28

In the preceding reading, Jerry Viscione argued that managers of small ventures must pay particular attention to the targets they set when formulating budgets. While agreeing that targeting is important, Neil Churchill maintains that budgets should be considered from a broader perspective. He views them as having two primary functions: planning and control. Managers must decide which function is more important and then resolve a number of formulation issues: the initiation process, implementation, the period covered, whether the budget should be fixed or flexible, and how it should be used to evaluate performance. He concludes that large companies concerned about operational efficiency should focus on the control aspects of budgeting while small, innovative companies should be concerned with planning aspects. Whatever the focus, budget preparation and implementation are important in carrying out company strategy and in professionalizing the smaller company.

start my classes on budgeting by displaying two situations on the blackboard:

EXPENSES

	Budgeted Amount	*Actual Results*
Budget 1	$1000	$950
Budget 2	$ 750	$850

Then I ask the class, "Which budget is better, assuming in both cases that the manager gets the job done in time, that the end result is the same quality of performance and customer satisfaction, and that the manager doesn't develop ulcers in the process of implementation?"

A heated argument usually follows. Most class participants eventually choose Budget 2 after being assured of equal results. A minority, however, hold out for Budget 1, which seems to them the "most reasonable."

These opposing views come together when I ask, "Which would be best for borrowing money on a one-loan-a-year basis?" In this case, the choice is almost always Budget 1. And when I ask, "Which would be best for motivating performance?" the majority of participants usually select Budget 2.

As this example shows, budgets can be used both for planning (Number 1) and for control (Number 2), although the same budget is not always optimal for both purposes.

Occasionally a company uses a budget with "stretch" in it for motivating performance—sales, for instance—and a more "realistic" budget for planning—expected sales, for example. More commonly, companies use the same document for both purposes.[1] Large companies tend to use budgets mostly for control and smaller entrepreneurial companies use them primarily as planning tools.

But no matter whether it is used for planning or for control, a budget is more than a forecast. A forecast is a prediction of what may happen and sometimes contains prescriptions for dealing with future events. A budget, on the other hand, involves a commitment to a forecast to make an agreed-on outcome happen.

Budgets come in several variations. Cash budgets are especially important to new and growing businesses, whereas capital budgets are widely used if capital expenditures are important and recurring. Human resource or "headcount" budgets (the capital budgets of service companies) serve as means of control in labor-intensive companies. But generally when the term *budget* is used, it refers to an operating budget containing an organization's detailed revenue and expense accounts grouped either by operating units, such as divisions or departments, or by products and product lines. Such a document is a central part of the management control system of many companies.

In preparing a budget, a company can proceed in a number of different ways. Some companies use a top-down and others a bottom-up approach in budget preparation. Some revise their budgets quarterly and others never change them. Some use flexible budgets to evaluate managerial performance while others compare results against original estimates. These and other differences in budget structures and processes largely determine the effectiveness of budgeting and whether it accomplishes management's objectives.

In this reading I consider eight managerial concerns in preparing budgets. The concerns vary according to whether the company intends to use its budget primarily for planning or for control.

PLANNING ISSUES

From a planning perspective, a budget is the glue that makes the different parts of the organization fit together. It harmonizes the enterprise's strategy with its organizational structure, its management and personnel, and the tasks that need to be done to implement strategy.

---

1. *See* M. Edgar Barrett and LeRoy B. Fraser, III, "Conflicting Roles in Budgeting for Operations," *Harvard Business Review* (July–August 1977): 137.

When well done, it translates the strategic plans of the organization and its implementation programs into period-oriented operational guides to company activities.

INITIATION AND PARTICIPATION

Who should initiate budgets? What should be the role of top executives? Should they start the process with tightly specified objectives? Or should they set forth the basic planning premises, competitive assumptions, economic forecasts, and so forth, and then play a relatively passive role in formulating the budget? And what should be the role of operating managers? Should they fill in the blanks of a tightly specified budget structure or take responsibility for initiating budget assumptions and calculations?

One of the first issues to be settled is the extent to which budget formulation involves all management levels. Both the top-down and bottom-up approaches have advantages whose importance varies in accordance with the nature of the business and the company's stage of development (see *Exhibit 1*).

The top-down approach allows the owner-manager and others at the top to put forward their comprehensive views of the organization and its economic and competitive environments. Top management knows the company's goals, strategies, and available resources. Indeed, in a small company the owner-manager may be the only one with such knowledge as others are almost totally involved with day-to-day operations.

Several situations call for a top-down approach—when business unit managers must be given explicit performance objectives because of economic crises, when unit managers lack the perspective to participate in budget setting, and when the nature of the business requires close coordination between units. In these situations, the knowledge necessary for good budget preparation usually resides at a managerial level one or two steps above that of unit managers.

EXHIBIT 1
Top-down and Bottom-up Budgeting

WHAT TOP-DOWN BUDGETING INCORPORATES BEST	*WHAT BOTTOM-UP BUDGETING INCORPORATES BEST*
Economic and industry projections	Operational plans
	Information on competition, products, and markets
Company planning parameters	
Corporate goals	Alternative courses of action
Overall resource availability	Specific resource requirements

The bottom-up approach, on the other hand, makes use of operating management's detailed knowledge of the environment and the marketplace, knowledge that is available only to those who are involved on a daily basis. The more responsibility unit managers have for innovation, the more their inputs are needed in budget formulation, for they are best able to decide courses of action and targets for their units. They know what must be done, where the opportunities lie, what weaknesses need to be addressed, and where resources should be allocated.

Furthermore, a budget prepared at the level at which it is to be implemented is more likely to evoke commitment than one imposed from on high. Moreover, only when unit managers contribute to budget preparation can they be held accountable for the long-term performance of their operating units.

For companies requiring quick responses to competitive pressures, top-down budgeting can be disastrous. But companies with a considerable degree of interdependence among operating units need top-down budget guidance for coordination. Perhaps this is why the extensively integrated smokestack industries have found it so difficult to adapt to the rapidly changing environment in which they find themselves. They may have to adopt a different set of budgets and other management controls in order to prosper—or even to exist.

IMPLEMENTATION

Simple top-down or bottom-up approaches to budgeting are rare. The decision is not either-or but rather how much of each type of approach is appropriate.

Blending the overview of top management with the experience of business-unit operating managers presents a major challenge in budget preparation. A cyclical process whereby the initial budget formulation is done in broad terms, with details added after everyone agrees on planning assumptions, can be quite effective. The cycle for companies without a strategic-business-unit (SBU) structure has six steps. (If the company has a SBU structure, a cyclical approach entails additional steps involving SBU management.[2]) These six steps are as follows:

1. Top management sets forth in broad terms, and sends to the operating-unit managers, an overview of the environment, the corporate goals for the year, and the resource constraints.
2. Each operating-unit manager formulates in broad terms the unit's operating plans, performance targets, and resource requirements.
3. Top management collects, combines, and evaluates information from all the operating units.

---

2. *See* Richard F. Vancil and Peter Lorange, "Strategic Planning in Diversified Companies," *Harvard Business Review* (January–February 1975): 81.

4. Top management assesses and revises targets and resource availabilities, and assigns preliminary estimates to each operating unit.
5. Operating-unit managers plan their activities in detail, determine their resource needs, and prepare their final budgets, which are sent to top management.
6. Top management combines these unit budgets, tunes them where necessary, approves them, and sends them back to the operating-unit managers for implementation.

This type of budgeting provides initial top-level input into the process and allows top management to retain overall control. It also permits operating-unit managers to make contributions before detail has been built into the budget and before all management levels are committed to estimates that no doubt will be revised anyway.

TIMING

Most operating budgets are based on the passage of time, with revenues and expenses related to calendar periods. In the uncertain atmosphere of start-up companies, the budget might better be related to important actions or events because the organization often takes longer than anticipated to get products perfected, to land the first big order, or to get financing in place.[3] In other than start-up situations, budgets are related to time periods in several ways.

For budgets based on calendar periods, the length of the operating period is usually a month, although smaller companies often prepare budgets for calendar quarters, particularly when they first begin the process. One common variation in monthly budgeting is dividing the year into thirteen four-week periods both for budgeting and reporting. This reduces inequalities in sales or production days between periods within the year and between similar periods in consecutive years. There is no *one* best budget period or interval—the period should fit the needs of a company, in terms of its planning horizon, the difficulties of budget preparation, and the link of the budget to strategic planning.

The period covered can range from three to six months in very small companies to two or three years in large corporations. Operating budgets usually cover one year, although some companies also include a general forecast for the second year. Such forecasts normally do not involve the same commitment as operating budgets.

Budget preparation should begin as near the start of the period as possible while still allowing enough time to do a thorough job. A participative

3. *See* Zenas Block, "Can Corporate Venturing Succeed?" *Journal of Business Strategy* (Fall 1982): 21.

process takes longer than a top-down budget. A small company using the top-down approach might initiate the budget process one or two months before the start of the fiscal year, whereas a large company might start six to nine months earlier. The more complex the company's products, processes, and environment, of course, the longer the whole process takes. As companies grow and change the nature of their budget processes, they may find that more time is needed for formulation.[4]

While small companies usually do not have formal strategic planning, this procedure may develop as they grow and decentralize. In such cases, the longer the period covered by the operating budget, the closer will be its links to the strategic plan and the greater the pressure to synchronize at least the first year of the plan with the budget. Moreover, if the budget and the strategic plan are prepared during the same time period, the links between them will be close. Usually, however, the strategic plan precedes the budget and the linkage is less pronounced.

CONTROL OPTIONS

Large corporations with sophisticated formal planning systems use budgets extensively for control—first for coordinating dispersed business units and later, for evaluating units' performances. Small company managers have less need to use budgets in this way since they control their businesses informally and personally.

But small companies also need up-to-the minute planning since they must react to events. Having less control over their environment than large corporations, they are more prone to seize opportunities than to make them. Thus, many of them stress the planning side of budgeting and revise their budgets while also rolling them forward on a monthly, quarterly, or semiannual basis.

ROLLING BUDGETS AND REVISION

Companies can choose to budget annually for the year ahead or opt for a "rolling budget" always looking ahead 9 to 12 months. The latter system involves budgeting an additional quarter at the end of each quarter, and then adding this on to the existing budget. As shown in *Exhibit 2*, on April 1, 1984, a three-month period, "Quarter 5," is added to the 1984 calendar-year budget to extend it to April 1, 1985. Another quarter is added on June 30, 1984. In this way, management always has a 12-month budget at the beginning of each quarter.

---

4. For a discussion of the different stages of development of small companies, *see* Chap. 21, "The Five Stages of Small Business Growth."

EXHIBIT 2
Rolling Budget

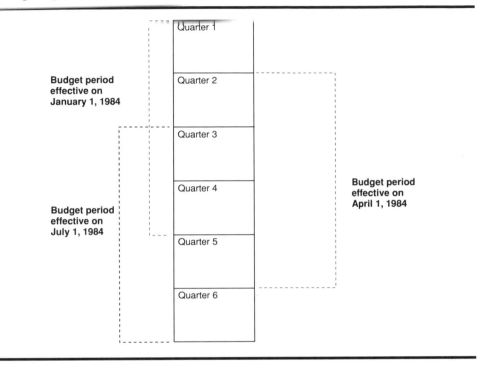

The advantage of a rolling budget is its coverage. As one company president stated in early 1983:

"We would have cut our inventories and production early last fall if we then had a budget that looked out into the first quarter of this year. As it was, we moved too late and it cost us a lot of money. That's why we're changing to a rolling budget as of next July 1."

On the negative side, a rolling budget takes more of management's time to prepare and, moreover, operations are disrupted four times a year, rather than once, for planning.

Those who prefer rolling budgets argue that managers get better at budgeting with practice, and therefore need no more time to do quarterly budgets than one annual budget. And, as operating managers should always be engaged in planning, budgeting four times a year is not a disruptive process for them.

While a company could have a rolling budget without revising its existing fixed-period budget, most companies that use rolling budgets revise their budgets at least once during the year as they roll forward.

Budget revision, however, is a highly controversial issue. Should a company revise its annual budget during the course of the fiscal year as conditions change? Revised budgets are more accurate, since they embody the best knowledge available, but revision makes a budget a rubber yardstick that cannot accurately measure performance or evaluate management.

Consider the budget program of Corcom, an electronics manufacturer with $30 million in sales and owning four plants, one in the United States and three offshore. The company sells three-fourths of its products to American manufacturers of electrical and electronic equipment and the remainder abroad. For competitive reasons, it tries to maintain an inventory of finished goods of seven and ten weeks of sales. It uses skilled labor, and since it is subject to restrictions on layoffs and terminations, it is reluctant to vary production levels more than necessary.

Because of uncertainties in demand, Corcom cannot project revenues accurately very far into the future. It can only watch carefully what is going on and try to react rapidly. It depends on forecasting and quick responses throughout the organization.

Management prepares an annual budget, composed of four quarterly budgets of thirteen weeks—the "original budget." Every six months it revises the annual budget for the remaining six months and adds on a new six-month budget—the "revised budget." At the end of each month, it also prepares a revised forecast for the next 13 weeks, altering the existing quarter budget when necessary, and adding an additional month. (For example, at the end of January, April is added to February and March to form a new quarter and estimates are revised, if necessary.) This becomes the so-called "current 13-week budget."

Results are compared with both current and revised budgets and, since Corcom is a publicly held company, with the original budget for each quarter to see if a revision of the forecasts made to the financial community is necessary. Top management also compares current budgets to check the accuracy of planning assumptions and to see if operating units throughout the company are using the same common assumptions.

Both the president and the financial vice president of Corcom readily admit that having so many budgets creates confusion as to which one is most important in evaluating results. They hasten to add, however, that the benefits of having a detailed plan for action (the current 13-week budget) that is up-to-date and comprehensive and prepares managers to deal with a rapidly changing environment far outweigh the ineffectiveness of their budget system as a means of control.

Companies like this electronics manufacturer, which are concerned with external developments and with seizing the opportunities that arise, use budgets mostly for planning, in order to have current thinking implemented throughout the company and to compare performance with plans. Large companies use budgets for annual planning and then for control to ensure that operations go according to the original plan. On the other hand, a trade-off exists between continually revised budgets that permit innovation but are not effective in ensuring efficient operations, and rigid budgets that exert tight controls over operations but hamper innovations.

FIXED OR FLEXIBLE BUDGETS

Successful management through delegation requires a clear set of objectives for individuals responsible for the various tasks in an organization. These objectives can be production standards, sales quotas, or budgets containing estimates of the level of production and the costs and revenues involved—all variables. Periodically, results are compared against estimates to determine if corrective actions or revised plans are needed.

When fast-changing markets force small companies into such uncertainty that they seldom achieve even the most precisely calculated sales and production forecasts, a flexible budget is a powerful tool for analyzing performance. This can separate the effects of variations between actual and estimated costs, between actual and estimated revenues, and so forth. For companies in uncertain environments, particularly those in manufacturing or distribution, the flexible budget is one of the most important control tools available.

For an example of how it works, assume a delivery budget of $1,000 for a sales level of 200 units. If the delivery cost was $900 for 175 units, the budget would show a $100-delivery-cost underrun or favorable variance. But if delivery costs average $5 a unit, the company should have spent only $875 for 175 units—thus indicating a $25 unfavorable variance.

A flexible budget would substitute results in terms of units or services produced or sold for estimates; use estimated costs and prices, thus providing a standard of comparison; and compare results with estimates on a "flexible" basis, isolating variances in terms of changes in costs, revenues, price levels, and use of resources.

BONUSES BASED ON BUDGET

Most companies use budgets to evaluate, to some extent, managers' performance. These evaluations result in bonuses based on the attainment of targeted goals or on achieving a certain percentage of budget, with extra bonuses for exceeding estimates. While bonuses based on budgets can have positive effects, they introduce the possibility of "budget games." Managers playing these games aim to influence the budgeting process by setting revenue targets low and costs high, thus making goals much easier to meet.

If control is the thrust of a company's budget, evaluating and rewarding performance against estimates is appropriate as long as steps are taken to detect and counter budget games. To do this effectively, top management must have considerable knowledge of the activities being budgeted to determine the extent of any games and to take corrective action. Using the budget as a basis for evaluation and compensation is very risky for managers who lack the requisite knowledge.

Managers should be wary of rewarding performance against budget in a new business or where an acquisition in a new area of activity has been made. To use budgets for compensation, a manager must know the territory well.

If the major purpose of the budget is planning, then using estimates as a basis for compensation, by encouraging budget games, can detract from accuracy. For a successful planning budget, compensation should be based on other criteria, such as current achievements compared with previous ones, profits, return on investment, or other agreed-on objectives. Just setting goals and measuring their achievement is itself a powerful motivational force.

EVALUATION CRITERIA

When using budgets to evaluate performance, top management must decide whether to focus on final net profit or only on the revenues and expenses for which the business unit is responsible. Final net profit includes expenses that a business-unit manager cannot control.

This problem is illustrated in *Exhibit 3*, where the performance of the managers of departments A and B can be judged on several levels:

- Contribution to overhead and profit—the direct costs and revenues that each manager controls in the short run.
- Department profit—contribution to overhead and profit less the fixed costs that are directly attributable to each department's operation. The department manager may control these fixed costs either by deciding to replace equipment or to move to a new location or by increasing or decreasing the department's use of a corporate

EXHIBIT 3
Actual and Budgeted Performance[a] (in thousands of dollars)

	COMPANY		DEPARTMENT A		DEPARTMENT B	
	Actual	*Budget*	*Actual*	*Budget*	*Actual*	*Budget*
Budget sales	$400	$400	$300	$200	$100	$200
Variable cost of sales	200	200	150	100	50	100
Contribution to overhead and profit	200	200	150	100	50	100
Department fixed expense	50	50	25	25	25	25
Department profit	150	150	125	75	25	75
Corporate overhead	120	120	90	60	30	60
Corporate profit	**$ 30**	**$ 30**	**$ 35**	**$ 15**	**$ –5**	**$ 15**

a. Income taxes ignored.

resource such as a central computer, legal department, or building space. In the latter case, allocations should be made, where possible, on a predetermined basis so that department managers can control use and costs.

· Corporate profit—the final "bottom line" after all costs have been deducted, including costs over which department managers have no control and for which they have no direct responsibility.

In *Exhibit 3*, the department A manager exceeds budgeted sales by 50%, while the department B manager falls 50% behind the sales goal. The entry entitled "Contribution to overhead and profit" shows the achievements of both department managers if budgeted volumes, costs, and prices are constant. If fixed expenses remain within budget, the departments' profits rise and fall by the same amount as their contributions to overhead and profit.

If corporate profit is used to evaluate department management performance, however, the results are different. Because corporate overhead is allocated on the basis of either department sales or variable costs, department A's profit before taxes is $20,000 higher than the budgeted sum, while that of department B is $20,000 lower. The higher sales of department A increased corporate overhead charges and reduced profits.

If a company uses incentive compensation, then department profit appears to be a better measure of performance than corporate profit, and operating managers are apt to perceive it as more fair.

Yet two arguments exist for using corporate profit. This is the measure used to evaluate overall company performance, particularly that of public corporations. Thus, the company's control system should reinforce the importance of this measure, with budgets and bonuses reflecting the economic reality facing the company. This is important when evaluating a manager responsible for a large or important business unit. The need for bottom-line orientation is not as necessary with first- and second-level supervisors and managers.

Moreover, when department, division, or product managers are evaluated and compensated on bottom-line profits, they are prone to question corporate expense allocations and thus exert a control on corporate spending.

HOW TIGHT A BUDGET?

When individuals are given a goal that is a bit beyond what they initially expect, they will often accept the goal as achievable and then work hard to attain it. But if the goal is set too high, they will probably reject it as unattainable and perform poorly. In budgeting, then, a key question is how tight a manager can set a budget and still make it useful in encouraging good performance.

As the example at the beginning of this reading showed, the best budget for control may not be the best one for planning. This is particularly true if only one budget is used that has considerable stretch built into it. If a budget is revised, adjusted, and readjusted until it contains the profit top management desires, it can be useless or even harmful to the business by breeding mistrust and insecurity among unit managers. There is a lot to be said for starting the budget process with an honest statement of what those at the top see as the market and what performance they think is needed. There is also a lot to be said for a corporate culture that encourages unit managers with knowledge of operations and opportunities to put together a realistic budget that takes both long- and short-run considerations into account.

UNUSUAL USES OF BUDGETS

In addition to the purposes previously discussed—planning, communicating goals, evaluating performances, and motivating managers—budgets can be used to accomplish three other goals not normally associated with budgeting: delegation, education, and better management of subordinates.

Delegation is something that few owner-managers do well. When managers grant authority to other individuals to make and implement decisions without obtaining approval beforehand, they need to be able to check that the results are what they want. Without this feedback on performance, "abdication," not delegation, is occurring.

A good budget is among the best means both for communicating instructions and for evaluating what is being done. A budget can support delegation better if the need for performance feedback is considered in its design and construction. The budget should carefully pinpoint delegated responsibilities. Its preparation should involve the managers who will assume authority to ensure that they understand the objectives, think they are reasonable, and are committed to their attainment.

The educational effect of a budget is perhaps most evident when the process is introduced in a company. Operation managers learn not only the technical aspects of budgeting but also how the company functions and how their business units interact with others.

Budgets enhance the skills of operating managers not only by educating them about how the company functions, but also by giving them the opportunity, and the spur, to manage their subordinates in a more professional manner. This aspect of budgeting is often overlooked because the budget is viewed essentially as a tool for the owners and top management of a company. A business unit manager can use a budget as an excuse to call on their customers and talk to them about their advertising needs and plans. Operating managers can, in their turn, use the budget as an excuse to accomplish distasteful things. They can, as is often done, "blame it on the budget."

A POWERFUL TOOL

A budget is an important means of accomplishing an assortment of managerial goals. Budgets also have various ramifications, some subtle and some not so subtle. For maximum effect, keep the following in mind:

- A budget is a plan.
- A budget is a control.
- It can guide corporate operations.
- It can extend the reach of top management by supporting delegation.
- It can coordinate company activities.
- It can communicate company objectives and activities during its preparation and serve as a basis for communication throughout its term.
- It can direct, guide, and reward operating managers and form a basis for performance evaluation.
- It can educate company employees as to what is to be done and assist them in doing it.
- It can lead to "games" involving false estimates and other counterproductive behavior.
- How it works depends on other management systems in place.
- Its effectiveness depends on the way it is used by top management.

DISCUSSION QUESTIONS

1. In organizations where you have worked, has the budget played a central role in guiding operations and coordinating activities? What conditions either encourage or discourage people to take budgets seriously?
2. The author describes the budget as "the glue that makes different parts of the organization fit together"; later, he adds that a budget's effectiveness depends on other management systems being in place. What other systems are essential in a new venture to make the budget process work?
3. The reading offers one means for combining a top-down and a bottom-up approach to budgeting. In what situations would the approach described be suitable? If your company's strategy depended on the expertise of operating managers, how would you design a process that would keep top management involved while giving operating managers more responsibility?
4. Do you agree that managers of new ventures should be wary of rewarding performance against budget? Why or why not?
5. What are the benefits and risks of revising budgets? Under what circumstances would you encourage or discourage budget revision?

29   How Long Should You Borrow Short Term?

JERRY A. VISCIONE

According to the matching principle, long-term needs should be financed with long-term capital and temporary requirements with short-term loans. Small companies, which usually lack long-term funds, can rarely adhere to these guidelines, however. More important than perfect matching, suggests Jerry Viscione in this reading, is calculating how much risk is involved in violating the principle and determining when the risk becomes excessive.

Small companies that use short-term capital to finance long-term needs must be flexible enough to eliminate the debt in a reasonable amount of time without disturbing operations. Using a case example, Viscione describes the risks these companies can incur and proposes different ways that companies can deal with them. Above all, he urges small businesses to make sure that financial policy is an integral part of their strategic planning process.

Small companies often use short-term loans to finance permanent investments in working capital. Unfortunately, this strategy is very risky. Small companies have enough operating risks—they do not need to compound their exposure by taking on more financing risk.

How can small companies maximize their ability to tolerate short-term debt? Equally important, how can they determine when the financing risk from short-term debt is great enough to warrant forgoing profitable opportunities?

The answers to these questions lie in the matching principle, a guide well known to financing experts. It argues that long-term needs ought to be financed with long-term capital and temporary requirements met by short-term loans. The experience of the Anderson Company (not its real name), a small distributor of industrial products, will help illustrate the principle.

In 1984, Anderson, whose sales at the time were about $200,000, was given a sudden opportunity to make a $1 million sale. To make the sale, though, Anderson needed about $970,000 of inventory—a huge credit risk, especially since the customer would pay about 30 days after Anderson had to pay its suppliers. Anderson convinced the customer to obtain a letter of credit from a commercial bank to virtually eliminate the credit risk and also pave the way for a short-term bank loan.

This transaction illustrates appropriate use of the matching principle. Anderson would invest $970,000 in current assets for two months, with trade creditors financing the investment for the first month and a bank loan covering the second. It was a temporary investment because the company would not be purchasing this amount of inventory regularly.

To see the distinction between temporary and permanent capital, assume the customer intended to buy this amount every month on terms of net 60 days, and Anderson had to pay its suppliers in 30 days. This investment of $1.94 million ($970,000 x 2) would be a permanent one because the working-capital cycle would continuously repeat itself. Trade credit would supply half of the financing, and Anderson would need a long-term source of capital for the remainder.

With a short-term loan, say a 30-day note, the company would have to refinance the loan every month. The arrangement could be likened to financing a $970,000 plant with a 30-day mortgage and getting a new mortgage every month. (The analogy is not perfect because if Anderson could not refinance the working capital loan, it could stop doing business with the customer, which would be a less painful retrenchment than the forced liquidation of a plant. If, however, the new sales represented 1,000 customers buying $1,000 apiece, cutting back would likely not be so easy.)

Small companies often find it unfeasible to adhere to the matching principle because of their well-known difficulties raising long-term capital. Hence Anderson, like many other small businesses, gave up on the notion of strict matching long ago. Moreover, use of a line of credit, rolled over repeatedly, to finance working capital (including permanent components) is an accepted practice to lenders.

Perfect matching is not essential. The important questions are: How much risk is involved, and when does the risk become excessive? The answers depend on the extent of mismatching, the way financings are structured and managed, and the particular circumstances—like the operating risks—of the business. My view is that Anderson was not overextended. I will explain why later, but first I want to consider the risks created by failure to adhere to the matching principle.

THREE RISKS

When a business (or a nonprofit organization) violates the matching principle, it incurs the following three related risks:

1. Interest rate risk
2. Refinancing risk
3. Risks of loss of operating autonomy

When the time for loan renewal comes, interest rates can easily be higher. Because working-capital arrangements like the one described previously usually involve a floating interest rate, the issue may seem academic. But it is not academic at all for companies that cannot afford the risk. Ask yourself, for instance, what impact a prime increase to 15% or 20% would have on your company. If you do not like what you see when you push the numbers, action is necessary.

Here is what a government report on the state of small business said about this issue: "The amount of funds borrowed on a long-term basis increased but still remained smaller than funds borrowed on a short-term basis. The exposure to high and fluctuating interest rates strongly affects the failure or survival of small businesses."[1]

Businesses relying heavily on working capital loans that are rolled over each year should consider the question of refinancing risk: What will we do if the lender terminates the arrangement? If you do not have a good answer, then action is necessary. If your response is, "Our lender would never do that," then you do not have a good answer.

Most lenders do not usually terminate borrowing arrangements on short notice, and, in fact, they often are very supportive. Still, when problems arise they expect corrective action and sometimes make "suggestions" that you might find unpalatable. They may even insist on revised terms such as more security, personal guarantees, or higher charges. For the unhappy owner of the business, the deterioration of the relationship with the lender, signaled by the change in terms, could not come at a worse time.

In discussing the financing of a new enterprise, two partners of a Big Eight accounting firm had this to say about financing working capital:

> Identify the term over which you actually need the financing. If, in fact, you have a permanent capital need to support working capital growth, admit the need and approach lenders on that basis. Too often entrepreneurs try to start with short-term or other loans requiring a fixed payback, failing to recognize that increased volume as they grow creates greater financing demands. As a result, the entrepreneur spends too much time worrying about financing matters, specifically in trying to arrange new financing instead of concentrating on the basic problems of the business. It is good to follow the principle, "Do not finance long-term needs with short-term money."[2]

—— DEALING WITH THE RISKS

In addressing the risks of violating the matching principle, it is usually helpful to have a frank talk with your lender and, if appropriate, with the

---

1. *The State of Small Business: A Report of the President* (Washington, D.C.: U.S. Government Printing Office, 1984).

2. Seymour Jones and M. Bruce Cohen, *The Emerging Business: Managing for Growth* (New York: Ronald Press, 1983), 39.

company's owners who are not involved in operations. Such discussions may yield more suitable terms. In any event, they promote a clear understanding of each party's position, which reduces the probability of unpleasant surprises.

My view is that businesses that violate the matching principle need enough flexibility to be able to eliminate the short-term debt within a reasonable period of time without seriously disrupting operations. The flexibility can be provided by contingency sources of capital and/or an action plan that will free up working capital. A key aspect of maintaining flexibility is to plan for contingencies before problems arise.[3]

To see how managers can plan for contingencies, it is worth exploring Anderson's situation further. Anderson borrowed an average $75,000 on its line of credit to finance permanent working capital. Management sought this amount based on the company's original sales-growth target. More important, management had assessed the risks previously discussed and decided it wanted to be prepared to pay off the line in a very short time. To accomplish this, the owners committed themselves to lending the company money and relying on funds set aside for a new retirement plan in case liquid reserves were necessary.

I am not saying that this is an ideal level of flexibility. In maintaining its capacity to eliminate the short-term debt within days, Anderson takes a very conservative approach—perhaps more conservative than necessary. The key point, however, is that in developing its plans the company has a clear understanding of the risk involved and has made a decision about how much risk to assume.

Part of Anderson's process includes discussions with its owners and banker. The loan officer was well aware of company officials' views on flexibility; together they had worked several years to develop financial policies that would enable the company to sustain growth while maintaining flexibility. In 1985, the bank granted Anderson a five-year term loan to sustain sales growth for the next three years without undue reliance on the credit line. (Luckily, the term loan actually had more favorable terms than the line of credit.) Such an arrangement would likely not have occurred without a regular dialogue.

Anderson's careful attention to its policies for financing working capital is no accident. When the company was much smaller, it relied heavily on short-term debt to finance working capital. When it suddenly encountered operating problems, Anderson discovered it could not meet the repayment provision on its line of credit.

To make matters worse, a new loan officer took over the company's account, and the owner did not get along with her. Although the bank did not call in the notes, the owner did get warnings and suggestions he did not appreciate. In the end, he obtained a second mortgage on his house to clean up the line of credit. He determined not to let this traumatic experience happen again.

---

3. A classic book on financial flexibility is Gordon Donaldson, *Strategy for Financial Mobility* (Boston: Division of Research, Harvard Business School, 1969).

I cannot underscore enough how important it is for lenders, owners, and managers to arrive at a consensus on appropriate financial policies for working capital. Anderson has derived many benefits from its efforts. For instance, it once faced a situation that could easily have created a serious problem because it relied on direct shipments from suppliers for certain items instead of maintaining a complete inventory.

Late in the year, a large competitor decided to stock a key product line that would enable it to gain a considerable competitive advantage in delivery time. Anderson decided that it had to match this action or suffer a severe erosion of sales. To meet the challenge, Anderson needed to invest about $100,000 in working capital as a permanent investment. In consultation with its banker, Anderson decided to use its credit line to buy the inventory immediately and then arrange for more permanent financing.

The attention Anderson pays to its financial policies enables the business to confront challenges that would probably present insurmountable obstacles for many other small companies. Moreover, its high degree of financial flexibility enhances its effectiveness in competing with larger companies.

—— ANALYZING THE OPTIONS

Some small businesses cannot raise long-term capital (on reasonable terms) and, unlike Anderson, their owners lack the resources to invest. In such cases, some owners conclude that they have no choice but to depend on short-term debt for permanent working-capital requirements. In my view, an opposite conclusion is in order: the inability to raise capital indicates a low degree of flexibility that, in turn, implies that the business should adhere closely to the matching principle.

To illustrate why, consider the experience of a company I call the Nelson Company. When John Nelson formed his retail business, he relied on debt financing, including some short-term debt, for permanent working capital. The company immediately made a profit and had no difficulty paying off the indebtedness. In fact, it paid several installments of the long-term debt in advance.

After a couple of years, Nelson opened a second unit, which was almost as successful as the first. The business employed short-term debt to fund permanent working capital and, once again, repaid the loans on schedule. Within five years, the company had six units and plans for more, all based on a one-year working-capital line (with no cleanup provision), which the enthusiastic banker routinely renewed. Investors were waiting in line to buy a piece of the business, and several banks were also anxious to establish a relationship.

Suddenly the company felt some growing pains. While not serious at first, the monthly operating profits soon turned into monthly losses. At about the same time, the economy sank into a recession; it was especially serious in the area in which Nelson's units were located. The company began to stretch its payables, but before long it became virtually impossible to rely on this source. John Nelson did not have the funds to invest and could not raise capital. The bank was patient for a while, but then insisted that he do something. By liquidating several units at great cost, Nelson was able to save his company.

Violating the matching principle was not the only cause of Nelson's problems, but it helped make a bad situation much worse.

—— RELY ON YOUR OWN JUDGMENT

Bankers who read this article may feel that I am being too hard on them. They might argue that the head of a small business can count on the maturity of the loan officer and the integrity of the institution. The small business, they might claim, should not worry that the loan might be called on short notice or that new, more onerous terms might be imposed.

Some bankers do give their clients more support than the business relationship mandates. But I believe it is a mistake to rely too much on lenders, for they have a different perspective from their borrowers about what constitutes a tolerable risk level and reasonable corrective action when trouble looms.

Recall that Anderson was able to turn to its owners for financial support. While this is not always possible—or desirable—it is important for small companies to involve the owners in the process of setting financing policy.

Take the case in which three partners contemplated buying an established business. Most of the financing would consist of long-term debt and equity, but some short-term indebtedness would be necessary to underwrite inventory. It was clear (at least to this observer) that if projections fell below target by more than 5% to 10%, the company could not repay the short-term notes on time. Because the owners could afford to invest more, this was not a serious problem—provided they agreed on the potential problem and how to solve it. The owners, however, never confronted the possibility in advance, and when the business could not meet its short-term debt payment the owners were unable to agree on how to resolve the matter—that is, whether to borrow or invest more. The company eventually satisfied all its debts, but at a price of great, and avoidable, emotional stress.

Too often financing issues arise and are addressed during a period of crisis—the worst possible time. People do not think clearly when resources are leaving the business as if they were being sucked up by a vacuum cleaner.

—— CAPITAL ISSUES

Lenders and other investors seek a proper balance between risks and return. Two factors that are often unfavorable for a small business in an assessment of the risk-return trade-off are these:

- Small businesses tend to have more operating risks than larger companies. For instance, they normally lack the breadth and depth of management that investors and lenders desire.
- The administrative costs for suppliers of capital decline in percentage terms as the size of the transaction grows, which can drastically affect the net returns on small loans and investments.

Yet smaller businesses often underrate their ability to raise long-term capital. As competition in the financial services industry sharpens, banks are increasingly seeking to attract small, growing businesses as customers. Small companies worrying about too much short-term debt should approach their current lenders, as well as other banks promoting themselves as specialists in small-business financing, about transforming at least some of those loans into long-term funding. There's nothing wrong with shopping around or with letting bankers know you are shopping around.

Then there's always the equity option. Many owners of smaller companies shy away from selling stock to outsiders because they fear giving up control and diluting ownership. But sophisticated investors are much more interested in making money on their investments than in having control of the companies they back. (Of course, if the company suffers a business downturn, the outsiders may be tempted to step in.) Besides providing badly needed funds that don't have to be repaid out of cash flow, an equity sale sometimes convinces banks to make long-term money available.

Growing amounts of venture capital—from established venture capital firms as well as from wealthy individuals—have become available in recent years, thanks in part to reductions in the capital gains tax. In seeking such funds, though, business owners should be prepared with a convincing business plan that emphasizes marketing considerations and return to investors.[4]

Moreover, selling equity to the public in recent years has become less burdensome as the Securities and Exchange Commission eased the requirements. Now companies seeking to raise up to $7.5 million can fill out a newly simplified form, S-18, before offering shares to the public.[5] Owners of established companies are likely to find investors more receptive to buying shares in a small, growing company than once was the case, thanks to the growing amount of interest in the publicity surrounding entrepreneurship and small business.

Apart from financing considerations, business owners can take actions to reduce administrative costs by calling in the help of creative people in the financial community when structuring transactions. Small businesses can be profitable, and this potential does not elude individual investors and financial institutions.

---

4. *See*, for example, Chap. 10, "How to Write a Winning Business Plan" by Stanley R. Rich and David E. Gumpert.

5. *See*, for example, "An Easier Way to Go Public" by James G. Manegold and Jerry L. Arnold, *Harvard Business Review* (January–February 1986), 28.

Devote time to exploring potential sources of long-term capital even if an assessment of risk indicates that your business does not rely too much on short-term debt. Access to capital is a key part of financial flexibility. Hence developing alternative sources and relationships will probably enable you to deal more quickly and effectively with unexpected problems.

Do not compound existing operating risks with unsound financing policies. Make the financing of working capital an integral part of your company's planning process to maintain the flexibility your business requires.

────── DISCUSSION QUESTIONS

1. Throughout the reading, the author emphasizes the importance of paying attention to financial policies. What measures can small companies take on an ongoing basis so that they will be prepared to manage problems before they become emergencies?

2. To finance permanent working capital with short-term debt, the Anderson Company developed a contingency plan to ensure flexibility. Do you find Anderson's approach too conservative, as the author suggests? What alternative contingency plans could a company design?

3. How could John Nelson have averted the losses that nearly bankrupted his company?

4. What strategies can small companies use to raise long-term capital?

5. "Some bankers," the author points out, "do give their clients more support than the business relationship mandates." How can entrepreneurs cultivate the trust and goodwill of their bankers?

30   Bankruptcy: A Debtor's Perspective

HOWARD H. STEVENSON AND MARTHA GERSHUN

Even the most optimistic, determined entrepreneur must contemplate the possibility and consequences of financial failure. A bad decision or a miscalculation can lead to financial adversity or an impossible burden of debt. While there are many solutions short of bankruptcy, the entrepreneur who clearly understands the bankruptcy laws will be best able to pursue the most appropriate route for the company.

This reading discusses bankruptcy from the point of view of the individual or corporate debtor. First, it describes the Bankruptcy Reform Act of 1978 and the legal jurisdiction for bankruptcy law in the United States today. It then examines bankruptcy in general and three particular forms of bankruptcy: liquidation, corporation reorganization, and debt adjustment for an individual with a regular income. Finally, it looks at some of the ways debtors can protect themselves from being forced to take this step.

For the most part, government in America treats the private sector with cautious noninterference. Direct public participation in the economic affairs of an individual or a corporation is limited to a monitoring function through such bodies as the Internal Revenue Service, the Securities and Exchange Commission, and the Federal Trade Commission. Only when things go wrong does the government step in to take action. In the case of financial failure, public policy has dictated that the legal system act as a buffer between debtors and creditors, seeking to maximize both economic efficiency and equity. Thus, bankruptcy laws have been passed to ensure that resolutions to situations of financial adversity maximize the present and future value of the "estate" and deal fairly with all debtors and creditors.

Bankruptcy is by no means the obvious result of financial trouble. There are many types of financial adversity and many solutions to them other than bankruptcy proceedings. Individuals or firms that become insolvent—that is, lack sufficient cash to pay the bills—may simply stall creditors until the situation improves. They may also default on loan payments, negotiate reduced-payment schedules, or liquidate inventory to generate funds. The notion of bankruptcy, on the other hand, implies that someone, either debtor or creditor, decides that the individual or firm should not continue in its present financial incarnation. Bankruptcy then becomes an option utilized by either debtors or creditors to amend the situation.

For the debtor, bankruptcy provides a chance to crawl out from under an impossible burden of debts, to wipe the slate clean, and to start again. Often it provides an alternative to years of struggling to pay off angry and impatient creditors with an income—personal or corporate—that is insufficient to meet all obligations as they come due. For creditors, bankruptcy provides a chance to get back some portion of their claims on an equitable basis with all other creditors. Often it provides an alternative to continuously postponed payments and the fear of being treated unfairly vis-à-vis other creditors. Bankruptcy provides a means for creditors to hedge their bets: it gives them a guarantee of partial payment, rather than the timing uncertainty inherent in the gamble for full payment in the courts. The initiation of any type of bankruptcy triggers an automatic stop to all lawsuits against the company.

—— THE NEW LAW

Until fairly recently, the prevailing code for bankruptcy law in the United States was the Bankruptcy Act of 1898, also known as the Nelson Act. While this act was amended some 50 times and given a major overhaul under the Chandler Act of 1938, it remained in effect for 80 years until Congress passed the Bankruptcy Reform Act of 1978. The new code, Public Law 95-958, has eight odd-numbered substantive chapters. The first three concern administrative rules relevant to all bankruptcy proceedings; the remainder deal with specific types of bankruptcy.

- Chapter 1 sets forth general definitions and rules.
- Chapter 3 sets up case administration practices.
- Chapter 5 concerns such issues as creditors' claims, debtors' duties, and advantages, exemptions, and trustees' powers.
- Chapter 7 deals with liquidations.
- Chapter 9 involves municipal debts.
- Chapter 11 deals with reorganizing businesses, including railroads.
- Chapter 13 establishes procedures for a debtor with a regular income.
- Chapter 15 contains the necessary provisions to set up a United States Trustee Pilot Program.

Under the act, bankruptcy courts were established as adjuncts of each U.S. District Court. Until 1983 bankruptcy judges were appointed by the president, with the advice and consent of the Senate. Early that year the Supreme Court ruled that bankruptcy judges, as members of the judicial branch, had to be given the same guarantees of independence, including lifetime tenure, as all other judges.

Between 1946 and 1975 total bankruptcy proceedings of all types increased from slightly more than 10,000 cases to more than 254,000. They declined during the next three years to just under 203,000 in 1978, before soaring to approximately 298,500 for the year ending in September 1980, the first year under the new Bankruptcy Code; they reached 561,000 in fiscal 1987.

──── GETTING INTO TROUBLE

For an individual, the path to bankruptcy is often clearly discernible in retrospect; it is easy to see where a person made a bad decision, became overextended, and misjudged his or her financial situation. There are two ways individuals accumulate sufficient debt to contemplate bankruptcy. The first is painfully simple: they purchase more on credit than they can afford to buy. This happens because they either underestimate the amount of money they will have to pay for their accumulated credit purchases or overestimate their income. Thus, individual bankruptcies increase in periods of easy consumer credit and in periods of unemployment. The second road to individual bankruptcy is more complex. It occurs when an individual's personal finances are in order, but he or she chooses to act as guarantor for a business or for another individual whose situation may not be as fortunate. By agreeing to accept the burden of another's debts a person becomes legally responsible if the individual or firm defaults on payments. When this additional financial burden is more than the individual's personal budget can accommodate, bankruptcy is a way to eliminate the added debts, leaving the individual free to begin again.

For corporations, the path to bankruptcy is considerably more complicated. Ray Barrickman outlines 18 potential causes of business failure: excessive competition, changes in the general business cycle, shifts in consumer demand, governmental acts, adverse acts of labor, acts of God, poor overall management, unwise promotion, unwise expansion, inefficient selling, overextension of inventories, poor financial management, excessive fixed charges, excessive funded debt, excessive floating debt, overextension of credit, unwise dividend policies, and inadequate maintenance and depreciation.[1]

John Argenti, studying corporate failures in Great Britain, posits a chain of events, beginning with poor management, that usually precipitates a slide into bankruptcy:

> If the management of a company is poor then two things will be neglected: the system of accountancy information will be deficient, and the company will not respond to change. (Some companies, even well-managed ones, may be damaged because powerful constraints prevent the managers making the responses they wish to make.) Poor managers will also make at least one of three other mistakes: they will overtrade; or they will launch a big project that goes wrong; or they will allow the company's gearing [financial leverage] to rise so that even normal business hazards become constant threats. These are the

---

1. Ray E. Barrickman, *Business Failure, Causes, Remedies, and Cures* (Washington, D.C.: University Press of America, 1979), 28.

chief causes, neither fraud nor bad luck deserve more than a passing mention. The following symptoms will appear: certain financial ratios will deteriorate but, as soon as they do, the managers will start creative accounting that reduces the predictive value of these ratios and so lends greater importance to nonfinancial symptoms. Finally the company enters a characteristic period in its last few months.[2]

These are not all the root causes of bankruptcy, of course. The direct catalyst for bankruptcy proceedings is generally a person's or company's inability to pay debts on time. When this situation occurs, the individual or company may begin voluntary bankruptcy proceedings, or creditors may try to force them into involuntary bankruptcy. Any person, partnership, or corporation can file for voluntary relief under the bankruptcy code.[3] Even solvent entities can do so as long as there is no intent to defraud.

For example, Johns Manville Corporation filed for bankruptcy in late 1982, even though the company had a book net worth of nearly $1.2 billion. The manufacturer sought protection from an anticipated 32,000 lawsuits relating to the injury or death of workers who manufactured or installed Manville's asbestos products. At an average settlement of $40,000 per lawsuit, Manville calculated that it could not afford to stay in business and sought bankruptcy relief from these "creditors."[4]

Sometimes, the resort to bankruptcy is motivated more by strategic than financial issues. Wilson Foods, a producer of meat and food products, sought Chapter 11 protection to force down union wages. Wilson's chairman announced publicly that the firm did not intend to close any of its plants or lay off any workers. He further stated that the company had sufficient cash, receivables, and available credit to meet its short-term obligations. It was applying to the court to nullify a union contract that would otherwise have lasted until 1985. Basing its decision on what it deemed the best interests of the estate, the court allowed Wilson to institute sharply reduced hourly wage rates. In a similar case in 1986 the Supreme Court decided the issue of whether bankruptcy allows a firm to change union contract terms by permitting Bildisco to use Chapter 11 protection in this manner. Thus far union efforts for legislative relief from this decision have been unsuccessful.

In order to seek relief from debts, a person or corporation must file for bankruptcy in the office of the Clerk of the United States District Court in which the domicile, residence, principal place of business, or principal assets of the entity have been located for the preceding 180 days. The filing fee is $60 for commencing a bankruptcy case under Chapter 7 (liquidation) or Chapter 13 (adjustment of debts for an individual with regular income); the fee for businesses seeking relief under Chapter 11 (business reorganizations) is $200;

---

2. John Argenti, *Corporate Collapse: The Causes and Symptoms* (London: McGraw-Hill, 1976), 108.

3. The exceptions to this rule are banks, including savings and loans, insurance companies, and foreign-owned companies, which are all prohibited from declaring bankruptcy.

4. "Asbestosis: Manville Seeks Chapter 11," *Fortune*, September 20, 1982.

railroads must pay a filing fee of $500. A person or corporation can only file for bankruptcy protection once every six years.

In certain situations, creditors can force debtors to go bankrupt. An involuntary bankruptcy case can be commenced by (1) three or more creditors whose aggregated claims amount to more than $5,000 over the value of assets securing those claims; (2) one or more such creditors if there are fewer than 12 claim holders in all; or (3) fewer than all the general partners in a limited partnership.

Creditors do not have to prove that the debtor is unable to pay his or her bills; mere failure to pay on time, regardless of ability to do so, is sufficient grounds for involuntary bankruptcy. However, in an involuntary bankruptcy proceeding, the court can require petitioners to post a bond to cover the debtor's costs in the event that the court finds in the debtor's favor. Furthermore, if creditors are found to have petitioned in bad faith, the court may award the debtor damages caused by the proceedings, including punitive compensation. In practice, involuntary bankruptcy is uncommon.

—— CHOOSING YOUR POISON: WHICH CHAPTER?

The three chapters of the bankruptcy code that can shape the outcome of the bankruptcy proceedings are Chapter 7 (liquidation), Chapter 11 (reorganization), and Chapter 13 (adjustment of an individual's debts).

In theory, bankruptcy procedures can be concluded very quickly, but in practice they are often long, drawn-out affairs. Corporate reorganizations especially can take many years to complete. Speaking before the 94th Congress, Representative Elizabeth Holtzman reported that "the average corporate reorganization case in the Seventh District of New York takes eight years to resolve."[5]

In a Chapter 7 bankruptcy the assets of the individual or corporation are liquidated and distributed to creditors; in a Chapter 11 or Chapter 13 bankruptcy debtors keep their assets and arrangements are made to pay off their debts over time. The outcomes of these types of bankruptcy are radically different, affecting the form of the assets that the debtor keeps as well as the timing and amount of payments that creditors receive. Both debtors and creditors thus have some influence on the choice of relevant chapter.

When the creditor files for an involuntary bankruptcy case under Chapter 7 or 11, the debtor can convert the case to a bankruptcy under any of the other chapters. When a debtor files for voluntary bankruptcy under any chapter, creditors can request the trustee to convert the case to a Chapter 7 or a Chapter 11 bankruptcy. Only a Chapter 13 bankruptcy cannot be commenced without the debtor's consent. Before choosing a chapter for bankruptcy, debtors

---

5. House Report #686, 56.

should carefully consider whether they prefer to liquidate their assets entirely or continue conducting the business with personal finances, attempting through reorganization or adjustment to pay the debts over time.

CHAPTER 7: LIQUIDATION

Chapter 7 of the Bankruptcy Act provides for either voluntary or involuntary liquidation of the assets of the debtor and distribution of the proceeds to creditors. When a petition is filed under Chapter 7 it constitutes an order for relief and obliges the debtor to:

1. File a list of creditors, assets and liabilities, and a statement of financial affairs;
2. Cooperate with the trustee appointed to the case;
3. Give the trustee all property of the estate and all records relating to the property;
4. Appear at any hearing dealing with a discharge;
5. Attend all meetings of creditors.

As soon as possible after the order for relief, an interim trustee is appointed. Creditors holding at least 30 percent of the specified claims can request an election to choose the trustee in the case. The debtor himself or herself can serve as this trustee while remaining in possession of the business. If no trustee is elected, the interim trustee continues to serve. The duties of the trustee include:

1. Reducing the property of the debtor's estate to cash and closing up the estate as expeditiously as possible;
2. Accounting for all property received;
3. Investigating the financial affairs of the debtor and examining all claims for validity;
4. Providing information about the estate to any interested party, furnishing reports on the debtor's business if continued operation is authorized, and filing a final report to the court on the disposition of the estate.

Certain portions of the debtor's estate are exempt from liquidation; in many states, the debtor can choose between the federal exemptions or the relevant state exemptions. Other states, such as Florida and Virginia, require residents to adhere to the state exemptions, and South Carolina, Delaware, and Ohio are considering similar statutes. Under the current federal regulations permissible exemptions include:

1. An interest, not to exceed $7,500, in the debtor's or dependent's residence, in a cooperative that owns property used by the debtor or a dependent as a residence, and in a burial plot for the debtor or a dependent;
2. Interest, not to exceed $1,200, in a motor vehicle;

3. Interest, not to exceed $200 in value for any particular item, in household furnishings, clothing, appliances, books, animals, crops, or musical instruments that are kept for the personal, family, or household use of the debtor or a dependent;

4. The interest, not to exceed $500, in jewelry held for personal, family, or household use by the debtor or a dependent;

5. Interest, not to exceed $400, in property in addition to that listed in Item 1;

6. Interest, not to exceed $750, in any implements, professional books, or tools of the trade of the debtor or a dependent;

7. Any insurance contract, other than a credit contract, that is not mature;

8. The debtor's interest, not to exceed $4,000, in any accrued dividends or interest or loan value or any nonmature life insurance contract under which the debtor or a dependent is insured;

9. Prescribed health aids for the debtor or a dependent;

10. The debtor's right to receive social security benefits, unemployment compensation benefits, local public assistance benefits, veterans' benefits, and illness or disability benefits;

11. The debtor's right to receive alimony, support, or separate maintenance;

12. The debtor's right to receive a payment, stock bonus, pension, profit-sharing annuity, or similar plan on account of illness, disability, debt, age, or want of service;

13. The debtor's right to receive an award under a crime victim's reparation law; a payment on account of a wrongful death of an individual of whom the debtor was a dependent; a payment under a life insurance contract that insured the life of an individual of whom the debtor was a dependent; a payment not to exceed $7,500 on account of personal bodily injury, not including pain and suffering or compensation for actual pecuniary loss, of the debtor or an individual of whom the debtor is a dependent; or a payment in compensation of loss of future earnings of the debtor or an individual of whom the debtor is or was a dependent.

The remainder of the debtor's estate is distributed, first to secured creditors and then to priority claimants. These claims include, in order: administrative expenses and filing fees assessed against the debtor's estate; certain unsecured claims arising before the appointment of a trustee in involuntary cases; wages, salaries, or commissions, including vacation, severance, and sick leave pay to the extent of $2,000 per individual earned within 90 days of the date of filing or the date of cessation of business, whichever occurred first; contributions to employee benefit plans up to $2,000 per employee earned within 180 days; claims of individuals, up to $900 each, arising from the deposit of money in connection with purchases of property or services that are not delivered; claims of governmental units of taxes and custom duties.

Next come the general unsecured creditors and the general unsecured creditors who filed late claims. Punitive penalties are next in distribution,

EXHIBIT 1
Distribution of Assets in Cases Closed in 1977

	PAYMENT	PERCENT OF TOTAL
Paid priority creditors	$ 27,799,506	12.1%
Paid secured creditors	77,479,621	33.8
Paid unsecured creditors	61,109,352	26.6
Other payments	10,612,376	4.6
All administrative expenses	52,534,678	22.9
Total distribution	**$229,535,533**	**100.0%**

Source: Table of Bankruptcy Statistics with reference to bankruptcy cases commenced and terminated in the United States District Courts during the period July 1, 1976 through June 30, 1977. Administrative Office of the United States Courts.

followed by claims for interest accruing during the bankruptcy case. Interest is paid at the legal rate on the date the petition was filed. If there is any surplus after these six classes are paid, it goes to the debtor. If the funds are insufficient to pay a class in full, claims within the class are paid pro rata. *Exhibit 1* shows how assets were distributed in cases closed during 1977 under the old Bankruptcy Act. It is interesting to note that fully 22.9 percent of the assets in bankruptcy cases were used to pay administrative expenses. Recent studies show similar results when the size of the bankruptcy is taken into account.

When the debtor is an individual, the court usually grants a *discharge.* This means the debtor is discharged from all past debts except those arising from alimony, child support, and taxes, or from debts that were not listed on the debtor's financial statements when bankruptcy was filed.

CHAPTER 11: REORGANIZATION

The purpose of Chapter 11 of the new Bankruptcy Code is to provide a mechanism for reorganizing a firm's finances to continue operations, pay its creditors, provide jobs, and produce a return to investors. Usually debtors and creditors opt for this form of bankruptcy if they think a business or estate has more value as a going concern than as a pile of liquidated assets. The objective of the reorganization is to develop a plan that (1) determines how much creditors will be paid and (2) in what form the business will continue.

Any individual, partnership, or corporation that can file for liquidation under Chapter 7 can file for reorganization under Chapter 11, except stockbrokers and commodity brokers. Furthermore, railroads, which are prohibited from seeking liquidation, can proceed under Chapter 11.

Like a Chapter 7 case, a reorganization can be either voluntary or involuntary. After the entry of an order for relief, creditors and debtor must meet within 30 days to discuss the organization of the business. Under the new Bankruptcy Code, the court may not attend a creditors' meeting; instead, the interim trustee or the U.S. trustee presides. This procedure follows from the new code's attempt to correct previous problems caused by having bankruptcy judges serve as both judge and administrator in bankruptcy cases.

After the order for relief, the court appoints a committee of general unsecured creditors, usually those holding the seven largest claims—although the court has great latitude in composing the committee so as to make it representative of the different interests in the case. This committee is primarily responsible for formulating a plan for the business and collecting and filing acceptances of the plan. The debtor keeps possession of the business unless creditors can show that he or she is guilty of fraud, dishonesty, incompetence, or gross mismanagement, or otherwise prove that such an arrangement is not in the interests of the creditors. If the court upholds either of these objections, a trustee is appointed. Unlike a Chapter 7 trustee, a Chapter 11 trustee is not elected and cannot be a creditor or an equity holder of the business. The Chapter 11 trustee is accountable for all of the information and records necessary to formulate the reorganization plan and for filing the plan with the court. Or, alternatively, he or she can recommend conversion to a Chapter 7 or a Chapter 13 case or dismissal of the case altogether.

If a trustee is not appointed, the debtor possesses these powers. No court order is necessary for the debtor to continue to run the firm; in fact, the business is to remain in operation unless the court orders otherwise.

The debtor has 120 days to file the reorganization plan and 60 more days to obtain acceptances. The plan must designate the various classes of creditors and show how they will be treated. The plan can also be a liquidation; thus, a business can be liquidated under Chapter 11 as well as under Chapter 7. The plan must be accepted by half of the creditors affected by the plan and by creditors holding two-thirds of the debt in dollar amount. When the court confirms a reorganization plan, the debtor is discharged from past debts except as stipulated in the new plan.

CHAPTER 13: ADJUSTMENT OF DEBTS OF AN INDIVIDUAL WITH REGULAR INCOME

Chapter 13 of the new Bankruptcy Code covers individuals with regular income whose unsecured debts are less than $100,000 and whose secured debts are less than $350,000. This includes individuals who own or operate businesses. It does not include partnerships or corporations. There cannot be an involuntary Chapter 13 bankruptcy.

The purpose of Chapter 13 is to allow an individual to pay off debts with future earnings while the court protects him or her from harassment by creditors. Furthermore, it allows the debtor to continue owning and operating a business while Chapter 13 is pending. Under Chapter 13 a plan can be an *extension*—creditors paid in full—or a *composition*—creditors paid in part. The debt is payable over three years, with a two-year extension allowed for cause.

In a Chapter 13 case the property of the estate includes property and earnings acquired after commencement of the case but before it is closed. The court appoints a trustee, who administers but does not take possession of the estate.

For the debtor this chapter has several major advantages.

1. Once it is filed, all the debtor's property and future income are under the court's jurisdiction. An automatic stay order is issued against litigation and collection efforts.
2. Unlike Chapter 7, the trustee does not take possession of the debtor's property. The debtor can increase his or her estate while the plan is in effect.
3. Chapter 13 can help preserve the debtor's credit. Also, the six-year ban on filing for bankruptcy can be avoided in an extension plan and some compensation plans.
4. Since only the debtor can file a plan, there are no competing proposals.
5. The court can still convert a Chapter 13 case to a Chapter 11 case or a Chapter 7 case if it determines it is in the best interests of the creditors or the estate.

Once it is drawn up the court holds a confirmation hearing on the plan, at which secured creditors can stop confirmation if they (a) are denied the lien securing their claims, or (b) do not receive the property securing their claims. Unsecured creditors have no voice in the confirmation process. After all payments under the plan have been made the court grants the debtor a discharge.

——— POWERS OF TRUSTEE

In addition to the responsibilities enumerated in Chapters 7, 11, and 13, the trustee in a bankruptcy case has broad powers to determine how assets are allocated and debt restructured. Note that in some instances, the debtor himself (debtor-in-possession) functions as the trustee. Chapters 3 and 5 of the Bankruptcy Code authorize the trustee to employ professionals to help carry out the duties of trustee, to use, sell, or lease property, to obtain credits secured by priority claims and new liens, to reject or assume contracts and unexpired leases, and to avoid preferences and fraudulent transfers (known as the avoiding powers). These powers can change the status of certain classes of creditors, depending on how they are applied. For instance, by rejecting an unexpired lease, the trustee can convert a long-term leaseholder into just another unsecured creditor. If a trustee is not appointed, then the debtor in possession of the estate assumes these powers.

━━━ NEGOTIATIONS AND SETTLEMENTS

Debtors may feel persecuted and helpless, but they actually have a great deal of power to negotiate with creditors for arrangements that will leave the firm intact, either before or after bankruptcy is declared. This power stems from several sources: the incentive for all creditors to reach a speedy and workable solution to the debtor's financial problems; the differing interests of various classes of creditors; and the ultimate protection provided by the bankruptcy laws. The Bankruptcy Code was designed to give both debtors and creditors motivation for seeking a solution that will maximize the settlement for both parties, although the effect has been to shift power to the creditors.

A debtor in serious financial condition may find that he or she has considerable leverage with creditors who fear recourse of bankruptcy. Such creditors may be willing to undertake voluntary arrangements to restructure loans, postpone payments, relinquish lease obligations, or ignore accrued interest in order to help the debtor avoid bankruptcy. Creditors may decide that they have a better long-run chance of repayment if the firm continues to exist than if it is dissolved and the assets are sold at low liquidation values under Chapter 7. They may also fear the high administrative and legal costs of bankruptcy proceedings, particularly in a complicated case; these costs may be incurred by the creditors directly or be charged against the debtor's estate, thus reducing the money available for distribution to creditors. When, for example, Itel Corp., the computer leasing company, filed for bankruptcy in January 1981, it took two years for the company to be reorganized under Chapter 11, and the first four months of administrative and legal expenses cost the estate $6.7 million.[6] Creditors may also prefer a voluntary arrangement to avoid the adverse publicity of a liquidation, to maintain prospects of future business with the debtor, or because such an arrangement can be concluded faster than a court- supervised plan. Sometimes creditors who want a voluntary settlement even pay off the debtor's liabilities to other creditors simply to avoid legal proceedings.

Debtors can also derive power from the differing interests of creditors. As noted above, creditors for whom speed of settlement is more important than full payment may negotiate with others whose interest lies in full payment rather than a quick solution. Both groups of creditors can be satisfied if the first pays the second's claims in order to expedite a settlement. Trade creditors and money creditors might have varying interests too, with trade creditors preferring a settlement that leaves the firm intact to do business in the future, and money creditors preferring a liquidation that provides as much cash as possible. Debtors can use this conflict to their advantage, paying off money creditors with

---

6. Jim Drinkhall, "Fees Charged by Itel's Overseers Suggest Bankruptcy Can Be Enriching Experience," *Wall Street Journal*, June 5, 1981, p. 27.

available cash while asking trade creditors to forbear in the hope of putting the firm back on solid financial ground.

Of course, creditors do not have to be conciliatory. In 1978, Food Fair, Inc. ran into cash shortages, and its suppliers refused to extend credit beyond their normal terms. Angered by what they perceived as preferential treatment to suppliers with family connections to Food Fair's management, the other suppliers refused to extend trade credit, even after the company had significantly reduced its outstanding obligations. As a result the firm was forced to seek bankruptcy protection under Chapter 11.[7]

In his book, *Corporations in Crisis*, Philip Nelson notes that the measures available to debtors and creditors short of filing for bankruptcy can lead to economic inefficiencies:

> Focusing for the moment on the triggering decision, it appears that, because bankruptcy is only triggered when economic actors perceive that bankruptcy promotes their interests, social losses may easily accumulate as a firm struggles on outside the court's protection. In most sample cases, no economic actor had the incentive and the knowledge to trigger bankruptcy when it was needed. Executive preference for continued salaries, the distaste for the stigma of bankruptcy, inadequate information flows, and ignorance of the advantages offered by bankruptcy combine to encourage delays. Only at the few firms where the controlling executives associated relatively little stigma with bankruptcy and understood its advantages was bankruptcy triggered promptly. As a result, bankruptcy often comes after the resources of the firm are largely expended.

Debtors also derive power within the framework of formal bankruptcy proceedings. Freed from turmoil and harassment by unpaid creditors, the debtor who has filed for bankruptcy is suddenly in a position to bargain, and the automatic stay against all lawsuits provided by the bankruptcy law is an additional incentive for creditors to reach agreement. Here again the debtor's leverage lies in the creditors' wish for a speedy, efficient plan that maximizes the wealth of the debtor for distribution or future payment. If creditors retain faith in the firm, there is usually a strong incentive to seek Chapter 11 relief to negotiate a deal that will get the firm back on its feet without litigation.

When Itel Corp. filed for bankruptcy, the firm received four 60-day extensions from the Bankruptcy Court to work out a reorganization package acceptable to creditors. In the final deal, Itel's Eurobond holders were allowed $110 million of claims, although that class of creditors only had $91 million in principal and accrued interest outstanding when Itel filed for reorganization. The distribution to Eurobond holders per $10,000 of claim was estimated by Itel's reorganization plan as shown in *Exhibit 2*.

---

7. "Food Fair Inc. Seeks Protection under Chapter 11," *Wall Street Journal*, October 3, 1978, p. 2.

EXHIBIT 2

SECURITY	FACE AMOUNT	MARKET VALUE
Cash	$3,690	$3,690
14% secured notes	2,035	1,689 – 1,780
10% notes	1,032	443 – 501
New preferred stock (11.5 shares)	——	259 – 305
New common stock (124.3 shares)	——	186 – 311

One of Itel's main reasons for increasing the amount of these creditors' claims was to avoid possible delays in the reorganization plan from pending litigation involving the Eurobonds.[8]

——— DEBTOR'S OPTIONS

Even though the new Bankruptcy Code deals generously with debtors, providing a chance to discharge debts and begin again, no debtor wants to be thrown into bankruptcy proceedings against his or her will. There are several steps a debtor can take to ensure against involuntary bankruptcy. These include being sure that the number of creditors always exceeds 12 and that no 3 creditors' claims amount to more than $5,000. This could mean paying off some creditors in full while not paying others all they are due. If there are more than 12 creditors in a case, 1 or 2 claimants cannot force an individual or a corporation into involuntary bankruptcy.

There are also many steps a debtor can take to maximize the amount of exempt assets that can be retained in a bankruptcy case. When contemplating bankruptcy, the debtor should examine exemptions closely and arrange his or her affairs to provide the best chance to recover following declaration. These measures should not be considered cheating or violating the law; the regulations were written to give debtors the opportunity to regain financial stability while treating creditors fairly.

However, there are many actions a debtor cannot take under the law. Besides the obvious violation of hiding assets or liabilities, the most important prohibition placed on debtors is that of preferential treatment. Once a debtor has filed for bankruptcy, the trustee has the power to disallow any payment to a creditor that enables that creditor to receive more than others in the same class. Any payment made 90 days prior to the bankruptcy can be considered a preferential payment. If the creditor is an insider, this limit extends to one year

---

8. Disclosure Statement for Itel Corporation's Amended Plan of Reorganization, Case No. 3-81-00111, December 1982.

if the insider had cause to believe the debtor was insolvent. Any creditor who manages to extort a larger share than others of the same class prior to the bankruptcy is forced to return it to the general pot for fair allocation. This provision limits the debtor's ability to play one creditor off against others in an attempt to avoid bankruptcy, since creditors know that such settlements could be disallowed if bankruptcy is declared within three months.

There are many avenues open to the savvy debtor to pursue, either before filing for bankruptcy or after such proceedings have been initiated. Debtors in financial trouble would be wise to seek competent legal counsel early so as to devise the best way out of their predicament.

—— DISCUSSION QUESTIONS

1. Compare the advantages and disadvantages for debtors of filing for bankruptcy or seeking alternatives. What are the psychological consequences for the debtor of pursuing each route?
2. Under what circumstances as a debtor would you seek alternatives to bankruptcy? At what point would you forgo these alternatives and initiate bankruptcy proceedings?
3. Compare the outcomes for the debtor of filing under Chapters 7, 11, and 13. Envision the scenarios under which each of these alternatives would best serve the debtor's interests.
4. For what financial or strategic reasons might a solvent company choose to file for bankruptcy?
5. Suppose your business is thriving—sales right on target, bills paid, morale high, and investors eager to do business with you. What mechanisms would you put in place to protect your business from financial difficulty at some time in the future?

31   Going Public

SEYMOUR JONES, M. BRUCE COHEN,
AND VICTOR V. COPPOLA

*In determining the best ways to fund growth, the entrepreneur may well
consider the possibility of selling shares of the company on the public market.
Going public is a milestone in a venture's life, a symbol of achievement for
many entrepreneurs. It is also time consuming, complicated, and expensive.
By reviewing the process of going public and describing its advantages and
disadvantages, this reading can help the entrepreneur make this crucial
decision wisely and deliberately.*

The expression "going public" describes the process of offering for
sale to the general public securities—generally common or preferred stock or
bonds—of a privately owned company.

Usually a company begins to think about going public when the funding
required to meet business growth has exceeded the company's debt capacity.

In an Initial Public Offering (IPO), a company may sell its unissued
securities to raise additional capital, so the company receives all of the proceeds—called a primary offering. Alternatively, securities that belonged to the
owners of the company may be sold, whereby the owners receive the proceeds—called a secondary distribution. Sometimes the offering may be a combination, for the benefit of shareholders and the company.

The President of the United States in a recent report to Congress on the
state of small business noted that small companies with total assets under
$500,000 issued more than 68% of all IPOs. The typical issue from this group
had a median value of $2 million, or four times the companies' preoffering asset
value.

Although small corporations did not participate in the public equity
market for many years, these statistics indicate that many are now active. The
President's report stated a major contributor to this activity is the effort by the
Securities and Exchange Commission (SEC) to reduce issuing costs and registration and reporting burdens on small companies. The SEC began simplifying
the registration process by adopting Form S-18, which applies to offerings of
less than $7,500,000, reduced disclosure requirements. It was intended to reduce
costs and accelerate the registration process. Regulation D continued the trend
that started with the adoption of Form S-18 by establishing exemptions from

registration for offerings up to $500,000 over a twelve-month period as well as larger offerings described in this reading. By these actions, the SEC has made access to equity markets easier for smaller companies.

Owners of growth-oriented closely held companies who read this may begin to have visions of their company's name appearing in the New York Stock Exchange listings. Equity capital from the public is very attractive. After all, the purchasers of a company's common stock are paid no interest on their investment. The corporate officers do not guarantee its repayment, marketability, or value; and, as far as the corporation is concerned, the investment is permanent.

An investor is motivated to purchase a new stock issue only if it appears to be a better investment than a low or no-risk alternative, such as an insured certificate of deposit or Treasury Bill. A stock's value will increase only if, over time, the public places a higher value on the security than at the initial offering. Although the market value of a company's stock is affected by many factors, performance is the major factor. Since the company's performance may be dependent on its access to capital for expansion, equipment needs, acquisitions, major sales or distribution, investors want all or a major portion of an offering's proceeds to be available. An IPO is much less attractive when a substantial amount of the proceeds go to the present owners. Consequently, IPOs are almost always primary offerings or offerings where only a small number of shares held by owners are included.

In this reading, only federal government regulations are discussed. Anyone considering issuing securities should be sure to comply with appropriate state and federal securities laws. We intend to provide you with the benefit of our experience by reviewing the process of going public, informing you of the pros and cons and removing some of the mystique that surrounds this major event in a company's life.

THE DECISION

The decision to go public requires in-depth analysis. Although going public offers many attractive advantages, it also has many disadvantages to be weighed carefully. Once you make the decision, it's time-consuming and costly to retreat to nonpublic status. Some of the principal advantages and disadvantages that must be considered before making the decision are summarized here.

ADVANTAGES

ACCESS TO LONG-TERM CAPITAL

A privately owned company may have limited sources of capital. For the most part, a company expands by reinvesting its undistributed earnings and by looking to its owners, banks, or institutional lenders for additional capital funds. Without more capital, the company's earning capacity may be restricted, the ability of the owners to provide capital may be limited and borrowing must be repaid with interest. Sale of the company's stock, however, provides permanent non-interest-bearing capital. Furthermore, once the company and its securities are known to the investing public, future stock offerings may be easier to sell, assuming no adverse change in its affairs.

SUBSEQUENT CAPITAL NEEDS

When securities are offered for sale to the public, they must first be registered with the SEC. Once the company has gone through the SEC's registration process, succeeding issues ordinarily take less to process. Registered companies may, under certain circumstances, also qualify to use simplified registration forms when offering additional securities.

EXPANSION THROUGH BUSINESS COMBINATIONS

When a company's securities have an established market, it's easier to negotiate mergers or acquisitions using the company's own securities. When a privately owned company wants to acquire another business, it's difficult to trade stock for the acquired entity since it's impossible to measure clearly the market value of the stock. With publicly held shares, however, the value of those shares is easier to determine, since the daily market stock quotations show the value that the investing public places on the shares. All other things being equal, the owners of a private company are often more interested in merging with a public company than with another private company because the shareholders may prefer to exchange their holdings for a readily marketable security.

OWNER DIVERSIFICATION AND LIQUIDITY

If all or most of your wealth is invested in your business, going public offers a chance to sell part of those holdings for cash and diversify your investments. Most owners would like to limit the number of shares sold to raise enough cash yet retain control of the business.

ESTATE-TAX PLANNING

In the event of your death, your shares in the company you own must be valued to determine the taxable value of your estate. If substantial estate taxes are due, your executors could be forced to sell the company to raise the cash needed to pay estate taxes. When a company's shares are widely owned by the public and the stock is actively traded on an exchange or in the over-the-counter market, the value and marketability of the securities for estate-tax purposes can be more clearly established—and the estate's liquidity increased.

MARKETABILITY OF INVESTMENTS

You want to dispose of a part of your holdings during your lifetime to be in a more liquid position. This is, of course, easier if there are established markets for your company's securities. It's also easier for you or any other shareholder to borrow money with collateral consisting of securities that have an established market than with securities having no market.

EMPLOYEE BENEFIT PLANS AND INCENTIVES

When a company is publicly owned, it's possible to establish stock compensation arrangements that will serve to attract and keep key personnel. Stock option plans, for example, may be more attractive to officers and other key personnel than generous salary arrangements, since these plans provide the employee with a sense of ownership and the opportunity to share in any stock price appreciation as well as tax advantages.

PUBLIC AWARENESS OF BUSINESS

Every shareholder is a potential customer. The company often benefits when its shares are owned by the public, especially if the company sells a consumer product or service. The more widespread the distribution of shares, the greater the public's awareness of the company's products or services.

—— DISADVANTAGES

LACK OF OPERATING CONFIDENTIALITY

The registration statement and subsequent reports to shareholders require disclosure of many facets of your company's business, operations, and finances that may never before have been known outside the company. Some particularly sensitive areas of disclosure are the remuneration of officers and directors; the security holdings of officers, directors, and major shareholders ("insiders"); details regarding stock option plans and deferred compensation plans; and extensive financial information, including sales, costs of sales, gross profits, net income, borrowings, and sales to major customers.

PRESSURE ON SHORT-TERM PERFORMANCE

Prior to going public, you can operate your business independently—taking whatever risks you wish, secure in the knowledge that it's only your money (or the bank's) at stake. Once the company becomes publicly owned, you acquire as many partners as you have shareholders and are accountable to them.

In a closely held company, management has the flexibility to focus attention on long-term goals, even if earnings in the near term suffer. In a public company, the investor's return depends on the company's performance, as well as the overall market's performance. Shareholders expect steady growth in areas such as sales, profits, market share, and product innovation. Management must balance short-term strategies to achieve growth with long-term goals. For example, management may believe that a substantial advertising and marketing campaign will result in a profitable product line within a year or two. In the interim, however, the cost of the campaign will depress earnings. Management must weigh the potential long-term benefits against shareholder reaction, the effect on the market value of the stock and the risk that the long-term sales goal may not be achieved. Finally, business flexibility may be limited, such as in sale of the company and election of officers, which may require the vote of the shareholders. In addition, the ability to act quickly is inhibited because management must wait on voting to take place.

RESTRICTIONS ON MANAGEMENT

After the public offering, the officers, directors, and principal holders of the company's equity securities and their relatives will probably become subject to insider trading provisions under SEC regulations. Because they have access to information before the public does, they must exercise caution in trading in the company's equity securities and discussing the company's affairs. For example, gains they realize in closed transactions (purchase and sale or sale and purchase) within a six-month period may be recoverable by the company if gains are from insider information.

INITIAL COST OF OFFERING

The process of going public is expensive and time-consuming. Preparation of the registration document is a complicated process that occupies the time of many people within the organization and several outside experts. Ordinarily, the documents must pass critical review by two different lawyers, the company's and the underwriter's. The financial statements must be audited by an independent public accountant. In addition, the printing bill alone is often quite substantial.

POSSIBLE LOSS OF MANAGEMENT CONTROL

If more than 50% of the company's shares are sold to the public, the original owners could lose control of the company. This is especially likely if most of the shares sold to the public are in the hands of a few individuals who could challenge management, and possibly obtain control of the company by voting themselves on the board of directors at the annual stockholders' meeting. If, however, the shares held by the public are widely distributed, management could exercise control, even though it owns less than 50% of the shares.

ACCOUNTING AND TAX PRACTICES

Owner-managers are typically more concerned with tax savings than with earnings per share and their accounting practices may be designed solely for the purpose of minimizing taxes on income. Their financial statements may not have been audited or even prepared in accordance with generally accepted accounting principles (GAAP). If this applies to you, be prepared to put your "accounting house" in order before going public. Conforming financial statements to prescribed rules and GAAP is a condition of filing with the SEC, and the cost and other implications of the changes you might have to make to meet the SEC standards could be significant.

ONGOING COSTS

After going public, companies become subject to the SEC's periodic reporting requirements, which vary with the number of shareholders and major company changes. The reports are designed to keep the information in the registration statement up-to-date—requiring maintenance of adequate financial staff and professional assistance, and adding significantly to the company's cost of doing business.

DEMAND FOR DIVIDENDS

As the owner of a private company, you may have declared dividends depending on your needs or sections of the Internal Revenue Code dealing with unreasonable compensation or accumulations of earnings. As a public company you may have to adopt a regular dividend policy if shareholders demand it. Generally, investors in companies that have "gone public" do not expect a dividend during the first several years of public life. They expect earnings to be reinvested to ensure long-term viability.

WHO SHOULD GO PUBLIC

Many companies may have capital needs that could be satisfied by going public. Individual, institutional, regional, or industry-specific investors also have needs. After evaluating what it offers to the investing public and the demands of investors, management may decide that traditional debt financing or owner capital infusion can satisfy their capital needs.

Here are some questions you should ask to determine whether your company is a public offering candidate:

- Has the company demonstrated a sustained or increasing growth rate high enough to attract investors? Generally, a company that outpaces the industry average in growth will have a better chance of attracting prospective investors than one with marginal or inconsistent growth. Many companies that have successfully gone public have shown market support for their product or service that would sustain a 25%–50% annual growth rate for a five-year period. This growth potential should be even larger if institutional investors are expected to buy shares in the company.

- Has the company reached the point where prospects for maintaining a strong sales and earnings growth trend in the future are reasonably good? Underwriters usually consider a company as an IPO candidate when it has at least $10 million in sales and profitability of approximately $1 million or more. The exception: the early stage company that has mitigated the investment risk.

- Are the company's products or services highly visible and of interest to the investing public? The established company can satisfy these requirements with historical data while the early stage company must use projections. Usually, the early stage company qualifies as an IPO candidate based on the uniqueness of its product or service. In addition, it should have reached the stage in its development where the risks usually associated with a venture capital investment—product development, manufacturing capability, market acceptance, and market size—have been reduced.

- Does management believe it can meet the disclosure and financial reporting requirements and other associated demands that will be made by the newly acquired "business partners" and the regulatory authorities? In an established company as well as an early stage company, the quality of the management team is a key factor. Since registration requirements and analyst meetings require detailed analysis and descriptions from executive management, they must have credibility to the investing public; the organization must have depth and quality in leadership and skill. Financial reporting requirements for both the SEC and shareholders must be provided on a timely basis. To meet these requirements, a system of management controls and financial reporting is necessary to maintain credibility and investor confidence after the IPO.

If you can answer these questions or have put together a plan to improve the company's ability to qualify as an IPO candidate, then the remaining portion of this reading provides information necessary to understand the process and consequences of going public.

———— HOW TO GO PUBLIC

The Securities Act of 1933 requires that a registration statement, such as Form S-1 or S-18, be filed with the SEC before an offering to sell securities is made public. It also prohibits the actual sale of securities unless the required registration statement has become effective.

The registration statement has two parts. Part I is the prospectus, which must be provided to anyone who has been made an offer to purchase the securities or ultimately buys them. Part II contains supplemental data and is available to the public at the offices of the SEC or by mail.

An offering of more than $7.5 million must be registered using Form S-1, and offerings of up to that amount can be filed using Form S-18. There are several exemptions from registration requirements. For example, regulation A is for certain public offerings not exceeding $1.5 million, used infrequently because underwriters' opportunities are reduced due to the limited amount of capital that can be raised. Regulation D rules 504, 505, and 506 are for offerings that do not exceed $500,000, $5 million and unlimited respectively.

A registration using Form S-1 includes business information in both narrative and financial format.

REGISTRATION STATEMENT: PART I

Part I of the registration statement, also known as the prospectus, contains basic information including:

- Company business and properties
- Degree of risk associated with the company's business
- Use of proceeds
- Underwriter's compensation
- Significant legal proceedings
- Extent of the company's competition
- Securities being offered
- Names of directors and officers and their remuneration
- Options outstanding to purchase securities
- Company's financial history, as follows:

    Detailed financial statements that include a balance sheet for each of the last two fiscal year-ends and other statements for each of the last three years that have been audited by an independent

> public accountant and, depending on the timing, interim un-
> audited financial data.
>
> Selected financial data, for five fiscal years and possible interim
> periods, including such items as revenues, net income, earnings
> per share, and long-term debt.
>
> Management's description of the company's financial condition
> in terms of liquidity and capital resources, and its explanation of
> any factors that have significantly affected or may affect the
> company's operating results.

The prospectus generally serves two purposes. The first is as a selling document to prospective buyers of the securities. The second is as a basis of legal protection for the issuing company and its officers. It ensures that a prospective purchaser has been provided with relevant information about the company so he or she can make an informed judgment with respect to his or her investment.

The dual functions that the prospectus serves may, however, be in conflict with each other. Management naturally wishes to tell the prospective investors about the company's past achievements and to predict successful operations. At the same time, to guard against possible litigation from purchasers of the securities who may claim they were misled, management must make sure that it adequately discloses the risks.

REGISTRATION STATEMENT: PART II

Part II of the registration statement contains supplemental data, which is not required to be provided to each prospective investor, including such items as:

- Listings of the registrant's subsidiaries
- Certain data on recent sales of unregistered securities
- Listings of financial statements and copies of certain documents filed as exhibits
- Descriptions of marketing arrangements
- Details of the expenses of the offering
- Supplemental financial statement schedules supporting certain financial data

Form S-18 reduces disclosure requirements and has resulted in a more timely and less expensive registration process for many companies. While many requirements of Form S-18 are the same as for Form S-1, the major differences to consider are:

- *Financial Statements.* S-18 requires that two fiscal years are audited and prepared in accordance with GAAP, while S-1 requires three fiscal years audited and presented in accordance with more detailed SEC regulations.
- *Narrative Disclosures.* S-18 requires less detailed description of business, operations, and performances than S-1 does.
- *Filing.* S-18 allows for regional filing in one of the nine regional offices of the SEC, while all S-1 filings are made with the SEC's Division of Corporate Finance in Washington, D.C.

The appropriate form to file depends generally on the size of offering and interpretation by legal counsel specialized in securities.

——— WHO CAN HELP

Once you've decided to go forward with a public offering, the next task is to assemble the registration team. It consists of management, your legal counsel, the underwriter, the underwriter's legal counsel, your independent accountants, a financial printer and, in some cases, a financial public relations firm. In addition to the help provided by the team, the SEC can also assist through the Division of Corporate Finance Office of Small Business Policy. The personnel of the SEC's regional offices can respond to any questions on federal securities laws. In addition, SEC rules and regulations are available through the U.S. Government Printing Office.

THE UNDERWRITER

The principal role of the underwriter is to sell securities to the public. The underwriter also plays a significant role in advising you on the financing opportunities, structuring the transaction, and determining the proper timing of the offering. The choice of underwriter is important because the investment bankers who perform these services vary widely in quality, cost, and range of services. Most companies will have established a relationship with an investment banker or had preliminary discussions prior to selection. It's usually a good idea to make contact with an underwriter a year or two before the offering. Here are some of the factors to be considered in selecting the underwriter.

Reputation The underwriter should have a good reputation in the investment community and among others who have used its services. The firm should be particularly well known in the company's target market—institutional investors, for example.

Experience   The underwriter should have experience and success with underwritings similar to yours in number of shares and dollar amount. The underwriter should also have experience analyzing and understanding your industry, since it must communicate the IPO opportunity and support the after-market through investor analysis.

Market-Making Capabilities   The underwriter should be able to attract a large number of investors and to generate enough interest in the stock to maintain a good market after the initial offering. Furthermore, the underwriter's distribution network should support the nationwide or regional image of your company and the appeal of its stock.

Ability to Provide Other Investment Banking Services After the Offering The underwriter should be prepared to assist in locating additional sources of public or private capital and general financial counseling.

Fees to be Charged   The underwriter's commissions and expenses for performing the brokering functions should be competitive.

The best way to gather information on the underwriter's capabilities is to ask the officers of other companies who have used its services. Your accountant and lawyer—both have frequent contact with underwriters on a regular basis—should also be reliable sources of recommendations. Ultimately, management must interview several underwriting firms and ask for proposals from each. References of other offerings the firm has underwritten should be obtained and contacted.

The underwriter's commitment to your stock is crucial, considering the time, effort, and money invested in the public offering process. You should fully comprehend different types of underwriting available before you choose an underwriter.

Types Of Underwriting   When the underwriter is selected, a letter of intent should be signed that outlines the proposed terms of the offering and acknowledges the underwriter's intention to execute an underwriting agreement before the conclusion of the registration process. The letter of intent is not a binding agreement to underwrite the offering, but rather a preliminary understanding of the terms of the offering. It outlines the underwriter's compensation, any reimbursement for expenses and defines the type of underwriting. The following types of underwriting may be entered into:

- *Best Efforts.* The underwriter agrees to use its best efforts to sell as many shares as possible and is not obligated to purchase any unsold securities. This means you incur the time and cost to prepare to go public with no guarantee the shares will be sold. Even if the company's shares are not sold, outside members of the team are still compensated on an hourly basis, except for the underwriters. In addition to their commission for a successful offering of generally up to 10% of the amount raised, underwriters normally require a nonrefundable fee on their engagement to cover initial expenses. Should the deal fail to close, you remain responsible for a substantial bill for professional services in addition to the nonrefundable fee.

- *Best Efforts, All or None.* The offering is cancelled if the underwriter is unable to sell the entire issue. Should the deal fail to close, you are responsible for the cost of professional services in addition to the nonrefundable fee.

- *Firm Commitment.* The underwriter agrees to buy all of the stock being offered for sale and thereby assumes the risk for any unsold securities. You are responsible for the cost of professional services, but the offering proceeds are guaranteed when the underwriting becomes effective.

The Underwriting Agreement   Regardless of the type of underwriting, the actual underwriting agreement generally is not signed until the registration statement becomes effective. It's important to understand that even though your company may incur considerable expense in anticipation of an offering, there is no advance assurance that the offering will actually take place. A reputable underwriter, however, will generally not turn away without a valid reason.

Normally, the underwriting agreement is a document of 10 to 15 pages that covers various matters including:

- The type of offering.
- Agreement by the company to sell and the underwriter to purchase a certain number of shares at a designated price.
- Warranties by the company on the completeness and accuracy of the information included in the registration statement.
- Indemnification of the underwriter against liabilities arising under federal securities laws.
- Conditions or events that must occur before the underwriter is obligated to pay for the securities, normally including receipt of an acceptable "comfort letter" from the company's independent accountants and a representation letter from the company's counsel stating that the company has met all legal requirements to complete the offering.
- Time and location of the closing.

Many of the factors that should be considered in selecting the underwriter—such as reputation, experience, service, and fees—are for the most part applicable to the selection of the other team members.

COUNSEL FOR THE COMPANY

The competence of company legal counsel and its familiarity with SEC rules and regulations and the registration process are critical to timely and effective coordination. Counsel's principal role is to advise the company on compliance with provisions of the securities acts and with the various state and federal laws the company and the offering will be subject to. Counsel also oversees the progress of the various members of the registration team, ensures the timeliness and completeness of the process, and coordinates the resolution of any questions arising from the SEC review and the filing of the necessary amendments. Should any conferences with the SEC be necessary, counsel would be expected to attend them with the company's representative.

COUNSEL FOR THE UNDERWRITER

Counsel for the underwriter is selected by the underwriter and is generally responsible for drafting the underwriting agreement and reviewing the registration statement and any related agreements and contracts that are filed as exhibits. Counsel's principal objective is to ensure the registration statement is complete and not misleading.

THE INDEPENDENT ACCOUNTANT

The independent accountant's principal responsibilities in preparing a registration statement are:

- Examining and expressing an opinion on the various financial statements that must be included in the document
- Reading, in depth, the text portion of the registration statement in order to identify any inconsistencies that may require changes or corrections to the text or the financial statements
- Issuing a letter (called a "comfort letter") to the underwriters, covering, in general, the financial statements' compliance, in both form and content, with applicable SEC regulations and describing any adverse changes in the company's financial position since the last audited balance sheet.

THE FINANCIAL PRINTER

The financial printer is responsible for having the prospectus printed and ready for distribution. A printer that is convenient—since most printing will be done overnight—aware of SEC regulations and sensitive to the accuracy and speed required in a public offering is a necessary and important member of the team.

—— THE PROCESS

Once you've selected the underwriter and the other members of the registration team, you can start the public offering process. It generally commences with an organizational conference attended by the members of the registration team, including:

- The chief executive and financial officers of the company
- Counsel for the company
- A representative of the underwriters
- Counsel for the underwriters
- The independent accountant
- The financial printer

Matters usually discussed at the organizational meeting include the nature of the offering, the appropriate SEC registration form, and the anticipated filing date. A detailed registration timetable for each member of the team, which indicates the date each step is to be completed, is also developed.

At this first meeting it's important to assess your ability to make the transition. The systems and controls that support your financial statements must be reliable and in place. This is important because at the time of the offering the underwriters or the SEC may require accurate interim or stub information in addition to annual financial statements to proceed with the offering.

This is also your last opportunity to estimate what the process will cost, and what portion of the company will be sold. The underwriter's discount or commission can range from 5% to 15% of the total funds raised. The amount you agree to will depend on the total offering amount, the market rate for current offerings, and the underwriter's effort to sell the stock. Also, depending on the total discount amount, certain expenses may be reimbursed and warrants (subscription rights to buy stocks) provided. While the underwriter's discount is not a cost until you close, all other services must be paid even if the offering does not close. Legal fees, depending on the extent of disorder (housekeeping) and state security filings (called Blue Sky), could range from $50,000 to $150,000. Accountants' fees, depending on the audit requirements and scope of the underwriter's comfort letter, could fall in the same range. Printing costs, based on length of the documents, color and picture use, and revisions could reach $100,000. If the offering is successful you will also be faced with SEC, NASD, Blue Sky, and registrar and transfer agent fees.

Based on a survey of IPOs, total expenses for underwriters, attorneys, accountants, and printers ranged from less than 10% to over 35% of the gross offering.

The entire process generally requires several months and in capsule form consists of the following:

- The initial registration statement
- Filing and SEC review
- The amended registration statement
- The preliminary ("red herring") prospectus
- Financial analyst meetings (road shows)
- The due diligence meeting
- The price amendment and the underwriting agreement
- Closing

Once a preliminary understanding with the underwriters has been reached, a "quiet period" begins when the company is subject to SEC guidelines regarding publication of information outside of the prospectus. The opportunity to enhance awareness of the company, its name, products, and geographic markets will be limited, since any publicity that creates a favorable attitude toward the securities could be considered illegal. However, continuation of established, normal advertisements and financial information is acceptable. The timetable should include strategies for enhancing company visibility, as market awareness and acceptance of the offering could reduce an underwriter's sales efforts and, as a result, lower offering costs.

THE INITIAL REGISTRATION STATEMENT

The form and content of the registration statement are prescribed by the SEC. The type of information included in the statement will vary to a certain extent depending on the particular registration form called for in the filing.

Generally, the responsibility for the preparation of the nonfinancial portions of the registration statement falls upon counsel for the company. Preparation of the financial portions usually rests with the company's financial management in consultation with outside accountants.

FILING AND SEC REVIEW

Registration statements filed by first-time issuers are subjected to review by SEC staff specialists—generally consisting of a lawyer, accountant, and financial analyst. The group may also consult with other staff experts depending on industry specializations. The staff reviews the documents filed to determine full and fair disclosure, particularly whether the document contains any misstatements of fact or omissions of material facts. The SEC review, however, cannot assure accuracy or completeness of the data.

The review of financial data is performed by a staff accountant who reads the entire prospectus and remainder of the registration statement to become familiar with the company and its business. The staff accountant may also refer to published annual and interim reports and newspaper articles for information regarding the company and its industry. The accountant's review is primarily directed at the financial statements and other financial data and the independent accountant's report. The purpose is to determine whether the data comply with SEC requirements and the applicable pronouncements of the American Institute of Certified Public Accountants and the Financial Accounting Standards Board, as well as with the various SEC staff interpretations and policies dealing with accounting and auditing issues.

Although the securities laws contemplate a review of registration statements filed with the SEC, they do not specify the review procedures to be followed by the SEC in processing these documents. The "informal" procedures followed have been developed by the SEC to make comments available to registrants and to permit necessary revisions of a registration statement without formal proceedings. The informal-comment technique has proved to be an effective method of communicating and resolving questions and defects before permitting a registration statement to become effective.

After the review, the SEC generally issues a letter that sets forth questions, deficiencies, and suggested revisions found in its review. The letter, referred to as a letter of comment, is generally mailed to the company's counsel.

To save time in the registration process, company counsel generally maintains close contact with SEC staff while the registration statement is being reviewed. Counsel often arranges to receive staff comments by telephone to expedite preparing the required amendment and/or response. Sometimes, a formal letter of comment is not even issued. Telephone contact is often used in connection with review of a registration statement amendment that has been prepared in response to comments raised by the SEC on a previous filing. This method to communicate SEC comments is generally used by registrants and their underwriters as a time-saving measure.

For a carefully prepared document, staff comments are usually relatively few in number and minor in character. Whatever the nature of the comments, each must be addressed and resolved before the registration statement can become effective. If the comments are well-founded and significant, the registration statement must be appropriately amended. Although differences of opinion sometimes exist as to the propriety of a particular comment or request, comments and suggestions made by the SEC often prove to be constructive and appropriate and, in the effort to save filing time, are usually complied with rather than challenged.

THE AMENDED REGISTRATION STATEMENT

After necessary revisions have been identified, preparation of a revised statement begins. Amendments to the initial registration statement may also be necessary as a result of significant business developments occurring subsequent to the original filing date—for example, a material change in the business or financial condition of the company. If the change is materially adverse, the underwriter could stop the offering since it could render the stock unsalable. On the positive side, a major pending lawsuit could be settled favorably and disclosure would remove any uncertainty about the company and its future. Generally, the changes that go into the revised registration statement require reprinting the statement.

THE PRELIMINARY ("RED HERRING") PROSPECTUS

Even before the amended registration is filed, a preliminary prospectus is sent to brokers and prospective purchasers. Circulation of the preliminary prospectus is important to forming the underwriting syndicate of various brokerage companies that the underwriter assembles to distribute the stock. SEC rules require that this prospectus substantially conform to the requirements of the Securities Act and that the cover page bear, in red ink (hence the term "red herring") the caption "Preliminary Prospectus." The following statement must be printed on the cover in type as large as that generally used in the body of the prospectus:

> A registration statement relating to these securities has been filed with the Securities and Exchange Commission but has not yet become effective. Information contained herein is subject to completion or amendment. These securities may not be sold nor may offers to buy be accepted prior to the time the registration statement becomes effective. This prospectus shall not constitute an offer to sell or the solicitation of an offer to buy, nor shall there be any sale of these securities in any State in which such offer, solicitation or sale would be unlawful prior to registration or qualification under the securities laws of any such State.

The SEC rules also stipulate that the preliminary prospectus may omit the offering price, underwriting discounts or commissions, discounts or commissions to dealers, amount of proceeds, or other matters dependent on the offering price.

FINANCIAL ANALYST MEETINGS (ROAD SHOWS)

Timing plays as important a part as any other factor in determining the final price of the shares. Almost any company that went public during the late 1960s and mid-1980s (great bull markets) would have done so at a higher offering price than in the mid-1970s (the worst bear market since the 1940s). In addition to cyclical market factors, particular industries go through "hot" and "cold" periods. Unlike the private sale of stock, where negotiations can be in the form of face-to-face meetings, stock sold through the public market is basically priced by market psychology.

For potential investors to learn about the company, the underwriter will arrange for financial analyst and brokers' meetings—usually called road shows. These meetings are usually handled by the president and key management (such as the chief financial officer). The credibility you project through your presentation and ability to respond to potential investors' and brokers' questions will be a major influence in the success of your offering.

THE DUE DILIGENCE MEETING

After the registration statement is filed, but before it becomes effective, the principal underwriter holds a due diligence meeting.

The reason can be found in a provision of the SEC rule stating that, except for the company and its principals, no person will be held civilly liable in connection with untrue statements or material omissions in SEC filings if he or she can prove that he or she had, after reasonable investigation, reasonable ground to believe and did believe, at the time such part of the registration statement became effective, that the statements therein were true and that there was no omission to state a material fact required to be stated therein or necessary to make the statements therein not misleading.

The meeting is attended by the principal underwriter and often by members of the underwriting group, as well as the company's principal officers, counsel for the company, counsel for the underwriter and the independent accountant. The usual procedure is for the underwriters to question the company representatives on the company and its business; products; competitive position; recent developments in finance, marketing, operations, and other areas and future prospects.

THE PRICE AMENDMENT AND UNDERWRITING AGREEMENT

When a registration statement has been filed, the registrant and the underwriter have generally agreed on the securities—both in number of shares and dollar amount—to be sold. In almost all cases, however, the issuer and the underwriter have not yet determined the final price to offer the securities to the public, the exact amount of underwriter's discount or commission, and the net proceeds to the registrant. The negotiation and final determination of these amounts depend on a number of factors, as discussed earlier, including past and present performance of the company and conditions in the securities markets and prices of securities of companies in similar industries at the time the registration statement becomes effective.

The agreed-on price should reflect a discount amount based on anticipated after-market share value of the company. An offering at the high end of a range may not provide adequate investor return, resulting in a weak or depressed after-market. While pricing at the low end may result in a run-up immediately following the offering, after a period of trading the stock should settle at the anticipated after-market share value. The price per share and number of shares will also have an impact on the after-market.

Market perceptions of the risk inherent in a stock are sometimes related to the per-share value. A company with a market value of $5 per-share value may be perceived to be speculative, while a $10 stock may not. An IPO of $15 may be considered overpriced. In addition to the price, the number of shares offered should be sufficient to ensure broad distribution and liquidity.

Upon completion of negotiations with the underwriter—usually about the time the registration statement is ready to become effective—the agreement is signed by authorized representatives of the company and the underwriter. At this time, the final amendment to the registration statement is prepared, including as applicable, the agreed-on offering price, underwriter's discount or commission, and the net proceeds to the company. This amendment is called the price amendment. If the staff of the SEC's Division of Corporate Finance has no important reservations with respect to the registration statement, the registrant and underwriter will customarily request that the offering be declared effective immediately—referred to as requesting "acceleration." If acceleration is granted, the underwriter may proceed with the sale of securities to the public.

CLOSING

The closing date—generally specified in the underwriting agreement—is usually 10 days to two weeks after the effective date of the registration statement. At the closing, the company delivers the registered securities to the underwriter and receives payment for the issue. Various legal documents are also exchanged as well as an updated comfort letter prepared by the independent accountant.

——— AFTER YOU GO PUBLIC

Once you have gone public it takes considerable effort to maintain your company's market position. The excitement of an IPO must be maintained or trading will decline and liquidity for the owner through a future secondary offering, as well as other IPO benefits, will not be realized. Effective distribution and support of the stock and continuing security analyst interest is necessary after you go public. A strategy for after-market support can be determined with the assistance of a financial public relations firm. It usually includes choosing an individual within the company to handle shareholder relations.

The SEC will require the company to file certain periodic reports to keep the investing public informed. This requirement will continue as long as certain investor and asset tests are met.

REPORTING REQUIREMENTS AFTER GOING PUBLIC

No discussion of going public would be complete without consideration to the obligations of the now-public company to provide information to its shareholders.

Legal counsel should be consulted about when a company is obligated to file a particular report with the SEC or the type of report to be filed. The following is an overview of the general filing requirements and common reports.

- *Form 10K.* Annual report to the SEC. It discloses, in detail, information about the company's activities, financial condition, and results of operations. It also contains the company's annual financial statements.
- *Form 10-Q.* Quarterly report required for each of the first three quarters of the fiscal year. It includes condensed financial data and information on significant events.
- *Form 8-K.* Report filed in the case of a change in control, bankruptcy or a change in independent accountants.
- *Proxy or information statements.* Data furnished to shareholders so they can decide how to assign their proxies (votes).

In addition, public companies must provide annual reports to shareholders with financial information similar to that included in Form 10-K.

To meet the various reporting requirements imposed on them, public companies must maintain an adequate financial staff, support by legal counsel, and knowledgeable independent accountants.

———— EXEMPT OFFERINGS

The importance of small businesses to the U.S. economy and their ability to gain access to equity markets is a major concern of the Congress and the SEC. Congress enacted the Small Business Investment Incentive Act in 1980 to expand exemption of certain public offerings or private placements from registration with the SEC.

In 1982, Regulation D was adopted by the SEC to coordinate limited offering exemptions and streamline the existing requirements, which reduce the cost of compliance applicable to private offerings and sales of securities. So if you are in need of limited capital, you can still sell stock in your company under an exempt offering and avoid the cost of a public offering.

While Regulation D simplifies the process, the company is not exempted from the antifraud provisions of the securities laws. You must still provide the prospective investor with adequate information to make an informed decision. In addition, while the offering may be exempt from federal registration, it may be subject to state requirements. Regulation D permits the following offerings:

- Sale of securities totalling up to $500,000 over a 12-month period.
- Sale of securities totalling up to $5,000,000 over a 12-month period. Investors must meet the SEC's definition of "accredited investor," except for up to 35 of them which the SEC allows to be non-accredited. An accredited investor, in general, is an individual or institution that is knowledgeable and has adequate net worth to make such investments.
- Sale of an unlimited amount of securities if all the investors, except for the up to 35, are accredited. The nonaccredited investors must meet the definition of a "sophisticated" investor. In general, a sophisticated investor is one who is capable of evaluating the merit of the investment venture.

WHY USE AN EXEMPT OFFERING?

There are advantages as well as disadvantages to raising money through an exempt offering.

ADVANTAGES

Business Strategy   Investors in exempt offerings are generally long-term oriented. In addition, you will probably know them as individuals. This could mean less pressure on management to obtain short-term results at the expense of long-term growth.

Time   With fewer requirements and no SEC review, an exempt offering can be completed more rapidly than a registration statement.

Disclosure   Continuous reporting requirements are necessary only for certain issuers. The limited number of investors also limits disclosure of information that you may prefer to keep confidential.

Cost Because the compliance regulations are reduced, so are the related professional fees. Also, the exempt offering documents can be produced on the company's word processor, allowing you to avoid substantial printing costs.

DISADVANTAGES

Offering Limitation   Exempt offerings limit the amount of capital that can be raised and could restrain the company's growth potential.

Price Generally your company's market valuation will be higher using an IPO. Investors in exempt offerings will demand a substantially larger share of ownership to offset the lack of liquidity and the risk that the company may never go public.

Investors   Investors in an exempt offering will want eventually to liquidate their holdings at a profit. Investor exit can be realized by participating in a public offering, a sale of the company or by having the company buy the shares back.

Liquidity The shares of an exempt offering cannot be freely traded. They are therefore less desirable for use as loan collateral, since value based on a market price per share is not readily available.

Selling a portion of your company to raise needed capital is a major decision. An exempt offering may be the appropriate decision for the company that has limited capital needs and is not ready to go public.

Copyright © 1988.

▬▬ DISCUSSION QUESTIONS

1. An alternative to equity financing is debt financing. Compare the advantages and disadvantages of going public with financing growth through short- and long-term debt.
2. Under what circumstances might a company that has not attained the sales and profit levels cited in the reading consider going public?
3. The quality of the management team is a key factor in the decision to go public. In view of what you have read here about the responsibilities of a public company, what do you consider to be the most important attributes of the management team?

4. The road show is an opportunity for potential investors to learn about your company. How would you prepare for these meetings? What subjects would you expect to cover? What other means would you use to raise your company's public profile?

5. The decision to go public calls for a more formal management style. What procedures and operational changes would you implement to prepare your company for going public?

INDEX